Professional Office Procedures

Hamilton Sorter Co., Inc.

Professional Office Procedures

Jolene D. Scriven, Ed.D.
Director of the Doctoral Program,
College of Business
Associate Professor of Management
Northern Illinois University

Charles E. Kozoll, Ph.D.
Professor of Education and Associate Director,
Continuing Education and Public Service
University of Illinois at Urbana-Champaign

Judith K. Myers, M.S., C.P.S.
Consultant, Private Industry

Gail L. Hapke, M.A.
Editorial Consultant

GLENCOE
McGraw-Hill

New York, New York
Columbus, Ohio
Woodland Hills, California
Peoria, Illinois

Library of Congress Cataloging-in-Publication Data
Professional office procedures/Jolene D. Scriven . . . [et al.].
       p.   cm.
    Includes bibliographic references and index.
    ISBN 0-02-650863-X (text with no disk).
— ISBN   0-02-819911-1 (text w/5¼ disk). — ISBN 0-02-819910-3 (text w/3½
disk).   — ISBN 0-02-650864-8 (manual to instructor)
    1. Office practice. 2. Secretaries—Vocational guidance—United
States. I. Scriven, Jolene D.
    HF5547.5.P69   1991 <MRCRR>
    651.3'74—dc20   90-25637
                                                   CIP

Professional Office Procedures

Imprint 1999

Send all inquiries to:
Glencoe/McGraw-Hill
936 Eastwind Drive
Westerville, OH 43081

0-02-650863-X

7 8 9   026/043   02 01 00 99

ACKNOWLEDGMENTS

The authors and the publisher wish to thank the following educators whose comments and reviews of earlier drafts provided many useful suggestions:

Nancy Barnett, Business Department Manager, National Education Center, San Bernardino, CA

Marion Coleman, Cuyahoga Community College, Cleveland, OH

Dr. Linda Kavanaugh-Varga, Robert Morris College, Pittsburgh, PA

Dr. Jacqueline D. Myers, Alabama State University, Montgomery, AL

Dr. Terry Roach, University of Central Arkansas, Conway, AR

Mary Sharifzadeh, Director of Curriculum, Cambridge Business School, Detroit, MI

Carolyn Webb, Chairperson, Secretarial Science Department, Robert Morris College, Chicago, IL

We would also like to express our thanks to the following educators who reviewed *Top Performance: A Decision-Making Simulation for the Office*, the software designed to accompany this book:

Dr. Rosemarie McCauley, Chairperson, Department of Business Education and Office Systems Administration, Montclair State College, Upper Montclair, NJ

Marilyn Mihm, Danville Area Community College, Danville, IL

Shawnna Patterson, The Bradford School, Portland, OR

Suzanne Vinitsky, Educational Consultant, Chicago, IL

Marlynna Schaefer, an office professional in every sense, entered and revised drafts of every aspect of this project. We appreciate her patient assistance.

Our families provided immeasurable amounts of support and enthusiasm during our labors. They deserve a collective note of thanks.

Photo Credits

Cover: From top to bottom: Pete Saloutos; Ronnie Kaufman; Henley & Savage
Frontispiece, p. i, Hamilton Sorter Co., Inc., 3158 Production Drive, Fairfield, OH 45014.

Unit 1: International Business Machines Corporation
Chapter One: Pp. 18, 19, International Business Machines Corporation, 1133 Westchester Avenue, White Plains, NY 10604 (914–642–3000, ext. 6438); p. 13, photos of equipment from International Business Machines Corporation, from Barbara Logan, C·I Photography, 275 Santa Ana Court, Sunnyvale, CA 94086 (408–733–5855); p. 7, Library of Congress; p. 7, Marketing Concepts Ltd., 150 Pine St., Suite 302, Manchester, CT 06040 (203–649–5885).
Chapter Two: Pp. 28, 38, Microcomputer Accessories, Inc., 5405 Jandy Place, PO Box 66911, Los Angeles, CA 90066-0911; pp. 29, 31, 42, Apple Computer, Inc., 20525 Mariani Avenue, Cupertino, CA 95014 (408–974–5191); pp. 29, 32, 33a, 33b, 36, 41, 41, International Business Machines Corporation; p. 32, Maxell Corporation of America, 22-08 Route 208, Fair Lawn, NJ, 07410; pp. 34, 45, Curtis Manufacturing Company, Inc., 30 Fitzgerald

Drive, Jaffrey, NH 03452 (603–532–4123); p. 39, TAB Products Co., 1400 Page Mill Road, Palo Alto, CA 94304 (415–852–2425).

Chapter Three: P. 56, DAROME (teleconference equipment), 8750 W. Bryn Mawr Avenue, Suite 850, Chicago, Illinois 60631 (1–800–Darome–1); p. 63, Curtis Manufacturing Company, Inc.; pp. 63, 64, International Business Machines Corporation; p. 65, Hamilton Sorter Co., Inc.; p. 67, General Electric Company, Nela Park, Cleveland, OH 44112.

Unit 2: The Stock Market
Chapter Four: Pp. 77, 87, 90, International Business Machines Corporation; pp. 78, 82a, 82b, 83, 85, Day-Timers, Inc., One Willow Lane, East Texas, PA 18046 (215–398–1151); p. 86, Magna Visual, Inc., 9400 Watson Road, St. Louis, MO 63126-1596 (314–843–9000).
Chapter Five: P. 122, Federal Express Corporation, 2005 Corporate Ave., Memphis, TN 38194.
Chapter Six: Pp. 135, 147, Day-Timers, Inc.; pp. 131, 138, Ameritech Mobile Communications, 1515 Woodfield Rd., Suite 1400, Schaumburg, IL 60173; p. 137, DAROME; p. 145, ROLM Company, an IBM and Siemens Company, P.O. Box 5017, Norwalk, CT 06856-5017 (203–849–6000).
Chapter Seven: P. 158, Day-Timers, Inc.; p. 171, Ameritech Mobile Communications.
Chapter Eight: P. 177, International Business Machines Corporation; p. 178, Day-Timers, Inc.
Chapter Nine: P. 199, International Business Machines Corporation.

Unit 3: International Business Machines Corporation
Chapter Ten: Pp. 216, 224, Lanier Voice Products, 1700 Chantilly Drive, Atlanta, GA 30324 (404–329–8000); p. 220, *The Administrative Secretary*, Second Edition, Ruth I. Anderson et al., p. 126; p. 223, Day-Timers, Inc.
Chapter Eleven: Pp. 246, 251, 255, International Business Machines Corporation.
Chapter Twelve: P. 268, Packard Bell, 9425 Canoga Ave., Chatsworth, CA 91311 (818–773–4400); pp. 269, 272, Eastman Kodak Co., 901 Elmgrove Rd., Rochester, NY 14650; pp. 270, 271, 271, Canon USA Inc., One Canon Plaza, Lake Success, NY 11042.
Chapter Thirteen: P. 286, Kardex Systems, Inc., Marietta, OH 45750 (614–374–9300); p. 309, Westinghouse Furniture Systems, 4300-36th St., S.E., Grand Rapids, MI 49508; p. 310, Robert P. Gillotte Company, Division National Service Industries, 2230 Commerce Drive, Columbia, SC 29205; Visual Planning, division of MagnaPlan Corporation, 184 N. Main St., Champlain, NY 12919; p. 312, Esselte Pendaflex Corporation, Clinton Road, Garden City, NY 11530. Pp. 289–308, Association of Records Managers and Administrators, Inc. (ARMA) p. 311, Pollack.
Chapter Fourteen: P. 321, Minolta Corporation, 101 Williams Drive, Ramsey, NJ 07446; p. 323, Curtis Manufacturing Company, Inc., 30 Fitzgerald Drive, Jaffrey, NH 03452 (603–532–4123).

Unit 4: Aaron Haupt/Glencoe
Chapter Fifteen: Pp. 339, 340, 341, John H. Harland Company, Drawer CS 100252, Atlanta, GA 30384-0252; p. 354, International Business Machines Corporation.
Chapter Sixteen: Pp. 363, 370, International Business Machines Corporation; p. 373, Esselte Pendaflex Corp.
Chapter Seventeen: Pp. 395, 410, International Business Machines Corporation.

CONTENTS

INTRODUCTION

"My assistant is a true professional! Nothing leaves our office unless it has been rechecked and is totally correct."

"You handled the arrangements for the annual meeting magnificently. I particularly appreciated the way you managed those two unanticipated crises."

"Could you take on this special report? It's very important to the company, but we're convinced that you can do a superb job!"

"Thanks so much for helping to resolve the disagreement between the other two secretaries. Your diplomacy and compromise solution were exactly what we needed!"

"We appreciate your extra hard work in mastering the new word-processing system. Your suggestions for programs to be developed were wonderful!"

Each of these well-deserved compliments focuses on a different aspect of a single office professional's responsibilities. That person is praised as a "professional," one who takes pride in consistent excellence, one who overlooks not a single detail. The office professionals described in this textbook are self-motivated, diplomatic, precise, cool under pressure, and confident of their ability to perform a myriad of diverse and demanding tasks.

Regardless of title and size of organization, your colleagues contribute each day to the achievements, productivity, and overall success of their employers. By way of emphasizing that point, each chapter begins with a brief example of how an office professional's knowledge, skill, and ability solved a problem, provided valued assistance, or identified a new approach.

This textbook describes how you can demonstrate your professionalism—and richly deserve such compliments yourself. In it you will find information, procedures, and suggestions that will increase your knowledge and skill in all areas of office responsibility and help you build a more positive attitude and develop greater enthusiasm for your work.

As you know, computer-based technology has affected our lives in significant ways. It is highly probable that, as a computer-age professional, your work will be made easier by equipment that integrates word processing, filing and financial management functions, and many other applications. You will be better able to complete such traditional duties as arranging meetings, scheduling appointments, and planning trips. In this text, you will learn to benefit from computers in all phases of your work—and you will learn what technological innovations to expect in the future.

While we emphasize the importance of technology, we haven't forgotten about the important role human relations will play in your success. We will suggest ways to develop effective working relationships with one or more managers, establish a pleasant office environment, handle problems among co-workers, and cultivate your own potential leadership roles.

We begin the text by looking at the history of your profession: how technology is affecting it, where positions can be found, and what duties your position will entail. We will then examine the necessary attributes of an office professional and how technology can contribute to your productivity, before addressing the specifics of your varied and often challenging responsibilities.

Through our research preparing this textbook, we have learned how much managers and others depend upon office professionals. Equally important, we now realize how many opportunities for growth exist.

Every position is a unique one, depending upon the organization, manager, and, of course, the person occupying it. By blending the information, procedures, and suggestions in this text, you will be able to build a solid foundation on which to base your professionalism. With knowledge, skill, and a positive attitude, you will experience many successes and know the satisfaction that results from consistent excellence.

Professional Office Procedures

UNIT 1

UNDERSTANDING YOUR PROFESSION

CHAPTER

1

RECOGNIZING YOUR OPPORTUNITIES AS AN OFFICE PROFESSIONAL

Chapter Objectives

- To learn how the responsibilities of an office professional have developed and changed over the years (circa 1870–present)

- To understand the importance of exhibiting the following professional qualities: a positive attitude, loyalty to the organization, diplomacy, and problem-solving skills

- To develop the ability to make decisions; knowing when to ask for help and when to "do it yourself"

- To understand how your personal appearance (as well as your work area) makes a statement about you

- To understand that although it takes time to become a professional, you can learn a great deal by observing others and learning from their criticism/suggestions

Examples of Excellence

Lauren Gomez had worked for a large bank for more than a year. Then she decided she would find greater opportunity in a small firm. When she joined Electronic Optics as assistant to the president, Lauren took on major responsibilities, including assisting the vice presidents and controller. She supervised the receptionist in her duties as telephone operator and shipping clerk. Finally, she hired and supervised temporary office workers.

At Electronic Optics, which manufactures scientific equipment, Mondays and Fridays tended to be the most hectic days. Lauren had learned to expect the unexpected on those days. One Monday morning, when Lauren had to make several copies of a major proposal, the primary office copier began chewing up paper, then stopped running altogether. Lauren quickly put up the "out of order" sign. Returning to her desk, she pushed a speed dial number on her telephone console to contact the copier service office for repair. Then she found a quick-copy outlet. She asked the mail clerk to take the proposal over there, then called the copier shop to ask for a rush job.

The next call was from the executive assistant to the president of a company that was a major client. "Lauren, my boss has to make an emergency trip to Canada next week and wants to see E Optics' plans for the new microanalyzer *before* she goes. Can your manager make the presentation this Friday in our office instead of next Wednesday?"

"I'll check and get back to you by 2 PM," Lauren promised. She made quick notes of what had to be done and started making calls.

First, Lauren got her manager's approval to work on the scheduling change and reviewed for him what had to be done. "Go ahead and leave a note on my computer of what the new plans are," the manager said. Then Lauren contacted a travel agent to make the flight and hotel reservations. Next, Lauren asked the marketing vice president whether one of his part-time employees could help with the preparation of a group of overhead transparencies. Copying and preparation of written material were delegated to an outside service, with the receptionist in charge.

Lauren kept a record of all the requests and underlined her promise to call back the customer in the early afternoon. She put that information in her daily "to do" file.

While sorting out this assignment, Lauren took a call from a supplier who was anxiously awaiting a large check. "Lauren, I need that money to buy some priority equipment! Can you help me out?"

"Bob, this has been a terrible day! I'll try to track down the check and call you back before 5 PM. But that's not a guarantee!" She called the controller and asked his assistant to let her know about the check. This note also went into her "to do" file.

Although Lauren concentrated on the upcoming presentation, she found time to check the task list she had made the previous Friday. Given how fast the day was moving, she picked out three tasks that had to be done before the close of business on Monday.

The first task was to make sure the board had the financial report a week before their next meeting. The second, given her by the president and controller, was to track down an employee who had made several unauthorized long-distance calls. The third was to fill out a lengthy form for a government agency that would certify Electronic Optics to bid on certain projects. Lauren hid out in her manager's office to work on the form without interruption—to "get it right the first time." She had finished only one page when a call came from another customer regarding the whereabouts of a promised replacement part for an expensive piece of equipment.

With a number of jobs uncompleted, Lauren left the office at 1 PM for a quick lunch. Her personal life had priority too. Except on the most hectic days, Lauren would leave her office around noon and find an empty office to sit in quietly for a few minutes to regroup and slow down.

Lauren split the remainder of that afternoon between following up on work assigned to others and handling her own assignments. She reviewed over fifty purchase orders and checks for signature by the controller and president. She updated the mail log and annotated several letters so that her manager could respond to them quickly. Most important, she found time to call back the first customer about the missing part, the second customer about the presentation, and the anxious vendor about the status of his check. So far, however, she had only written a note requesting information for the financial report and done nothing on the unauthorized phone call problem.

Although Lauren had spent the entire day working at full speed, not once had she turned to her computer. The screen remained the same except for the blinking of a Q-mail icon, indicating unanswered messages. "But tomorrow the computer could consume my day!" she thought. "The only constant in my work here is the unexpected."

The numerous challenges of Lauren's job point out the variety of tasks office professionals are expected to handle and show why the success of companies depends on the competence and enthusiasm of their office staffs. Lauren's activities may change from day to day, but each day is equally full and complex.

Here is how Lauren's supervisor regards Lauren's work: "Lauren is committed to our success. No matter what the task, she approaches it with determination, energy, and attention to detail. I can pay more attention to running the company because she manages our central office so effectively."

The pattern to Lauren's success is clear: her ability to listen carefully, consistency in following up, understanding that memory alone can't be trusted, skill in organizing and time management, and steadiness under pressure. Finally, Lauren makes no demands of others that she doesn't make of herself.

You are unlikely to begin in a position comparable to Lauren's. Within a short time, however, you could be handling as many tasks as she does. Regardless of your position, you will likely spend many busy days dealing with a great deal of detail management.

The Office Profession through the Years

Ever since written records have been kept, office professionals have been indispensable to their managers. In earlier years, some were called **secretaries** because they were relied on to record and protect important secret information. Early definitions of that title emphasized confidentiality. Businesspeople, public officials, and military leaders depended on those who could keep and find letters, bills, records, and confidential information.

With the development of industry in the United States, offices have greatly increased in size and many people have been needed to prepare correspondence, pay bills, and keep employee records, among other tasks. For example, clear records are essential for tax and general financial reporting. Certain laws require that other information be collected, reported, and stored for possible future use. Further, lawsuits are very common today. A business can be sued for something it did or failed to do. Accurate preparation and careful filing of mail and telephone logs, correspondence, reports, and financial statements are therefore crucial activities.

Figure 1–1 highlights the development of the office work profession since 1870. Figure 1–2 chronicles some of the costs of running an office from the mid-1870s to the present (with a prediction for the next century).

Thus, you can see how complicated office operation has become. Regardless of the organization, a great deal must be done to buy, sell, produce, hire, dismiss, complain, respond, and complete. As an office professional, you can become more productive with intelligent use of technology, but the *amount* of work you will perform is not expected to decline.

Figure 1-1
Highlights in the office work profession in America.

Library of Congress

1870   The number of female stenographers totaled seven.

1875   The earliest ad for female typists appeared in a New York newspaper: "Mere girls are now earning from $10 to $20 a week with the #'Type-Writer.'#"

1888   *How to Succeed as a Stenographer or Typewriter* by Arthur M. Baker was published; it was written mainly to men.

1900   The census reported over 100,000 women working as secretaries, stenographers, and typists; other estimates reached 200,000.

1911   The Katherine Gibbs Secretarial School was founded. Its aim was to allow more women to enter the field.

1920   One million women had entered the business world as clerical workers. These jobs required a high school education.

1973   WE (Women Employed) was organized by 1,000 women in Chicago to monitor the enforcement of affirmative action regulations requiring companies with federal contracts to set goals and timetables for firing, training, and promoting women and minorities. They subsequently won $500,000 in back pay for several hundred female employees. A new state rule banning the sale of discriminatory insurance policies followed.

1978   *Dun's Review* reported that secretaries changed jobs every eighteen months due to better offers.

1980   Working Women–National Association of Office Workers reached a membership of 10,000 in forty-five states.

1981   *The Wall Street Journal* reported that male secretaries were a rarity in the Midwest. A new national union local, District 925 (pronounced "nine to five") was organized.

1990   The U.S. Department of Labor predicted that the secretarial shortage will peak.

Courtesy of Marketing Concepts Ltd.

Figure 1-2

Sample office costs and salaries.*

1874	Mark Twain bought a typewriter for $25.
1878	A telephone guaranteed to work one mile cost $3; a five-mile model cost $5.
1892	"The Chicago" writing machine sold for $35.
1906	A six-week shorthand course cost $7; a beginning male stenographer's weekly salary was $20.
1930–	
1953	The cost of preparing and mailing a typical business letter rose from $.29 to $1.70.
1955	Women's wages averaged 64 percent of men's in all jobs.
1960	The cost of preparing and mailing a business letter rose to $1.83.
1961	One-third of almost 2,000 office managers surveyed reported that they always paid men more than women for the same job.
1964	Female clerks earned less than half of what male clerks earned.
1970	The cost of preparing and mailing a business letter rose to $3.05.
1976	The salary of the assistant to the mayor of New York City was $27,715.
1980	The cost of preparing and mailing a business letter rose to $6.07. Secretaries in Washington, DC, earned $243, 33 percent more than the national average; in Jackson, North Carolina, they earned 45 percent less than the average. Citibank reported using Mailmobile Robots, each of which replaced nine people.
1981	The average factory worker used $25,000 of equipment on the job; the average office worker used $2,900. Stenographers with the federal government started at $26,951; private secretaries earned $35,033.
1988	The cost of preparing and mailing a business letter rose to $9.89.
1990	The cost of preparing and mailing a business letter rose to $10.85.
2030	According to one book on predictions, a secretary will earn $600,000 (but a cup of coffee will cost $10).

*Figures for the costs of preparing and mailing correspondence courtesy of the Dartnell Corporation.

The Office Professional's Skills

A study by Professional Secretaries International (PSI) asked office professionals to rank fourteen tasks according to preference. Note that most respondents preferred the more demanding tasks and responsibilities:

1. Managing projects
2. Operating word processing equipment
3. Supervising people
4. Keeping financial records
5. Composing letters for executives
6. Making travel arrangements
7. Arranging and scheduling appointments and meetings
8. Typing
9. Taking shorthand/dictation
10. Answering and routing calls
11. Opening and sorting mail
12. Ordering equipment and supplies

13. Photocopying/duplicating
14. Filing

All these tasks are important in performing office work. Figure 1–3 summarizes the skills necessary for performing these and other office tasks.

Advances in technology have made completing some tasks easier. Nevertheless, telephones have to be answered, meetings arranged, business trips organized, records kept, and mail processed. These tasks have remained constant over the years.

Although you will use computer-based technology to complete much of your work, your human relations skills will be essential to office operation. Being able to work with different personalities, knowing how to solve problems, and making sound decisions are as important now as they ever were—and perhaps more so.

Research indicates that employers are eager to hire professionals with well-developed business skills, the ability to use computer technology to complete many assignments, and a positive attitude toward their work. Office professionals with the positive attitude, knowledge, and skills that Lauren Gomez demonstrates are in high demand and often have their choice of employers.

Your Title

Throughout the last one hundred years, office professionals who support one or more managers have been called *secretaries*. In many organizations, that title

Figure 1–3

Desirable skills and knowledge.

Knowledge

Typing/keyboarding	Office machines (copiers, fax, answering)
English language usage/spelling	Customer/client service
Computer operations	Cooperation with co-workers
Mathematics/some accounting	

Skills

Telephone, mail management	Written material preparation
Information management	(letters, memos, statistical reports)
(hardcopy and computer)	Recording of information
Greeting visitors, scheduling,	Management of financial records
making travel arrangements,	Employee supervision
meeting with management	

remains; but a new list of titles has emerged, reflecting the increased importance of the profession you have chosen. When you interview for a position or examine the classified ads in newspapers, you will likely see the following titles:

secretary	35%
executive secretary	25%
administrative assistant	15%
office manager	5%
assistant to . . . personnel assistant and program assistant	5%
other, including aide, associate, clerk coordinator, specialist, supervisor	10%
stenographer, typist, receptionist, operator	5%

Some ads will give no title but include only a list of the tasks; the person hired will determine what he or she will be called.

For consistency—and to emphasize how much a professional attitude will contribute to your success—we have chosen to call you and your colleagues **office professionals**. In an office, **professionalism** is highly valued and, to a substantial extent, rewarded. Throughout the remainder of this text, as you think about the specific "hard skills," such as keyboarding and filing, that will be required of you, keep in mind the other attributes of an office professional that employers value:

1. Appropriate overall appearance, especially attire
2. A sense of humor, used at the appropriate time
3. The ability to anticipate potential problems and take action in advance
4. Loyalty to both the employing organization and individual managers
5. Carefully chosen language, used in a natural way
6. Discretion concerning confidential matters
7. Neatness in work and other areas of responsibility

The Office Professional and Technology

Consider these common-sense suggestions as you examine how technology can contribute to your overall effectiveness:

- Many software programs allow you to input information once and then change parts of it regularly. It is unlikely that you will spend long hours typing and retyping drafts of letters, memos, and reports.
- Modern organizing systems for mailing lists, financial records, and general files will let you store and retrieve information easily and quickly.

- Computer technology can increase your organizing ability but can't substitute for a lack of it.
- It's best to learn what technology can do for you by applying new information slowly with assistance from co-workers.

Approached sensibly and with well-chosen hardware and software programs, your computer will be a mechanical assistant that will help you every day. You will explore its benefits in the chapters on mail management, organizing meetings, and financial duties. Chapter 2 overviews the technology and how to use computer hardware and software.

Elements of Success

Personal Attributes

What **attributes** do managers value most in their support personnel? A positive attitude and loyalty to the organization head nearly everyone's list. These two attributes are important in organizations of all sizes, whether clinics, manufacturing firms, airlines, insurance agencies, or universities.

Professional business education and management organizations such as the American Management Association periodically conduct surveys to determine the qualities managers value most in their assistants. According to these surveys, individuals with a **positive attitude** are easy to work with, willing to learn, and regular contributors to their offices. A positive attitude is infectious and creates the kind of atmosphere everyone appreciates. People with a positive attitude naturally project an upbeat outlook and confidence in their abilities. They also demonstrate **consistency** and **empathy**. Finally, they are likely to be goal-oriented and able to pinpoint daily accomplishments. Figure 1–4 summarizes these qualities.

Managers value **loyalty** for at least three reasons. First, a loyal employee is committed to quality work on all occasions and willing to exert extra effort when needed. Rarely does a loyal employee say, "This isn't my job!" Instead, he or she looks for ways to solve problems.

Second, loyalty brings **discretion**—the ability to handle (but not disclose) sensitive information and to work with (but keep silent about) confidential items. You may be called on, for example, to take confidential notes at an important meeting, type salary recommendations, or maintain sensitive financial or personnel records. In such situations, managers want to be sure that you are not discussing sensitive and private material with others in or out of the organization.

Third, loyal employees support both their managers and their organizations against outside critics who might do substantial damage or attempt to take advantage of situations or of others. Managers don't expect football-fan devotion, but they do want to see a willingness to emphasize positive over negative aspects

Figure 1-4
Elements of a positive attitude.

An Upbeat Manner

Managers appreciate an upbeat manner. A smile and a friendly "good morning" will make visitors feel comfortable about coming to the office. Remember to show appreciation to others for their assistance.

Consistency

Managers and co-workers want to be confident that your appropriate responses to questions, telephone calls, requests, and even crises can be counted on—every day. People with unexpected and substantial mood swings cannot be considered reliable on a consistent basis.

Empathy

What you do in the office affects others. Consider who will be affected by what you do or say and how they might feel before you speak or act. Empathy helps develop the skills of listening and observing, which are essential to an office professional's effectiveness.

Self-Confidence

Your positive attitude should be based on a strong belief in yourself. Psychologists suggest that people who focus on their accomplishments rather than on their shortcomings feel good about themselves, their work, and their associates. This satisfaction boosts the morale of everyone in the workplace.

Goal Setting

Setting realistic goals helps you focus your energies and increases your motivation. Establishing goals and developing a plan to reach them will encourage you to link daily activities to desired long-range accomplishments. At the end of each day and week, you can point to the progress you have made—progress that will give you satisfaction and pride.

of the organization. Managers also expect support against internal critics or employees who take advantage of the organization, such as those who habitually come in late, leave early, or take excessive breaks. Obviously, they also expect office professionals to report theft or unauthorized use of office equipment and materials.

In addition to the attributes of positive attitude and loyalty, employers value diplomacy. **Diplomacy**—the ability to listen, speak, and act in a manner appropriate to the situation—applies to answering the telephone, greeting visitors, working with a group of managers, or introducing a new employee to office personnel. A manager may hire an individual whose office skills are still developing if that person shows a clear ability to be diplomatic and tactful.

Managers appreciate an upbeat manner. *(Courtesy of Barbara Logan)*

Competition to gain and retain clients or customers is the nature of business and always will be. Providing necessary assistance to clients, helping out in special situations, or following up to determine customer satisfaction is essential. An office professional who knows what to say, how to say it, and when to say it will always be invaluable to employers.

Here are some tips for providing good service to clients:

1. Get to know who your customers are and what they need.
2. Make it easy for customers to come to you with their problems and concerns.
3. Make your customers' concerns your concerns (even if the details don't come under your job description).
4. Make customer satisfaction one of your top goals.

Still another valued attribute is **problem-solving skill**. Managers want to work with office professionals who can anticipate and solve a variety of problems, from breakdowns of copying machines to personality clashes. As you will see later in this text, problem-solving ability grows out of experience, requiring considerable common sense and a systematic approach.

Confident office professionals approach problems directly rather than allow them to grow and thus become even more difficult to address. They propose one or more alternatives; discuss those options with the people involved; listen; and, more often than not, compromise. Managers should be made aware of potential and actual difficulties their assistants face.

Office professionals with problem-solving skills are able to *anticipate* difficulties—a skill that managers appreciate. Remembering how sensitive situations were handled in the past is a valued ability. Some office workers keep written or computerized records of how they managed problems: the details of major meetings, important client visits, long and complicated trips, and extensive reports. As a result, they learn from the past and can address similar events calmly.

Managers demand the skills you will study and practice in your office procedures class and other courses. They expect you to understand how basic procedures are completed and to recognize that by establishing logical systems, you will be able to manage the hundreds of details an office professional confronts every day. Given their dependence on technology, businesses will likely require some level of computer literacy, including word processing, database management, and desktop publishing knowledge.

These skills will make you a valued employee. Further, when you have acquired the ability to work well with others, a knack for solving problems, solid listening and speaking skills, and the ability to work well under pressure, you will become indispensable.

Communication Skills

How you communicate is a central part of your overall image. What visitors, managers, and coworkers hear from you indicates the degree of professionalism you have attained. Following are a few simple guidelines for communicating effectively:

- Think before speaking, not only to organize what you say but to select the right words.
- Use proper grammar. If you're not sure, consult a dictionary or well-informed co-worker.
- Avoid profanity—it is offensive to many people (even if they don't tell you).
- Use humor when it can relieve tension or improve morale, but keep it appropriate. Never use humor to hurt another person.
- Remember that keeping silent is better than saying something inappropriate or in poor taste.

Listening is crucial to communication. Occasionally you will have to *work* to listen by (1) finding a location where paying attention will not be difficult;

(2) asking others to speak quietly; (3) indicating that you can listen to only one person at a time; (4) looking directly at the person talking; and (5) repeating what was just said for verification and then writing it down.

The Seven *C*s of Communication

1. **Completeness.** Provide all the information your readers/listeners need.
2. **Conciseness.** Keep your message brief.
3. **Consideration.** Be kind to your readers/listeners. Focus on the "you" (the reader/listener) rather than on yourself ("I").
4. **Concreteness.** Choose precise words; avoid vague words that may confuse readers/listeners.
5. **Clarity.** Double-check your message to ensure it is understandable. Ask yourself, "What do I expect them to understand from my message?"
6. **Courtesy.** Show sincerity, tact, and thoughtfulness by avoiding offensive words and expressions, placing blame, or demanding rather than asking for help.
7. **Correctness.** When writing, use an appropriate format; follow an acceptable writing style; proofread for spelling, keyboarding, or punctuation errors; and double-check the accuracy of facts and figures. When talking, use correct grammar; speak pleasantly and distinctly; and pay close attention to your listener's reactions.

Ethics

In your career, you will naturally want to follow the highest ethical standards. But what does **ethics** really mean? Recent evidence, including some well-publicized cases involving elected and appointed public officials, suggests that loyalty and ethical standards sometimes conflict. For example, a manager may ask an assistant to falsify certain records, destroy documents, or lie about the manager's whereabouts. This manager may believe that a loyal assistant is always supportive even if the request is inappropriate. These and similar requests may pressure office professionals to act in an inappropriate, if not dishonest, way. Knowing how to handle these situations is a clear indicator of professionalism.

No one can tell you which system of ethics to follow. Everyone is different and brings his or her unique values to every situation. We can tell you, however, that people who deal with ethical problems effectively have well-developed ethical systems.

One of the oldest ideas about ethics is "The Golden Rule": Treat others as you would like to be treated. Another basic idea is that ethical actions are those actions that benefit the most people without violating the rights of the few. The most important point, however, is that you should not attempt to "go it alone."

Decide on a system of ethics to follow and commit yourself to it. Then, if a problem arises that you can't comfortably interpret according to your ethical system, consult a counselor, rabbi, priest, pastor, teacher, doctor, or older family member.

If you follow your chosen ethical system in everything you do, you will be a valuable and trusted employee to the vast majority of managers, who themselves are generally honest, well-meaning people. If your beliefs place you in conflict with your employer, you may want to find a new employer rather than a new system of ethics. Remember: Your job is a lot easier to replace than your self-respect.

Self-Motivation

Office professionals are decision makers and must make many of their decisions independently. It is important to know when to ask for guidance and when to "do it yourself."

A truly **self-motivated** worker knows how and when to ask for help. That may sound like a contradiction, but it isn't. Passive people often let problems build up and pretend they don't exist. Strong, take-charge people get in and solve problems, either by themselves or with the help of others.

But it is also important to know the limits of your authority and your manager's patience. If you overstep your bounds and make decisions that require your manager's help or permission, you can end up in trouble. On the other hand, if you ask for permission or guidance every step of the way, your manager may as well do the job for you. So steer a middle course, be sensitive, and learn both the written and unwritten rules.

How do you learn what you should and shouldn't do? By learning everything you can about your manager's responsibilities. Read the materials you type, listen to phone messages and to others at meetings, and study the letters that cross your desk. You'll soon know what you can handle and what will require your manager's help. When you make your decision to step in and take charge, clear it with your manager first. Select with care the opportunities to demonstrate your leadership abilities so that you will use them successfully, learn your limits, and enhance your image as an effective office professional.

Overall Appearance

How you dress is very important. Some firms have a well-defined dress code; for example, they discourage female employees from wearing slacks and require men to wear jackets and ties. In other organizations, you will have to use your own best judgment to determine what is appropriate. However, subdued, well-pressed, and comfortable clothing is suitable in most office settings. If in doubt about appropriate attire, consult experienced co-workers.

Managers will also judge the appearance of your desk and work area. A neat, well-organized desk indicates that a professional uses it. With the increasing popularity of open-space offices, which offer no place to hide messiness, neatness and organization are becoming even more important. Further, because your assignments will continually change, you will have to find information quickly. Thus, be organized in anticipation of your needs so that frantic searches for documents won't add pressure to your day.

Becoming a Professional

Professionals don't develop their abilities overnight. They put a great deal of time and energy into mastering their fields. They learn from others and from experience, drawing strength as their confidence increases. Small improvements become significant accomplishments. Becoming an office professional takes hard work, but the rewards are great. Managers and others will recognize your achievements with promotions, increased salary and responsibilities, and greater opportunity. In addition, you will gain the personal satisfaction and pride that come from consistently excellent performance.

As you complete this and other courses, you may want to consider these suggestions from professionals for developing professionalism:

1. Study people with established records for excellence. Identify what they do, especially how they work with others. Look for the "little things" in action and language that set these individuals apart.
2. Become a positive self-analyst. Determine what you do well and what needs improvement.
3. Accept suggestions for improvement. Such suggestions will give you a more objective view about yourself. Also, if your manager makes suggestions, he or she believes your potential is worth developing.
4. Identify how formal education can contribute to your growth. Learn how to *learn* from educational activities.
5. Recognize that setbacks will occur, but balance them against your achievements to maintain a positive attitude.

Your Opportunities

Small business is the fastest growing sector of the U.S. economy. The Bureau of Labor Statistics estimates a 10 percent growth rate each year in the number of available positions for office professionals. Thus, there will be many opportunities for you to work in an office like the one in which Lauren Gomez is employed.

Various positions will offer you different opportunities and challenges. Consider the following possibilities:

- Secretary to a leading neurosurgeon who handles only the most difficult cases.

- Private aide to a nationally recognized television newscaster.
- Administrative assistant at a large two-year college located in a growing suburban community.
- Legal secretary to a partner in a firm that specializes in international law and handles lawsuits with millions of dollars at stake.

You are likely to find all of these positions in urban or suburban areas. A comparable list of attractive opportunities could be developed for smaller communities and rural areas. In short, opportunities are everywhere.

We've mentioned Professional Secretaries International (PSI) before. This organization is dedicated to the improvement and professionalism of office professionals. PSI defines *secretary* as an executive assistant who possesses a mastery of office skills; is able to assume responsibility without direct supervision; exercises initiative and judgment; and makes decisions within the scope of his or her assigned authority. But this general definition encompasses many kinds of office professionals.

You can choose to remain a "generalist," performing the tasks common to most offices. Each setting will vary to some extent, with a new set of terms, procedures, and personalities. But the basic skills—typewriting/keyboarding, organizing, communicating face to face or by telephone, managing records, and working with others (plus an ability to adapt!)—will likely suffice. There are probably more generalist jobs available than positions that require specialized training.

Some of you will decide to specialize as legal, medical, or education office professionals. Because of the knowledge and skills these positions require, you will need additional training and certification, but the opportunities are great.

Basic office skills of the generalist include typewriting/keyboarding, organizing, communicating face to face or by phone, managing records, and working with others. *(Courtesy of International Business Machines Corporation)*

(Chapter 17 discusses opportunities in more detail.) Those of you with an entrepreneurial spirit may start your own businesses to provide support to individuals and small companies. If you enjoy flexibility and variety, you may choose to be an office temporary.

In planning your career, you might ask, "Will I be replaced by a computer or some kind of robot?" Indeed, a few organizations have reduced the number of their support personnel. On the whole, however, the need for competent office professionals is greater than ever. *Newsweek* reports that 533,000 secretarial positions will become available every year over the next ten years (9/18/89, p. 2). In some cases, computers have actually spawned an increased need for office professionals.

In addition, completing office work with machines is only one aspect of the office professional's job. Recall all the tasks Lauren Gomez performed on that hectic Monday. The rest of her week was probably similar. Lauren had a great deal of technology available to her; but her knowledge and positive attitude, combined with a solid group of skills, made her the heroine of Electronic Optics.

The assignment sections in these chapters will give you an opportunity to learn more about how offices operate. As you gather information, note to what extent daily accomplishment and success are tied to the contributions office professionals make to today's businesses.

SUMMARY

People who work in offices have many titles. We use *office professional* to stress the importance of a professional attitude. The office professional's life is filled with diverse responsibilities, challenges, and potentially rewarding

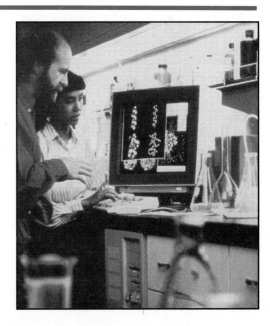

Various specialized fields open to the office professional include education and medical laboratory work.
(Courtesy of International Business Machines Corporation)

achievements. For both generalists and specialists, opportunities in the office profession are increasing continuously.

Office professionals need to possess "hard skills" such as typing or keyboarding, English language usage, office equipment and computer operations, and mathematics. They also need "soft skills," which are based on human relations. Soft skills include listening, communicating, empathizing, and working with others.

A cheerful, empathetic employee demonstrates the professional attitude so vital in organizing and managing an office. One way to develop a more positive attitude is to regularly assess your accomplishments. Also, establishing goals and developing a plan to attain them will give you a feeling of pride.

Other important qualities are a command of the English language and the ability to listen. These skills will constantly be tested in the many interactions you will have with others each day. With constant attention and the desire to do better, you can improve these skills.

A professional image demands that what you wear be appropriate. Likewise, you should maintain a well-organized work area. Good organization will demonstrate your competence and professionalism.

Office professionals who demonstrate loyalty, discretion, and support are greatly appreciated by employers. In addition, diplomacy and the ability to spot and solve problems are valued qualities.

As a professional, you must exert time and energy to develop the characteristics that lead to success. Others will recognize your achievement, and you will gain the personal satisfaction and pride that come from doing excellent work.

Key Terms

The following terms appeared in boldface type in this chapter. Do you recall what they mean? For a more complete definition, turn to the glossary beginning on p. 442.

attribute (p. 11)
consistency (p. 11)
diplomacy (p. 12)
discretion (p. 11)
empathy (p. 11)
ethics (p. 15)
loyalty (p. 11)

office professional (p. 10)
positive attitude (p. 11)
problem-solving skill (p. 13)
professionalism (p. 10)
secretary (p. 6)
self-motivation (p. 16)

Discussion Questions

1. Would you rank the fourteen tasks (p. 8) in the same order of preference used by Professional Secretaries International? If not, how would you change the ranking? How do you think your ranking might change after your first year on the job?
2. Which of the responsibilities of an office professional would you find

most attractive? Which ones would be least attractive? Explain your choices.

3. Review each major category of knowledge and skills (see Figure 1–3) needed in today's office. Which skills have you already developed? Which would you find the most challenging? Explain your choices.

4. Webster's *New Collegiate Dictionary* defines *professionalism* as "the conduct, aims, or qualities that characterize or mark a profession." What do you think of when you hear the term *professional*? Be prepared to discuss these qualities.

5. Think about loyalty for a moment. Are there any situations in which a manager's or co-worker's need for loyalty could exceed your limits? Consider and identify some specific cases.

6. Imagine you have access to certain confidential personnel records. Two co-workers continually pester you to see this material. What will you say to them to end their requests? What, if anything, will you say to your manager about this situation?

7. What an office professional says (or doesn't say) contributes a great deal to that person's image. The first words you say to a manager, co-worker, or visitor can be very revealing. How would you act in the following situations?
   a. Being introduced to a senior office professional the day you begin employment
   b. Greeting an unannounced and unknown visitor in the office
   c. Answering a phone call by an unknown person
   d. Asking a co-worker for assistance

8. Explain why your personal appearance is important in the work environment. How do you find out what is acceptable in your office?

9. Why do you think discretion is one of the most important attributes of a successful office professional?

10. Visitors judge an office professional on first impressions. They look for evidence of professionalism in both actions and appearance. List what you can do through your actions, appearance, work area, and phone manner to create a favorable first impression.

11. Explain the importance to on-the-job success of a positive attitude toward work, strong technical skills, and the ability to get along with co-workers.

Assignments

1. Ask a PSI member in your area (or, if there is no PSI chapter, a local businessperson) to speak to the class about professional image and the personal qualities and behavior necessary for success.

2. What skills and knowledge will you personally try to gain and/or improve upon within the next year? What goals do you have for your first year on the job?

3. Check your newspaper's "Help Wanted—Secretarial" (or "Office Professionals") advertisements to see whether they mention any of the skills you selected in question 2.

4. Make ten copies of the following list of personality characteristics. Distribute the copies to classmates, friends, and/or relatives, and ask them to circle the characteristics they would use to describe you. When you've completed one year on the job, have people in your organization do this exercise. Then compare their lists with those you obtained earlier.

accepting	cutting	kind	rude
adaptable	defensive	lazy	searching
affectionate	demanding	liberal	self-reliant
afraid	dependable	loyal	sensitive
aggressive	dependent	manipulative	serious
analytical	dominating	materialistic	shrewd
argumentative	easygoing	mature	shy
assertive	efficient	modest	sincere
athletic	emotional	naive	skillful
aware	energetic	observant	sociable
bewildered	enthusiastic	odd	stable
bitter	flexible	open-minded	straight
blunt	forceful	optimistic	stubborn
bold	frank	orderly	studious
bragger	free	organized	sympathetic
bright	friendly	original	tactful
brilliant	generous	outgoing	tender
carefree	gentle	passive	tense
careless	genuine	patient	thick-skinned
caring	gracious	perceptive	thorough
cautious	greedy	persistent	thoughtful
cheerful	happy	persuasive	thrifty
compassionate	helpful	pessimistic	timid
compatible	honest	powerful	tolerant
competitive	idealistic	practical	tough
complex	imaginative	precise	trusting
complicated	impractical	proud	trustworthy
conforming	independent	prudent	unassuming
conscientious	innovative	realistic	uncomplicated
conservative	intellectual	reasonable	understanding
controlled	intelligent	rebellious	unfriendly
cooperative	intolerant	relaxed	uninvolved
courageous	introverted	reliable	unpredictable
creative	involved	religious	vulnerable
critical	jealous	reserved	warm
curious	just	resistant	wise
		responsible	withdrawn

5. Using your experiences with part- or full-time employment or education, complete the following questionnaire regarding your professional image. Then discuss your responses with a few classmates who have completed the same self-analysis.

	Yes	No	Not Sure
I make sure to address my manager(s) in a formal manner.	———	———	———
I am not a party to office gossip about my manager or others in the organization.	———	———	———
If there is a controversy, I owe allegiance to the organization, first, then to my manager.	———	———	———
I help create and promote a pleasant working environment.	———	———	———
I continue to educate myself to increase my value to the organization.	———	———	———
I understand that my working equipment and materials belong to my employer.	———	———	———
When I must criticize, I do so in private; when I compliment, I do so in public.	———	———	———
I mind my own business.	———	———	———
I follow my organization's policies.	———	———	———
I am trustworthy and reliable.	———	———	———
I am self-assured when dealing with managers, co-workers, and clients.	———	———	———
I understand that my job is to support the work of one or more managers.	———	———	———
I take care of my health so that I can better perform my work.	———	———	———
I respect my employer.	———	———	———
I readily accept responsibility and handle it without supervision.	———	———	———
I perform my work with speed and accuracy.	———	———	———
My attire is appropriate for the office.	———	———	———
When I am at work, I work.	———	———	———
I make sure confidential work remains confidential.	———	———	———
I am punctual in arriving to work, arriving to meetings, and completing my work.	———	———	———
When I go to the office, I leave my personal life at home.	———	———	———
I exhibit a positive attitude toward my job.	———	———	———

6. Locate a manager who has worked with the same assistant for at least five years. Ask the manager which of his or her assistant's personal qualities are valued most. Then ask the assistant for a reaction to the manager's responses, as well as for any additional ideas about the qualities of professionalism.

Case Study
While completing his office procedures course, Henry Adams applied to a local law firm with three partners and two young associates, the latter recent law school graduates. No position was available at that time. Six months after Henry graduated and was hired elsewhere, the senior administrative assistant of the law firm called him to ask if he was interested in becoming an aide to the two associates. The responsibilities, location, pay, and fringe benefits made it impossible for Henry to pass up the offer.

After Henry began work, an unanticipated difficulty arose: The two associates took on a personal injury case involving several people whom Henry knew. These individuals were not close friends; Henry saw them at some social events, and two of their children had been in his high school graduation class. However, one of his responsibilities as an aide would be to transcribe their statements and perhaps have other on-the-job contacts with them. Thus, he would likely see a great deal of personal information about these people.

What can Henry do to be as professional as possible in this situation? What, if anything, should he say to the two attorneys preparing the case? How should he handle social situations in which he meets the people involved in the case?

2

USING TECHNOLOGY TO MA░░░░ YOUR WORK

Chapter Objectives

- To ░░░░░░░░░░░ ░░░░░░░ ardware: a keyboard, monitor, p░░░░░░░░ ░░░░░░░░░derstand each component's

- ░░░░░░░cessing software: to edit text; file; ░░ctions

- ░░░░░░░nputers includes all the functions of ░░░░░s, database management, statistical ░░░░shing, and information management,

░░░░n technology, including electronic mail, ░░░smissions, and voice messaging

░e hardware and software for your needs

Examp░░░░░
Excel░░░░

░░h Toys for Education, suddenly realized at 3:30 ░░error in a proposal mailed out that morning to ░ Margarita Sloan's office and asked if she would ░sed letter to each client. The letters had to be sent ░t the same time as the proposals.

░mly assessed the situation and asked Clayton these

░s' names and addresses? *(yes)* Were the names and ░a word processor or computer? *(no)*
░ ready for typing? *(yes)*
░e the recipient's name and address or omit the inside ░n only an announcement of the correction? *(use each*

░clude the client's name in a sentence within the body of the

░pany stationery suitable? *(yes)*

Because the names and addresses weren't in a computer file, they would have to be keyed. Margarita asked Robert to perform this task. After Robert finished keying the names and addresses into his desktop computer, Margarita hurriedly read through the letter checking for accuracy of content, grammar, and punctuation—how embarrassing it would be to make another error in the process of correcting the calculation error! Then Margarita discovered that the calculation error reappeared in a graph from a spreadsheet software program. Thus, that graph would have to be corrected in the revision letter too.

Margarita keyed the revision letter into her desktop computer. She used a spelling verification software package to identify keying errors, but she also proofread the letter for errors that the software could not find. Margarita printed one copy of the letter to make sure the spacing was correct and the letter easy to read. She also checked that the graph she had "called up" and corrected from the other software program was now placed at the appropriate point in the letter.

Margarita located a supply of company letterhead paper, second sheets, and envelopes and stacked them in the bins of the printer. She cleared the counter space near the letter-folding machine so that the printed letters could be quickly inserted. Then pages one and two could be matched and inserted into the correct envelope. The envelopes would be run through the postal machine, which would seal and put the correct postage on each envelope.

Robert brought Margarita the disk containing the names and addresses. She inserted it into her computer and started the printer to print the letters along with the matched envelopes. Margarita carefully examined the first printed letter and envelope to ensure that the final product was correct. Using her word processor, she had instructed the printer to merge the names and addresses Robert had recorded with the letter she had recorded. The merge function also allowed the computer to "remember" to insert the person's name at the predetermined point in the body of the letter. Minutes later, the printer had produced all the letters and the job was nearly done.

As she stacked the letters to take to the post office, Margarita glanced at her watch; it was 4:20, so she would not have to stay late. Once again technology, along with excellent organizational skills, has spared Margarita the tedious and time-consuming effort such a job would have required only a few years before.

Although managers recognize the need for office automation, it is office professionals who are affected by the technology. You will be deciding how to assign tasks and which operations to automate. Because the technology is constantly changing, working with it requires a positive attitude and a questioning, creative outlook. You will have the opportunity to evaluate and select electronic office equipment, maintain and care for it, and train others to use it. This chapter addresses these challenges as well as the following topics:

- How automated office equipment can help you in your work
- Basic computer hardware components
- Computer input and output devices
- Types of technological memory media
- How electronic typewriters increase office productivity
- Types of word processors and the advantages of each
- How word processing software can make your job easier

- How word processing integrates with data processing
- What data processing software does that word processing software doesn't
- How to train new employees in using word processing equipment

Innovation: The Human Element

Office equipment continues to become smaller in size, larger in capacity, faster in processing speed, and lower in cost. The new technology offers exciting potential. Nevertheless, each step in a newly automated procedure should be carefully checked to ensure that it matches the previous procedure. The best person to conduct this examination is an experienced office professional who has been following the approved procedure for many years.

Office professionals should remember that equipment designers usually know a great deal about technology but little about particular offices or businesses. Further, not even the latest hardware and software can solve all office problems. Many office tasks and problems require a responsible individual who knows how to use technology to perform office tasks in an efficient and effective manner. For example, only you can detect and correct all spelling, grammar, and logic errors in a business letter. Only you can distinguish a telephone call by your firm's most important customer from that of a pesky salesperson. No current technology can soothe an unhappy employee when the boss is out of town. In other words, *people* still need to be in charge.

Hardware

Hardware refers to computer equipment. *Software* refers to the programs that tell the computer what to do. This section introduces the various types of hardware.

A computer consists of five basic pieces of hardware: a keyboard, monitor, processing unit, disk drive, and printer.

Keyboard

The **keyboard** resembles a typewriter. It lets you type in data and commands to the computer such as Page Up, Page Down, Insert, Delete, Home, End, Print Screen, Scroll Lock, Pause, Center, Underline, and Bold. Each of these commands has its own key. Figure 2–1 shows a computer keyboard.

Monitor

The **monitor** is like a television screen; it shows what you have keyboarded. The monitor is also called a *cathode ray tube* or *CRT*.

Central Processing Unit

The "brain" of the computer is called the **central processing unit (CPU)**. The interior of the CPU consists of three sections:

1. The *internal storage area*, sometimes called the *memory*, contains the information you put into the computer along with your instructions to the computer. These instructions are in the form of prestored programs or software packages.
2. The *arithmetic unit* and the *logical unit* perform arithmetic functions such as adding, subtracting, multiplying, and dividing. This section of the computer system also performs logical deductions when you instruct the computer through a program.
3. The *control section* manages the often simultaneous functions of the computer. It ensures that the instructions from the internal storage area are understandable; then it interprets the instructions and notifies the arithmetic/logical unit to execute them. The control section also alerts the printer or other output device when the data are ready to be transmitted.

Disk Drive

Anything in the memory section of the computer can be stored on a disk (p. 30) and recalled later. The **disk drive** is a storage device that increases the computer's capacity for saving data. Typically, the disk drive on the top, sometimes the left, is the "A" drive and the one on the bottom, sometimes the right, is the "B" drive.

Businesses with moderate to heavy computer needs usually equip their computers with **hard disks,** which store more data than floppy disks. Figure 2–2 shows a computer with a hard-disk drive.

Printer

The **printer** (Figure 2–3) reproduces the information onto paper (the paper printout is also called *hardcopy*). Most computer systems can use many different kinds of printers. Printers vary in speed, print quality, and type of paper to be used. (Printers are explored in more detail on pp. 32–33.)

Auxiliary Technology

Input Devices

Entering a lot of information into the computer by keyboard can be expensive and time-consuming. Thus, some offices use auxiliary technology to speed up the process. We will discuss three types:

Figure 2–2
A computer with a hard-disk drive. The top slot, drive A, is filled.
(Courtesy of Apple Computer, Inc.)

Figure 2–3
Printer. *(Courtesy of International Business Machines Corporation)*

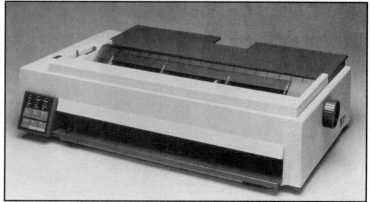

- An **optical character reader (OCR)** reads typewritten or handwritten documents and stores them on magnetic media.
- With **touch-sensing** technology, you point to words, drawings, diagrams, or symbols displayed on the screen. The screen responds to the touch as it normally would when information is keyboarded. Similar devices, **light pens,** allow you to write directly onto the screen or onto a data table that electronically senses what is being written and reproduces it on the screen.
- The popular **mouse** (Figure 2–4) is about the size of a deck of cards. You manually move the mouse in the desired direction on the table (it need not touch the machine) until the information is relayed to the computer. Then the computer moves a blip on the screen in the same direction. You then touch a button on top of the mouse to indicate that the decision has been made.

Machine-Readable Storage Media

Most information entered into the computer can be "filed" somewhere outside the computer so that it will not take up excessive space inside. Some *machine-readable storage media (MRSM)* are more cost-effective than others. Before purchasing MRSM, you should consider what will be stored, when it will be needed, and in what form.

Magnetic Tape

Magnetic tape is made from a strong but lightweight plastic. The rate at which data can be written on or accessed from magnetic tape depends on the *density* of the characters recorded (that is, how tightly packed together they are). As the density increases, the amount of data that can be stored increases. Density also affects the speed at which the data can be transferred from the main storage area in the computer to other storage media.

Data recorded on magnetic tape are written and retrieved in sequential order. If you want to access a document that is stored near the end of a tape reel, the machine must read all the previously recorded documents before it reaches the one you need. This procedure may take several minutes. Although magnetic tape may be ideal for sequentially recorded documents that are likely to be retrieved in a specific sequence (such as pension checks printed monthly), it is not a good choice in business operations such as airline reservation or bank teller transactions.

Disk

Disk storage is used for operations that need instant access—in fractions of a second. *Disks* are flat platters that resemble phonograph records. When stacked together, they form a disk pack. The platters are coated with a magnetized material, and data are recorded in circles called *tracks*. The density of the tracks determines how much information can be stored. The computer searches and finds data using **random access searching,** meaning that it can go directly to where the information is stored on the disk.

Figure 2–4
Hand-operated mouse. *(Courtesy of Apple Computer, Inc.)*

A **floppy disk** (Figure 2–5a), also called a *flexible disk* or *diskette,* can store up to several million characters of information. *Double-density (two-sided) floppy disks* can hold twice as much information.

A **Winchester disk,** a type of hard disk, may protect data from dust better than a floppy disk, because it is sealed in plastic. One Winchester disk can store what would take several dozen floppy disks to accommodate.

Figure 2–5
Floppy disks (a) can be two-sided. Hard disks (b) can store as much as 160,000 double-spaced typed pages of information. Businesses with moderate to heavy computer needs equip their computers with hard disks, which store much more data than floppy disks.

(a) Floppy disks. *(Courtesy of Maxell Corporation of America)*

(b) Hard disks. *(Courtesy of International Business Machines Corporation)*

Bubble Memory

Bubble memory stores data on a thin film of synthetic garnet. It stores more than magnetic tape or disk storage does. Other advantages are that bubble memory does not lose data when the power is turned off and it retrieves data faster. Bubble memory is currently expensive, but it is predicted that it will eventually replace disk storage.

Optical Disk

Optical disks store information in microscopic pits burned into them with laser beams. The pits then can be read by another laser beam in any sequence desired.

An optical disk can be used only one time to record information. It can be read many times, but nothing can be rerecorded on top of the first recording. Also, the data cannot be erased. Thus, optical disks are not recommended for records that will need constant updates or revisions.

Output Devices

The major types of computer output devices are printers, terminals, and computer output microfilm. Let's briefly review each of these devices.

Printers

There are two basic types of printer: impact and nonimpact. An **impact printer,** like a typewriter, has a ribbon. A hammer strikes the back of a raised or embossed character, leaving an imprint on the paper. A **nonimpact printer** makes images on paper through transfer, electrostatic, or photographic methods.

Printers may use either single sheets of paper or continuous-feed paper. Continuous-feed paper, which is frequently used for letterhead stationery and other business forms, has a perforated strip of holes along each side. These holes fit on pins that feed the paper into the printer.

A **dot-matrix printer** (Figure 2–6a) is a high-speed impact printer. The printing mechanism is a block of metal with many holes into which metal pins have been inserted. When a hammer strikes the back of the print block, the pins are forced against the ribbon, causing a series of very tiny dots to form the image of a character on the paper. Because the image on the paper is merely a series of dots, the quality of the printing is often unsuitable for sending to customers. However, it is satisfactory for most internal reports and memos.

A **daisy wheel printer** has a printing element that looks like a flower with long petals with a character embossed on the outer end of each petal. The printing element continuously whirls right and left to position the correct "letter petal" in the print position. A *thimble printer* works similarly except that the petals are cupped, making the printing element resemble a thimble. These printers, referred to as **letter-quality printers,** print only one character at a time and produce solid-line images. Thus, the print quality equals that of a good typewriter.

A *laser printer* (Figure 2–6b) is a type of nonimpact printer that uses regular bond paper. Laser printers are very fast, and most can be programmed to print in many different type fonts. They print about 18,000 lines per minute, or about two pages per second. Some print on both sides of a page, a process called *duplexing.* Laser printers offer five advantages for office automation: low cost, high print quality, very high printing speed, fewer moving parts to break down, and nearly silent operation.

Figure 2–6
Dot matrix and laser printers.

(a) **Dot-matrix printer.** *(Courtesy of International Business Machines Corporation)*

(b) **Laser printer.** *(Courtesy of International Business Machines Corporation)*

Terminals

Cathode-ray tube (CRT) terminals are often used by businesses. Most CRT terminals provide a wide variety of features, including paging, character or line blinking, scrolling, **cursor control** (a feature that allows you to move the cursor blip in all directions to indicate position on the screen), brightness, reversed and protected fields, underlining, and bold.

Portable terminals (Figure 2–7) are used to conduct business outside the office. They are lightweight and about the size of a briefcase. Some portable terminals include a CRT, a printer, a tape cassette or disk drive for storage, and a built-in attachment for interaction with the computer. Using a modem, you can connect a portable terminal to standard telephone lines to communicate with other computers or directly to a computer to enter or retrieve data over telephone lines.

Computer Output Microfilm

Computer output microfilm (COM) can produce output at 20,000 or more lines per minute. Most systems output information onto **microfiche film cards,** which

Figure 2–7

Portable terminal and workstation, interchangeable for right- and left-handed users. *(Courtesy of Curtis Manufacturing Company, Inc.)*

can hold hundreds of pages of output. This information can be read only by using special magnifying devices, hand-held microfiche readers, desktop readers, or reader-printers.

Advantages of this system include the high speed at which information can be retrieved, the ease and economy of producing multiple copies of needed information, and the far smaller storage space required. Also, microfilm can be mailed at a small fraction of the cost of mailing other output.

Word Processing

Today word processing depends on the microchip. The **microchip,** which is about the size of a matchbook, contains the software that allows the merging of word processing (words, sentences, and paragraphs) and data processing (mathematical calculations). A person may use both functions in one computer. Therefore, you should keep in mind that some older equipment will handle only word processing while most recent computers will accommodate both word processing and data processing functions.

Electronic Typewriters

Electronic typewriters are inexpensive word processors. Standard office electric typewriters are no longer being manufactured; instead, most offices are using electronic typewriters because of their greater capability and affordability. Like its predecessor, the electronic typewriter can be used to keyboard, correct errors, store data, and retrieve documents.

Electronic typewriters are a combination of the earlier electric typewriter and the **memory typewriter,** an earlier form of word processor. It is not unusual to find memory typewriters in use alongside newer machines, as few businesses can afford to throw out old equipment every time new technology becomes available.

Office professionals find electronic typewriters more convenient than computer equipment for some frequently performed tasks such as typing envelopes, preparing labels, and filling in multipage forms. For example, to address one envelope on a computer, you would have to start the computer, load the word processing program, adjust the paper guide on the printer, and remove the stationery to insert an envelope if the printer lacks a dual-sheet feeder that takes both stationery and envelopes. You could complete this task in a far shorter time on the much less expensive electronic typewriter.

Of the lower-cost electronic typewriters, compact models are more apt to be found in offices. They usually have one to two lines of memory, which allows you to correct many point-of-entry errors. Spelling verification programs are available for some compacts, as well as the capability to print in bold and italic. Another feature allows you to adjust the line spacing in increments of 1/20th of an inch, which is helpful when filling in forms where space is critical. A slightly more sophisticated model can be upgraded by adding video screens and additional memory.

The more costly electronic typewriters have much greater memory capacity and can be expanded with the addition of diskettes. They frequently have a video display screen that shows a full page just as it will appear when printed. The spelling verification checks typically allow you to insert industry-specific terms and names of clients, products, or other short segments of information into the program. The more recent addition of "window" technology allows you to switch into a new program while using the text-editing function. For example, the document will continue to be displayed while you check the meaning of a word in a "window" by calling up another program. Frequently used copy that has been recorded in memory can be easily inserted into a document by keying a simple instruction.

Some machines allow you to switch back and forth from an electronic typewriter to a personal computer. Experts predict that the future for electronic typewriters will include the capability of using software packages as well as connecting with additional printers, a fax, or a telex machine. Figure 2–8 shows an electronic typewriter with a monitor.

Dedicated Word Processors

A **dedicated word processor,** also called a **stand-alone word processor,** is a single unit with one keyboard and video display screen. Only one operator can

Figure 2–8
Typewriter with monitor.
(Courtesy of International Business Machines Corporation)

use it at a time. Its functions include automatic margin adjustment with wraparound capability, automatic centering, global search, spelling verification, dictionaries, automatic underscoring and boldfacing, format storage, blocking and moving of segments of information within a document, and reformatting of paragraphs.

Shared-Logic Word Processors

A **shared-logic word processor** looks like a dedicated word processor, but it shares the memory and logic of one central processing unit. A shared-logic word processor is designed for a word processing center in which several operators work on different tasks at the same time. It consists of a single large-memory unit that may have several diskette drives and one or more printers. Each operator uses a separate display screen and keyboard attached to the word processor memory unit by a telephone wire. Since the memory unit is the most expensive part of the equipment, this arrangement allows the company to invest considerably less money in equipment while leaving several workstations available for simultaneous keyboarding. These units show copy on the screen or provide printouts. Most of these systems store information on floppy disks.

A disadvantage of this system is its total dependence on the functioning of the central processing unit. If the CPU breaks down, no one can work until it is fixed.

Microcomputers

Microcomputers (Figure 2–9), also called *personal computers (PCs),* consist of a keyboard, screen, microprocessor, and printer. These "desktop" microprocessors can be used as stand-alone computers or as communicating computers. When a microcomputer is used as a stand-alone computer, all entry, storage, and retrieval are housed within one machine. Some microprocessors can be linked to a large computer, allowing for easy transfer of data from the point-of-entry microprocessor to the larger machines.

A great deal of software designed to increase office productivity is available for microcomputers. Most software companies sell ready-made packages for functions such as word processing, payroll, inventory control, file management, and graphics. These packages allow a microprocessor to serve as both a word processor and a data processor (able to perform arithmetic functions).

Equipment Compatibility

Office professionals who perform word processing often differ from those responsible for data processing. If each department selects a computer without consulting the other, they may find that their hardware selections cannot

Figure 2–9
Microcomputer. *(Courtesy of Microcomputer Accessories, Inc.)*

communicate with each other without additional hardware and wiring. It is best for the departments to confer with each other before buying equipment.

Typically a workstation has a microcomputer (or word processor) with the ability to store and use its own files and programs. Some of these files are text files created by the word processing software and some are collections of numeric data stored as tables by the spreadsheet software. Although it may sound simple to exchange floppy disks among different workstations, there are three complications: (1) The workstation equipment must be the same; (2) the software station must record files on disks in a standard form; and (3) the workstations must be located near one another.

The need to exchange files or data among workstations usually arises after several employees with different jobs have become comfortable using their word processors or microcomputers. For example, Judy keyboards a monthly progress report using word processing software. The report is to contain several large tables of numbers that Dan has entered using spreadsheet software in the accounting department, which is located in the next building. If Judy can borrow Dan's floppy disk, she can move the tables directly into the body of the report text, eliminating the need to rekeyboard.

In this example, Judy and Dan can work efficiently only if their microcomputers and software are compatible, that is, if Judy's word processing software can read Dan's spreadsheet software. It will also be convenient, since Judy and Dan work in different buildings, if the information can be transferred electronically from Dan to Judy.

Local Area Networks (LANs)

Local area networks (LANs) make data exchange among workstations easy. A LAN connects several workstations by wire or cable. This connection enables the workstations to "talk" to one another. Employees exchange items such as letters, reports, files of data, and even personal memos.

A local area network can serve up to thirty workstations located in the same building or in adjacent buildings (see Figure 2–10). Workstations that are farther apart can be connected by a **remote user network** or a multiuser computer network. Both types of network require larger, more expensive computer equipment and network management software.

Some networks require all workstations to be operating when messages are being sent or received. The requirement may be inconvenient for the user who works at night or on weekends. Thus, a network may expand its hours of service by installing electronic mail software (discussed later). Then a user may send a message to another workstation even if the receiving workstation is not active; the receiver will see the message as soon as he or she turns on the workstation. Most office networks start with a collection of individual microcomputers and add a LAN within two or three years. A company's decision to use electronic mail depends on its need to communicate rapidly and its commitment to use less paper.

Figure 2–10

Multiple users accessing document information via a local area network (LAN). *(Courtesy of TAB Products Company)*

Another way to transmit a report between workstations is over the phone using a modem. A **modem** translates computer signals into signals that will travel over a telephone line. In the future, companies will likely use fiber optic cables, which are like modems but use light signals.

Software

Software programs tell the computer system what to do and when to do it.

Word Processing Software

Software for word processing should be able to (1) edit text, (2) file, (3) mix/match/merge/sort, and (4) perform utility functions.

Some packages include graphics, statistical functions, and special printing functions; however, the typical package has only these four functions. If an office does not need all four functions, it can buy software that performs only what it needs. For example, an office that needs only the text-editing function for letters, memos, and reports can save money by using a smaller software package that is not designed for filing or preparing intricate form letters for mass mailings. Also, an office that has a machine with a small memory should purchase a package that fits the machine's capabilities.

The **text-editing** function allows you to (1) insert characters or lines; (2) delete characters or lines; (3) move or copy lines or paragraphs within the body of the text; (4) justify the margins and set tab stops; and (5) center the copy on a page or center columns within a page. These are the most basic text-editing functions, but more elaborate software packages do more.

The **filing** function stores and recovers addresses for mass mailings. It automatically creates form letters and merges specific address lists when used in conjunction with the **mix/match/merge/sort** function. You can store form letters with general paragraphs to be sent to all addressees, as well as special paragraphs to be included only for specific recipients. (Such preformed paragraphs are sometimes called *boilerplate*.)

A company can choose from a wide range of **utilities** for inclusion with the word processing software, such as (1) automatic page make-up and page numbering; (2) an automatic spelling checker; (3) the ability to add and print totals of columns of numbers entered through the text editor; and (4) the ability to print side headings in boldface type.

Microprocessing Software

Computer software for microcomputers (Figure 2–11) generally includes all the functions found in word processing software, plus several additional ones. The most common software packages used in business are spreadsheets, word processing, database management, statistical packages, graphics software, desktop publishing, and information management.

A **spreadsheet package** (Figure 2–12) displays the largest "sheet" of columnar accounting paper imaginable—at least 250 columns and 500 rows. Not only can you list data, you can also instruct the computer to perform basic arithmetic functions. Spreadsheet software is helpful if you must account for funds or prepare reports based on sales or budget records.

Database management packages can file large numbers of records in files that can be easily searched in order to display or print one or several records. This software can merge several files into a single file to print summary reports automatically.

Figure 2–11

Computer software. Software for microcomputers commonly includes word processing software for text editing plus other functions such as information management. *(Courtesy of International Business Machines Corporation)*

Figure 2–12

Spreadsheet. Spreadsheets list, in columns, data such as company finances. *(Courtesy of International Business Machines Corporation)*

Statistical packages are used to prepare reports such as comparisons or projections of income, costs for project operation, and estimates of profits based on a comparison of income and expenses. The formulas for calculating these statistical summaries are sometimes simple, such as the calculation of the average of a series of numbers. However, additional, complex formulas are needed to produce certain statistical information. Most office employees may understand the method used but often forget the exact formula because they do not use it every day. Statistical packages store these formulas and calculate the answers automatically.

Some spreadsheet and statistical software packages are designed to work together. For example, you may enter the company's daily income into the spreadsheet; then your manager uses the statistical package with these income amounts to predict income for the following year.

The attractive reports applauded by managers today are the result of graphics and desktop publishing software. You can easily produce a wide range of charts, graphs, and other illustrations on your microcomputer (Figure 2–13). You can also print reports and documents with software that paginates material, includes headings, and prints various typefaces. With **desktop publishing software,** you can produce newsletters and other documents with the same professional appearance as those produced by commercial print shops.

A **graphics package** uses output from a statistical package to represent the results as graphs or charts. Some graphics packages even help you prepare simple illustrations or design business forms.

Figure 2–13

Desktop publishing software. The office professional can use desktop publishing software to prepare attractive reports with a wide range of charts, graphs, and other illustrations.
(Courtesy of Apple Computer, Inc.)

Microcomputers with large amounts of memory can handle a single software package that will automatically combine all necessary functions into one program. For example, Li Ming prepares a monthly report that follows the same format each month. The package allows her to create paragraphs and insert numbers from a spreadsheet at the proper place in the report. She uses a statistical forecast as well as a graphic representation of the monthly sales. These combined functions make the monthly report preparation relatively easy.

Information management software can help you keep other important office records up to date. For example, you can maintain appointments and daily "to do" lists on your desktop computer, and these schedules can be printed as a daily, weekly, or monthly calendar (Figure 2–14).

Appointment calendar software is probably one of the most useful packages available. This program will not allow conflicting appointments for the day. It is also available for laptop or briefcase computers used by managers outside the office. When the manager returns and connects the briefcase computer and the office computer, all appointments he or she has made are transferred electronically to the master appointment file in the office microcomputer. Any conflicts can be resolved at that time. This software also includes a simple accounting function that lists managers' expenses. When this information is transferred to the office microcomputer, a spreadsheet package can be used to prepare expense accounts.

Transmission Methods

In this section we will explore today's newest communication technology, including electronic mail, electronic notebooks, facsimile (fax) transmissions, and voice messaging.

Figure 2–14
Software that includes a "To Do" list, calendar, and organizer for expenses, contacts, and projects. *(Courtesy of International Business Machines Corporation)*

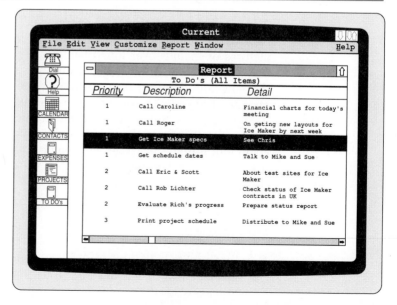

Electronic Mail

Electronic mail blends the telephone with the computer. Both the sender and the receiver must have a computer. Messages travel back and forth via the telephone, which is connected to the computers. For example, the traveling executive uses a briefcase-size electronic notebook (discussed next) for writing memos and letters in her hotel room at the end of the day. She uses the telephone to send the contents of her electronic notebook to the office electronic mail system. Her assistant can retrieve the letters at the beginning of the next workday. In turn, the assistant can store and relay memos addressed to the manager, who reads and responds to them from her hotel room that evening.

Some organizations are expanding their personal electronic mail systems into centralized networks by using special electronic mail software or by subscribing to a public electronic mail system. These are expensive options, but they allow microcomputers to interact throughout the organization as well as with other firms.

Electronic Notebooks

The **electronic notebook** is a relatively inexpensive computer designed to fit inside a briefcase. Your electronic notebook could include a word processor for memos, a petty-cash accounting program, an appointment calendar, a telephone and address directory, and a "tickler" file to display reminders of tasks to be completed on specific dates. The notebook replaces the steno pad, card file, desk file, desk drawer files, and task schedule board. The cost of electronic notebooks is so low that many employees purchase their own.

Facsimile (Fax) Transmission Machines

A **facsimile transmission (fax)** or **transfax** (Figure 2–15) transmits a picture of a page by telephone. Some fax devices operate like copying machines to send pictures or memos over long distances. The user inserts a document into the machine and dials the telephone number of the receiver. Then the user places the telephone handset in a coupler cradle and presses a "send" button. The machine transmits the document to the receiving fax machine.

Some fax machines can send electronic data stored in the memory of one typewriter directly to the memory of a typewriter in a distant city—usually in about four minutes per page. The major limitation of this form of transmission is that it is received on paper rather than on a computer display and is difficult to correct on the receiving end.

Voice Messaging

Voice messaging is like an answering service. You leave a spoken message that the recipient may listen to later. You can send the same message to several

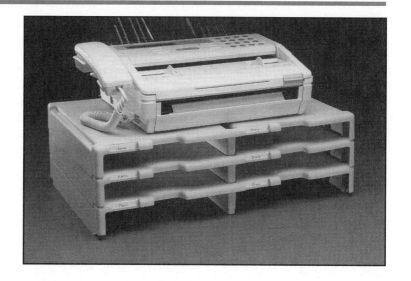

Figure 2–15
**Fax device and expandable fax
holder.** *(Courtesy of Curtis
Manufacturing Company, Inc.)*

persons at the same time. You can arrange for future delivery and notification of delivery.

However, with voice messaging there is no immediate feedback and no printed copy. You cannot leave complex or lengthy messages. Also, some people dislike talking to a machine.

The cellular phone is a new technology that is gaining in popularity. With this device, you can make and receive calls from your car rather than having to stop at a pay phone.

Choosing Hardware and Software

If you are asked to help select an office system, remember to choose the software first, then the hardware. The reason is that most programs will work only on a limited number of computers. The software you choose will narrow your choice of computer.

To begin the selection process, consider the following questions:

- What are your needs—word processing, data processing, electronic mail?
- How heavy do you expect the workload to be?
- What are your printing needs?
- Will you have any need for graphics or desktop publishing?
- Will you need computers with communication capability?
- Is convenient, reliable repair service available?
- Are the instructional materials clear and easy to understand?
- How many people will be using the machines? How easy are the machines to operate?
- How will employees be trained?

Once you have found a few software packages you like, check the throughput time for each task with each software package. (By *throughput* we mean the amount of time between starting and finishing the task.) Find out which package is fastest. Identify a few tasks that most resemble your normal business transactions, and ask to see these tasks demonstrated with each proposed software package. Then multiply the time taken for one demonstration transaction by the number of similar tasks that characterize your business processing. The following list includes some typical tasks:

Daily tasks	Entering customer charge sales Entering bills to be paid Posting sales to inventory and accounts receivable files
Weekly tasks	Entering employee time cards Posting payroll costs to various general ledger files Printing checks

Monthly tasks	Summarizing all charge sales and printing monthly statements
	Summarizing all unpaid bills; posting these
	    bills to the proper general ledger
	    accounts; printing checks
	Printing trial balances; closing general
	    ledger accounts; preparing
	    financial statements

It is best to buy from software vendors who have been in business for several years. This strategy will allow you to obtain occasional service assistance from the vendor who developed and sold the software package.

After exploring all these issues, you will be ready to purchase the computer system. Typically, you will select those items listed under the software first, followed by the equipment listed under the hardware.

Software

1. Application programs
2. Word processing package
3. Spreadsheet package
4. Database management package
5. Desktop publishing package
6. Appointment calendar package

Hardware

1. Operating system with programming languages
2. Central processing unit (CPU)
3. Hardware repair and maintenance service
4. Printer
5. Video display terminal(s)
6. Keyboard

Teaching Others

Office professionals often help teach employees new skills such as operating and maintaining equipment, understanding office procedures, completing forms, and handling difficult customers. Many office professionals find the following four-step process for teaching employees valuable:

1. Preparation for learning
   a. Put the employee at ease. If the employee is afraid of you, it will be more difficult for him or her to learn.
   b. Tell the employee what you want him or her to learn. Start by determining how much the employee already knows.
   c. Explain the benefits of what you are teaching. Once the employee wants to learn, your job will be much easier.
   d. Place the learner in the best position to learn. If equipment is involved, be sure the employee is seated and has all the necessary materials.
2. Presentation of skill/knowledge
   a. Describe, demonstrate, and illustrate one step of a task at a time. Use simple words; speak clearly and slowly. Define any technical terms.
   b. Emphasize key points. Determine one key point for each step of a procedure. This strategy will help the employee recall each step later by remembering the key point.
   c. Be patient. Do not present too much information at one time. Most people tend to try to teach too much too fast; learners become confused and frustrated. Present the information in a recognizable sequence, and wait until each step is mastered before continuing.

When teaching someone how to use a computer, determine one key point for each step of a procedure.
(Courtesy of International Business Machines Corporation)

3. Performance of skill/knowledge
   a. As soon as possible after teaching a new skill, give the employee an opportunity to perform the skill on a trial basis while you observe. If errors occur (and they will), patiently and tactfully correct them and encourage the employee to try again.
   b. Ask the employee to verbally explain the procedure. This method will help clarify his or her understanding. Encourage the employee to ask questions.
   c. Provide the employee with sources of help should you be unavailable. For example, show him or her where a manual is kept or provide the name of a co-worker who would be willing to help. You can also supply the name and telephone number of the vendor.
4. Evaluation of skill/knowledge

After a training session, follow up to ensure that all is going well. Encourage the employee to ask questions. However, do not undermine the person's confidence by oversupervising; taper off when you think he or she has reached a satisfactory performance level.

Most training problems are due to insufficient time allowed to teach, failure to follow the above four steps, and/or a lack of patience and unreasonable expectations. Fortunately, such problems can be avoided with careful preparation and a positive, helpful attitude.

Remember that as an office professional you must keep up to date to be able to share your knowledge with others in the organization. To do this effectively, you will need to continue to learn through self-study, formal coursework, and practice.

SUMMARY

Technology has vastly increased the productivity and independence of workstations. Today's typewriter can add computer memory for storage, editing capabilities, video displays, magnetic media, and the ability to transmit documents via telephone lines.

Word processors are available as shared-logic processors or stand-alone processors, depending on their memory, and may be linked to computers.

Microcomputers can be both computers and word processors. With the appropriate software, they can replace stand-alone word processors while providing executives and office professionals with flexibility and computing power right at their desks.

Office software includes word processing software with text editing, filing, mix/match/merge/sort, and utility functions. Other programs useful in the office include spreadsheet, statistical, graphics, desktop publishing, information management software and appointment calendar software. Computer-based technology continues to make managing office work easier, less repetitive, and more error-free. Spreadsheet software makes producing figures, statistics, budgets, and financial reports a simple activity. Graphics software allows the creation of charts, graphs, and other illustrations. With desktop publishing software, formats for long reports can be set up once and used repeatedly.

Recordkeeping, appointments, and office communications now move more efficiently with electronic notebooks, electronic mail, and fax machines. Various types of printers produce documents in draft or letter-quality form.

Key Terms

The following terms appeared in boldface type in this chapter. Do you recall what they mean? For a more complete definition, turn to the glossary beginning on p. 442.

appointment calendar software (p. 43)
bubble memory (p. 32)
cathode ray tube (CRT) (p. 34)
central processing unit (CPU) (p. 27)
computer output microfilm
   (COM) (p. 34)
cursor control (p. 34)
daisy wheel printer (p. 33)
database management package (p. 41)
dedicated (stand-alone) word
   processor (p. 36)
desktop pubishing software (p. 42)
disk drive (p. 28)
disk storage (p. 30)
dot-matrix printer (p. 33)
electronic mail software (p. 44)
electronic notebook (p. 44)
electronic typewriter (p. 35)
facsimile transmission (fax) or
   transfax (p. 44)
filing (p. 40)
floppy disk (p. 31)
graphics package (p. 42)
hard disk (p. 28)
hardware (p. 27)
impact printer (p. 32)
information management
   software (p. 43)
keyboard (p. 27)

letter-quality printer (p. 33)
light pen (p. 30)
local area network (LAN) (p. 39)
magnetic tape (p. 30)
memory typewriter (p. 35)
microchip (p. 35)
microcomputer (p. 37)
microfiche film card (p. 34)
mix/match/merge/sort (p. 40)
modem (p. 40)
monitor (p. 27)
mouse (p. 30)
nonimpact printer (33)
optical character reader (OCR) (p. 30)
optical disk (p. 32)
portable terminal (p. 34)
printer (p. 28)
random access searching (p. 30)
remote user network (p. 39)
shared-logic word processor (p. 37)
software (p. 40)
spreadsheet package (p. 40)
statistical package (p. 41)
text editing (p. 40)
utility (p. 40)
touch sensing (p. 30)
voice messaging (p. 44)
Winchester disk (p. 31)

Discussion Questions

1. What types of reports have you seen that were probably prepared with spreadsheet software? What types of office reports and other documents would be more efficiently prepared using spreadsheet software?
2. When might you want to use a stand-alone electronic typewriter to complete assignments?

3. Outline the basic elements you would select for a computer system.
4. What are the advantages and disadvantages of participating in a local area network (LAN)?
5. How can electronic mail improve communication between an office professional and one or more managers?
6. Explain how you would send a fax (facsimile transmission). Why do you think this method is becoming more popular?
7. How would you explain a word processing program to a newly hired office professional? What would you suggest this person do to become familiar with this technology?
8. Why should you take the time to become acquainted with software before trying to think of more applications (ways to use it)? What makes this a time-consuming task in the beginning?

Assignments

1. Become acquainted with current word processing equipment and software by reviewing office personnel and information periodicals. In outline form, write down the brand name and number, manufacturer, and a description of the features listed. For software, include the equipment on which it could be used. What are the similarities and differences among the brands?
2. Form groups of five. Each group member calls two office professionals at different businesses and asks what types of word processing equipment and software they use. How did they learn the software? How long did it take before they felt comfortable operating it? Add any other questions you like, but be sure all five people in the group ask the same questions. Give your findings to the class.

Activity

Calculate your technological ("techno") coefficient score as follows. In column 1, record how many times you use each piece of equipment each day. Multiply this number as shown, and record your answer. Then total the points.

telephone	____	× 2 = ____
color television	____	× 3 = ____
black-and-white television	____	× 1 = ____
video tape machine	____	× 4 = ____
video camera	____	× 5 = ____
CD player	____	× 4 = ____
computer with word processing	____	× 10 = ____
modem	____	× 10 = ____
boom box	____	× 4 = ____
		Total ____

Techno Coefficient

$$
\begin{array}{rcl}
0 - 10 \text{ points} & = & \text{beginner} \\
11 - 25 \text{ points} & = & \text{on your way} \\
26 - 35 \text{ points} & = & \text{average} \\
36+ & = & \text{techno wiz} \\
0 - 10 \text{ points} & = & \text{beginner}
\end{array}
$$

 Those instructors using *Top Performance: A Decision-Making Simulation for the Office* should consult the *Instructor's Guide* at this point for support material regarding use of the software in the classroom.

Case Study

Lisa Dooley's manager is a diehard computer addict. He firmly believes in keeping up with changes in hardware and software. He also wants Lisa and other office personnel to become skilled in using spreadsheets, producing charts and graphs, and formatting reports.

The administrative clerk who handles office finances has mastered the spreadsheet program loaded into the office computers and volunteered to help others learn how to use it. Seven training sessions were scheduled. But they were a disaster. It wasn't that the clerk demonstrated the software improperly or was uninterested in training others. The problem was that explanations were unclear and the clerk seemed impatient with the questions asked.

Lisa doesn't want to continue with the training, but her manager wants to start using the spreadsheet program very soon. What are Lisa's alternatives? How can she become familiar with the software on her own? How should she approach the administrative clerk?

CHAPTER

3

ORGANIZING FOR PRODUCTIVITY

Chapter Objectives

- To understand the importance of an organizational chart so you know where the various responsibilities of the company lie

- To be aware of your manager's responsibilities, which generally include planning and setting goals; organizing the work; directing to complete the tasks; and controlling the work flow

- To comprehend your responsibilities in the role of support personnel as secret keeper, sounding board, coordinator, and assistant

- To learn how to develop a good working relationship with your manager and to understand how your position fits in with the total picture of the company

- To understand how the physical characteristics of your office, such as sufficient space, optimal lighting, adherence to safety features, and well-designed furniture increase productivity

---

Examples of Excellence

"Ms. Blanton is the person who can best answer your question. She'll be back at 2 PM. Can you call back then? Or may I have her return your call?" Ann Watanabe told a client calling long-distance. Then she helped two visitors use audiovisual equipment in the firm's conference room and located a corporate officer with authority to sign travel advance checks for sales staff going to a national convention.

As executive secretary to the president of Heartland Insurance, Ann frequently works on her own, making decisions about priorities. "All in a day's work," Ann tells managers who admire her detailed knowledge of all aspects of company operations. But what she modestly shrugs off now actually took months of hard work to learn: how the firm operates and how to keep up with changes in people, products, and policies. As Ann's manager points out, "We can concentrate on work outside the office, particularly with clients. Ann and her co-workers are in charge of what happens inside."

The keys to the high productivity Ann regularly achieves are

1. Understanding the organization's products and/or services
2. Understanding her manager's principal responsibilities

52

3. Having access to a comprehensive office manual that details important procedures
4. Organizing her work area with attention to details that help reduce stress

In this chapter, we will examine each of these four factors. You will learn how organizing skills, combined with the skills described in Chapters 1 and 2, will contribute to your success.

Understanding Your Part in Productivity

Know Your Company's Goals

Knowledge about your organization will help you see how your work contributes to the organization's success. Become familiar with the organization's basic purpose, structure, reporting lines, and key personnel, specifically those to whom your manager reports and those with responsibilities similar to your manager's. It's a good idea to obtain a copy of the organizational chart.

All organizations have clearly defined objectives, whether they produce a product, a service, or both. A profit-oriented business can be a single proprietorship, a partnership, or a corporation that sells stock. Read your organization's newsletter, annual report, and public relations material to learn more about its objectives.

Here are some things you will want to know about your employer:

1. Who was the founder? When was the company founded?
2. How many people work there? (Keep a list of personnel and update it periodically.)
3. Who owns the company now—a single person, partners, or stockholders?
4. How many stockholders are there?
5. What goods (services) does it produce (provide)?
6. Who are its competitors?
7. Which products or services are the most profitable?
8. What does your department do?
9. What does your manager do? What are his or her goals?
10. Who is your manager's boss?
11. How do you help your department achieve its goals?

Become familiar with how the firm is structured. The three most widely used organizational structures are (1) line, (2) functional, and (3) line and staff. Figure 3–1 illustrates all three structures.

In a *line structure*, one person directs one or more operating units. In other words, this person has authority and responsibility for the performance of the position below hers.

Larger organizations are more likely to use a *functional structure*. This structure is designed around an expert in a specialized field. Thus, the manager of a functional area has overall responsibility but assigns specific duties to employees.

A business that produces one or more products typically uses a *line and staff structure*. Managers in such an organization direct employees much as they would in a line organization, but they also have "staff" who can provide assistance when needed.

Know Your Manager's Work

Once you understand your organization's goals, your next task is to identify the responsibilities of your unit or department. Part of this task is knowing what your manager does, and part of it is knowing your job description.

The main person you will work for will obtain, control, and use information. With these data, your manager will develop and monitor policies; make financial, personnel, marketing, and product development decisions; and handle crises or unexpected situations. These responsibilities are the same whether your organization is a financial institution, manufacturing company, or real estate firm and whether it is located in a city or small town or in the southern or northern part of the United States.

Although the specific duties of each manager differ, managers generally have four responsibilities:

1. *Planning* involves determining goals and methods for one or several employees. It includes establishing specific goals, determining the tasks needed to reach them, setting a time frame for completion, and assigning responsibilities. Planning should always precede action; it requires time to think, read, and select alternatives. While planning, a manager may work alone or with selected staff members. Planning may require meetings, draft plans, and data collection.
2. *Organizing* usually follows planning. Some work will be done by the manager; other tasks will be delegated to other units inside (or even outside) the organization. Plans made must be put into operation, with clear deadlines set.
3. *Directing* involves motivating oneself and others to complete various tasks effectively.
4. *Controlling* keeps everyone's efforts on target. Managers monitor how closely events conform to plans and where unanticipated changes are occurring. This information helps them determine what alterations might be needed "midstream." For example, such monitoring might show that a certain task should be rescheduled to begin sooner or that more staff should be assigned to the project.

Your manager may ask for your support in several ways:

- *Secret keeper.* Office professionals have access to lots of information, much of which must be held in strictest confidence. Managers also expect you to protect their privacy.

Figure 3–1
Organizational structures.

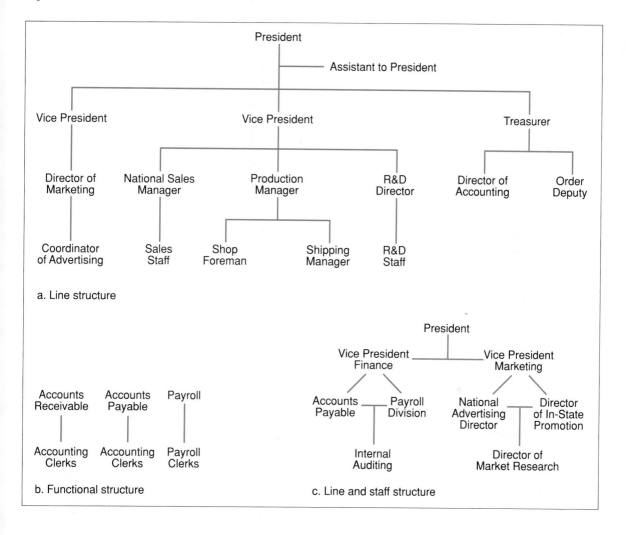

a. Line structure

b. Functional structure

c. Line and staff structure

- *Sounding board.* Managers may try out their ideas on an assistant while they are thinking and planning.
- *Coordinator.* Office professionals must pull together many diverse tasks and tie up loose ends. This includes scheduling appointments; placing, receiving, and screening phone calls; and greeting visitors. As part of coordinating, an office professional will be responsible for seeing that a major report is completed or all details of a meeting handled.
- *Assistant.* Office professionals try to anticipate their managers' needs. They organize and conduct routine work with minimal supervision while eliminating as many disruptions for their employer as possible (Figure 3-2).

Ten Tips for Developing a Good Working Relationship with Your Manager

1. Visualize your manager's job.
2. Be reliable.
3. Know your stuff.
4. Anticipate.
5. Take charge.
6. Don't be a pain.
7. Communicate.
8. Be your own toughest critic.
9. Don't have too many "new ideas."
10. Stretch yourself.

(Roy C. Smith; Goldman, Sachs & Company)

Figure 3–2
A good assistant makes things happen or can get others to make things happen. Managers depend on assistants to develop effective working relationships with other employees so that together they can achieve the organization's goals. (*Courtesy of Darome Teleconference Equipment*)

Gaining Your Manager's Confidence

Over one-half of office professionals assist more than one manager. Further, over one-quarter help four or more managers! Thus, learning to work effectively with several people at a time is an important goal.

As we've mentioned before, it's good to know what each manager does and how he or she prefers to get work done. Each manager may have different ways of preparing reports, making telephone calls, scheduling appointments, seeing unexpected callers, organizing offices, maintaining records, and keeping you informed. Add a list of these inevitable preferences and differences to your job manual, which is described on pages 58–60.

Managers and office professionals can develop a sound working relationship. However, this requires effort by both individuals. With a positive attitude and professional behavior, you will enjoy your current assignments and have opportunities for promotion, growth, and continuing challenge.

Managers place the highest value on the ability to

1. Follow directions
2. Accept criticism
3. Keep information confidential
4. Continue to work despite interruptions
5. Communicate well verbally
6. Maintain a professional appearance
7. Work well under pressure
8. Be flexible and adaptable
9. Be a team member
10. Work alone (in a nontraditional office setting)
11. Be creative and able to understand technological processes (such as machine logic)
12. Base decisions on careful analysis of data

Writing Your Job Description

Some organizations will have a job description for your position already in place. However, job descriptions must be updated regularly to reflect evolving changes.

Writing or modifying a job description for yourself will allow you to work effectively and comfortably in either a large or small office. We recommend the following steps in preparing a job description:

1. Make a list of your duties as you interpret them (see Figure 3–3).
2. Submit the list to your manager for review; perhaps the two of you will need to discuss and clarify the list.
3. Draft a revised job description.
4. Follow the draft closely for one to three months.
5. Make any necessary changes after the trial period and further discussion with your manager.

Most job descriptions contain a sentence similar to the following: "Perform other duties as assigned or as necessity dictates." That's because the unexpected does happen. But with specific information on what your manager does and what your major responsibilities are, you will be better able to develop and follow a realistic job description even when the unexpected arises.

Figure 3–4 illustrates a highly specific job description. The office professional who uses it will know what to do, when, and for whom. Responsibilities of the job are listed in order of importance.

Office Manuals

Many organizations have an **office manual**—a guide that explains policies and provides general information that affects all employees. Some large companies also supply style manuals so that all correspondence can be prepared uniformly. In addition, as mentioned earlier, you should maintain your own **job manual**, which contains information about normal office procedures, including how your manager prefers to set up meetings, travel, appointments, and files.

This manual will jog your memory for duties performed occasionally, such as filing a manager's quarterly income tax report or organizing an annual staff seminar. If you are new on the job, such a manual saves time because it reminds you about what to do next. For the experienced office professional, it is a handy

Figure 3–3
Guidelines for describing your position.

1. *Education.* What are the minimum educational requirements for adequate performance in the position? Include specialized courses, training, specific college degree, professional license, or certificate required.
2. *Related experience.* What is the minimum amount of experience necessary for adequate performance in the position? Include any on-the-job training required. What special skills, such as operating computers, are required?
3. *Problem-solving skill.* What types of problems (setting work schedules, responding to customer complaints) must a person in this position handle?
4. *Teamwork.* To what extent does the position involve working with others inside your function to get the job done?
5. *Inside contacts.* What other positions of employees outside your function do you come in contact with in person, by phone, in writing; daily, weekly?
6. *Outside contacts.* What types of contacts with persons outside the organization or with other organizations (customers, vendors, government agencies, business and professional organizations) does the position require in person, by phone, in writing; daily, weekly, occasionally?
7. *Supervision.* How many employees are supervised directly or indirectly by the person in the position?
8. *Accountability.* What is the responsibility (if applicable) for which the position is accountable in the current fiscal year?
9. *Summary of function and responsibilities.* List the five or six main responsibilities of the position in order of importance. Use statements that start with action verbs—*supervise, initiate, develop, analyze, plan.* Also, estimate the percentage of time devoted to each responsibility in a typical month.

Figure 3–4
Sample position description.
The American Bank

Title: Commercial Lending Secretary   **Department:** Commercial Lending
Division: Lending   **Reports to:** Vice-President, Commercial Loans

This position description has been read and accepted by:

_____   _____   _____

Signature of Incumbent   Signature of Supervisor   Date

Summary Description

Provides secretarial and administrative support to the Commercial Lending Department, including handling confidential information and typing letters, documents, and reports. Relieves and assists Real Estate Lending Secretary as receptionist for the Lending Division.

Specific Duties and Responsibilities

1. Provides administrative support to Commercial Lending officers by answering telephone, handling routine calls, routing mail, and scheduling appointments and meetings. (40% of the time)
2. Relieves and assists Real Estate Lending Secretary in directing flow of traffic through division; directing walk-through customers to appropriate personnel; answering phones for department and directing inquiries to appropriate personnel. (30% of the time)
3. Prepares loan review and documentation checklist forms. Prepares minutes for Loan Review Committee meetings.

Supervises

Has no supervisory responsibility.

Accountability

Recommends department's purchasing needs to supervisor.

Position Requirements

A high school diploma or equivalent is required. Employee must be skilled in communication and customer relations; be able to operate business machines; desire to learn commercial loan policies and accounting procedures; and become familiar with the bank's lending services.

reference guide for working efficiently and productively. It provides a basis for setting priorities—for deciding which tasks have immediate priority, which are routine, and which can be postponed.

Your job manual will change over time, so it's a good idea to arrange it in a looseleaf notebook according to categories. Use the following guidelines to prepare your manual:

1. Make a rough draft of the index.
2. Write complete instructions for each procedure.
3. Create a title page, a table of contents, and an alphabetical index. Cross-reference related material.
4. Organize the manual so that you can make revisions as you learn new procedures or as your responsibilities change.
5. Proofread the manual to ensure that your English is correct and that the manual is organized and accurate.
6. "Pilot test" all procedures with a co-worker to ensure that a temporary replacement will be able to follow them as written.

Figure 3–5 suggests some topics to include in your job manual.

Ergonomics

Ergonomics refers to how the workplace is set up (*ergon* means "work" and *nomes* means "laws"; thus, *ergonomics* means "laws of work".) Specifically, ergonomics is the science of designing machines, operations, and work environments that best meet employees' needs.

A comfortable work environment contributes to overall productivity. Efficiency is increased by ready access to necessary equipment and materials, proper lighting, some degree of privacy, and appropriate arrangement of desks, chairs, and files. Office professionals spend more time at workstations than anywhere else; thus, this area can have major effects on their physical and psychological well-being. The following sections discuss ergonomic issues.

Working with Your Computer

A current controversial ergonomic question concerns the long-range effects of video display terminals (VDTs). You should be aware that potential health problems have been linked to the use of these terminals. The research has been inconclusive; however, some users complain of visual disturbances such as "seeing pink," which sometimes requires the use of tinted lenses. Headaches, eyestrain, and back, neck, and wrist pain have also been reported. Others are concerned about potential radiation effects from cathode ray tubes (this problem is highly debatable). Because of these concerns, you should be aware of how long you sit in front of your VDT.

Figure 3–5
Suggested topics for a job manual.

Company Description

Company literature and history
Organizational chart (list the purpose of each department and the names of department
  heads)
Summary of company's service or products

Your Job Description

Personnel Policies

Starting and ending time each day
Length and number of breaks and lunch periods
Time allowed for leaves (sick time and personal business)
Tuition reimbursement
Overtime
Vacations
Insurance benefits
Dress code
Safety precautions

Manager's Style or Preference

Preparing correspondence (sample letter and memo format showing preferred style,
  signature line, stationery)
Making and receiving telephone calls (how to answer, telephone message system,
  long-distance reporting system)
Greeting visitors (office etiquette, screening, frequent visitors)
Establishing periods to think and plan (interruptions, decision making)
Memory aids (pocket and desk calendars, manager's whereabouts, tickler file)

Mail

Incoming
    Opening the mail
    Sorting mail for manager to read
    Annotating mail
    Using a mail digest
    Handling routine inquiries
    Routing procedures and forms
Outgoing
    Displaying correspondence for manager's signature
    Mail pickup times
    Special services frequently used (express, certified)
    What shipping services are used, for what, how they are done)
    Where fax machine is located and fax number

Continued on page 62

Figure 3–5 continued

Files

Alphabetic, numeric, geographic
Color coding
Types of files—lateral, etc.
Arrangement

Cross-referencing
Record retention system
Locking files
Filing oversize items

Forms

Purchasing procedures (include a completed form explaining when it is used, how many
    copies are made, and where they are sent)
Payroll
Duplicating services
Office supplies
Forms and procedures unique to your responsibilities

Office Equipment

Inventory of serial numbers; repair service contracts; instruction manuals

Meetings and Travel Arrangements

Steps to follow in setting up routine meetings
Taking minutes; typed format
Handling travel arrangements (by you, a travel agency, or the company traffic depart-
    ment)
Preparation of itinerary
Manager's preference for monetary advances, mail and phone calls
Expense reports

Miscellaneous

Publication subscriptions
Petty cash
Bank statement reconciliation

Names of co-workers
Location of checkbook

Here are some ways to avoid problems:

1. Place reference materials as close to the screen as possible, preferably using a document holder (Figure 3–6).
2. Organize your work area so that bright overhead light or natural light doesn't cause screen glare (Figure 3–7). If the light source is behind you or off to the side, glare will be reduced. If you can't cut down on the glare, consider using a visor.
3. Tilt the terminal up to cut down on glare, or purchase a hood or antireflective glass to reduce eyestrain.

Figure 3–6
Document holder.
This clip attaches with Velcro fasteners to either side of the monitor, to be rotated out of the way when not in use. *(Courtesy of Curtis Manufacturing Company, Inc.)*

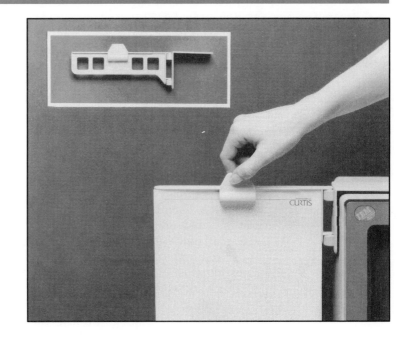

Figure 3–7
Preventing computer screen glare. This work area avoids screen glare by using under-shelf lights. *(Courtesy of International Business Machines Corporation)*

4. Position the terminal so that you are looking down at it (e.g, at a 10- to 15-degree angle). This strategy reduces both eye and neck strain.
5. Adjust your chair so that your feet are flat on the floor, forming a 90-degree angle at your knees. This position reduces back strain.
6. Take a fifteen-minute break once every two hours, especially to change posture, move around, and do a few stretching exercises.
7. Try to keep the terminal at least an arm's length from you. With that distance, you'll be less bothered by glare.

Office Design

Some offices employ only one assistant; others have one thousand or more office professionals. Each office type has its advantages and disadvantages. Let's look first at the small office.

In a small office (Figure 3–8), you may work in a semiprivate area. The typical one- to three-room suite is likely to be filled with traditional office furniture (desk, work table, file cabinets, and a small computer system). You will be close to materials and equipment, but that very compactness could produce a feeling of overcrowding. If there are two or more employees, space will be at a premium, minimizing or eliminating privacy. Conversations will be overheard, and interruptions will be numerous. If personalities conflict, nearness may bring the situation to a boiling point. On the other hand, if temperaments are compatible, a small office can be pleasant and productive. The close quarters may enhance communication between manager and assistant.

In contrast, if you work in a large office, you will likely have an "open-space" or "landscaped" setting with movable partitions that divide work areas and

Figure 3–8

Semiprivate office. *(Courtesy of International Business Machines Corporation)*

control noise (Figure 3–9). A "new" office can be created simply by rearranging partitions. This system offers great flexibility. Modular furniture is used because it is easy to move and makes good use of available space. Some organizations "pipe in" soft music to contribute to the sense of privacy these open-space offices require.

Strategically placed green plants not only soften the institutional look of many offices but also act as noise barriers. Carpeting also helps keep down noise levels. Most open-space offices have many windows that let in natural sunlight.

Thus, open-space offices provide savings as well as increased flexibility. Although this plan offers less privacy and presents some security problems, many employees like the more spacious look and often prefer it to an office with built-in walls.

To improve work flow, some offices partition off **workstations** for groups of employees with similar responsibilities. For example, your workstation might share a computer terminal, storage cabinets, and files with the workstations of three managers. Special areas may be set aside for computer terminals connected to a mainframe or stand-alone system; these stations are usually placed near the largest number of computer users.

Lighting

Good lighting helps people work faster and more accurately; poor lighting can lead to health problems, errors, and absenteeism. Fluorescent ceiling lights, while designed to light an entire room uniformly, can be extremely uncomfortable due to glare on desks, files, and screens. Task lights and ambient fixtures produce softer lighting.

Task lighting fixtures are placed directly above the work surface; they distribute light evenly on the surface, making it easier for you to work, read, and type. *Ambient lighting* fixtures (Figure 3–10) direct light to the ceiling and back down to the floor. Proper positioning of these fixtures—on the ceiling or on

Figure 3–9
Open-space office with movable partitions. *(Courtesy of Hamilton Sorter Company, Inc.)*

walls—distributes the amount of light according to need. If you can prevent eyestrain from bright lights, the glare of highly polished surfaces, or the effort of trying to read papers that are partially in shadow, you may be able to avoid the "trailing off" of productive work that occurs just before noon and again at the end of the day.

Furniture

Because you will spend a lot of time sitting, your chair must provide comfort and support, regardless of what you are doing. Posture chairs that reduce strain on neck, back, and thighs are available. Such a chair will give your lower and middle back constant support. Regardless of your task, you will work more productively and feel much better at the end of the day.

If you work in a carpeted office, you might want a hard, plastic floor pad that fits underneath your desk and chair. This flooring will allow your chair to move around more easily.

Here are some questions to ask when buying furniture to ensure that it meets your needs:

1. Will it fit in with the other furniture in the office?
2. How much space will it take up?
3. Is it easy to move?
4. Is it worth the money?
5. Is it well constructed?
6. Is it already assembled? If not, is it easy to assemble?
7. Can it be adjusted to individual or office needs?

A Healthy Office Environment

Comfortable temperature and clean air contribute to employees' well-being. As businesses continue to conserve energy, offices will be cooler in the winter and warmer in the summer. Many companies have reduced the hazards of cigarette smoke by designating smoking areas or banning smoking altogether.

Noise control is crucial to concentration. Many businesses are installing noise-masking devices such as "white sound" and low-key music. Other strategies are acoustical panels and noise-reducing floor, ceiling, and wall treatments.

Attractive colors can also enhance comfort. Drapes and artwork can help create a professional image for employees and visitors alike.

Work Area

Work Area Arrangement. Being visible and accessible is part of your job, but allowing yourself to be distracted easily will "eat away" time needed to finish work. Consider the following suggestions for organizing your work environment to help you concentrate. These may require some changes in your present arrangement and should fit into your working style.

Figure 3–10

Ambient lighting. Ambient lighting directs light to the ceiling and back down to the floor, preventing glare. *(Courtesy of General Electric Company)*

1. Remove "eye-catchers" on your desk that grab attention and interrupt concentration. Items such as a postcard from a friend or a seashell paper-weight may be pleasant, but they can also distract you. Put your stapler, calculator, and other equipment within reach but out of sight. Keep pencils, pens, paper clips, and rubber bands in special compartments in your top drawer. Make sure your desk isn't a "holding area" for other people's items.
2. Assemble what you need for a task before starting it. This will reduce "up and down" time.
3. Cover papers not in use; if you see them, you may be tempted to read them. Place them in folders, put them away, or throw them out. Items not used at least twice a day should be kept in a drawer or cabinet.
4. Turn your back on the flow of traffic whenever possible, perhaps by placing your typewriter or computer against the wall behind your desk.
5. Store stationery in a deep drawer with slats to separate the various types you use.
6. Place business envelopes in a separate drawer with flaps down; keep larger ones in a nearby file cabinet.
7. Group regularly used files in one desk drawer.

Reference Materials. Reference materials should be readily accessible so that you'll be more likely to use them. These basic reference books are helpful:

- Complete and unabridged dictionary to check spelling and word definition
- Thesaurus for finding synonyms that escape your memory
- Instant word guide to quickly check spelling and word division
- Job/office manual
- Office professional's handbook that answers common questions about the English language, style, and formatting of business documents
- Local directory or phone book

Storing and Ordering Supplies. Usually one person—often a senior assistant—is responsible for ordering and replenishing office supplies and materials. If the supply cabinet is kept well organized and careful records of items removed are maintained, shortages of important items can be avoided. Some suppliers, such as paper vendors, require advance notice of orders.

If maintenance of office supplies becomes one of your responsibilities, develop the habit of checking supplies two or three times each week. Besides identifying items to be reordered, you will see if any supplies are being used more often than usual. Routinely encourage co-workers to suggest new office products they would find helpful in doing their work.

Obviously a neatly organized cabinet is easier to use. An effective technique is to keep a list of the cabinet's contents taped to the inside of the door. Place frequently used materials at the front so they can be reached quickly; put small items at eye level and bulky supplies and extras on lower shelves.

Identify packages with oversize lettering or a sample of the contents; this method prevents employees from needlessly opening extra supplies. Keep loose stationery in open boxes so that people can remove it easily without messing up the cabinet. Display small supplies such as paper clips or rubber bands in open boxes.

The following suggestions will make ordering supplies easier:

1. Have one person do all the ordering.
2. Develop an internal requisition form.
3. Develop a list of all items used regularly.
4. Place orders periodically.
5. Take regular inventory.
6. Keep all supplies in one central location.
7. Before placing an order, check to see if it is on sale.
8. Pass catalogs and sale fliers along to the people who need them.
9. Order items in standard packs.
10. Whenever you place an order for one item, check all supplies to see if anything else is needed.
11. When placing an order by phone or mail, have all the necessary information available, such as your account number, the item (catalog) number, and color.
12. Use the phone, telex, or fax machine to speed up orders.

13. Learn what the normal delivery time is from your vendor. In an emergency, request an express service.
14. Keep a copy of your order form, and check the received merchandise and the invoice against it.

Additional Equipment Storage. Your work may require you to use the following equipment, which should be positioned within easy reach:

- Electric or manual paper cutter with margin guides to ensure evenness.
- Three-hole paper punch to use when preparing material for a ring binder or similar container.
- Electric pencil sharpener.
- Electric collator, perhaps attached to a convenience copier, to help you sort material quickly and correctly.

If you need more complicated equipment, such as an electric folding or laminating machine, you may have to set up an in-house duplicating service or hire an outside service.

Accident Prevention

Not all on-the-job accidents happen in factories or places where heavy equipment is in use. Many accidents occur in offices, because little attention is paid to potentially dangerous areas and equipment. To prevent accidents, be watchful of these hazards:

1. Extension cords, carpets, and objects placed where they may cause falls
2. Wet or recently waxed floors
3. Electrical equipment left on during minor repairs
4. Clothing items, hair, or jewelry caught in equipment
5. Improperly used paper cutters, especially when the lever is not secured
6. Space heaters left on when no one is around or placed too close to people or draperies
7. Coffee makers, hotplates, copiers, typewriters, and computers not turned off at the end of the day
8. Ashtrays placed too close to papers and lit cigarettes left unattended
9. Flammable liquid improperly stored
10. File and desk drawers left open
11. Overcrowded storage drawers that can crash to the floor when opened

Periodically review your work area with co-workers to spot these and other potential hazards.

In addition, you should learn the best way to exit in case of a fire, where to go for shelter when severe weather threatens, and how to contact local emergency assistance.

SUMMARY

To be an effective office professional, you will need to know the company and the manager(s) you support, including the company's purpose, structure, major products or services, and the specific responsibilities of your unit or department. With this information, you can more easily define your responsibilities to your manager. If this information is organized into a job description and job manual, you will be able to locate and use it easily.

Managerial responsibility is generally grouped into four categories: planning, organizing, directing, and controlling.

The number of managers you support will vary, as will their working styles. Identify their working style preferences and try to accommodate them. Make a special effort to focus on protecting a manager's privacy; scheduling appointments; placing, receiving, and screening telephone calls; and greeting visitors. By handling these activities thoughtfully and calmly, you will be able to work productively.

Small offices hold space at a premium. Large offices often have an open design, with partitions that separate work spaces, offer privacy, and reduce noise.

Optimal lighting and well-designed furniture, especially a comfortable chair, will increase your productivity. Other important considerations include the flow of information to employees working together, paper control, and maintenance of necessary supplies. Safety precautions are another necessity in today's office.

Key Terms

The following terms appeared in boldface type in this chapter. Do you recall what they mean? For a more complete definition, turn to the glossary beginning on p. 442.

ergonomics (p. 60)	office manual (p. 58)
job manual (p. 58)	workstation (p. 65)

Discussion Questions

1. Refer to the personal characteristics of an office professional described on page 57. Rank them from most to least important in your opinion.
2. Which type of office environment—small and semiprivate or open—most appeals to you? What advantages and disadvantages are you likely to encounter in your preferred environment?
3. You work in a small (three-assistant) office. How can you deal with constant conversation between the two other assistants?
4. What is task lighting? Ambient lighting? How do they differ from conventional lighting? How can those differences benefit you?
5. What elements of an office chair are most important to your comfort? Why?
6. What can you do to reduce the strains associated with regular computer use?

7. Why do organizations have organizational charts? How would you obtain information about your organization's structure if none were provided?

8. How would you encourage a reluctant manager to help you write a complete job description?

9. Where would you put the following procedures in your job manual? Use the categories suggested in this chapter.

    a. Information on assistants to corporate management (names, phone numbers, general duties)

    b. List of hotels managers prefer to use

    c. Newsletter routing procedure

    d. Date on which certain files can be cleared and contents thrown out

    e. Deadlines for submitting certain kinds of financial information

    f. Names of equipment repair services

10. You need some part-time assistance to transcribe tapes of meetings conducted by managers in the office, prepare preliminary drafts of long reports, and type form letters. The part-time assistant will report to you. Draft a job description that you could give to a personnel officer or temporary-help firm. Be as specific as possible in describing what you want this person to do.

11. As an assistant to two managers, you are asked to anticipate what they will need you to do to accomplish an assignment. What do you think is meant by "the skill of anticipation"? How can you work on improving that skill?

Assignment

Visit three businesses in which office professionals work. Compare the following facts:

1. Type of organization
2. Approximate amount of work space for assistants and managers
3. Color of room or partitions and components
4. Plants and other decorating devices
5. Type of lighting
6. Chairs for assistants and managers
7. Information exchange methods

Ask the office professionals you meet about the advantages and disadvantages of their work areas. Prepare a brief report of your visit.

Those instructors using *Top Performance: A Decision-Making Simulation for the Office* should consult the *Instructor's Guide* at this point for support material regarding use of the software in the classroom.

Case Study

In every respect but one, Aaron Freund's position as legal secretary was terrific. Aaron liked the size of the firm, the partners, the type of practice, and his co-workers. The office location couldn't have been better—close to his apartment and the main shopping areas.

The one problem was that two of his co-workers insisted on giving him endless information about their personal lives. At first he had welcomed their openness as a sign of acceptance. He found their revelations interesting—until their problems and quest for solutions took over. "What do you think, Aaron?" had become a frequent entreaty accompanying problems of aging parents, troublesome teenagers, and an upcoming family reunion. Because the office was small, Aaron couldn't pretend not to hear; he had to respond, regardless of what he was doing.

"The thought of their upcoming questions actually makes me jumpy," he thought. "I don't know what they will ask next. These interruptions are slowing down my work!"

What can Aaron do to get the peace and quiet he needs to do his work?

UNIT 2

CRITICAL SUPPORT RESPONSIBILITIES

CHAPTER

4

SCHEDULING, MAKING APPOINTMENTS, AND RECEIVING VISITORS

Chapter Objectives

- To understand your critical responsibilities in supporting one or more managers

- To learn the essential elements in effective communication

- To understand how to schedule appointments and meetings effectively for one or more managers

- To understand how calendaring can be done, checked, and changed, and to identify what aids will assist in completing this task

- To be aware of your various responsibilities for greeting and introducing visitors, as well as handling difficult ones

Examples of Excellence

"All my scheduling is done in pencil," Anthony Duke emphasizes. "My managers change their plans often, sometimes with little notice."

As assistant to two corporate vice-presidents, Anthony is constantly alert to these changing conditions. One exceptionally busy Wednesday, he worked with two other assistants to arrange an important staff meeting and acted as the host for an out-of-town client who had to wait nearly an hour for a delayed appointment.

"Tony handles these situations beautifully for us," his two managers agree. "He's tactful with others. He's also protective of the time we need for thinking."

Managers in both private and public organizations have busy schedules, and the office professionals working with them must be able to handle the details of arranging and rearranging. With such support, managers can fulfill commitments and operate at a sane daily pace.

This chapter will show you how to assist one or more managers in planning their days, arranging appointments, and handling visitors. You will learn how to

- Establish realistic schedules for one or more managers
- Make and confirm appointments involving one or more managers
- Use appropriate memory aids
- Greet and direct visitors
- Maintain office security

Organizing Realistic Schedules

Regular Communication

Regular communication between you and your manager is necessary to achieve realistic scheduling. Some managers prefer to make most of their appointments themselves, while others delegate this responsibility to assistants. In either case, regular discussions (at least three times a week) between the two of you about schedules are vital.

Set a regular time to meet with your manager to examine the daily schedule. Some managers prefer to do this during the first hour of the workday; others prefer to review the next day's schedule at the end of each day. Ask your manager for preferences about scheduling, length of appointments, and arranging meetings.

At these regular meetings, one constant item for discussion will be appointments or meetings that have been previously scheduled or need to be scheduled. By meeting regularly, you can keep your calendar up to date with arrangements your manager may have made personally. Careful planning will also help you limit the number of meetings during a day and give your manager welcome time alone.

If you assist several managers, it is important to routinely ask them about their arrangements so that their whereabouts will not become a mystery (or an embarrassment). Figure 4–1 illustrates a form used for tracking several managers' activities.

At the end of each workday, Judy and Ray review the next day's schedule. *(Courtesy of International Business Machines Corporation)*

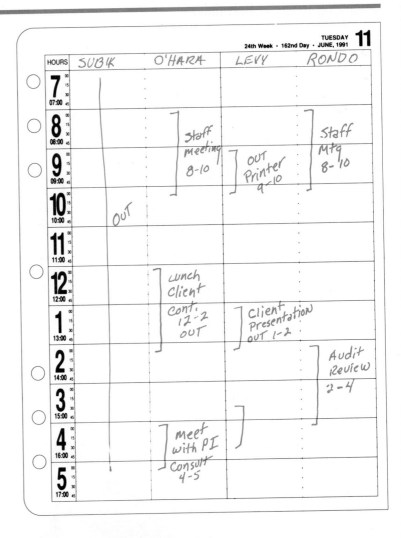

Figure 4–1

Daily tracking form for four managers. *(Courtesy of Day-Timers)*

TUESDAY **11**
24th Week · 162nd Day · JUNE, 1991

HOURS	SUBIK	O'HARA	LEVY	RONDO
7 07:00				
8 08:00		Staff meeting 8-10		Staff Mtg 8-10
9 09:00			OUT Printer 9-10	
10 10:00	OUT			
11 11:00				
12 12:00		Lunch Client cont. 12-2 OUT		
1 13:00			Client Presentation OUT 1-2	
2 14:00				Audit Review 2-4
3 15:00				
4 16:00		meet with PI Consult 4-5		
5 17:00				

Calendar Updates. You should emphasize to your managers the importance of keeping you up to date about their schedules. Indicate how this information will help keep the office better organized and the staff more effective in assisting the managers. By establishing a routine method for handling appointments, you will increase the chances for a workable schedule.

There are no foolproof methods for keeping informed. However, one helpful tactic is to ask each manager you assist for a calendar update twice a week. Getting this information should take only a few minutes and could provide an opportunity to discuss other pertinent matters. If you do this regularly, your managers may even develop the habit of keeping you informed on their own.

You should be forgiving when a manager forgets to advise you and give praise when he or she remembers to do so. Maintaining a positive attitude when handling these difficulties will eventually yield improved communication.

Appointments

Just as important as keeping informed about your manager's daily schedule is learning how to control that schedule. The following sections suggest some procedures you can use to establish control.

Establishing Quiet Times. Managers need quiet times for thinking and planning. Establish times of the day when your manager's door will be closed and no calls taken except in emergencies. Monday mornings, Friday afternoons, early mornings or late afternoons, periods before and after lengthy trips, and the days just before or after major meetings are particularly desirable times to protect. When you call another manager for an appointment, keep in mind that that person's assistant is likely to protect the same time slots.

You can also help your manager pace each day by allowing sufficient time between appointments. During a half-hour break, for instance, your manager can review a meeting just completed, think about the next meeting, return phone calls, or read correspondence. Some managers may want appointments to end by 11:30 AM or 4:30 PM—another aspect of scheduling to consider. You can also give your manager a break between appointments by establishing times for him or her to work away from the office while you take phone calls.

Unexpected Visitors. It is a good idea to have all visitors check in with the primary assistant, who then announces them to the manager. Many busy managers want to be protected from unexpected visitors or staff seeking an unscheduled meeting. Be sure your role in screening these two types of drop-ins is clear.

Some managers may tell you how they want interruptions handled. Depending on their style and position, some may want to be available at all times to all personnel and customers. On the other hand, some managers may prefer tight scheduling with no drop-in visitors. Be sure you understand these preferences so that you will protect your manager's privacy most effectively.

Limiting Length of Meetings. Determine how much time your manager prefers to set aside for each routine appointment and what time of day is preferred. Depending on schedule and style, a manager may limit meetings to thirty minutes, allow more than an hour, or ask the person making the appointment to determine the length. Or a manager may have you set aside a specific amount of time according to the nature or complexity of the topics to be covered.

It is also important, especially when you work closely with one or more managers, to help bring unexpectedly long meetings to a close. For example, if you sense that your manager is running behind schedule because of a talkative visitor, you can either call on your intercom or local line to report an unexpected request or hand your manager a note indicating another engagement. Either method will allow the manager to conclude the meeting diplomatically. Check with your manager about when and how you are to use these tactics.

Scheduling Appointments. When your manager wishes to see someone, either in or out of the office, make the arrangements according to his or her instructions. Before you can schedule an appointment, you need to know

- Who is expected
- The organization the person represents
- The telephone number at which the person may be reached
- What the appointment is about and whether special material such as a report or financial figures needs to be prepared
- The preferred date, time of day, and length of time required
- The best location for the appointment (the manager's office, conference room, other person's office, restaurant, hotel)

Arranging Appointments. Once you have obtained the information you need to schedule the appointment, you can telephone the person(s) and make the arrangements. When they learn the specifics of the meeting from you, they will have the information they need to make their own preparations. When you call them or their assistants, use a script similar to the following:

> Good morning! This is Elaine Williams, assistant to Carlos Olmo of Phuong Construction Company. I would like to arrange for Mr. Olmo to meet with Tom Davis of your marketing staff some time next week. He has time on Tuesday or Wednesday afternoon. About an hour will be needed to discuss plans for an upcoming promotional campaign. Can you confirm a time now?

Confirming Appointments. Depending on the importance of the appointment, your manager may wish to send a written confirmation similar to that in Figure 4–2. Or he or she may want you to call the invitees the day before the meeting to confirm their attendance. Similarly, if someone requests an appointment with your manager and you set a tentative time, you should call the person to confirm the time after your manager has approved it.

Refusing Appointments. If you must refuse to schedule an appointment, tact and honesty are equally important. Tell the caller that your manager will be busy for an upcoming period of time, and indicate politely that you will relay the caller's message to your manager as soon as possible.

Scheduling Changes. Occasionally a manager's schedule changes for various reasons. If an appointment is running over the allotted time, inform the person(s) who have the next appointment of the delay; these people may need to reschedule their appointments. Similarly, if your manager will be late for a meeting at another office, a call to report the delay will be appreciated.

Figure 4–2

Written confirmation of a meeting.

To:	Tom Davis
From:	Carlos Olmo
Date:	June 18, 19—
Subject:	Southfield Meeting

This confirms our meeting next Tuesday, June 24, at 3 PM in the conference room to discuss the upcoming promotional campaign for the Southfield real estate development. I have attached some of our preliminary thoughts on the subject and look forward to working with you on this project.

jah

Attachments

Scheduling Aids

You can use several scheduling aids to keep track of your own and your manager's schedules.

Calendars. When your manager has given you all the necessary information, fill in two calendars: yours and the manager's. Enter the arrangements in pencil so that it will be easier to make changes. Block out times for regularly scheduled meetings or appointments, and mark in desired times for special events.

Several types of calendars are available. Select the one that will work best for you and your manager.

Monthly and daily calendars. *Monthly calendars* (Figure 4–3, p. 82) can help you plan long-range schedules. With a monthly calendar, you and your manager can anticipate busy periods, days out of the office, and appointments that need special preparation. When items on a monthly calendar are transferred to a *daily calendar*, more detailed information, such as time and location, should be added. Figure 4–4, pp. 83–84, shows two typical forms of daily calendars.

Pocket calendar. A *pocket calendar* (Figure 4–5, p. 85), similar to the calendars shown in Figure 4–4, is carried by each manager. It is an effective way to keep your manager aware of time commitments. You can offer to update the pocket calendar on a weekly basis.

Electronic calendar. Many managers have desktop computers and programs to help them plan their schedules. One of the most sophisticated scheduling tools is *electronic calendar* software (Figure 4–6, p. 85). When this program is initiated, several items of data may need to be entered to identify the user. After the data are entered, the screen displays a portion of a one-month calendar

Figure 4–3
Monthly calendars.
(Courtesy of Day-Timers)

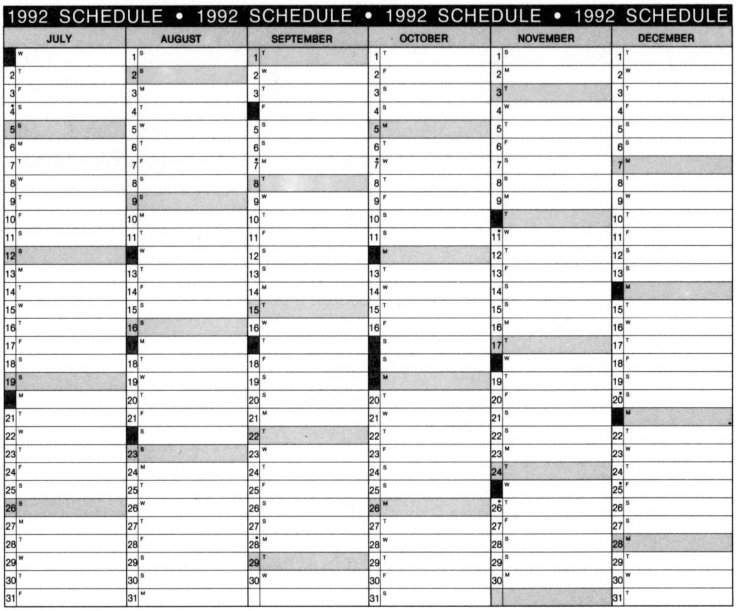

a. Half-year monthly planner.

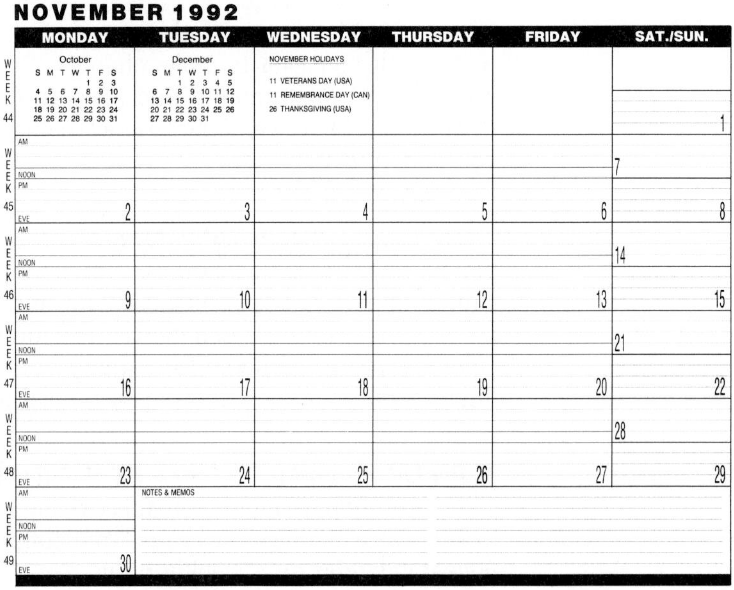

b. One-month planner.

Figure 4-4
Daily calendars. *(Courtesy of Day-Timers)*

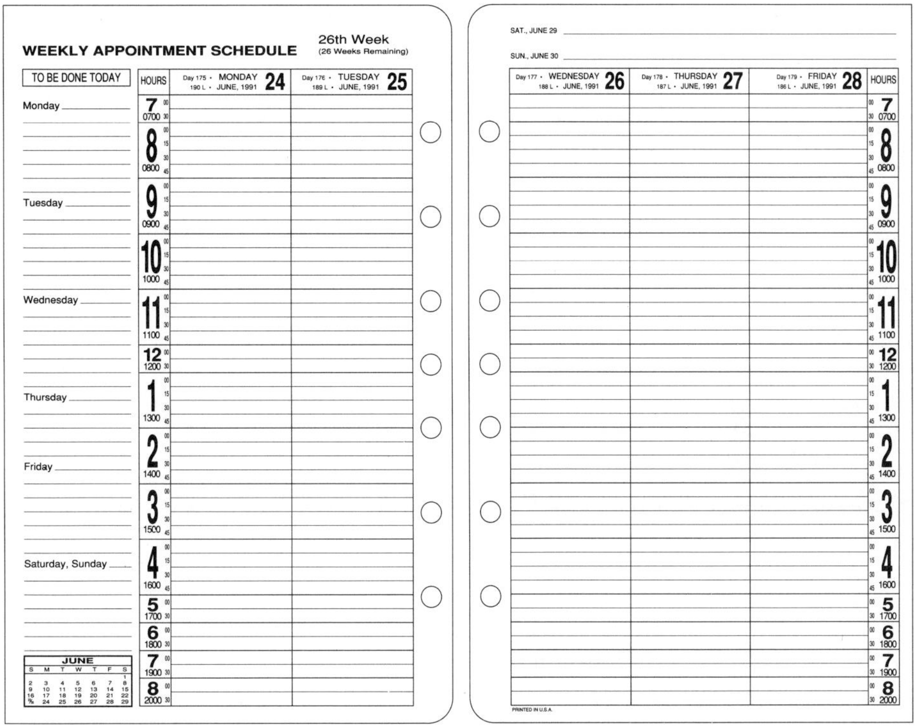

a. One week at a glance.

listing a schedule of previously entered appointments. Additional weeks and months can be reviewed by vertical scrolling (moving up or down the computer screen to examine information previously entered). If you have access to the information in the calendar through your own personal computer, your manager will not have to take time to share this information with you.

Calendar software offers special advantages when it is part of a network such as an office local area network (LAN). For example, appointments or notices can be inserted into any employee's schedule. Managers can review their calendars from any computer terminal in the network, make changes, and print copies.

This software will also accommodate a request for the first available time slot for participants to schedule a meeting. Then, with a single instruction, the meeting can be added to everyone's calendar. Of course, this technology requires that all employees keep their calendars current; otherwise, it is no more effective than keeping a manual calendar.

Both manual or electronic calendars must be protected. When calendars for one or more managers are on a computer network, other staff could reserve

Figure 4–4 Continued

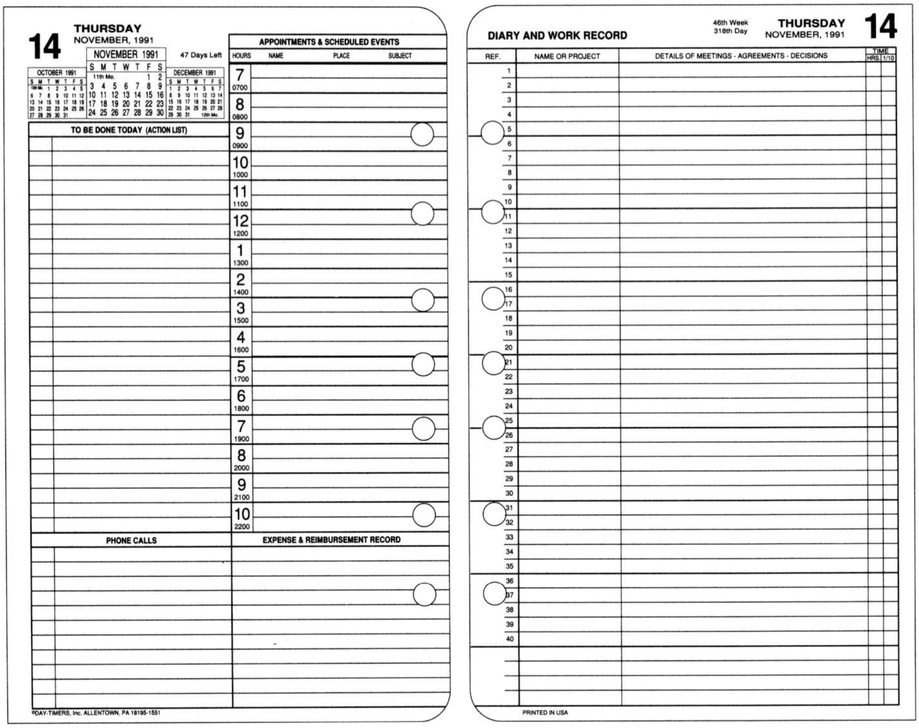

b. Expanded daily schedule and log.

blocks of time without the managers' approval. To be an effective assistant, therefore, you must restrict access to and constantly monitor your manager's calendar.

Appointment Board. An *appointment board* (Figure 4–7) contains the schedules for several people and should be placed in an easily accessible location. It is especially useful when managers and other staff are frequently away from their offices for long periods. They can indicate when they will be gone and their expected time of return.

Reminder Pad. Managers can use a *reminder pad* (Figure 4–8) to record appointments already made or to request that you arrange a meeting.

Teleconferencing

Given today's computer technology, you may be scheduling teleconferences as often as you do face-to-face meetings. Teleconferencing requires coordination with conference operators as well as with meeting participants.

The chief advantage of teleconferencing is that several participants can talk on the phone at once to discuss important items. Even with long-distance telephone rates, the cost of a teleconference can be lower than that of a traditional meeting, which usually involves travel and other expenses. Nevertheless, some kinds of business are best conducted face to face. Common sense should dictate the most efficient method.

Figure 4–5
Pocket calendar.
(Courtesy of Day-Timers)

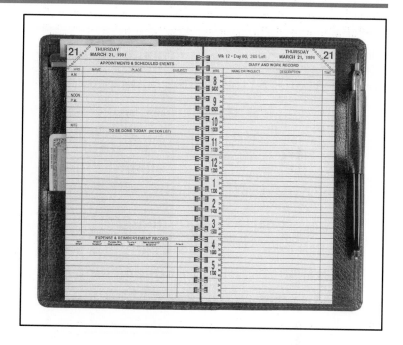

Figure 4–6
Electronic calendar. *(Courtesy of International Business Machines Corporation)*

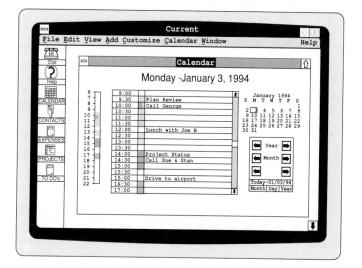

Planning Sessions for You and Your Manager

We have discussed a great deal about scheduling appointments. While scheduling, it's important to plan sessions in which you and your manager work together. Office professionals who enjoy their work report that they hold regular meetings with their managers to discuss schedules, priorities, upcoming major events, and the status of office operations. In contrast, assistants who do not have that regular contact feel left out and uninformed.

Figure 4–7
Appointment board. *(Courtesy of Magna Visual, Inc.)*

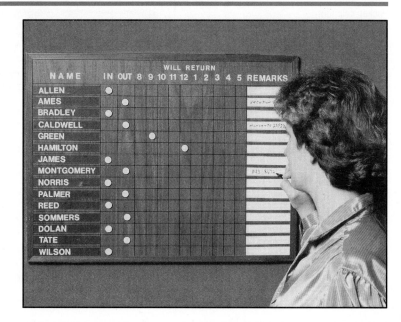

Figure 4–8
Reminder pad.

Date	*March 3, 1992*
Appointment with	
John Pelzl, Margaret Green, and Cecil Ngala	
Date	*March 10*
Time	*2–3 PM*
Place	*Margaret's office*

Some managers will ask to meet with you each day or a few times during the week, but in most cases you will have to request meetings yourself. Schedule the meeting on both of your calendars rather than set it up on a "when possible" basis. In preparation, make a list of topics to cover, especially calendar appointments, priorities, and information you need to do your work effectively. By planning ahead, you can accomplish a great deal at a five- to ten-minute meeting. Your efficient organization will show your manager that you do not intend to waste valuable time.

Suggest to your manager that you will need occasional "quiet" periods free from interruptions. Obviously your responsibilities and physical location make ongoing privacy impossible. Let your manager know that there will be times when you must work alone to complete major assignments on time. Your manager is more likely to understand your need for privacy when made aware of its importance.

Memory Aids

This section profiles various **memory aids** that will help you manage the details of scheduling. These aids include calendars and various types of files.

Calendars

As mentioned earlier, you and your manager should have identical monthly calendars for long-range planning. Update these calendars daily with plans for meetings, out-of-town travel, important events, holidays, vacations, conferences, and regular business meetings.

So that regularly scheduled meetings with your manager cover all the points you want to discuss, prepare a list of topics—appointments, priorities, and what you need to do your job well—ahead of the meeting. *(Courtesy of International Business Machines Corporation)*

In addition, both of you should use a daily calendar that clearly shows your manager's plans during his or her eight to ten hours on the job. Figure 4–9 provides an example of one manager's carefully planned day. Some managers prefer to have a typed list of all appointments on their desks the night before or each morning with information on participants, lengths of meetings, locations, and subjects.

Files

Tickler File. Another indispensable memory aid is a **tickler file,** or long-range planning card file (Figure 4–10). This file "tickles" your memory about upcoming due dates for assignments such as writing monthly or quarterly reports, organizing periodic meetings, and making payments. A tickler file is placed on cards because cards are easy to locate, move around, and replace; don't get lost as easily as random notes; and can be color coded so that a single file will serve the long-range planning needs of several managers.

You can make a tickler file with 3″ × 5″ cards. Organize them with dividers into three parts: (1) cards for each month, with the guide for the current month at the front of the file; (2) date guides (numbered from 1 to 31) behind the current month; and (3) one card labeled for future months. File individual cards with the required information and reminder date at the top behind the appropriate divider. These cards will serve as a reminder to you of what needs to be done on specific days. Turn over dates falling on a Saturday or Sunday so that you don't mistakenly file a reminder for those days. "Tickle" an important event a few days before it occurs to allow for preparation time. If you write it down on a tickler, you won't miss it.

Both you and your manager should learn to rely on the tickler file and refer to it regularly. Develop the habit of checking it every morning.

Figure 4–9
Typed list of a manager's appointments for the day. Note that time has been set aside for the manager to work alone. This schedule was given to the manager the night before on 3″ × 5″ cards.

```
SCHEDULED APPOINTMENTS

  9:30 AM        meet with the president concerning sales projections

 11:00 AM        meet with sales staff

 12:00 noon      lunch with Paula Nichols, executive director, Economic
                 Development Corporation

  2:00 PM        meet with Robert McFadden, advertising director,
                 News Gazette

  3:00 - 4:00 PM prepare quarterly sales report


SPECIAL REMINDERS

Call Agnes LeBon, 555-0310, about speech for Business & Professional
                 Women.

Develop Goldman contract.

Discuss personal investment plan with Michael Andretti.
```

Figure 4–10

Tickler file. In the card file, items should have complete information. In the folder file, the information is repeated on letter-sized paper. You should not have to refer elsewhere to complete the task.

```
Meeting with District Sales Manager


Monday, February 4
9:30 AM
Mr. Nelson's office needs January sales report and analysis.


Project February figures.


Discuss expense reporting procedure for spring traveling.
Compare travel expenses for this month, last two years;
project February expenses.
```

Pending File. A **pending file** supports the monthly and daily calendars by identifying major tasks to be completed by specific dates. This file contains reminders concerning material to read, letters to answer, reports to finish, orders to place, and meetings to organize. You and your manager should check the pending file regularly to be sure nothing has been overlooked or to include additional priorities.

Special-Events and Crisis Files. Another useful memory aid is a **special-events file,** which contains the timetables and details of major events such as an annual staff review of sales or a board of directors' quarterly meeting. You may also want to keep a **crisis file,** which details how difficult situations were handled, along with suggestions for improving future management. For example, your crisis file may include the specifics of completing a major proposal or report requiring many steps and a great deal of cooperation from different units. Naturally, it should also contain suggestions for improving the process in the future.

Chronological File. Many assistants make an extra copy of each piece of correspondence they type and place it in a monthly chronological file. The **chronological file** (often called a *reading file*) is kept for at least six months; the most recent documents are placed at the front of the folder. Some offices maintain a chronological file in a three-ring notebook for easy reference. This file can be invaluable when a document has been misfiled and you don't have time to search for it.

The use of memory aids will help you control details that could otherwise clutter up your time. By clearly scheduling appointments, you can relieve time pressures and allow for courteous handling of expected and unexpected visitors.

Handling Visitors

When a business appears disorganized, unprepared, and unprofessional, potential clients or customers are unfavorably impressed. An office professional contributes significantly to the company's image—for better or worse. First impressions are critical; it is during these first few minutes that the "little" details—appearance, tone of voice, and consideration for visitors' needs—register.

Greeting Visitors

To maintain a professional atmosphere in your office, you should have a simple but effective routine for greeting visitors. This routine might include the following steps.

Welcome all visitors in a courteous but businesslike fashion. Stop what you are doing, turn to face the visitor, and begin with "good morning" or "good afternoon."

First impressions are critical; they are the first step toward appearing to visitors that your business is worth their time.
(Courtesy of International Business Machines Corporation)

What if you are in the middle of working?

- If you are talking on the phone, excuse yourself to the caller to greet the visitor.
- Remember not to judge the importance of visitors by their appearance.
- Pay close attention to a first-time visitor's name so that you repeat it correctly. In some instances, you may have to ask for the spelling of the name. To help you put the correct name with the right face, you can provide memory cues about callers by describing them with details such as height, dress, or products/services they sell. Note these cues on their business cards or on a 3″ × 5″ card kept in your desk drawer.

Take care not to discuss with visitors any dissatisfactions you may have with your company. Comments such as "the air conditioner never works" or "the computer terminal is down again," or "no one told us when the remodeling will be finished" are not appropriate for customers/clients to hear.

Refer to the manager's calendar to see if the visitor has an appointment. If a visitor is scheduled, notify your manager. If waiting is necessary, ask the visitor to wait in the reception area; offer coffee or other refreshments if that is standard procedure. When the manager is ready, escort the visitor into the manager's office or work area, making any necessary introductions. (Before leaving your desk, be sure all material is covered or filed.) If possible, check ahead of time whether any calls are to be put through to either the manager or the visitor and obtain the names of those to be connected. The forwarding of calls may be a routine procedure in your office.

Obtain necessary information about unscheduled visitors. Ask for the visitor's name, organization, purpose of visit, and time needed. Write down this information and take it to the manager. The manager will then decide whether or not to see the visitor. Certain co-workers, family members, or close friends may be allowed to drop in unannounced. Try to determine the preferences of each manager in handling such unscheduled interruptions.

Establish with your manager whether and when to allow drop-in visitors. During certain times of the day, for example, your manager's door may be "left open." This means that anyone can see the manager—no appointment is needed. You will need to understand such signals, so if you are unsure about what is expected, ask your manager. Some managers prefer to keep the doors to their offices closed even if they are available so that they won't be bothered by noise or other distractions.

Refer visitors to others when appropriate. Encourage visitors, especially unannounced ones, to explain their business. In some instances, you may be able to provide the needed information or indicate another person who can be seen immediately. You may need to call someone in another department about seeing these visitors. Then take the visitors to the correct department and introduce them to the person who can help them. Every visitor should receive high-quality, courteous treatment.

Develop interruption procedures. Discuss with your managers when you should interrupt lengthy meetings and what approach you should use. For example, you may be expected to call the manager, bring in a note, or mention other commitments.

Keep records. Your company may require you to keep a visitors' log similar to the one in Figure 4–11. Some professionals, such as attorneys, architects, consultants, and physicians, keep detailed records for billing purposes. Such records can also be used for security purposes.

Making Introductions

When visitors arrive, introduce them properly (Figure 4–12). For example, when conversing with visitors or addressing your manager in their presence, refer to your manager by his or her last name, preceded by the proper title (*Ms. Chan, Dr. Morrell*). Sometimes you will sense that additional information will be needed

Figure 4–11
Visitors' log.

Visitors' Register

DATE	NAME	FIRM	ADDRESS: STREET	ADDRESS: CITY	ADDRESS: STATE	TO SEE	TIME IN	TIME OUT
12/14	Chris Meyers	ABC Vending		Chicago	IL	Pat Howard	8:35	9:15
12/14	Sharon Brown	Mid-City Copiers		Chicago	IL	George McClain	8:40	10:00
12/14	Sarah Havelin	Barrington		Washington	DC		8:40	4:00
12/14	Mike Brick	Acme Interiors Design, Inc.		Indianapolis	IN		8:45	10:15
12/14	Evan Harrison	Quick Courier		Chicago	IL		9:10	9:15
12/14	Diane Klasak	Manchester Printing		Boston	MA		10:15	11:45
12/14	Michael Koss	BL Graphics		Paterson	NJ	Jerold Watkins	10:30	1:00
12/14	Deb Bowers	Bowers Construction		Chicago	IL		2:00	3:15
12/14	Allison Gibson	Ward's Flowers and Gifts		Chicago	IL		2:10	2:20
12/14	Beth Anderson	Office Supplies, Inc.		Chicago	IL		2:40	3:15
12/14	Bruce Albrecht	Arts & Stuff	2110 5th Ave	Cols	OH	Betty Booth	4:20	4:35

during the meeting. Gather the material in a folder, and present it to the manager as you make introductions.

Difficult Visitors

Occasionally you will have to deal with difficult visitors. Problem visitors may include

1. Insistent salespeople or fund raisers who refuse to identify themselves to you, hoping that once they get a foot in your manager's door, they will be able to describe their product, service, or charity.
2. Angry clients or customers who use inappropriate language, disrupt the office, or try to force their way into your manager's office.
3. People who ask questions about sensitive company matters or personnel. These people may be competitors, industrial spies, or individuals involved in lawsuits against the company or one or more of its employees.

You'll be able to recognize problem visitors as those who

- Refuse to give their names, whom they represent, or the nature of their business
- Demand to see your manager or another person in the office
- Attempt to engage you in conversation to obtain information about business operations
- Try to get past you to see a manager or wander about the office
- Talk loudly, use inappropriate language, and generally act unpleasant

In addition, you may have to deal with visitors whose mannerisms, language, or attitude is unprofessional. Respond in a friendly but businesslike way to lessen their potential impact.

If possible, your manager should let you know ahead of time who is expected and how they should be treated. Ask your manager how you should deal with insistent salespeople, visitors with no appointments, angry or uncommunicative visitors, and people with requests for information about the company or staff.

Your Image

How you appear to visitors is at least as important as what you say. Nonverbal actions can speak louder than words. Sit up straight in your chair with feet flat on the floor. Make eye contact with the visitors, and maintain a pleasant expression. Appear to like the work you are doing. No matter how rushed you are, give visitors the impression that everything else can wait while you help them; they will appreciate your attention. Keep personal items out of sight, and take care of grooming matters (hair combing or tie straightening) out of the visitors' sight.

Look directly at visitors as you greet them to increase your concentration on them. It may be appropriate to extend your hand to the visitor's hand. If the visitor speaks too softly or unclearly, politely ask him or her to repeat the name, affiliation, or purpose of visit. In addition, write down and practice saying all

Figure 4–12
Proper introductions.

Individual Introductions

1. People of lower rank introduced to those of higher rank: "Mr. President, this is Mrs. Vice-President."
2. People of equal rank introduced in no special order (although it is courteous to introduce the younger person to the older person).
3. Additional information about the people being introduced included: "Mrs. Jones, this is Mr. Rodriguez. He's the new store controller in our Houston branch."

Group Introduction

1. Group of men introduced to a woman or women: "Mrs. Owens, Mrs. Chen, this is Mr. West . . . and Mr. Starr."
2. Group of men and women introduced to men: "Mr. West, Mr. Starr, this is Miss Schwartz . . . Mrs. Weiss . . . Mr. O'Leary . . . and Mr. Alphonse."

Self-Introduction

1. Use your full name.
2. If you know the person's name, address the person by name: "Mr. Nguyen, I'm Miss Tanaka, Mrs. Schultz's assistant. Please be seated."
3. If you don't know the person's name, give your own name and title first: "I'm Miss Tanaka, Mrs. Schultz's assistant. May I help you?"

Acknowledging Introduction

1. "I'm pleased to meet you."
2. "Hello, I'm glad you could come."
3. "How do you do?"
4. "Mrs. Pratt."

---

names; keep on file the names of people who visit regularly. If you must make visitors wait, explain the delay as tactfully as possible. If the waiting time will be long, check back with them occasionally; never let them think they've been forgotten.

Use a pleasant speaking voice. Speak distinctly, slowly, and loudly enough to be understood. Pronounce names clearly when making introductions. Avoid speaking to co-workers about office problems or personal matters in front of visitors.

Office Security

Your office's security arrangements will depend on managers' personal preferences, the product or service involved, and the office location, among other factors. A high-technology firm manufacturing classified computer circuitry for the U.S. Air Force has very detailed procedures. Security arrangements in a small business that sells prepackaged software to the general public may be less complex. Offices located in some urban areas emphasize security a great deal.

Increasingly, businesses are keeping an entire office suite or some part of it locked at all times. Visitors are admitted only after being identified visually or presenting proper credentials. A staff member escorts all visitors in and out and does not allow them to wander around. More and more companies are adopting the general office security procedures outlined in Figure 4–13.

In addition to internal office security, be alert to your own safety after leaving the office. Some employers, especially those in high-crime areas, provide escorts for those leaving the office after regular working hours. You may ask to be walked to your car or to the nearest transportation.

SUMMARY

It will be your job to help your manager develop a realistic schedule, make and keep appointments, and handle visitors. These tasks will require a good working relationship and communication between you and your manager. Regular meetings are vital to establishing how each of these responsibilities will be managed.

Even if your manager does a great deal of self-scheduling, he or she should keep you informed. Frequent communication with your manager will help you determine priorities and make more informed decisions in scheduling work. You should develop ways to obtain this information, such as asking, using an appointment board, or having your manager fill in appointments on a reminder pad. You should also obtain information about the person(s) involved, subject, date, length, and location.

Figure 4–13
General office security.

Every office should post a set of security procedures like these:

1. Purses, wallets, desk clocks, and other items attractive to thieves should be put out of sight, preferably locked up when personnel are absent.
2. Desks, file cabinets, and storage cabinets should have working locks and be kept locked when staff are away from them.
3. The doors to unoccupied offices should be locked when vacant.
4. An office or organization decision should be made concerning who has access to files and other material. A list of those persons should be posted. The same procedure can be followed for computer terminal use.
5. All visitors should show some form of identification, including those coming to repair equipment. They should be escorted in and out of the office. If suspicious persons are loitering about, the police or building security should be notified.
6. Security procedures should be reviewed regularly.

Another important responsibility is to protect certain times for your manager to work alone and to pace each day to avoid back-to-back appointments. You should also inform others who are involved of changes in the manager's schedule, such as a meeting running late. Finally, you can help your manager bring a meeting to a close diplomatically by mentioning another engagement.

Certain memory aids will help you schedule your manager's time effectively. These aids include identical, regularly updated calendars for you and your manager; a tickler file of reminders; a pending file identifying major tasks to be completed by specific dates; special-event and crisis files containing the details of important events and the handling of unexpected occurrences; and a chronological file of documents typed.

Greeting and conducting visitors is another responsibility in overall office management. You should work with your manager to establish procedures for handling visitors and protecting office security.

Key Terms

The following terms appeared in boldface type in this chapter. Do you recall what they mean? For a more complete definition, turn to the glossary beginning on p. 442.

chronological file (p. 89)   pending file (p. 89)
crisis file (p. 89)   tickler file (p. 88)
memory aids (p. 87)   special-events file (p. 89)

Discussion Questions

1. Realistic scheduling for a busy manager is critical. What steps would you use to
   a. Break a manager's habit of providing information about appointments needed while rushing off to the next appointment?
   b. Reduce overscheduling so that your manager will not be constantly behind and have no time for thinking, planning, and tending to personal matters?
   c. Encourage three managers for whom you work to provide more lead time in scheduling appointments?
2. One of your responsibilities is to greet visitors to the office. Most of them are salespeople calling on the three managers who regularly purchase equipment and supplies from the salespeople's firms. Develop a set of procedures you would follow to ensure that all visitors get equal treatment and are kept at a distance until ready for their appointment. The procedure should also let you deal with unannounced visitors seeking an appointment on short notice.
3. Your office is open to the public from 8:00 AM to 5:00 PM five days a week. Lately, small items have disappeared from desktops, money has been taken from purses, and desk drawers have been opened by unauthorized persons. There is no security officer available, and the number of clients constantly entering and leaving makes control difficult.

What realistic suggestions could you make to other employees for protecting their possessions and watching out for other difficulties?

4. An important responsibility for an office professional is protecting the manager's time. How would you protect your manager from the following potential interruptions? What would you do in each instance?

   a. A personal long-distance call from the manager's sister while he is in a crucial staff conference
   b. A long-distance call from the home office while the manager is talking with a major customer
   c. A visitor from a branch location who has no appointment and wants to ask the manager "a few questions" before leaving
   d. A colleague of your manager who tends to wander past your desk and into the manager's office at any time of the day

5. Which of the memory aids discussed in the chapter—calendars, special-events and crisis files, pending files, tickler files, and chronological files—would you use to record the following?

   a. A list of individuals to be called during the coming week to arrange for an all-day meeting next month
   b. Details on how a major quarterly program and financial report must be completed in the next week
   c. Instructions from the purchasing department on how to submit special orders (one copy is already in your job manual)
   d. A trip report from your manager citing difficulties experienced at the hotel at which he or she stayed
   e. A seminar your manager will be attending next month
   f. A pricing memo that must be reviewed before a senior management meeting in three weeks

Assignment

As administrative assistant to Eileen O'Connell, the president of a growing publishing firm, you must pay particular attention to her busy schedule. Ms. O'Connell travels a great deal, sees prospective authors, meets with editorial staff, handles routine administration, and must find blocks of two hours at least twice each week to review manuscripts. Using the following weekly calendar, suggest a daily schedule designed to include these activities for the week of June 18–22.

Business trip to Chicago—1 day
Meetings with editors Ed Simon and Irene Papadopoulos—1 hour each
Meetings with four prospective authors—1 hour each
General staff meeting—2 hours
Two trips to printing plant—half-day required for each
Three 2-hour periods for reading manuscripts
Daily blocks of 1 hour for general administration
Time for you to meet with Ms. O'Connell at least 3 hours during the week for information updates

(Note: While Ms. O'Connell can handle this busy schedule, she needs some "quiet" and unscheduled time between appointments. Remember: You could recommend that some meetings be delayed until the following week.)

Those instructors using *Top Performance: A Decision-Making Simulation for the Office* should consult the *Instructor's Guide* at this point for support material regarding use of the software in the classroom.

Case Study

Amy Williams took great pride in the fact that visitors could get complete and current information about her two managers' schedules. Setting up appointments and meetings were two responsibilities she handled easily and well. Both her managers and co-workers had commented on how her assistance helped smooth operating schedules. "I don't know how she fits so much into my day," one manager had remarked.

Three months ago, a third manager had joined Amy's department. This manager was somewhat secretive about appointments made and seemed reluctant to seek Amy's assistance in scheduling or to keep Amy informed of her whereabouts. Amy found this lack of information frustrating. On a few occasions, customers had been angry because Amy didn't know when the manager would be back. Also, Amy had been surprised by visitors who didn't have an appointment and wanted to see the manager.

One of Amy's goals is to develop a good working relationship with her new manager, and she wants to begin with a positive experience. How can Amy obtain information about her manager's schedule? How can she suggest to her manager that she provide assistance in scheduling?

CHAPTER

5

INCOMING AND OUTGOING MAIL

Chapter Objectives

- To understand the importance of completely and effectively handling incoming and outgoing mail

- To be aware of procedures for completely organizing the various types of incoming mail, including keeping a mail log, routing mail, and acknowledging certain correspondence

- To understand procedures for preparing mail to be sent, especially correct addressing, appropriate mail class, and special services

- To recognize the value of electronic mail systems to rapid communication

- To become familiar with other rapid and special methods of delivering mail and other items domestically and internationally

Examples of Excellence

Todd Watkins, a successful insurance representative, spends at least five hours a day visiting current and prospective clients. "Getting out of my office is essential," Todd emphasizes. "I can't sell policies on the telephone." So that he can leave the office by 10 AM, Todd and Jan Domenico, his assistant, have developed an efficient system for processing all incoming mail.

Jan takes care of much of the mail-generated work independently. Mail is ready for each department by 8:30 AM. As soon as it arrives, Jan sorts it into four piles: work she handles automatically, including checks to deposit, forms to fill out, and policyholder requests; mass-mail announcements, flyers, and similar items; first-class mail for Todd's immediate attention; and magazines and other publications. Each item is logged in and date-stamped. Jan also attaches files to important correspondence. Todd and Jan make contact twice a day to handle special problems and requests.

Todd credits Jan with keeping the firm up to date and keeping policyholders satisfied. "Very few deadlines are missed or requests forgotten," Todd says. "Jan's efforts really impress our customers."

In the competitive world of business, timely information is a key to success. Essential reports, letters requiring immediate responses, important announcements, and routine bills and other items arrive each day. One of your duties will be to process all incoming mail rapidly and correctly.

Because methods of sending all types of material have become more complex and costly, your outgoing-mail responsibilities will be even more important. Items not only need to arrive on time but must be sent by the most effective means and at the lowest cost.

In this chapter, you will learn how to

- Receive, open, and sort incoming mail
- Stamp, log, and deliver different items to the proper individuals or offices
- Sort incoming mail in priority order
- Organize letters, memos, and other incoming mail while your manager is away
- Handle special requests
- Prepare outgoing mail and select the fastest and safest form of delivery
- Classify mail according to correct postage and delivery designations
- Process outgoing international mail
- Avoid the common pitfalls of domestic-mail delivery

Mail Processing and Delivery

In most large organizations, mailroom personnel initially sort mail by department. If mail is addressed to the organization rather than to an individual or department, mailroom personnel open, time-stamp, and forward it to the appropriate destination. Then all mail is delivered or placed in designated locations for pickup. In a smaller organization, mail may be delivered to a post office box or an area in which several offices share mail delivery.

Some managers request mailroom personnel to sort and deliver their mail first. One of your responsibilities may be to receive this mail once or twice each day and see that it gets to the manager promptly. When that mail does not arrive, you will have to call or visit the mailroom to obtain it.

In addition to processing incoming mail from outside the company, you will have to open, sort, and deliver interoffice material.

Sorting

The first step in processing mail is to sort it by each employee in your department. Then divide each individual's mail into the following categories:

1. Specially marked mail, including certified, registered, special delivery, express, and mailgrams
2. First-class mail, including letters, invoices, statements, orders, payments, and business-reply mail
3. Personal or confidential mail, which can often be determined by the return address on a personal rather than a business envelope (if *personal* or *confidential* doesn't already appear on the envelope)
4. Interoffice mail, such as memos, announcements, and reports from other individuals or offices within the organization
5. Advertisements, catalogs, and brochures
6. Newspapers and magazines
7. Packages

If you know that a manager is eagerly awaiting a particular piece of mail, you should give it top priority and bring it to that person's immediate attention. If mail for another person or unit has been delivered to you by mistake, it is your responsibility to forward it.

Opening Mail

In large organizations, mailroom personnel open all mail with an automatic opener that quickly feeds, opens, and stacks the items. Smaller organizations often use a manually operated letter opener.

If you open all your manager's mail, these tips will speed up the process:

1. Tap a few envelopes on the desk so that the contents fall to the bottom of the envelopes. This method will help you avoid damaging the contents.
2. Stack the envelopes face down on your left so that all flaps are to the right.
3. Place the letter opener under the flap and slit the envelope open. Slit three sides of the envelope to avoid overlooking any enclosures.
4. Lay the envelope flat when removing the contents.
5. Open all the envelopes before removing the contents of individual envelopes.

As you remove the contents of an envelope or package, place them face down on your right and the envelopes face down on your left so that the envelopes and contents are in the same order. Interoffice envelopes should be kept and reused.

When opening packages, be alert to any first-class letters attached or notations stating that a letter is enclosed. After you have verified the contents of the package with the packing slip, place the letter with the other first-class mail. You can attach a sample of the contents to the letter to notify the recipient that these materials were received. Secure items in a package by tying or clipping them together.

Handle all remittance enclosures carefully. For example, check a payment against the accompanying invoice or an earlier invoice to verify that the amount is correct. Next to the enclosure notation, write *OK* or *Accurate*. When a remittance is not attached to a letter as an enclosure but has been sent directly to the business office or cashier, note the amount, indicate where it went, and initial it. You might also keep a log of payments received.

When a remittance is sent without an accompanying letter, reinsert it into the envelope and forward remittance and envelope to the business office or cashier. If the enclosure requires a verification of date, amount, or billing procedure, provide whatever information you can.

If you mistakenly open personal or confidential mail, reseal the envelope with tape, attach a note to the front of the envelope saying "opened by mistake," and sign your name.

After unwrapping and opening newspapers and magazines, arrange them in a reading file in the order you believe the manager will find most useful.

Many organizations require envelopes to be stapled to the back of all correspondence. Others want envelopes saved for at least one day. If your organization doesn't require envelopes to be saved, check inside each envelope again before throwing it away.

Dating and Time-Stamping Mail

All incoming mail should be **dated** and **time-stamped**. Dating can be done manually or with an automatic time stamper with a built-in clock.

When a date stamp is used, the word *received* and the date and time can be stamped in the upper right-hand corner or between the letterhead and body on correspondence. Bulky mail (newspapers, brochures, periodicals, catalogs) should be stamped on the front or back cover.

Registering Mail

Many assistants are encouraged to keep a mail register for the receipt and disposition of special mail—certified, registered, special delivery, insured, remittances, mailgrams, and packages. (Mailroom personnel may also record receipt.) A *mail register* is a form listing the date and time an item was received; sender's name and address; date sent; to whom it was addressed; description; mail service used; items being sent later; and routing information, including addressee and date. Mail registers are usually kept in a looseleaf notebook or easily accessible file. Figure 5–1 illustrates a sample mail register.

When items are being sent under separate cover, note that fact in the mail register. That way, the date of arrival can be anticipated and mailroom personnel alerted and asked to deliver the expected item upon receipt.

Reading and Annotating Mail

Naturally you must read all the mail you open. Some mail will be confidential or sensitive—dealing with personnel or financial matters, for example. Treat these items with extreme care. Put them in a special folder, and give them directly to your manager. If your manager is away, put them in a locked drawer or file cabinet.

Figure 5–1
Mail register.

Date and Time Received	Sender's Name/Address	Date Sent	Addressed to Name/Dept.	Item and Class of Mail	Separate Cover	Routing Date/Name
7/19 9:45 AM	Centerville Chamber of Commerce	7/18		Retail sales brochure	Package shipped 7/19	Eloise Day, Marketing Dept.
7/19 9:45 AM	HyperSoft, Inc., LaJolla, CA	7/17	Y.M. Chan, Economic Institute	Letter, first class		
7/19 1:00 PM	Professor James Saxton, Tulane University	7/18	C.Z. Martin, Accounting Office	Letter, first class		

You may also be required to **annotate** mail, that is, mark or highlight certain portions of correspondence for a manager's immediate attention. Familiarize yourself with individual managers' preferences before adopting this procedure.

If your manager wants you to annotate mail, carefully underline important dates or facts and note them on your calendar or tickler file for appointments. Also note items being sent to you separately, dates for particular follow-up action, and other notes that will aid your manager.

Annotations can be made in the margins of letters or memos. For example, an annotation to your manager might point out that a meeting date in a letter conflicts with one already arranged. Or you could state that you have already taken action independently, such as mailing a requested item to a client.

Figure 5–2 shows a letter that has been time- and date-stamped, underlined, and annotated.

You may be required to prepare a package of related materials. For example, if previous correspondence must be attached or other items gathered to help the manager write a follow-up letter, put them with the letter. Do not hold up presenting the mail, however, while trying to locate background information. Collect and bring these items to your manager as soon as possible.

You can help a manager handle the bulk of advertising, periodicals, newspapers, and other professional business mail by reading the tables of contents and highlighting special articles or sections. Attach a note to the front cover or page listing relevant articles and page numbers, and paper-clip and highlight the articles.

Routing Mail

After reading and annotating mail, you may find items addressed to your manager that others should see or could handle more effectively. As you gain experience, your manager may wish you to routinely send such mail on to the correct person.

Although managers should see all the mail before it is circulated, you might prepare a **routing slip** or make the necessary photocopies to speed up the procedure. Confidential mail is best routed in an interoffice envelope. Figure 5–3 shows a sample routing slip. Figure 5–4 contains a variation of a routing slip on which a manager lists actions to be taken on an attached item.

Presenting Mail

After the mail has been properly processed and recorded for one or more managers, one final sorting step is necessary. All items received should be placed in one of four categories:

1. *Top-priority correspondence*—personal/confidential, specially marked mail, first-class letters, and interoffice memos requiring your manager's immediate action

Figure 5–2
Annotated letter.

January 21, 19XX

Ms. Amelia Nair
The Citizen's Bank
21 Front Street
Quincy, IL 62301

**RECEIVED
1/23/xx 10:30 AM**

Dear Amelia:

Here are the February and March radio and television schedules for your review.

Because the dates fall the same on the calendar for February and March, I made only one radio schedule for both months. With the bank sponsoring the seminar "Financing a Small-Business Venture," I think we should include the "Venture Capital" spot in the rotation with the two spots we ran in January.

Ken feels the television spot should be ready to start on February 10, so I have scheduled it to begin on that day.

I've made a tickler. ✓

If you have any questions regarding these schedules, please feel free to give me a call. If I don't hear from you by Friday afternoon, January 24, I will assume these schedules have met your approval for placement.

Sincerely,

Sandy Montoya

Sandy Montoya
Media Director

SM/kew
Enclosures

2. *Routine correspondence*—items you can handle, items requiring instructions or short personal notes, routing, or someone else's action
3. *Correspondence handled by an assistant*—routine inquiries and requests with your rough drafts attached
4. *Informational material*—announcements, policies and procedures, periodicals, advertisements, brochures, newspapers

Figure 5-3
Routing slip. If the same information is routed regularly to the same people, you may want to duplicate a form. After the first person has seen the material, he or she initials it and forwards it to the next person on the list.

Date: 10/23/XX

Route to: Initials

Smits _____   _____

Nguyen _____   _____

Crippen _____   _____

Etienne _____   _____

Barr _____   _____

To keep mail organized, place it in pocket notebooks or colored folders labeled with each of the four categories. You can present it to a manager in this order, dealing with the highest priority first. If time is limited, put aside lower-priority items.

Some assistants collect informational material and give it to a manager once or twice a week. Busy managers may want to see these items less frequently.

Handling Mail When Your Manager Is Away

Depending on your manager's preference, you may be required to make decisions about mail received in his or her absence. In any case, when your manager is away, you are responsible for seeing that mail is handled properly. Follow the steps mentioned earlier exactly as if your manager were present. You must, however, follow certain additional steps to ensure that mail is handled properly in your manager's absence.

Routing to Others. When letters must have your manager's immediate attention, forward them to the person designated by your manager for action. Before forwarding, make a photocopy for your manager and attach a dated note stating to whom you forwarded it. If the person answering the letter sends a copy to your manager, attach it also.

Writing Acknowledgments. First-class letters that will need your manager's attention when he or she returns should be held. As a matter of courtesy, however, write the sender and acknowledge receipt of the letter, explaining that the manager will be back on a certain date after which a reply will be written. Remember: You do not need to say where your manager is.

Figure 5–4

Action-to-be-taken slip. **Answering Routine Mail.**   If you frequently write letters on your own verifying the receipt of material, answering routine requests and inquiries, and setting appointments, continue doing so while your manager is away.

Forwarding Correspondence.   Some managers who are away for long periods will want their mail forwarded. Find out from your manager what to send and

DATE _____   SIGNED _____

TO _____

Refer to the attached materials and

_____   RUSH—handle immediately.

_____   File.

_____   Read and return to me.

_____   Read and file.

_____   See me about this _____ AM _____ PM.

_____   Mail to _____.

_____   Write reply and give copy to me.

_____   Write reply for my signature.

_____   Handle appropriately.

_____   Make _____ photocopies.

_____   Please sign.

_____   For your information.

_____   For your comments.

_____   For your approval.

Remarks: _____

when. Never forward an original copy; make a copy of the correspondence for mailing, and note on the original the date the copy was mailed. Personal mail can be held or forwarded unopened in a fresh envelope if it will reach the manager in time.

Be sure to record the action you've taken in a *mail digest*. A mail digest prepared each day will enable your manager to quickly learn what was received in his or her absence. In the digest, list the date the mail was received, note the sender, summarize the main idea, and indicate what action was taken. In general, do not list advertising materials, periodicals, catalogs, and similar items in the mail digest. Forward these materials or hold them until your manager returns. Figure 5–5 shows a sample mail digest.

When mail requires immediate attention, contact your manager by leaving a message at the hotel or airport terminal. Before your manager goes on vacation, find out whether someone can be designated to handle this type of correspondence. If your manager calls you daily to check on office operations, you can review the mail digest at that time.

Presenting Mail to a Returning Manager

Your manager will welcome returning to a well-organized collection of mail. Mail should be grouped by (1) the mail digest; (2) correspondence the manager must answer; (3) correspondence you have answered or forwarded to associates (the originals and the replies); (4) correspondence to be read for information; and (5) advertisements, catalogs, periodicals, and newspapers grouped in a separate folder to be read when convenient.

Figure 5–5
Mail digest.

Date of Receipt	Sender	Description or Summary
3/17	Business Dept., Auburn University	Need to send congratulatory letter to retiring professor
3/17	American Tortilla	Wants proposal for sales training for employees
3/17	Julia Vandermeer	Requests meeting to discuss budget cuts
3/17	Y. Z. Bonnelli	Needs more information on American Society for Training and Development's yearly convention
3/17	Higrade Mfg.	Notice of stockholders' meeting in St. Louis on 4/15

Multiple Managers

If you assist two or more managers, they may want you to use different procedures. Some may want all mail opened, while others prefer that mail be left sealed. Include the procedures you follow in your procedures manual and review them periodically. This strategy will allow a substitute to handle incoming mail correctly.

Preparing Mail for Sending

Experienced office professionals suggest that you follow certain established procedures in preparing all outgoing mail.

Before folding a document, make sure it has been signed, is neat in appearance, contains necessary enclosures, and requires no corrections or revisions. Then check the inside address against the address on the envelope. Make sure the document is enclosed in the correct envelope. Before filing the copies, be sure they have been corrected to show any personal notes or additions the manager made to the original.

Fold enclosures separately and insert them in the last fold of the letter. If an enclosure is stapled to the letter, it is called an *attachment*; in that case, type the notation *Attachment* on the letter instead of *Enclosure*.

Be alert to mail cost-cutting procedures. Look for the safest and most economical methods for sending items. Figure 5–6 lists some suggestions.

Figure 5–6
How to cut mail costs. *(Adapted from* The Secretary's Desk-Top Resource File, *Bureau of Business Practice, Waterford, Connecticut.)*

- Use third- and fourth-class mail for supplies and forms. These classes are less expensive than first class, but be sure to allow enough shipment time because they are slower.
- Use certified mail instead of registered mail. It costs less but still provides you with a receipt and a notice of delivery.
- Use regular postage on mail addressed to a post office box. It will get there just as fast as special delivery.
- Make the most of your per-ounce cost. One ounce of mail is approximately three sheets of bond paper plus the envelopes. Therefore, don't send information going to the same place in separate envelopes.
- Minimize enclosures, attachments, and photocopies. Before mailing, check to see if they are necessary, can be clipped, reduced in size if in large print, or printed on both sides.
- Use lightweight material for large mailings; you might be able to break into a lower-rate category. Also, beware of close weights. Items such as staples, paper clips, stamps, and metered tapes add to the weight of the finished product.
- Check the accuracy of your postal scale. An inaccurate one can cost you money, especially when you weigh mail that's on the borderline between two rates.
- Don't throw away damaged meter-posted tapes or envelopes. Unused meter postage can be reclaimed at 90 percent of its face value.

ZIP Codes

The **Zone Improvement Program (ZIP) code** is a five-digit number that identifies each postal delivery area in the United States (Figure 5–7). Today more than 95 percent of the mail handled by the U.S. Postal Service has a ZIP code.

Each of the ten geographic areas shown in Figure 5–7 consists of three or more states or possessions and is given a number between 0 and 9. The first three digits of any ZIP code number stand for either a particular sectional center or a metropolitan city. Each sectional center post office receives and transmits all mail moving between post offices in the section and all mail moving into and out of the section. The last two digits of a sectional center ZIP code number stand for one of the associated post offices served by the sectional center. The last two digits of a metropolitan city ZIP code represent one of the delivery areas served by the city post office, its branches, and its stations.

ZIP Plus 4. In the **ZIP plus 4** system, four numbers are appended to the original five-digit ZIP code. The first five digits of the expanded ZIP code number remain the same; then comes a hyphen and four more digits. The first two numbers represent a sector: 00–09 means boxes or box sections; 10–97 designates streets, firms, and rural routes; and 98–99 represents business-reply and special codes. The last two new numbers indicate a delivery segment and range from 00 to 99. The delivery segment identifies a specific house or address. The segments are identified and made a part of a sector as follows:

Expanded ZIP code:	61821-1234
Delivery zone:	61821
Sector:	12
Segment:	34

ZIP plus 4 is designed for large business mailers. Use of the four-digit code numbers is voluntary, but the U.S. Postal Service offers a postage discount for

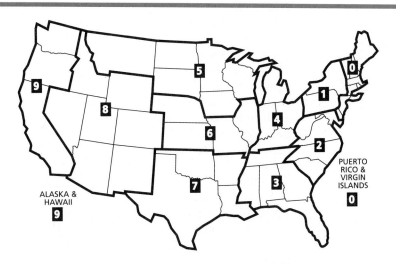

Figure 5–7
ZIP code map.

each plus 4 piece of mail numbering over 500. Upon request, your local post office will update your employer's mailing list to reflect the ZIP plus 4 code. This service is available free of charge once a year.

Automated Sorting Equipment

Post offices in major cities use the **optical character reader (OCR),** a machine that reads addresses electronically. Because the OCR reads the last two lines of the address, the mail it sorts must have nothing typed below the address. The ZIP code must be used with the two-letter state abbreviation, and the address must be single-spaced and in block format. When everything is correct, operators at sorting machines can send items to the proper bins rapidly.

Bar codes printed by an attachment to the OCR speed delivery at the destination post office. These codes represent machine-readable numbers. You will find these lines most often on business-reply mail.

Procedures for Speeding Up Mailing

Mailing regulations and procedures change periodically, but the following processing methods are likely to remain the same.

Addressing Envelopes. When both a street address and a post office box number are provided, put only the box number on the envelope. When both addresses are shown, delivery may be slowed down. The U.S. Postal Service will direct the mail according to the last address shown. If you use both the street address and the box number, the box number goes below the street (Figure 5–8).

The U.S. Postal Service offers these tips for accurate addressing:

1. Try to avoid using dual-delivery addresses, such as a street address and a post office box number.
2. Place the name of the intended recipient (business or individual) on the line above the delivery address line.
3. When a business name is on the name-of-recipient line, use the information/attention line to direct the material to a specific person.
4. Place any nonaddress data lines, such as account numbers, subscription codes, or presort codes, above the name-of-recipient line.
5. Be sure the building number is correct, and include any suite, apartment, or floor number.
6. Add directional abbreviations (*E, W, S, N,* etc.) to the street name when applicable (see Figure 5–9a).
7. Use the correct state abbreviations (Figure 5–9b).
8. Place the ZIP code or ZIP plus 4 immediately after the state abbreviation.
9. Put city, state, and ZIP code, *in that order,* on the last line of a piece of domestic mail. Use no punctuation.
10. Use simple, clear type.
11. Type the destination and return address in single-spaced block format. Place the destination address no more than 1 inch from the left and right edges of the envelope and at least ⅝ inches—but no more than 2¾ inches—from the bottom.

Figure 5–8
How to address an envelope for automated processing.

MARIO DOMINGO
PO BOX 112
BERKELEY CA 94701   *information/attention line*
                                  ↓

CONFIDENTIAL   *name of*   DR JANICE AMATO, PRESIDENT
                 recipient line → CENTERVILLE AREA COMMUNITY COLLEGE
                                2222 EAST MAIN STREET
       delivery address line → PO BOX 1
                         ↗ CENTERVILLE ME 04621
         post office, state,
         ZIP code line

1. Type on-arrival directions, such as *Confidential* or *Please Forward*, in all capital letters with a triple space below the return address.
2. For safety's sake and for standardization, leave one space before a ZIP.
3. Use the two-letter abbreviations (listed in Figure 5–9) for the state names.
4. Block the address lines, placing the return address no more than one inch from the left edge and the destination address no more than one inch from the right edge. The destination should be at least ⅝ inches but no more than 2¾ inches from the bottom of the envelope. Do not arrange the addresses in indented form.
5. Single-space the address lines, no matter how many there are.
6. Place the name of the person or department immediately above the name of the business.
7. Omit punctuation in the address, and type all words in capital letters.
8. Spell out in full the name of any foreign country on the last line of the address.
9. The size of the envelope should be no smaller than 3½″ × 5″, nor larger than 6⅛″ × 11½″. If it's too small it will be returned. If it's too large you will be charged extra.

    Preparing Postage. Postage takes one of three forms: stamps, precanceled stamps and stamped envelopes, and metered postage.

    Stamps. When using stamps, place the correct amount of postage in the upper right-hand corner of the envelope or parcel. Stamped envelopes may be purchased at the post office for an additional fee. When purchasing a large quantity, you may have a return address printed on the stamped envelopes.

    Precanceled stamps and precanceled stamped envelopes. Before buying precanceled stamps and precanceled envelopes, you must obtain a permit. Pieces must be mailed at the post office that issued the permit.

Figure 5-9
Directional and state/territory abbreviations.

a. Directional abbreviations for streets

North	N	West	W	Southwest	SW
East	E	Northeast	NE	Northwest	NW
South	S	Southeast	SE		

b. Two-letter state/territory abbreviations

Alabama	AL	Kansas	KS	Northern Mariana Islands	MP
Alaska	AK	Kentucky	KY	Ohio	OH
Arizona	AZ	Louisiana	LA	Oklahoma	OK
Arkansas	AR	Maine	ME	Oregon	OR
American Samoa	AS	Marshall Islands	MH	Palau	PW
California	CA	Maryland	MD	Pennsylvania	PA
Colorado	CO	Massachusetts	MA	Puerto Rico	PR
Connecticut	CT	Michigan	MI	Rhode Island	RI
Delaware	DE	Minnesota	MN	South Carolina	SC
District of Columbia	DC	Mississippi	MS	South Dakota	SD
Federated States of		Missouri	MO	Tennessee	TN
Micronesia	FM	Montana	MT	Texas	TX
Florida	FL	Nebraska	NE	Utah	UT
Georgia	GA	Nevada	NV	Vermont	VT
Guam	GU	New Hampshire	NH	Virginia	VA
Hawaii	HI	New Jersey	NJ	Virgin Islands	VI
Idaho	ID	New Mexico	NM	Washington	WA
Illinois	IL	New York	NY	West Virginia	WV
Indiana	IN	North Carolina	NC	Wisconsin	WI
Iowa	IA	North Dakota	ND	Wyoming	WY

Metered postage. **Metered postage** may be used on all classes of mail. Because metered mail does not have to be canceled or postmarked at the post office, it can be distributed sooner than nonmetered mail.

The postage meter machine prints a postmark and the correct amount of postage on each piece of mail. The machine you use may be a desktop or a fully automatic model that feeds, seals, and stacks envelopes. The postage meter is leased from the manufacturer and licensed at no charge from the U.S. Postal Service. Also with the license, the postal service issues you a meter record book. When you buy the postage, the detachable meter is set for the amount purchased. As you use the meter, it automatically records the amount of postage used on each piece, keeps the dollar balance remaining on the meter dials, and counts the number of pieces being processed. Each day the amount of postage used and the balance remaining should be recorded in the meter book.

If you use a postage meter, keep in mind the following tips:

1. Check the meter date daily. Metered mail must be deposited on the date shown.
2. Print the amount of postage in the upper right-hand corner of the envelope.
3. Batch together all mail requiring the same postage.
4. Set the meter dials for the correct amount of postage.
5. Process pieces of mail requiring irregular amounts of postage last.
6. Return the meter setting or display to zero for the next user.
7. Bundle metered mail with addresses facing one direction, and group them by the amount of postage and class of mail.

If meter stamps are illegible, you can apply at the post office for a refund of 90 percent of the postage value.

First-class permit imprints (see Figure 5–10h, p. 118) may be used on all classes of mail after obtaining a permit from your post office. The minimum number that must be sent under these permits is set by the postal service. The first-class permit imprint must show the city and state, the "first-class mail" designation, postage paid, and permit number.

Second-, third-, and fourth-class mail must show the same information as first-class with the words *first class* omitted.

Presorting Mail. **Presorted mail**—mail that has been sorted by ZIP code—is delivered before unsorted mail. Even if you have just a few pieces of mail, sort them into local and out-of-town mail; then classify them according to ZIP code, and separate out the metered mail. Five or more pieces of metered mail must be bundled. First-class mailing volumes of 500 or more copies presorted according to specific procedures qualify for a postage discount of 3¢ per piece. Check with your post office for exact directions.

Domestic Mail Classes

Domestic mail is transmitted within the United States, its territories, and its possessions; post offices of the Army/Air Force (APO) and Navy (FPO); and the United Nations in New York City.

To learn about the domestic-mail services available, visit your local post office and obtain copies of its latest pamphlets. You can purchase the *Domestic Mail Manual* from your post office or from the Superintendent of Documents, Washington, DC 20402.

The following categories of domestic-mail service have remained constant; the rates for each will change periodically.

First-Class Mail. **First-class mail** is sealed or closed against postal inspection, weighs 12 ounces or less, and includes the following kinds of mail:

- Handwritten or typewritten letters and copies
- Postcards
- Business-reply mail
- Bills and statements of accounts
- Checks, price lists, printed blanks, invoices, and other matter partly printed and partly written or typed

Letters or other documents enclosed in odd shapes or sizes of envelopes should be clearly marked *First Class*. You can also purchase envelopes with a preprinted first-class notation.

Express Mail. Express mail designates one of four guaranteed overnight and one-day delivery services: *Next Day Service, Express Mail Custom Designed Service, International Express Mail,* and *Express Mail Same Day Service.* Consult your local post office for details on these services. Currently there are plans to upgrade what each service offers.

Priority Mail. Priority mail designates first-class mail that weighs one-half of an ounce or more—up to and including 70 pounds—and does not exceed 100 inches in length and girth combined. Send priority mail in envelopes with a green diamond border. These envelopes cannot be used by other classes of mail and must always carry first-class postage. Priority mail is less expensive than express mail services.

Second-Class Mail. Second-class mail includes newspapers and periodicals regularly issued at least four times a year. A permit or notice of entry must be obtained from the U.S. Postal Service, which computes the rate.

Third-Class Mail. Third-class mail includes items not required to be sent first class, not entered as second class, and weighing up to 16 ounces per piece. Third-class mailable matter includes

- Books and catalogs with twenty-four or more bound pages
- Seeds, bulbs, plants
- Photographs, keys, drawings
- Circulars, booklets, films, calendars

Third-class mail may be sealed but must be marked *Third Class* on the address side. Sealed third-class mail may be opened and examined by the post office. Third-class bulk-mail rates apply to mailings of 50 pounds or 200 pieces of identical matter mailed at one time. A permit must be obtained from the post office and a bulk-rate statement-of-mailing form submitted with each bulk mailing.

Postage for third-class bulk rate usually includes an imprinted *Bulk Rate Postage Permit* designation or precanceled stamps. Permit-imprinted mail of any class may not be dropped into mail collection boxes; it must always be presented at the post office with a statement of mailing.

Fourth-Class or Parcel Post Mail. **Fourth-class** or **parcel post mail** includes all mailable material weighing 16 ounces or more and not included in first, second, or third class. The weight of the material and its destination determine the rate. When you mail sealed parcels at fourth-class rates, it is understood that you consent to a postal inspection of the contents.

Two special rates are available for fourth-class material. The special fourth-class rate applies to

- Books
- 16mm or narrower-width films, film catalogs
- Objective test materials
- Printed music
- Sound recordings
- Manuscripts
- Playscripts
- Educational reference charts
- Medical information

These parcels must be marked *Special Fourth-Class Rate Books*. Library-rate materials (items loaned or exchanged among libraries, colleges, schools, museums, and nonprofit groups) also qualify for a special rate; such parcels must be marked *Library Rate*. Before using the special fourth-class or library rate, check with your local post office for details.

Mixed Class of Mail. If you enclose letters with first-class postage in a third- or fourth-class parcel, you must mark *First-Class Mail Enclosed* above the address and below the postage. If you send a first-class letter with a third-class enclosure, you can use a combination mailer. The combination mailer is a large envelope with a number 10 envelope attached. The enclosure is sent at the third-class rate and the letter at a first-class rate. It is also permissible to tape an envelope to the exterior of a third-class envelope and mark *First-Class Mail Enclosed*.

Special Mailing Services

Special mailing services (Figure 5–10, pp. 117–118) are available for a specified fee in addition to the regular postage fees. These special services speed mail delivery or help ensure receipt of mail.

Insured mail (*a*, p. 118) carries insurance of up to $500; third- and fourth-class mail qualify. Extremely fragile items and items inappropriately packaged are not accepted for insurance. Merchandise insured for more than $15 qualifies for a receipt of delivery signed by the receiver and kept on file at the delivering post office. Irreplaceable items (or those with values over $500) should be mailed by more secure means, such as registered mail.

Registered mail (*b*, p. 118) provides protection for valuable mail and evidence of mailing and delivery. To be registered, the items must be sealed and have the first-class or priority postage rate paid in addition to the registry fee. At the time you register the item, you must declare its value. Insurance coverage carries a maximum liability of $25,000.

Certified mail (c, p. 118) lets you know that first-class mail with no intrinsic value has been delivered. A certified-mail fee must be paid in addition to the first-class postage rate.

A **return receipt** (d, p. 117) provides the sender with a signed receipt of legal evidence that the mailable matter was delivered to the addressee. Return receipts are available for all registered mail, certified mail, and mail insured for more than $15. A fee is paid when the return receipt is requested. If delivery of the return receipt is restricted to the addressee only, there is an additional charge; when delivery is not restricted, anyone can sign a return receipt. Return receipts requested after the mailing require a much higher fee. Be sure to complete the front and back sides of the return receipt.

Certificates of mailing (e, p. 118) are used when only proof that the item was sent is needed. These certificates can be used for any kind of mail, domestic and international. The certificate of mailing does not insure the item or provide proof of delivery.

Collect-on-delivery (COD) service is available only for a bona fide order or articles that the addressee has agreed to accept. The addressee pays for the items at the time of delivery. The maximum amount that can be collected is $400. Payments by check for CODs should be made payable to the mailer.

Special-delivery (f, p. 118) service can be used for any class of mail any day of the year. It is delivered by messenger during prescribed hours within designated special-delivery areas. Such mail must be marked *Special Delivery*. This service is recommended for perishable material or items that would otherwise be likely to reach the destination post office after hours, on Sundays, or on holidays. Use this service when you know the addressee must receive the mailing promptly.

Special handling is available for third- and fourth-class mail only. Items should be marked *Special Handling*. Special handling is valuable because for a small amount of additional postage for items up to 10 pounds, the third- or fourth-class piece is handled along with second-class mail. This keeps the material out of the bulk mail centers, which obviously speeds up delivery considerably.

General-delivery mail may be addressed to individuals in care of the general-delivery window of main post offices. This service is convenient for individuals who have no established address in a city. Such mail is held for a specified number of days and, if unclaimed, is then returned to the sender. A manager on a touring vacation or a sales representative who will be driving for several days might ask to have mail addressed in care of general delivery to a city en route.

Mailgrams (g, p. 118) can be sent by calling Western Union. Your mailgram message will be transmitted electronically to the post office nearest the addressee for guaranteed delivery in the next day's mail.

Money orders are used to transfer money from one person or business to another. Money orders can be purchased at all post offices. They are often used by people who do not have a checking account.

Figure 5–10

Special domestic-mail service logos and first-class imprints are shown on this page and on page 118. (See text discussion, pages 113–116.)

UNITED STATES POSTAL SERVICE

OFFICIAL BUSINESS

SENDER INSTRUCTIONS
Print your name, address and ZIP Code in the space below.
• Complete items 1, 2, 3, and 4 on the reverse.
• Attach to front of article if space permits, otherwise affix to back of article.
• Endorse article "Return Receipt Requested" adjacent to number.

PENALTY FOR PRIVATE USE, $300

RETURN TO ➤

Print Sender's name, address, and ZIP Code in the space below.

d (front)

● **SENDER:** Complete items 1 and 2 when additional services are desired, and complete items 3 and 4.
Put your address in the "RETURN TO" Space on the reverse side. Failure to do this will prevent this card from being returned to you. <u>The return receipt fee will provide you the name of the person delivered to and the date of delivery.</u> For additional fees the following services are available. Consult postmaster for fees and check box(es) for additional service(s) requested.

1. ☐ Show to whom delivered, date, and addressee's address.   2. ☐ Restricted Delivery
   (Extra charge)   *(Extra charge)*

3. Article Addressed to:	4. Article Number
	Type of Service:
	☐ Registered ☐ Insured
	☐ Certified ☐ COD
	☐ Express Mail ☐ Return Receipt for Merchandise
	Always obtain signature of addressee or agent and **DATE DELIVERED**.
5. Signature — Address X	8. Addressee's Address *(ONLY if requested and fee paid)*
6. Signature — Agent X	
7. Date of Delivery	

d (reverse)

PS Form **3811**, Mar. 1988   ★ U.S.G.P.O. 1988-212-865   **DOMESTIC RETURN RECEIPT**

INSURED
922503
U. S. MAIL

a

REGISTERED
NO.

b

CERTIFIED
No. 148001
MAIL

c

SPECIAL DELIVERY

f

certificates of mailing

CERTIFICATE OF MAILING

Received From:

Affix postage and postmark. Inquire of Postmaster for postage

One piece of ordinary mail addressed to:

MAY BE USED FOR DOMESTIC AND INTERNATIONAL MAIL. DOES NOT PROVIDE FOR INSURANCE   — POSTMASTER

e

western union Mailgram UNITED STATES POSTAL SERVICE

g

CHICAGO
If you wish
PUT DATE
HERE
ILL.

DETROIT
MICH

DETROIT
MICH

FIRST CLASS MAIL
U S POSTAGE
PAID (Rate goes here)
PERMIT No. 00

First Class Mail
U.S. POSTAGE
PAID 1 oz
PERMIT 00

First-Class Mail
U.S. POSTAGE
& PAID
PERMIT 37

PRESORTED
FIRST CLASS MAIL
US POSTAGE PAID
NEW YORK, NY
Permit No. 1

h

Figure 5–10, continued

Rapid-Delivery Services

Because information must move very rapidly today, both the U.S. Postal Service and a number of private companies now offer rapid-delivery options. These include same-day, overnight, and twenty-four-hour guarantees. Costs will vary depending on location and the nature of the request. You may have access to the following options:

- *Messengers.* You can have letters and packages picked up and delivered to locations within a defined area (usually a major city). Some services offer "bonded messengers," which allow you to send currency, financial documents, or confidential material to another location rapidly. A large firm may have its own messengers available for these special requests.
- *Van, limousine, or bus service.* In addition to providing local service in metropolitan areas, companies with either vans or buses deliver letters, packages, or other items to hard-to-reach locations. Scheduled and special service are available. Items can be insured, but there are some size and weight limits.
- *Air delivery.* The fastest and most expensive service is by air. Major air carriers guarantee time of delivery, often within a few hours. Fees depend on distance. Some firms involved in delivery specialize in this aspect of transportation, as do major commercial carriers. These companies also include pickup and delivery in their fee.

Mail-Handling Variations

Several variations in traditional mail-handling procedures are available.

Electronic Mail. Various forms of electronic mail make communication with one or more individuals easy and fast. In addition to sending a message, you can transmit computer files that include mailing lists and spreadsheets. Some systems allow you to order materials from a central unit; modems let you reach suppliers in distant locations. You and your managers may also be able to obtain financial information, up-to-the-minute news, credit reports, and access to bank accounts.

Regular users of electronic mail (regardless of the software used) recommend the following procedures:

1. Check messages regularly and respond to them in a timely fashion.
2. File messages you want to save in the appropriate storage section of your electronic mailing system.
3. Delete messages no longer of value to you in the "send" portion of your system.
4. Print messages containing information you want to save in hardcopy form.
5. Be careful when sending confidential material so that unauthorized individuals do not obtain access to electronic mail files.

Some mail systems produce a distinct sound, such as a bell or whistle, that tells you when there is a message for you and another sound when you indicate that a message will be deleted. These systems can store up to one hundred messages in various files. However, check electronic mail files periodically to delete messages no longer of value; the more information these files contain, the slower the system will operate.

Users of electronic mail claim that it significantly increases their productivity and the amount of communication among co-workers. Instead of being passed around by hand, messages can be sent to a number of individuals simultaneously. Messages can be left for those out of the office for a short period or sent to them at a distant location via modem.

Forwarding Mail. There is no charge for returning first-class or priority mail. You simply write the correct address on the front of the envelope and deposit the item in the mail. Forwarding second-, third-, and fourth-class mail requires additional postage.

Returning Undelivered Mail. First-class undelivered mail will be returned at no charge. Third- and fourth-class undelivered mail require the sender's return address and the statement *Return Postage Guaranteed* in the upper left-hand corner. Services requesting a new address or the reason for nondelivery are also available for a fee.

Remailing Returned Mail. Mail that has been returned and rubber-stamped *Return to Sender* and the reason for the return (undeliverable as addressed; moved, left no address; forwarding address has expired; no such street or number) must be put in a new, correctly addressed envelope and postage paid again.

Recalling Mail. When you must recall a piece of mail, immediately contact your local post office for a locally delivered piece or your sectional post office for an out-of-town delivery. Request that the piece be held. Type the envelope address and go to the appropriate post office. There you will complete a form entitled *Sender's Application for Withdrawal of Mail.* Give the form and the envelope address to the postal clerk.

Refusing Mail. When you receive mail of value that you did not order, you do not have to pay for the item or return it. If you want to return the unopened item, you may do so at no charge.

Changing an Address. Notify your local post office of any change of address. You can complete a change-of-address form giving the old and new address and the effective date of change.

Updating a Mailing List. For a fee, the post office will furnish new addresses and names and correct addresses on your mailing list. You should type each name and address on a separate 3″ × 5″ card, with your company's name and address in the upper left-hand corner. Many organizations update their mailing lists yearly.

International Mail

If you are responsible for handling international mail, get a copy of the international mail rate chart at your local post office. More detailed information appears in the *International Mail Manual,* kept at most post offices. Because international regulations, services, and rates change frequently, check periodically with your local post office for any recent changes or revisions.

International mail is divided into two categories: postal union mail and parcel post.

Postal Union Mail. *Postal union mail* consists of two categories: LC mail and OA mail.

LC mail (Letters and Cards) includes letters, letter packages, all handwritten and typewritten correspondence, Aerogrammes (air letters), and postcards. All mail destined for countries other than Canada or Mexico are charged international postal rates. Mail to Canada and Mexico carries the same rate as that for the United States. Letter packages (small sealed packages) should be sealed and marked *Letter* so that they will be treated as letters. An *Aerogramme* is a lightweight, prestamped single sheet, marked *Air Mail,* that forms an envelope when folded. It can be sent by air to any country with air service.

OA mail (Other Articles) includes printed matter, materials for the blind, merchandise samples, and small packets. OA mail by air is the cheapest and fastest international postal service. It is ideal for shipping small articles. Dutiable printed matter and merchandise, maps, drawings, and similar items subject to duty (tax paid to the U.S. Customs Service) must have a green customs label (Form 2976) affixed.

All postal union articles, even if registered, must be sealed. Special delivery and special handling are available to most countries. Insurance, certified, and COD services are not available outside the United States.

Parcel Post. International *parcel post* must have a completed parcel post sticker and a customs declaration (Form 2966-A) affixed. Some countries require additional forms. Because the destination country's weight and size limitations vary, check with your local post office before mailing.

Packages may be registered or insured; they must be sealed. Special handling is also available; certified and COD services are not.

Addressing International Mail

When addressing international mail, address the envelope, package, or card using the same guidelines as those for domestic mail. In addition, you must write the post office and country in capital letters and include the postal delivery zone. Open-panel (window) envelopes are not allowed in international mail.

Figure 5–11 contains examples of international addresses.

Shipping Services

In addition to using the U.S. Postal Service, you are likely to be responsible for shipping articles through private services. This section lists and briefly describes the services available.

Figure 5–11

Samples of international addresses.

Miss Heidi Strum	Mr. Shaun Bernard	Jacques Miele
2300 Hamburg 54 (Lakstedt)	Strand Stamp Center	Rue de Champaign
64 GRANDWEG	84 Oxford Street	06573 St. Paul
WEST GERMANY	LONDON WIE 322	FRANCE
	ENGLAND	

Exception: Mail addressed to Canada may use either of the following formats when the postal delivery zone number is included in the address:

Mrs. Jane Mellen	OR	Mrs. Jane Mellen
1259 Oak Street		1259 Oak Street
Ottawa On K1A 0B1		Ottawa On Canada
CANADA		K1A 0B1

United Parcel Service

United Parcel Service (UPS) delivers to a wide range of rural and metropolitan areas; it does not deliver to post office boxes. If the recipient is unavailable, UPS attempts to make the delivery two more times; in some cases, a UPS driver will leave a package(s) at an address when no one is there. Proof of delivery is provided on request. Use ZIP codes, and call a day in advance for pickup.

UPS Blue Label is United Parcel Service's air service. It is a good alternative for fast (but not overnight) service.

Air Express

Federal Express Priority One provides pickup on the same day called. It is especially designed for business documents but not for sending valuables. Federal Express uses its own planes and provides computer tracking. Documents are sealed in a protective package that holds up to 8 ounces. This service is available for both domestic and international deliveries. Next-day delivery may be guaranteed depending on the destination. Centers are available for after-hours mailing. For information, call the Customer Service Hotline at 1-800-238-5355 (in Tennessee, 1-800-542-5151).

Federal Express Standard Service provides pickup on the same day called. It is a good, inexpensive alternative for fast (but not next-day) delivery.

Federal Express Economy Two-Day Service provides pickup on the same day called. It is a proven, inexpensive alternative for fast (but not next-day) delivery. The destination determines when a package will be delivered over a two-day period.

Federal Express Overnight Letter Service provides next-day delivery. You can drop off a letter at any of the 1,500 Federal Express offices or have it picked up by

Federal Express planes at the Memphis Super Hub. *(Courtesy of Federal Express Corporation. All rights reserved.)*

courier. This service provides special 9½″ × 12½″ envelopes designed to contain up to thirty typewritten pages.

Emery Worldwide Urgent Letter provides pickup on the same day called. It is designed for business documents but not valuables and provides a computerized tracking system. Service is available in the United States, Amsterdam, Basel, Brussels, Frankfurt, Geneva, London, Madrid, Paris, Rotterdam, and Zurich. Quick European delivery is limited to items not subject to duty.

Emery Worldwide is a full-service air cargo shipper. Articles must clear customs.

Emery Special Air Courier is designed for packages or articles so valuable that you would carry them yourself. The sender pays the price of an airline ticket plus the carrier charge.

Emery Worldwide Constant Surveillance Service is designed for articles so valuable that you would prefer to hand-carry them yourself. A courier carries the item and will reach the destination on the same day called. Items are limited to those that can be hand-carried. For this service, you pay a surcharge along with the normal freight rate.

Emery Worldwide Signature Service is for items of considerable value. All individuals who handle the item at various stages of the delivery sign to indicate that they have completed their portion of the delivery. Same-day or overnight service is available using air, train, or truck.

Airborne Express Overnight Service serves the United States and Europe. It is designed for business documents. This service provides pickup on the same day called; proof of delivery is available.

Commercial airlines provide rush delivery of packages. Most airlines offer twenty-four-hour pickup and proof of delivery upon request. For international shipments, be sure to mention deadlines. Some airlines offer Telex confirmation plus guaranteed time limits on international shipments.

Train

Amtrak Rail Express delivers articles that arrive at the station one hour before train departure. Items can be sent anywhere in the United States where baggage check service is available. Boxes are provided for oversize items.

Bus

Greyhound and *Trailways* provide station-to-station service. You must take your item to the station thirty minutes ahead of bus departure. Trailways and Greyhound have reciprocal agreements for transporting packages.

Messenger

Regional messenger services provide pickup on the same day called. Some offer twenty-four-hour answering service. Regional deliveries or tie-ins with other services (buses, trains, planes) are sometimes available.

Cab and Truck

Cab delivery can be very reasonable. Its feasibility depends on the town you are in and where you want to send the item.

Moving companies are typically used only for transporting whole offices; the cost of moving individual articles is very high. These companies will do your packing, but of course this service increases the cost.

Trucks and *freight forwarders* often provide package-shipping services. However, you must package articles yourself.

Increasing Your Mail-Handling Efficiency

This section offers some tips to help you manage your mail-handling responsibilities effectively and efficiently.

UPS provides a booklet called *Priority vs. Price* to help office personnel make efficient decisions. It suggests using delivery logs for both incoming and outgoing packages and recording all delivery charges.

Keeping a log will help you determine whether there is a seasonal pattern to your deliveries; if you could save money by using other carriers; if you are experiencing excessive breakage or late deliveries; and whether you are paying for pickup or inside delivery, tracking, or rural delivery.

Communication Tips

- Prepare a list of items to discuss with your manager(s) when you meet to review correspondence.
- Jot down your manager's responses to your questions about mail-related work.
- If you have annotated mail, ask your manager if any additional work is needed.
- Ask your manager if any other people in the organization should see certain correspondence.
- Define procedures for reviewing, organizing, and responding to correspondence that arrives while your manager is away; include a time for you to contact your manager by phone to review correspondence, if desired.
- Be sure you understand which items can be sent first class besides those normally sent that way.
- Ask your manager(s) which rapid-delivery method to use in rush situations.
- Review options for sending various items, and suggest to your manager(s) less costly but equally efficient delivery methods.
- Determine from more experienced co-workers the most effective ways to send material, including the best special-service options.
- Recheck instructions for special-service drivers or messengers to be sure they are clear.

SUMMARY

For incoming mail, use the following procedures:

1. Obtain mail directly or from a mailroom.
2. Sort items into groups according to class and level of importance for one or more managers; forward incorrectly delivered mail.
3. Open envelopes and remove the contents, paying special attention to enclosures.
4. Date and time-stamp the mail.
5. Register all mail in a log, if such a record is required.
6. Read and annotate the mail, respecting each manager's preference.
7. Route mail to the appropriate people and present each manager's mail in priority order.

For outgoing mail, follow these procedures:

1. Check all documents for signature, appearance, and necessary revisions.
2. Match the letter address with the envelope before inserting items into it.
3. Insert all enclosures.
4. Determine the most economical yet efficient way of sending an item.

All mail should carry the ZIP codes of addresser and addressee to speed delivery. In some cases, the expanded ZIP code should appear on the envelope. Nothing should be typed below the last lines of the address. Bar codes speed the identification and sorting process.

Correct postage reduces the cost and speeds delivery. If you use a postal meter, mail on the date metered, make sure each item contains the date and correct amount, and bundle the mail by ZIP code.

Mail can be classified as local or out-of-town, grouped by ZIP code, and then separated by metered and unmetered. Large mailings that are presorted go out at a lower rate than unsorted mailings do. Special mailing services can be used to speed up delivery and provide insurance and proof of delivery. International mail requires following special addressing and customs-clearing procedures.

A number of private shipping services are available for sending items domestically and internationally. You should become familiar with those in your area.

Key Terms

The following terms appeared in boldface type in this chapter. Do you recall what they mean? For a more complete definition, turn to the glossary beginning on p. 442.

annotate (p. 103)
bar codes (p. 110)
certificate of mailing (p. 116)

certified mail (p. 116)
collect-on-delivery (p. 116)
date/time stamp (p. 102)

domestic mail (p. 113)
express mail (p. 114)
first-class mail (p. 113)
fourth-class (parcel post) mail (p. 115)
general-delivery mail (p. 116)
insured mail (p. 115)
mailgram (p. 116)
metered postage (p. 112)
money order (p. 116)
optical character reader (p. 110)
presorted mail (p. 113)

priority mail (p. 114)
registered mail (p. 115)
return receipt (p. 116)
routing slip (p. 103)
second-class mail (p. 114)
special delivery (p. 116)
special handling (p. 116)
third-class mail (p. 114)
Zone Improvement Program (ZIP) code
    (p. 109)
ZIP plus 4 (p. 109)

Discussion Questions

1. Your company requires assistants to keep a mail register. You always update the register within a half-hour of receipt of mail. Two new associates always take mail out of the stack delivered to your desk before it has been stamped and recorded. You have politely requested them to stop, but with no results. What is your next step?

2. In today's mail, your manager received a letter marked *Urgent and Personal* on the envelope. She is out of town for the remainder of the week and may not call in. You were asked to open and sort all mail. What will you do with this letter?

3. You support four managers. Each day each manager receives at least five first-class letters, three to four interoffice memos directed to them, three to four interoffice announcements, *The Wall Street Journal,* and fifteen to twenty mass mailings. Two of the managers want a record of all mail directed to them personally. In addition to the sorting and routing steps suggested in the chapter, what other actions can you take to avoid mixing up their mail?

4. Into which of the seven categories presented in this chapter would you put the following items? In what order would you arrange them to ensure that your manager receives the most important items first?
   a. Letter containing a price quote for new factory equipment
   b. Request to your manager to attend a regional convention of a trade association
   c. Complaint letter addressed to the company president and routed to your manager for immediate reply
   d. New supplement to a catalog the manager uses routinely
   e. Trade journal
   f. Interoffice memo from the comptroller requesting information by noon the day after tomorrow
   g. Six brochures advertising new equipment

5. Choose the most effective way to send the following items.
   a. Travel expense vouchers for a regional sales manager

b. Brochures announcing a conference to staff members who work in different cities
c. Ten-ounce package containing an important letter and enclosures that must reach Washington, D.C. by noon tomorrow
d. Twenty-five first-class letters with metered postage
e. Six overdue bills whose importance you wish to emphasize
6. A newly hired assistant regularly forgets to include the necessary enclosures in first-class mail. What reminder steps would you suggest she follow to prevent that from happening?
7. Name the special service you should use to protect each of the following when mailing it.
   a. Certified or cashier's check
   b. Ten stock certificates
   c. Last will and testament
   d. Five U.S. Treasury notes
   e. Deed to a building
8. What special procedures should you follow when preparing first-class mail, including packages, for international delivery?

Assignments

1. You keep a mail register for items expected under separate cover, cash received, and special mail services. You then prepare routing slips for certain pieces of mail. Record on the mail register the information for each of the following pieces of mail:

   April 10: A letter from Juan Hernandez refers to brochures sent under separate cover on March 31 to the advertising department.

   April 10: A letter from Jeanine Turner of The Gourmet Shop, dated April 8, states that she returned that day by UPS a package of our merchandise. The package should be referred to our shipping department.

   April 11: A letter dated April 9 from Illinois Bell Telephone Company states that they are sending a film catalog to our public relations department.

   April 12: At 1:00 PM, a registered letter was received from Kester-Henderson, Chicago, Illinois, for the accounting department.

   April 16: Received Illinois Bell Telephone Company film catalog.

   April 17: Brochures from Juan Hernandez were received.

   April 17: Received Jeanine Turner's returned merchandise.

   April 20: Received a letter from John Fujiyama with $3.50 enclosed for a handbook on listening skills.

   April 30: At 4:15 PM, received a certified letter from Scott Shapiro, Cincinnati, Ohio, for Mary McMahon.

2. Categorize the following material according to class of mail and special service, if required.

	1st	2nd	3rd	4th	Special Services
Letter					
Mail-order catalog					
Magazine					
Circular					
Package weighing 80 pounds					
Mimeographed bulletin					
Sale announcement					
Unsealed greeting card with no message					
Sealed greeting card					
Package of seeds weighing 4 ounces					
Statement of account					
Postcard					
Photocopy					
Newspaper					
Book					
Business-reply card					
Merchandise weighing 9 ounces					
Negotiable bonds					
Certified check					
Form letters, not individualized					
Photograph					

 Those instructors using *Top Performance: A Decision-Making Simulation for the Office* should consult the *Instructor's Guide* at this point for support material regarding use of the software in the classroom.

Case Study

As office manager in an engineering consulting firm, Tom O'Brien controls expenses. For the past four months each monthly statement shows an increase in mailing costs, mainly because of the number of priority-mail and express-mail items sent to meet deadlines. Also, some consulting engineers have been sending some items with first-class letters that Tom believes could be sent at a lower rate. Further, other employees have been using first-class mail to send copies of newspaper and magazine articles to clients or colleagues along with short notes.

The firm's owners are cost-conscious, but they have not established clear-cut guidelines regarding either mail or long-distance telephone calls. Business has been brisk and cash flow good, so these matters have not been a concern. When Tom approached the firm's vice-president about them, she appeared somewhat interested but seemed unwilling to talk to the consulting engineers, whose work she valued.

What should Tom do at this point to continue cost-cutting activities? Describe the steps he should take if he decides to proceed.

CHAPTER

6

USING THE PHONE

Chapter Objectives

- To know how to control telephone costs

- To learn how to organize and place outgoing calls, and how to place domestic or international long-distance calls

- To become familiar with domestic and international telegram and mailgram services

- To develop an effective system for answering calls

- To understand how to handle various types of calls

Examples of
Excellence

The telephone bill shocked everyone in the office. As a small (ten-person) organization, Graphics Resolutions couldn't afford to spend over $900 each month on special charges. An analysis of the bill revealed many operator-assisted, person-to-person, and direct-dial calls, along with hefty directory assistance costs.

Beth Schoenfeld, a new office staff member, volunteered to find specific ways to reduce telephone costs. She obtained telephone directories from the major areas most often contacted, assembled a list of useful 800 numbers, and began putting together a company-wide list of frequently called clients, vendors, and other contacts.

With strong support from Graphics Resolutions' owner, the information Beth assembled gradually began to reduce the monthly telephone bills. "Little steps mean a lot," the owner said happily.

Managers in both public and private organizations continually look for ways to control costs. In recent years, charges for telephone equipment, service, and calls have risen greatly. Yet businesspeople, educators, government officials, and professionals continue to rely on the telephone to reach clients, obtain information, and perform many other tasks. As a result, economical and efficient methods of using the telephone have become increasingly important.

Just as you and your organization rely on the telephone to communicate with other firms, they use the telephone to contact you. A constantly ringing telephone can be stressful and cut productivity. As one administrative assistant put it, "You can't concentrate, because the phone goes off just as you are trying to start."

In this chapter, you will learn

- How to control telephone costs
- How to organize and place outgoing calls
- What steps to take when placing a domestic or international long-distance call
- How to use domestic and international telegram and mailgram services
- How a system for answering incoming calls can reduce telephone-related stress
- What specific steps to use to handle all types of calls, including problem ones

Becoming Cost Conscious

Becoming familiar with the most effective but least costly telephone options will save your firm money. Cost-saving telephone features such as WATS (Wide Area Telephone Service) lines for long-distance calls or tie lines to specific offices are useful in large organizations.

Because telephone companies now charge for directory assistance calls, you can save money by assembling both local and out-of-town telephone numbers into your own call directory. You can further reduce time and charges if you know an individual's extension number.

Measured Service

Measured service is a method of charging that counts each call you make. Customers who choose measured service pay a lower basic monthly charge, but message units are counted for each call.

Call-Cost Records

One of your responsibilities may be to keep a record of all long-distance and credit card calls. You won't be able to obtain information on costs for direct-dial long-distance calls. When an operator assists with a call, indicate that you want the **toll charges** provided at the end of the call.

When a monthly bill arrives, you may have to review all calls made and assign them to the proper department or account, or check them against a printout of all long-distance calls by extension. Some of this billing may be done automatically.

Managers commonly carry credit cards that enable them to make long-distance calls from any location. Charges for these calls appear on monthly reports and are identified as credit card calls.

As you become more familiar with your organization's telephone procedures, it will be easier to select the best methods. Your company's procedures manual

A manager makes a long-distance credit card call using a mobile phone. *(Courtesy of Ameritech Mobile Communications)*

will probably describe how to make various types of calls, but your manager and co-workers will also be good sources. However, no techniques will succeed if you lack the up-to-date information that various directories provide.

Valuable Directories

The following directories will help you find both in- and out-of-town numbers: (1) public directories issued by the local telephone company; (2) special business telephone listings; (3) a city directory; (4) organizational directories; and (5) a carefully maintained personal directory. You should keep these items near your telephone.

A *public telephone directory* is divided into three sections: a call guide, an alphabetical directory, and a classified guide (yellow pages). Each section is distinct and contains valuable information.

The *call guide* or *customer guide* contains emergency numbers; telephone company services such as directory assistance, repair information, and special services for disabled persons; community service numbers such as city offices, civil defense, health care, libraries, post offices, and schools; area codes for large cities; and country and routing codes for international calls.

The *alphabetical directory* lists subscribers' names, addresses, and telephone numbers. Its alphabetizing system will enable you to find numbers quickly (Figure 6–1).

The *classified directory*, printed on yellow pages, lists businesses by field or product in alphabetical order. In addition, it usually includes a map of the city and a listing of ZIP codes for communities in your state.

Both the alphabetical and classified directories contain *special business telephone listings*—listings of businesses that want their telephone numbers

Figure 6–1
How to find numbers in the telephone book.

Abbreviations. Abbreviations appear alphabetically as though the name were spelled out. Example: *St. John* would appear as *Saint John*. Businesses starting with *U.S.* are found under *United* for *United States*.

Alternate listings. *John James Company* might appear as *James John Company*.

Ampersands (&) and apostrophes. Ignore them. Example: Bill & Bob's Shop would be listed alphabetically as *Bill Bobs Shop*.

Business names. Some business names use initials only. Most precede the regular listings under the appropriate initial letter. However, an "initials-only" company may prefer an alphabetical listing as though the name were spelled out. Example: JOT, Inc., may be listed at the beginning of the *J* section or may appear further down in *J* after other listings whose first two letters are *J* and *O*.

Government listings. Look in the white pages under the name of the appropriate government. Example: *(name), City of; (name) County; (name), State of; United States Government*.

Initials. Initials precede first names. Example: *Doe J.* would precede *Doe John*.

Letters used in names. Names consisting of all capital letters, such as radio and TV stations, are listed at the beginning of the alphabetical section. Example: *WABD* would precede *W & W Appliance* and *Wabash, D.* When letters precede a full name, check the beginning of the section. Example: *A-1 Garage Inc.* would be among the first listings in the *A* section, but *A-1 Construction Company* would be listed before it.

Numbers spelled out. When used as names, numbers are alphabetized as though spelled in full. Example: *123* (one-two-three) *Company* would appear under the letter *O*. However, numbers are usually listed in numerical sequence. Example: *100* (one-zero-zero) would come before *123* (one-two-three). Another exception is *First* (1st), which would be listed under *F* for *first* or *O* for *one* as the customer prefers.

Prefixes. Prefixes in names are alphabetized. Example: *MacNeil* would follow *Macnab*, and *Macoy* would follow *MacDonald*.

Schools. For public schools only, look under *Schools, Public*. For all other schools, look under the name of the school.

Spelling variations. Spelling variations are cross-referenced; cross-references are shown at the beginnings of the sections that include the names. Example: *Johnson* might appear as *Johnston*.

The. *The* usually follows the company name. Example: The Brown Fabric Company would be listed as *Brown Fabric Company, The*.

Titles. Titles are placed after the entire name. Example: *Smith Robert MD*.

Two-word listings. Two-word listings may appear in one of two ways. Example: For Jack Brown Company, look for the last name, *Brown*, first. If it's not in the *Bs*, try *Jack Brown* in the *Js*.

Unusual spellings. Business names can have unusual spellings. Example: *Kofy Kup Restaurant*. If you're not sure how to spell the name, look for it by category (*Restaurants*) in the yellow pages.

published in directories outside their local areas. These businesses usually provide an 800 area code, which allows their customers to contact them at no expense.

Sometimes an out-of-town company lists its name and address and a local phone number. Such a listing is called a *foreign exchange line*. The company pays to have calls switched to its out-of-town location. Here is an example:

Central Transport Inc
Hwy 237 South La Port Rd
New Buffalo, MI . . .
Evansville Tel No
433-4527

Although many firms list their 800 numbers in telephone directories, you can obtain others by calling **directory assistance** at 1-800-555-1212. Record these numbers in your personal directory for future use.

The *city directory* lists public and private organizations. It is divided into three sections: names, streets, and phone numbers. Items in the names and streets sections are listed alphabetically, and the phone numbers are listed in numerical sequence. This directory is printed by a private company and must be purchased. It is useful when you have only a name, street address, or phone number and need a more complete address.

Organizational directories consist of a staff phone number list. Regardless of the organization's size, the list should be updated regularly. The directory should include directions for using tie lines and other features. A **tie line** is a special, privately leased telephone connection to the company's offices in the same area or in distant locations; you will have to dial a special set of numbers to use it. Unlimited calling is available at a fixed monthly charge.

Your *personal telephone directory* should contain an alphabetical listing of people and organizations that you call frequently. Some people prefer desktop rotary card files that also list addresses. These files can be updated quickly by changing the information on the cards or adding new cards.

Your organization may require you to keep a log of local and long-distance outgoing calls. You might encourage staff to use a similar log if you are responsible for compiling their long-distance call records. Some systems provide printouts of long-distance calls from each extension if the individuals must enter their own extension numbers before the calls are completed.

Placing Outgoing Calls

Before placing any call, be sure to have a pen or pencil, pad of paper, and the appropriate telephone directory within reach. Next, plan the call. Write down the key points you want to cover in the conversation. Assemble what you need beforehand so it is available for reference during the call. Check off your points as you cover them, and make notes to yourself about important points discussed.

Unlike social calls, business calls require concentration. Preparation before dialing will focus your attention on the purpose of the call and improve your listening ability. If you get into the habit of writing down points to be covered and information received, you will need to rely on your memory less often. With a list, you can also summarize or review what was covered to ensure that all points covered are jointly understood.

Some managers will ask you to place calls for them (however, this practice is becoming less common). Use the following steps to perform this task effectively:

1. Obtain the name and number of the person to be called.
2. Make sure the manager is ready to take the call.
3. Identify the manager and the organization when the phone is picked up: "Dr. Habiby, please. Mr. John Allen of Lake View Hospital calling."
4. Comply with a request that the manager be put on the line.
5. Establish alternative times if the person called is not available.

If you support two or more managers, this service may be difficult to perform. Depending on your workload and other priorities, managers may have to make their own calls. In any case, try to accommodate preferences as often as possible.

Long-Distance Calling

The long-distance calls you will make most often are likely to be **station-to-station calls**. To place this kind of call, dial or depress the 1 plus the area code and local telephone number. You should make these calls when you are willing to talk with whoever answers the telephone. The charges for a station-to-station call begin when the phone is answered.

If you dial the wrong number or reach an incorrect number, end the call. Then contact your local operator to report what happened, and ask for a refund. If a call is cut off, inform the operator so that an adjustment can be made. If you get a message that the call can't be completed, you will have to redial. If you continue to experience difficulty, operators will assist you at no charge.

Your organization may decide to cut costs by subscribing to a special long-distance service that offers cost reductions to business clients. To use this service, call a special number, depress your special code, and dial the long-distance number.

Remember to be aware of any time difference in the area you are calling. The United States and Canada are divided into five time zones from the east to west coasts; there is a one-hour time difference between each zone. To check the area codes and time zones, consult the map found at the front of most telephone directories.

When you place a **person-to-person call,** depress the 0 (instead of the 1) to begin the call, followed by the area code and telephone number. When the operator comes on the line, name the person you wish to reach.

If the person you wish to contact cannot be reached, you will not be charged for the call. If you want the call to be returned, give the operator your area code and telephone number. Have the operator refer to this as a *collect callback number*. The number assigned—say, 65—depends on the type of billing and where the call originated. The person returning the call tells the operator the callback number and is not charged for the call. Figure 6–2 shows a sample callback form.

A person-to-person call can also be *collect*—if the person called agrees to pay for it—or charged to a credit card or another phone number.

The 0 is also used to begin an international call. In most parts of the United States, you can dial more than ninety countries directly through *international direct-distance dialing (IDDD)*. Your local telephone company can supply you with information on both country and city area codes, time differences, and rates. To dial an overseas call, you must use one of the **International Access Codes**. For a station-to-station call, dial or depress 011. For a call requiring operator assistance (person-to-person, collect, credit card, charge to another number, and requests for time and charges), use 01. Then dial the country code, the city code, and the local number.

Operator-Assisted Calls

If direct-distance dialing is not available in your area, or you want to place a collect or credit card (calling card) call from a rotary phone, you will have to contact an operator. Give the operator the area code of the city being called, your party's telephone number, the type of call, your party's name, and your telephone number.

Operator-assisted international calls are handled similarly: Dial 0 and tell the operator the country you wish to call, the city, person or organization, phone number, and type of call.

Figure 6–2
Telephone callback form.
(Courtesy of Day-Timers)

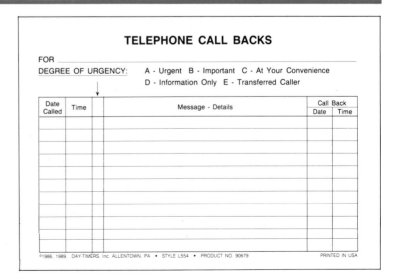

Call-Routing Systems

Deregulation of the telephone system has greatly intensified competition among telephone companies. You may now select the company that you believe provides the best service at the lowest rate. In addition to AT&T, major long-distance carriers include MCI, GTE, Allnet, and Sprint. A computer will automatically choose the most economical long-distance rate when more than one system is used. This routing system, called *equal access*, divides service among providers on a proportionate basis. The computers that assign calls also track the length of time used to calculate charges and issue bills.

Other widely used routing systems include Centrex (central branch exchange), PBX (private branch exchange), and PABX (private automatic branch exchange). Through the Centrex system, every telephone has its own number and can be reached directly from an outside phone. With PBX, a switchboard operator routes calls to their proper destination and processes external calls. PABX has more automated features, allowing an operator to monitor calls in progress.

WATS

The **Wide Area Telephone Service (WATS)** line provides reduced rates to businesses with a high volume of long-distance calls. There are both inward and outward WATS lines. Inward WATS is the familiar 800 number that allows callers to reach your company toll free. Outward WATS allows people in your company to call out at reduced rates. You can purchase full-service WATS at a flat rate or service limited to certain hours of the business day or to certain calling areas, depending on your long-distance needs. Remember: The WATS line is not free. Depending on the type of service you have, abuse of a WATS line can be extremely costly for your company.

Conference Calls

You may be called upon to arrange **conference calls** involving individuals in several locations. Your telephone may even have a conference call option that enables you to arrange the call yourself by depressing the numbers to be called and indicating to the conference call operator when the call will be held. In some cases a conference call operator will make all the arrangements, contact all the participants, and actually place the call.

You should treat your conference calls like face-to-face meetings. A good time to get people together from different time zones is 10:00 AM to 1:00 PM. Be sure to confirm the arrangements with all the participants. Your manager may also want materials such as agendas or reports to be discussed in advance.

Cellular Phones

Great advances have been made in cellular (mobile) phones (Figure 6–3, p.138). Keep a record of cellular-phone numbers you use regularly. Employees who

spend considerable time outside the office find the accessibility of cellular phones in their cars very convenient.

Telegrams and Mailgrams

Telegrams and mailgrams are public message services offered by Western Union. Their advantages over a long-distance phone call or business letter are that they provide a written record of messages, rapid delivery at low cost, and a format that will attract the recipient's attention. When you need to send a telegram or mailgram, call the local Western Union office.

Telegrams. Regular or overnight telegrams can be sent twenty-four hours a day, seven days a week, including Sundays and holidays. Overnight telegrams cost much less than regular ones.

Both messenger and telephone delivery are available; however, messenger delivery is not available everywhere at all times. Messenger delivery is guaranteed within five hours and phone delivery within two hours. A written copy of the message will be mailed for an additional charge. With an overnight telegram, the message delivery will arrive by 2 PM the next day.

Western Union offers many special services, including report delivery (a return telegram or mailgram sent to the originator stating the date and time the message was delivered); a **confirmation copy** (a written copy of the telegram sent to the originator by mailgram); alternate delivery (an alternate address given for delivery); personal delivery only (telegram handed directly to addressee by messenger); repeat-back and valued message (the telegram is of high monetary value, such as a contract for more than $500).

When writing a telegram, be clear and concise. Short sentences with action verbs are best.

Mailgrams. In 1970, the U.S. Postal Service and Western Union introduced the **mailgram**. This service allows a written message to be delivered in the next day's mail at a lower cost than a telegram. The mailgram message is sent directly to the U.S. post office nearest to the addressee. The message is transmitted by Western Union via its satellite and microwave networks. The message is typed by a high-speed printer at the post office on continuous-form letterhead, torn off, inserted into a blue-and-white mailgram envelope, and delivered in the next business day's mail. If you send a mailgram at the close of a business day, your addressee should have it the next morning.

The mailgram service offers four advantages: It adds urgency and importance to your message; it receives preferential treatment by the postal service; the cost is relatively low; and your mailgram message may be sent to Western Union by telephone, telex or TWX, computer, communicating typewriters, and facsimile.

A confirmation copy is also available for any mailgram message. It can also be sent certified; in that case, the addressee must sign a receipt.

Composing and Sending Telegrams and Mailgrams. To prepare a clear and concise telegram or mailgram, follow these steps:

1. Use active verbs, substitute numbers for words, and eliminate adjectives.
2. Type, rather than handwrite, the message on your company's or Western Union's forms to be sure you have all the necessary information in a clear, readable format.
3. If you phone in a message, an operator will type it as delivered. Before phoning it in, therefore, be sure you have the addressee's name and business title spelled correctly, the complete address, the telephone number, and the billing information (paid or collect). Figure 6–4 lists letters and sounds you can use to ensure correct spelling.
4. If the addressee's office has a telex or TWX and yours doesn't, you can phone in a message. Ask that it be transmitted to the addressee's teletypewriter terminal. (Western Union can get the telex or TWX number for you.)
5. To reach someone in transit on a ship, provide the person's name, the ship's name, the ship's approximate location, and the estimated time of arrival at its destination.

Cablegrams or International Telegrams. There is only one class of service for the cablegram or international telegram: full-rate international, with costs charged on a per-word basis. The rate depends on the country to which you are sending the message. Night service is no longer available.

You can send an international message through your office telex or TWX or by calling your local Western Union office. Your message will be transmitted by Western Union to one of five international record carriers. Because not all carriers operate in all countries, Western Union will relay the message to a carrier that does transmit to the destination country. The carrier then assumes responsibility for handling and delivering your message.

Handling Incoming Calls

In addition to placing calls using cost-effective and efficient methods, you will be expected to manage incoming calls in a professional manner. One responsibility will be to maintain a calm and businesslike response to the numerous work interruptions the telephone creates.

Few office professionals will ask a caller, "What is your name and what do you want?" Nevertheless, we all have experienced callers who had a hostile tone of

Figure 6–4

Making pronunciation clear.

Because some words and letters are difficult to understand, it is helpful to use words to identify the letters when spelling names and places. When pronouncing numerals, exaggerate certain letters.

Letter	As in	Letter	As in	Letter	As in
A	Alice	J	John	S	Sugar
B	Bertha	K	King	T	Thomas
C	Charles	L	Lincoln	U	Union
D	David	M	Mary	V	Victory
E	Edward	N	Nellie	W	William
F	Frank	O	Ocean	X	X-ray
G	George	P	Peter	Y	Young
H	Henry	Q	Queen	Z	Zero
I	Ida	R	Robert		

Numeral	Pronounced	
0	oh	Long *O*
1	wun	Strong *W* and *N*
2	too	Strong *T* and *OO*
3	th-r-ee	Single roll of the *R* and long *E*
4	fo-er	Long *O* and strong *R*
5	fi-iv	*I* changing from long to short, and strong *V*
6	siks	Strong *S* and *KS*
7	sev-en	Strong *S* and *V* and well-sounded *N*
8	ate	Long *A* and strong *T*
9	ni-en	Strong *N*, long *I*, and well-sounded *N*

voice. This makes us think negatively not only about the person but about the entire organization the person represents. In contrast, a "smiling" voice makes a favorable impression. We are more relaxed and willing to talk with the office professional who uses it. Our experience with the organization begins on a positive note.

No matter how hectic your day, keep in mind that your telephone is a major business tool and perhaps represents the most immediate way to present your office, organization, and manager in the best possible light. You should also remember that a ringing telephone is an indication of client or customer demand and, in some situations, of success. One office professional has said, "I appreciate some quiet, but if my phone stopped ringing there wouldn't be much for me to do!" Once you realize how much your telephone contributes to your company's success, you will be less irritated by its ringing.

Preparation, Pause, and a Positive Response

If you are prepared for calls, you can respond to them calmly and efficiently. Place a message pad close by your telephone. Some office professionals put their telephones on a special desk or credenza, away from other work. When it rings, their attention shifts to answering the telephone.

Before you lift the receiver, pause for a moment to relax, slow down, and think about what you just stopped doing. This will help you pick up where you left off after the phone call is completed. By pausing briefly, you can shut out any distractions before focusing your attention on the call. This will allow you to listen better, take down information correctly, and handle the entire call more professionally.

Correct Telephone Behavior

Correct telephone behavior isn't complicated, but it does require consistency and a positive attitude. Keep the following tips in mind every time you answer the telephone:

- Speak expressively, with feeling, friendliness, and interest.
- Use a natural tone of voice and grammatically correct, uncomplicated language.
- Speak directly into the transmitter; pronounce each word clearly.
- Include words and phrases such as "please" and "thank you for calling."
- Listen attentively and repeat important details such as names, telephone numbers, and messages.
- Put aside what you are doing so you will concentrate on the communication.
- Turn away from distractions; concentrate on listening to the caller and writing down important information.
- Use formal address, such as *Ms.* or *Mr.*, unless you are very familiar with the person.
- If you must put the caller on hold, check back with that person every thirty to sixty seconds.

The following techniques are simple but effective methods of preventing loss of valuable information and/or creation of a negative organizational image:

- Answer promptly—within the first three rings.
- Use a standard greeting. Identify your organization and yourself; then ask how you may help the caller. This will help you begin each call in a friendly and businesslike manner.
- As the call begins, concentrate on what is being said. Careful listening is extremely important. When necessary, repeat a phone number, ask for the correct spelling of a name, or summarize information.
- During the call, emphasize personal treatment, courtesy, and follow-up. Say the caller's name frequently, and use polite language. Close the call with follow-up responses such as

    I will give Ms. Boulanger the message as soon as she comes in.
    I will get the brochures you requested from our sales office and send the information out today.

I will check with our marketing department to see if someone there can call you back with those figures.

- If you must end a call abruptly, indicate the reason, for example, "I'm sorry, but I'll have to hang up now to deal with an emergency." Before hanging up, establish when you will call back if that is appropriate or necessary.

Effective calls generally are short and well organized. When you receive a call, encourage the caller to get to the point of the message or information. Summarizing what was said, followed by a polite "Do we have anything else to discuss?", will help bring the call to a close.

Figure 6–5 lists some recommended phrases to use in various telephone situations.

Figure 6–5

Recommended phrases for common telephone situations.

Situation	Possible Response
Greeting	Good morning! Mr. _____'s office. Mrs./Ms./Miss _____ speaking.
Placing on hold	This will take a moment or so; would you care to wait, or may I call you back? I have another call; would you mind waiting just a moment? Or may I call you back? Mrs. _____'s line is busy. Do you care to wait?
Breaking a hold	Mrs. _____ is still on the other call. Do you want to continue to wait, or may I have her call you? I'm sorry about the delay. We certainly can help you. I'm sorry his line has been busy, but he can help you now.
Transferring	The _____ department would be glad to help you. May I transfer you to Mrs. _____ in that department, or would you like her to call you?
Taking a message	He's not at his desk now. May I tell him who called? I expect him at 11 o'clock. I will give your message to him as soon as he returns. Would you repeat your name for me, please?
Indicating a called party is not in	Mr. _____ is not available right now. May I help you? Ms. _____ is out of the office. We expect her by 2 o'clock. Could Mr. _____ help you? Mrs. _____ was delayed unexpectedly this morning. May she call you when she arrives?
Closing	Thank you for calling, Mrs. Bates. That will be taken care of today, Mr. Alvarez. Goodbye. I'm glad we could be of service. Goodbye. Yes, sir, I'll be glad to do that for you. Goodbye.

Connecting Callers with Their Parties

Callers will often request a specific manager or staff member. You should already be familiar with how that person wants incoming calls handled. If you support one or more managers, you will need to make note of the following information:

1. At what time of the day calls are accepted
2. Which calls are to be put through immediately
3. Whether callers are to be identified before being connected with the manager
4. What information the manager wants recorded if he or she is unavailable to receive a call

When you take a message, be sure to indicate that you will give it to the manager as soon as he or she returns. Do not promise that a manager will return a call; at that point, it becomes your manager's responsibility.

To avoid having callers miss your manager on a second, third, or even fourth try, suggest a good time for them to return a call—when you know your manager won't be involved in a meeting, out to lunch, or otherwise unavailable. This will avoid "telephone tag." If your manager is to return a call, find out the best time for that as well.

Calls on Hold

If you answer two or more lines, you are likely to receive more than one call at a time. In that case, you should put the first call on hold, then answer each succeeding one as follows:

1. Name of the organization
2. Your name
3. Request "May I put you on hold?" or "Hold, please"

As soon as the first call is finished, return to those on hold with an apology for having kept them waiting. If more than one person is waiting, repeat the process. If you have a **call-waiting** option, you will hear a click indicating the second call. In that case, you can finish the first call or turn momentarily to the second one to indicate that you will call back or ask the caller to wait.

If the person to whom the call is directed cannot answer his or her phone, ask the caller if he or she would like to hold, call back, or have the call returned. If the caller wishes to hold, remember to check in every thirty seconds or so to report on progress and to ask if that person would like to continue to hold. To the person on hold, thirty seconds of silence seems a long time.

With the prevalence of direct long-distance dialing, it may be wise to ask where a call originates. Some managers give long-distance callers preferential treatment and may want to be interrupted for such calls. Some will cut short a local call to answer a long-distance one.

Providing Information

Just as you can't guarantee that a manager will return a call, you are limited as to the amount of information you can provide. You should be helpful but not explicit. It's better to give too little information than too much. Instead of indicating specifically where your manager is, say when he or she is expected to return. If the caller requests information that you can't give out because of organization policy, be honest and give a straightforward explanation.

If a manager has asked that you answer all calls for an entire day or a major portion of a day, you might say something like the following: "Mr. Idris is attending several meetings today. However, he will be in and out of the office. Would you like to leave a message?" This information is correct but not too detailed. The caller can then decide whether to call back or leave a message.

Answering Calls for Co-workers

When answering the phone for a co-worker, identify the office, then yourself. For example, you could say, "Mrs. Adams' office, this is Mrs. Lopez." Use the word *office* rather than *line* or *desk*. Let the caller know when you expect your co-worker to return, offer to be of assistance, or take a message. Your tone of voice should be the same one you use when answering your own phone.

Leaving Your Phone

When you must leave your desk, tell the person who will answer the phone where you will be and for how long. Be sure to give the person any special instructions for call screening. When you return, collect any messages and read them carefully. If there is any unclear information, be sure to ask the person who took the call for clarification as soon as possible.

Call Forwarding

Some phone systems are equipped with a **call-forwarding** option. To use this feature, you depress one or two function keys and the extension to which you want the call to go. To release call forwarding, you follow a release procedure on your phone.

Transferring a Call

Before transferring a call, explain why you are doing so, for example, "Ms. Tho is responsible for all payroll information. May I transfer you to her extension?" If the caller agrees to be transferred, give the caller Ms. Tho's extension, adding "in case you are disconnected while the call is being transferred." Then transfer the call following organization procedure. If the person to whom you are transferring the call is not available, offer to take the caller's name and number and have the appropriate person return the call.

Dealing with Complaints

Some calls may be from members of the general public or customers who have complaints about your organization's product or service. They will want something done as a result of the call. Some might be angry and direct their

Transfer a call only when you know someone is available to take it. *(Courtesy of ROLM)*

anger toward you. Experienced office professionals suggest the following steps to help you deal with this difficult situation:

1. *Listen* to the caller. Express interest and understanding, but let the person talk. Doing this will help the individual cool down and give you all the details you need to act. If the caller is confusing you or providing too much information too rapidly, politely ask him or her to slow down.
2. Take notes while listening. This will allow you to state the problem back to the caller so that he or she knows you understand what happened. The caller will also sense your interest and feel more satisfied that some action will be taken.
3. Despite what you hear and feel, don't assign blame by saying the incident was caused by another person or department. That approach indicates dissension in an organization and a less than professional way of operating. Your job is to listen, obtain correct information, and see that it gets to the proper person.
4. If the caller is extremely angry, ask whether you may look into the situation and call him or her back. During the interval, the caller may cool down. However, you need not listen to profane or insulting language. In that case, remain as composed as possible, say that you will not continue to listen now, ask the individual to call back when he or she is calmer, and hang up.
5. Initiate action to address or correct the problem by informing the appropriate people. You can return the call to report progress or a proposed solution. These actions will show that both you and your organization are caring and public-spirited.

Using an Answering Service

Your office may use an answering machine or answering service to take calls when it is closed. With an answering machine, an assigned staff member turns the machine on and off, listens to recorded messages each day, and makes sure the machine is in operating order. With an answering service, the service is called just before the office closes; a staff member contacts the service to begin receiving calls once again and obtaining messages.

Long-Distance Calls

When you answer a long-distance call, consider how much it costs. Work quickly to help the caller find someone who can assist or take a message. Most callers are positively impressed with this sensitivity to their needs.

If the long-distance call is person-to-person for your manager and he or she is not there, tell the operator when you expect the manager. If the operator asks that the call be returned, carefully record and repeat the caller's name, number, operator callback number, best time to return the call, and any necessary information about the purpose of the call.

If you know your manager would like to accept the call but is in another office, give this information to the operator. Policies on accepting collect calls vary among organizations. Be sure you know your organization's policy.

Message Reminder

Your phone can ring once an hour or once every two minutes. A *message reminder* (Figure 6–6) will allow you to record the following information:

1. Write the name of the person who called, paying attention to correct spelling.
2. Record the caller's company, firm, or department.
3. Write the caller's phone number, including the area code if different from yours, and the extension number.
4. Record the date and time you took the message.
5. Write the message.
6. Sign your name.
7. If you answer the phone for two or more people, write down whom the message is for.

Be sure to record your name and the date and time accurately to ensure clarification of the message and establish the correct sequence of events.

As you take a message, say "yes" or make some other affirmative comment while you're listening to directions, instructions, or ideas to let the caller know you are alert. Be sure the message is clear. If it isn't, ask questions. Repeat the details of the message, especially phone numbers, to ensure they are correct.

Place the message in the recipient's mailbox, on his or her desk, or in some other prominent location. It also helps to remind individuals to check for messages frequently. They should also be reminded to keep their assistants informed of their whereabouts and alert them to important calls expected, especially when a return call might be needed.

Figure 6–6
Message pad. *(Courtesy of Day-Timers)*

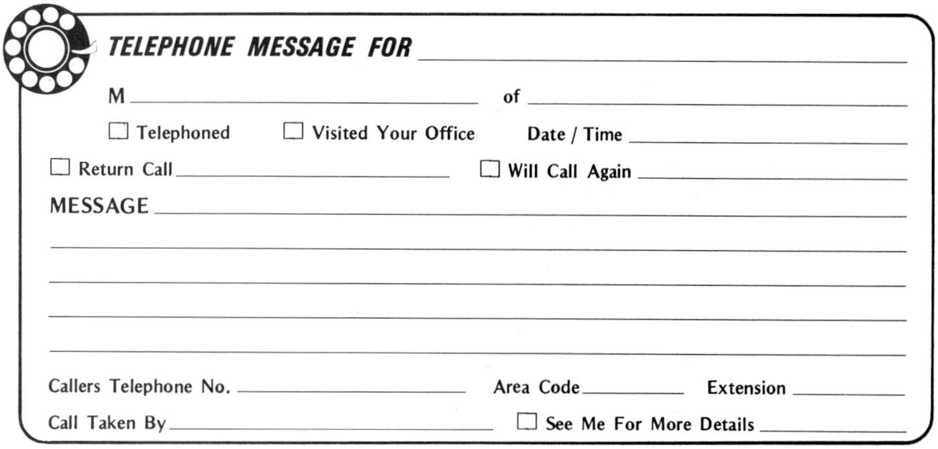
TELEPHONE MESSAGE FOR ______

M ______ of ______

☐ Telephoned ☐ Visited Your Office Date / Time ______

☐ Return Call ______ ☐ Will Call Again ______

MESSAGE ______

Callers Telephone No. ______ Area Code ______ Extension ______

Call Taken By ______ ☐ See Me For More Details ______

Your manager or organization may require a telephone log like the one in Figure 6–7.

Voice Mail

Voice mail is a computerized system for answering, recording, and directing calls that can't be taken immediately. Messages are recorded after an individual gains access to the system by entering a code. A recording indicates when to begin the message. The message is coded and then delivered, if possible. Messages can be held so that a user can retrieve them all at once.

Here are some tips for using voice mail—or an answering machine—effectively:

1. Make sure calls are returned promptly.
2. Don't insist that callers leave a response. Some people intensely dislike talking to machines.
3. Don't use voice mail when you can speak person-to-person.
4. Make your recording polite and friendly. But don't let it sound too much like your normal style of answering the phone. People feel foolish when they speak to a recording by mistake.

Figure 6–7
Telephone log.

Soderham and Associates

Telephone Log and Callbacks

Date	Time	Person	Message	Phone Number	Returned
6/8	10:15	Eleanor Phong	Call by 10:45 AM	446-1611	✔
6/8	11:25	Jim Johnson	Will be available all afternoon Call Friday morning	446-1000	✔
6/8	11:55	Hugo Hauser	Hauser, Inc. Call	442-4121	✔
6/8	12:00	Jaime Estevez	Gary cannot teach class in hospital		
6/9	8:50	Jim Johnson	Call before 9:15 AM	446-1000	✔
6/9	10:25	Lisa	Adm. Council—Wed., July 14, 9:00 AM		
6/9	1:40	Carolyn Hall	1st Nat. Would the Retail Sales program be of any benefit to them?	442-0362 Ext. 233	✔

SUMMARY

Telephone costs have become a major concern for both public and private organizations. You should monitor these expenses, particularly the costs of long-distance calls. By using a variety of directories, you can locate persons or organizations to be called, then develop your own personal directory of frequently called numbers.

When placing an outgoing local or long-distance call, double-check the number, dial carefully, and give the person who answers your name, organization, and purpose. When making long-distance calls, check the time zone you are calling and dial directly if possible. By preparing in advance, you can keep all calls brief and to the point.

If you have to place a person-to-person call and your party is not available, you can leave a callback number for the person to use at no charge. National and international calls can be placed with operator assistance. Operator assistance is also available for conference calls and for sending telegrams and mailgrams domestically and internationally.

A clear and pleasant telephone voice establishes a professional image for yourself and your organization. You should follow certain procedures to make each call effective. Likewise, you should use another set of procedures to establish when to screen calls for a manager(s), what basic message information to collect, and what call-transferring steps and long-distance calling methods to use. By planning, organizing, and using the most efficient and economical ways to handle different types of calls, you can help your organization conduct its transactions successfully.

Key Terms

The following terms appeared in boldface type in this chapter. Do you recall what they mean? For a more complete definition, turn to the glossary beginning on p. 442.

call forwarding (p. 144)
call waiting (p. 143)
conference call (p. 136)
confirmation copy (p. 137)
directory assistance (p. 133)
international access codes (p. 135)
mailgram (p. 138)
measured service (p. 130)

person-to-person call (p. 134)
station-to-station call (p. 134)
tie line (p. 133)
toll charges (p. 130)
voice mail (p. 148)
Wide Area Telephone Service
  (WATS) (p. 136)

Discussion Questions

1. Your manager says to you, "Please locate Director _____ at the U.S. Department of Commerce." How will you find that person's number and ensure that such a search mission won't have to be repeated?
2. One of your co-workers is abusing the firm's WATS service. She rationalizes this by asking, "What will a few calls cost?" How would you explain to her the real costs of this service?

3. How would you arrange a conference call involving your manager, two people in Chicago, one in San Francisco, and one in Tampa, Florida? Describe the steps you would take with your manager, the conference call operator, and the other participants.
4. Your telephone rings at nearly the same moment a visitor enters. Which should you attend to first? Why?
5. You have just begun an important long-distance call. The loud conversation between two managers standing near your desk is making listening difficult. Also, the caller is talking faster than you can record information. How can you deal with the managers? With the caller?
6. Your manager wants some quiet time and has requested, "No calls please, unless they are an emergency!" The phones rings. A person who refuses to identify himself asks for the manager, indicating that he has an important message. Should you put him through? Why or why not? If not, what should you do instead?
7. Your manager is twenty minutes late returning from lunch when the group vice-president calls. How would you respond to the question "May I speak to _____, please?"
8. As assistant to the president of a bank, you routinely receive calls from bond salespeople quoting the latest prices. What steps can you take to learn who should be put through to the president and when you should just take a message?

Assignments

1. In the alphabetical section of your local telephone directory, locate the following telephone numbers. Using three columns, show (1) the organization or department wanted, (2) the name under which the telephone number is listed, and (3) the telephone number.
   a. City clerk's office
   b. Western Union
   c. Fire department
   d. City park
   e. Police department
   f. City post office
   g. Public library
   h. Local hospital
   i. Community college
   j. Local office of the state employment service
   k. Tax assessor (local township)
   l. Driver's license examiner
   m. A store that begins with an initial (e.g., K's Convenient Mart)
2. Make an appointment at a local business to observe a switchboard operator to see the latest phone technology and a well-trained professional in action.

3. Indicate the heading in the yellow pages under which you would find the names of subscribers to each of the following services.
   a. Word processing equipment dealers
   b. Certified public accountants
   c. Advertising agencies
   d. Cellular-phone dealers
   e. Microcomputer dealers
   f. Income tax specialists
   g. Interior decorators
   h. Lawyers
   i. Ministers
   j. Video game dealers
4. Your office has just installed an answering machine to be used at three distinct times: when the office is closed at noon, at the close of each weekday, and over the weekend. What recorded message would you prepare for callers?
5. Call three or four public and private organizations, and note the various ways the telephone is answered. Explain to the person who answers the phone that your class is calling different businesses to compare methods of answering telephones. Thank the person for his or her time, then hang up. Compare what each person said and what you think his or her words indicate about professionalism. Present your findings to the class. Use the following rating sheet to gather your data:

	Excellent						Poor
Way phone was answered	7	6	5	4	3	2	1
Sense of welcome	7	6	5	4	3	2	1
Undivided attention	7	6	5	4	3	2	1
Clarity of voice	7	6	5	4	3	2	1
Voice tone	7	6	5	4	3	2	1
Obtained customer's name	7	6	5	4	3	2	1
Used customer's name	7	6	5	4	3	2	1

6. In small groups, discuss what could be done to
   a. Obtain a caller's name when it is not volunteered
   b. Indicate that a manager is unavailable
   c. Encourage a caller to ask the assistant rather than the manager
   d. Slow down a fast-talking caller
   Then present your suggestions to the class.
7. Tape record your voice using a variety of phrases that
   a. Greet a caller
   b. Put a caller on hold
   c. Ask for a telephone number at which to call back
   d. Indicate that a manager can't be disturbed now

Those instructors using *Top Performance: A Decision-Making Simulation for the Office* should consult the *Instructor's Guide* at this point for support material regarding use of the software in the classroom.

Case Study

As the newest assistant in the product development laboratory, Mary Farrell is responsible for answering four incoming lines and taking messages for the fifteen scientists and technicians who work there. They receive calls from colleagues throughout the United States and Canada. Many of the callers do not speak English well and are difficult to understand.

In addition to having problems with callers' names, Mary sometimes doesn't understand the telephone numbers they give; for example, she can't distinguish between the numbers 2 and 3. After asking some callers to spell names or repeat numbers once or twice, she senses their irritation; they believe they're speaking clearly. On a few occasions, Mary has written down the wrong number, causing considerable confusion.

The tension this problem has created makes Mary dread answering the telephone. Three of the fifteen scientists are particularly upset because they are originally from another country and Mary finds them hard to understand as well. They are proud of their English-speaking ability and are important to the laboratory's operations.

What are Mary's alternatives in this situation? How can she improve her recording of information from these callers? How can she work more effectively with the three scientists with whom she has difficulty communicating?

CHAPTER

7 ORGANIZING MEETINGS AND CONFERENCES

Chapter Objectives

- To learn the procedures for organizing meetings—before, during, and after

- To know how to use lists and other reminder tools to make arrangements

- To learn how to anticipate what can go wrong—and how to avoid these common pitfalls

- To understand how to take minutes and issue them in final form

Examples of Excellence

"Simply marvelous!" was just one of many compliments Eileen's boss had made at the weekly unit meeting. He was ecstatic because an important all-staff conference had taken place without a mistake. From advance materials through hotel reservations and specific arrangements for every session, each detail had been identified, handled, checked, and rechecked. Several participants had written notes of appreciation, stating that the arrangements had contributed to a pleasant and productive experience.

Eileen was not surprised that everything had gone so well. She had developed a methodical system for making the organization of meetings, one of her key responsibilities, easier to handle. She had begun her planning early, listed all details, and taken the time to work consistently on all phases of the meeting. Not only had she handled all the basics, she had also found an opportunity to add small fine touches such as a special folder for materials, flowers at the luncheons, and fresh fruit at breaks. As a result of her planning, she was able to complete the arrangements with a minimum of rush and tension.

Regardless of where you work, at some time or other managers will ask you to arrange a gathering, from a thirty-minute conference to a week-long national meeting. Whether two or two hundred people are involved, attention to details such as that Eileen demonstrated will be necessary.

In this chapter, you will learn

- What to do before, during, and after meetings of all kinds
- How to use lists and other reminders to check on arrangements
- Which procedures to follow when called on to take minutes and prepare them in a final form

153

Keys to a Successful Meeting

There two basic ingredients to successful meetings: *caution* and *courtesy*.

Caution

Most successful meeting planners take nothing for granted. They try to antici-pate everything that could go wrong—projector light bulbs that burn out, single electric outlets that must be reached by extension cord, refreshments that don't show up on time. Then they take steps to ensure that these nuisances don't cause a major difficulty. They bring extra bulbs and extension cords; they remind the caterers several times when the refreshments are expected. In other words, they check and double-check everything.

As your experience in planning meetings increases, you will develop a long list of things that could go wrong. If you write down these details or store them on a computer disk, you will be better able to repeat past successes and avoid mistakes the next time.

Most important, you must plan these events as far in advance as possible. Every arrangement will involve more time, forms, phone calls, and rechecking than you originally expected. Regardless of how well-organized an event is, unforeseen difficulties can and do occur. For example, suppliers may prove unreliable, as may the weather. Last-minute rushes can lead to embarrassing oversights, so take the extra time early on to identify and check on all details. If you follow the procedures suggested here, even unavoidable problems will be easier to handle.

Courtesy

Although Eileen is an expert meeting planner, she will be the first to admit that those who provide assistance both regularly and on special occasions contribute greatly to her success. These individuals include sales managers at hotels, travel agents, office workers, and caterers, to name just a few. Eileen always makes requests pleasantly and makes sure to thank them for their assistance afterward.

Eileen's unfailing courtesy has built up a reservoir of goodwill that she taps very carefully in times of crisis. Because Eileen is courteous, doesn't overask, and is available to assist others when called on, they are willing to help her when she needs them.

Before the Meeting

In planning the meeting, you will likely have several responsibilities. You will need to find out details such as the day, time, length, and location of the meeting; confirm the location; prepare an agenda; assemble necessary materials and equipment; and check last-minute details.

Initial Preparation

There are four items that should be finalized as soon as possible after a meeting has been decided on. Your manager should select the day, time, length, and location, plus two or three alternative times. After those decisions have been made, you should do the following:

1. Determine from the manager in charge pertinent details such as the topic and the participants.
2. Devise a scheduling form such as that in Figure 7–1. Across the top, write the names of the participants. In the left margin, list days of the week and, if appropriate, time of day.
3. Send the form to the participants, or call them, and request an immediate reply. Identify at least three alternative dates and times, and ask potential participants to hold those times open temporarily.

Figure 7–1
Scheduling form.

Time	Participants
Monday	
9:00 AM	Melinda Parker, Allison White, Bill Kraus
PM	
Tuesday	
AM	
PM	
Wednesday	
AM	
PM	
Thursday	
AM	
1:00 PM	Melinda Parker, Allison White, Bill Kraus
Friday	
AM	
PM	

4. Determine the best time for the meeting as soon as possible. Check the time with your manager, and confirm it with the other participants—preferably in writing. This meeting notice should include answers to *who, what, when, where,* and *why* questions. To avoid confusion, always give both the day and date of the meeting. Figure 7–2 contains a sample confirmation notice.
5. As the meeting nears, reconfirm the participants' attendance by telephone or mail. Reconfirmation is also useful for some regular meetings, such as a monthly staff conference.

Confirming the Location

Confirming the location of the meeting is your next responsibility. In many cases, all you will do is reserve a conference room. When a location is selected, you should make every effort to see where the meeting will be held. Obtain a diagram of the room or other facility to identify size, room arrangement alternatives, audiovisual aids, proximity to dining facilities, and so on. Larger meetings require careful arrangement of one or several rooms and clear instructions to hotel or conference center personnel. Detailed requests should be put in writing to remind those handling these arrangements. If these requests are not honored, the letter can be used to justify not paying a portion of a bill. Figure 7–3 presents a sample confirmation letter to a hotel manager.

You should also ask the sales manager which other groups will be using rooms adjacent to the meeting location. For example, they may be involved in noisy activities that would make concentration difficult. Planned construction is another concern; the resulting noise and inconvenience could have a negative impact on the meeting.

When you are confirming location, ask your manager if audiovisual equipment will be needed. Then reserve or rent the appropriate equipment for that date. Be sure to check that all equipment is working properly immediately before the meeting.

Figure 7–2
Confirmation
notice.

TO:	Washington, Oregon, and Idaho Regional Sales Managers
FROM:	James Arnaud, Vice-President of Sales
DATE:	March 9, 19XX
SUBJECT:	Quarterly Sales Managers' Meeting

This memo confirms that the quarterly sales managers' meeting will be held on Monday, March 23, in the conference room adjacent to my office. We will begin promptly at 9 AM and should be finished no later than 12 noon. A detailed agenda plus some material to be read in advance will be sent to you by March 16.

Juice, fresh fruit, and muffins will be available at 8:30 AM.

JA:jh

Figure 7–3
Confirmation letter.

January 8, 19XX

Susan Lee, Sales Manager
Welcome Inn
123 Main Street
Boise, ID 83707

Dear Susan:

This is to confirm the following arrangements for our staff meeting on Monday, March 23, 19XX:

1. Registration table in meeting hall
2. Coffee, rolls, and juice available by 7:30 AM
3. Room arranged for group to sit at banquet tables—eight to a table
4. Breaks at 10 AM and 2:30 PM—juice and fruit available
5. Lunch in adjoining room at 12:15 PM (order from the menu)

Please provide a screen, lectern, and chalkboard. We will bring our own overhead projector.

Call me if you have questions.

Sincerely,

Ellen Hall

Ellen Hall, Assistant
James Arnaud

Preparing an Agenda and Supporting Materials

Preparing an agenda and all necessary supporting materials is your next responsibility. Figure 7–4, page 158, illustrates a helpful form. A well-planned and complete agenda that sets the tone for an effective meeting includes meeting length; topics to be covered, their order, and the individuals responsible for each; and expected outcomes. Figure 7–5, page 159, contains a sample agenda. Although it is detailed, it is not excessively long. Encourage your manager(s) to put the most important items first.

If you prepare an agenda for a formal meeting such as an annual meeting of an association, the usual order of business is as follows (on top of page 159).

Figure 7–4
A form for planning an agenda.
(Courtesy of Day-Timers)

MEETING AGENDA

Title _____

Purpose _____

Results Desired _____

Date _____ Time _____ Location _____

SCHEDULED			ACTUAL			MEETING COST
Start	Stop	Total Hrs	Start	Stop	Total Hrs	

Persons Attending		✔	Value Per Hr	Total
1				
2				
3				
4				
5				
6				
7				
8				
9				
10				

Items To Be Discussed	(Sequence) →	✔
1		
2		
3		
4		
5		
6		
7		
8		
9		
10		

Material Needed (Number each item)	Person Responsible
1	

©1985, 1989, DAY-TIMERS, Inc. ALLENTOWN, PA • STYLE L535 • PRODUCT NO. 90608   PRINTED IN USA

Figure 7–5
Agenda.

Quarterly Sales Managers' Meeting
Monday, March 23, 19XX, Corporate Headquarters

8:30 AM	Coffee, tea, juice, fruit, and rolls available
9:00 AM	Welcome, introduction of new sales division staff—James Arnaud
9:15 AM	Review of sales figures—Lisa Schneider
10:00 AM	Presentation of new marketing plans for northern Idaho—Harry Ames
10:30 AM	Discussion of other new market possibilities—staff
11:30 AM	Examination of second-quarter goals—staff
12:00 noon	Adjournment

1. Call to order by presiding officer
2. Roll call (oral or recorded by the secretary)
3. Determination of a quorum, if necessary
4. Reading and correction of minutes
5. Approval of minutes
6. Reports of officers
7. Reports of standing committees
8. Reports of special committees
9. Unfinished business
10. New business
11. Appointments of committees
12. Nominations and elections
13. Announcements, including date of next meeting
14. Program
15. Adjournment

Preparing Materials

While you are setting the agenda, you should duplicate reports, minutes, and presentation outlines that must be available for the meeting. Also, send out any pre-meeting material at least five working days before the event. For those new to the meeting location or community, maps directing them to the site from an airport or nearby major highway will be helpful. Whom to call for directions or assistance is another valuable piece of information to include. Finally, be alert to any potential problems in reaching the location, such as road construction, so that you can inform participants and direct them to available alternatives.

Next, ask your manager if items such as charts and other graphics, pads, and pencils will be needed. Prepare all these materials ahead of the meeting to hand out or put at each participant's place. You can also provide a sheet informing participants about the locations of restrooms, telephones, refreshment or eating areas, and other necessary facilities. Smoking regulations should also be included. Attention to these items will demonstrate your sensitivity to participants' needs.

Increasingly, meeting facilities in hotels, conference centers, restaurants, educational institutions, and other locations are being outfitted with the latest equipment and technology. For example, you will be able to make arrangements to rent or lease the following equipment:

- Electrically operated screens
- Electronic copy boards that allow material written on them to be reproduced in moments
- Television cameras that will project overhead transparency images on one or more monitors
- Computer-transmitted images that can be sent to monitors for viewing by a large audience

Find out from the facility what will be available, inform your manager, and discuss how he or she wishes to use the equipment or technology.

Check the meeting room itself for chairs, ashtrays, working blinds or drapes, and so on. Some meeting rooms, particularly those in hotels, have outlets for piped-in music that you may want to tone down or shut off.

If a major meeting is being held at a hotel or similar facility, examine all facilities with the general manager, sales director, or person directly responsible for those rooms. Check all details with that person against agreements made at the time the facility was reserved.

If the meeting will be recorded or videotaped, you will have the following responsibilities:

1. Obtain a tape or video recorder
2. Identify one or more technicians to operate equipment (perhaps the facility's own employees)
3. Secure enough tape for the length of the meeting
4. Check equipment to ensure it is in operating order
5. Determine if an extension cord or special socket is needed to operate the equipment in the meeting room
6. Test the equipment; note particularly what sound level is needed for all voices to be heard on the tape
7. Set up the equipment and microphones

In some cases, you will have to use services approved by the facility.

When many topics will be covered with accompanying handouts, review your manager's folder to be sure all materials are included in sequence. Then see that copies for handouts are in the same order. If information packets have been assembled, recheck two or three of them to ensure that they are complete.

Checking Last-Minute Details

Your final responsibility before the meeting will be to check all last-minute details. Make a final visit to the meeting room just before the event to ensure that nothing has been changed. Then review the entire plan from start to finish to see if anything else is needed. Commonly overlooked items include

- Telephones
- Accessible copying machine
- Chalkboard, chalk, and erasers
- Extra bulbs for overhead projectors
- Extension cords
- Marking pens
- Tape recorder and blank recording tapes
- "No smoking" signs if that is the rule
- Extra copies of materials being used
- Video equipment
- Water glass for the speaker

You might ask a more experienced co-worker to suggest additional items.

Experienced meeting planners suggest paying special attention to the following details that are essential for successful meetings:

- Seating arrangements that promote communication and interaction, such as round tables for a seminar
- Temperature control—maintaining a cool (but not cold) room that will keep participants alert
- As much lighting as possible, particularly to allow speakers and audiences to see each other
- A troubleshooter available to handle problems that need immediate attention, from closing a door to getting help with a faulty sound system

Figure 7–6, page 162, provides a checklist for organizing long (over two days) or more complicated meetings and conferences.

During the Meeting

During the meeting, you may be responsible for greeting participants, taking minutes, and/or providing special assistance.

Greeting or Welcoming Participants

Most likely you will be asked to greet or welcome participants. This task can range from seating two people in a manager's office to registering a large group at a seminar. You may have to answer questions about the meeting's agenda and the location of facilities such as restrooms and phones. In this role, you act as the meeting's host and do as much as possible to make visitors feel welcome.

Taking Minutes

You may also be required to take **minutes,** depending on the complexity of the meeting and the need for a written record. This responsibility will vary according to the manager(s) and the organization. In general, you will need to record six basic facts:

1. Date, location, and time of day the meeting was held
2. Name of presiding officer
3. Kind of meeting (regular, special, board, executive, committee)
4. Names of members present and absent (groups of under twenty people)
5. Order of business as indicated on the agenda
6. Motions made, their adoption or rejection, and originators of the motions

As you record this information, remember to take enough notes, using each agenda item as a major heading. When unclear points are made, request an immediate clarification. You will find taking notes easier when you know the names of participants, particularly if motions were made and seconded at a small-group meeting. If necessary, prepare a seating chart.

At some meetings, **Robert's Rules of Order, Newly Revised,** are followed. Major Henry M. Robert, a U.S. Army engineer, originally developed these

Figure 7–6
Checklist for organizing meetings.

	Target Date	Date Completed
Speakers or participants		
___ Written acceptance	—	—
___ Written agreement on honorarium	—	—
___ Orientation to program	—	—
___ List of any special equipment needs	—	—
General meeting arrangements		
___ Site of meeting	—	—
___ Written confirmation of reservation	—	—
___ Written agreement on cost of meeting room(s)	—	—
___ Written agreement on cost of meals and menus	—	—
___ Decision and agreement on meeting facility	—	—
Promotion and publicity		
___ Biographical data on speakers	—	—
___ Photos of speakers	—	—
___ Advance copies of speeches or papers	—	—
___ Announcement of meeting	—	—
___ Contacts with reporters	—	—
___ Preparation of posters or flyers	—	—
___ Distribution of posters or flyers	—	—
___ Advance mailings	—	—
___ Phone follow-up	—	—
___ Preparation of printed program	—	—
___ Distribution of printed program	—	—
___ Secure and instruct photographer	—	—
Meeting facilities and room arrangements		
___ Seating arrangements	—	—
___ Check on speakers' table arrangement	—	—
___ Location of electrical outlets	—	—
___ Location of public address controls	—	—
___ Where special equipment will be placed	—	—
___ Arrangements for press	—	—
___ Facilities for social activities	—	—
General		
___ Prepare registration cards	—	—
___ Prepare badges or name tags	—	—
___ Prepare lists of complimentary and paid reservations	—	—
___ Prepare lists of materials, supplies, and equipment to be taken to the meeting	—	—
___ Prepare checks or honoraria for speakers	—	—

continued on next page

Figure 7-6 (Continued)

	Target Date	Date Completed
Time of meeting		
— Complete registration setup	—	—
— Set up identifying sign or poster	—	—
— Final check on arrangements and facilities	—	—
— Final check on special equipment	—	—
— Placecards at head table	—	—
— Set up exhibits or displays	—	—
— Distribute and collect evaluation forms	—	—
After the meeting		
— Tips to hotel staff	—	—
— Return borrowed or rented equipment	—	—
— Follow-up news story	—	—
— Thank-you letters	—	—
— Prepare and distribute minutes or proceedings	—	—
— Pay bills	—	—
— Summarize evaluation forms	—	—
— Report to board of directors	—	—

procedures in 1876 after having presided over several church meetings. He based these procedures, now a standard for meeting operations, using parliamentary law practiced by law-making bodies.

Most often, however, you won't have to work with this level of formality. Knowing the priority of motions outlined in Figure 7–7, page 164, and the short guide to commonly used motions presented in Figure 7–8, page 165, will be sufficient. Record all important points, decisions, motions, and resolutions **verbatim** (word for word).

Providing Special Assistance

Your third responsibility may be to provide special assistance. This may include copying, taking phone messages, relaying information, or locating files during the meeting. Again advance planning and preparation will help you deal with some of these requests more effectively.

After the Meeting

You may be assigned four duties after the meeting: preparing the minutes, recording the details of the meeting, filing the minutes and related material, and preparing acknowledgments.

Figure 7–7
Priority of motions.

1. Fix time for next meeting
2. Adjourn
3. Recess
4. Lay on the table
5. Close debate

6. Postpone to definite time
7. Refer to committee
8. Amend an amendment
9. Amend primary motion
10. Main motion

Types of Motions

1. *Main motion:* brings business before a meeting and can be made when no other is pending.
2. *Postpone indefinitely:* the group votes to put aside a motion for the remainder of a meeting so that no vote or stand on the question is taken.
3. *Amend:* modifies the wording of a pending motion.
4. *Commit or refer:* sends a pending motion to a permanent or temporary committee for review and possible change.
5. *Postpone to a certain time:* puts off a question until a certain time.
6. *Limit or extend limits of debate:* establishes time limits on discussion of a question.
7. *Previous question:* brings the meeting to an immediate vote on one or more pending motions.
8. *Lay on the table:* puts a pending question aside temporarily to consider an issue of greater importance.

Preparing the Minutes

If you are to prepare the minutes, assemble your notes into a rough draft as soon as possible after the meeting. Have your manager check your draft. Then prepare the final copy.

Although the format may vary, all minutes generally report events in **chronological order**—as they happened. They describe when, where, and at what time the meeting began and the conclusion, followed by a list of those who attended and possibly those who were absent. Figure 7–9, page 166, contains a sample set of minutes.

Headings identify subjects covered in the meeting. They may be numbered for easier, quicker reference or presented in an outline format. Subjects regularly discussed should be reported each time they arise under consistent headings, such as "President's Report," "Committee Report," or "New Business." Events should be reported factually, without any opinions.

Pay particular attention to **motions**. List all motions made and acted on, along with the type of action taken. Report motions that passed in full. Tally the number of votes each time, recording each member as voting for, against, or abstaining.

Figure 7-8
Commonly used motions.

Motion	When Used	You State by Saying . . .
Main motion to the assembly	To introduce a proposal	I move that . . .
Amendment	To change a motion before the house	I move to amend this motion by . . .
Request for information	To request information	I rise to request information on . . .
To postpone to a certain time	To delay consideration on a matter before the house	I move we postpone this until (state time).
To postpone indefinitely	To kill a motion	I move we postpone this matter indefinitely.
Refer to committee	When further study on a matter is desired	I move we refer this matter to committee.
Point of order	To call attention to an error in procedures	I rise to a point of order.
Question of privilege	To register a complaint concerning comfort or well-being of person or assembly	I rise to a question of privilege.
Previous question	To end debate and bring matter under discussion to vote	I move the previous question. . . .
Appeal ruling of chair	To call a vote on a ruling made by the chair	I appeal from the chair's decision.
Reconsider	To reconsider the vote on a matter already disposed of	I move we reconsider the vote on the motion to do . . .
Recess	When a recess in the meeting is desired	I move we recess until (state time, or for 15 minutes).
Adjourn	When you wish to end the meeting	I move we adjourn.

Depending on the formality of the meeting, you can record votes in several ways. A voice vote of those in favor or opposed is commonly used when the outcome is clear in advance. A show of hands will occur if the issue is in doubt. Paper ballots are used when privacy is important. For boards or elected bodies, roll call votes are used; then each person's vote is known. In all instances except the voice vote, you will record those for and against a motion. In the case of voice votes, the chairperson determines whether the motion has been accepted or rejected.

Figure 7–9
Minutes of a meeting.

Tri-State Management Consultants
Meeting of Executives, July 2, 19XX

Time and Place of Meeting

The regular monthly meeting of the executives of Tri-State Management Consultants was held in the conference room of the company on Friday, July 2, 19XX, at 2:00 PM with Chairperson Paula Simms presiding. Mr. Colin Gallagher acted as Recording Secretary.

Roll Call

The following executives and department heads were present:

Paula Simms, Chairperson   Elaine LaSalle
A. K. Alvarez   Joachim Mainz
Jacob Berns   Rosina Trotta
Millie Craig   Evelyn Young
David Gannon   Ada Zelle
Colin Gallagher

Approval of Minutes of Last Meeting

The minutes of the meeting of June 7, 19XX, were approved as read by the Recording Secretary.

Treasurer's Report

Ms. Elaine LaSalle, Treasurer, reported that the employees' entertainment fund was down to $173.62. The report showed a balance of $193.82 on June 7, expenditures of $20.20 during the month, and a balance of $173.62 as of July 2.

Reports of Committees

Mrs. Millie Craig, chairperson of the Employee Projects Committee, made a report on requests for bowling teams for women. She was appointed chairperson of a special committee to look into organizing bowling teams.

Unfinished Business

None.

New Business

Mr. A. K. Alvarez suggested that a speaker bureau be established so that the company could provide speakers free of charge to various groups. Mr. Joachim Mainz moved that such a speaker bureau be established. Ms. Rosina Trotta seconded the motion. The motion carried. The chairperson then appointed Mr. Alvarez chairperson of a committee to establish the bureau.

continued on next page

Figure 7–9 (Continued)

Time of Next Meeting

The next meeting will be held in the conference room on August 2, 19XX.

Adjournment

The meeting was adjourned at 3:15 PM.

Respectfully submitted,

Colin Gallagher

Colin Gallagher,
Recording Secretary

Paula Simms

_____
Paula Simms, Chairperson

July 3, 19xx

_____
Date

Figure 7–10
Correcting minutes.

After the minutes are read, the presiding officer asks for corrections and additions to them. This is usually a mere formality, and the voters approve the minutes as read.

In some cases, however, corrections or additions are made. When this happens, the minutes should not be rewritten. The changes should be made in red ink on the copy of the minutes as they were originally written; and, of course, the corrections and additions will become a part of the minutes of the meeting at which they were made.

When corrections of the minutes of a previous meeting are approved by the president, the secretary enters the corrections in red ink on the original copy, in the following manner:

1. Draw a line through the words to be deleted and write the substituted words directly above.
2. If a whole paragraph or section must be rewritten, neatly draw a straight line through each line of copy to be deleted. Rewrite or retype the new paragraph or section on a separate sheet of paper. A note in red ink on the original should make reference to the addition to the minutes. (Example: "Corrected Statement" on page 4)

For longer meetings or meetings addressing complicated topics, you may wish to tape record as well as take notes. The recording can then be played back to be sure no points have been missed. Figure 7–10 contains a guide for correcting minutes.

In addition to preparing minutes, you may be called on to prepare committee meeting notes of the **proceedings,** such as those in Figure 7–11, page 168. Note

Figure 7–11
Proceedings.

Quarterly Sales Managers' Meeting
Monday, March 25, 19XX

9 AM–12 noon—Corporate Headquarters

Welcome	The meeting was called to order at 9:00 AM by Vice-President Arnaud.
Sales figures review	After a brief introduction of new staff, Mr. Arnaud reported an almost uniform increase in sales for the past three months. Several sales managers observed that the smaller sales catalog contributed to the increases.
Marketing Plan—northern Washington	Harry Ames reviewed the planned marketing campaign for northern Washington. It was agreed that a Seattle marketing firm would be hired to smooth out portions of the planned campaign.
New market possibilities	Four new areas were identified for additional marketing: northeastern Oregon; the greater Boise, Idaho, region; suburban Seattle; and Portland, Oregon. Sales managers in those areas will work on marketing plans to be presented at the next quarterly meeting.
Second-quarter goals	Second-quarter goals were discussed. Mr. Arnaud agreed with the sales managers that the original projections should be maintained. The meeting ended at 11:40 AM.

---

that a chronological order is followed and events are described objectively. The person in charge should review your draft of the proceedings before the final copy is prepared and distributed.

You may also be required to prepare resolutions. Through a *resolution*, an organization expresses appreciation, congratulations, sympathy, or condolences; proposes an idea; and endorses or condemns an act or measure. Resolutions are signed by the president and the secretary. They follow a verbal ritual that consists of a series of paragraphs beginning with WHEREAS or RESOLVED, typed in all caps and followed by a comma. Figure 7–12 contains a sample resolution.

Recording Details of the Meeting

Your next step is to make a record of all the details of the meeting in your notes or on your computer. Record both successes and difficulties that occurred during the meeting. This will help managers make appropriate adjustments in future planning.

Figure 7–12
Resolution.

Adopted January 25, 19XX

WHEREAS, Mr. Charles Traurig has been for twenty years a member of the Board of Directors of Kempson Industries, Inc.;

WHEREAS he finds it necessary, because of ill health, to resign from the Board, effective February 1, 19XX; and

WHEREAS he has made large contributions of time and personal service to the work of Kempson Industries, Inc.;

RESOLVED, That the Board of Directors of Kempson Industries, Inc., accepts the resignation of Mr. Traurig with deep regret and wishes for him an early and complete recovery; and be it further

RESOLVED, That Mr. Charles Traurig be elected an Honorary Life Member of the Board of Directors of Kempson Industries, Inc.; therefore be it further

RESOLVED, That an engraved copy of this Resolution, suitably framed, be presented to Mr. Traurig.

Kristina Davis   *Paul Robertson*

Secretary   President

Filing Important Materials

Next, you will need to file the minutes and related materials. Some organizations require that a copy of the minutes be circulated among the members for their review. With this process, the minutes need not be read at the next meeting; rather, only additions and corrections will be made at that time.

Preparing Acknowledgments

Preparing acknowledgments and letters of appreciation will be your final duty following the meeting. These could include thank-you or complaint letters to hotels or conference facilities, follow-up notes to speakers, and other letters. Acknowledgments and letters of appreciation bring the meeting to a close and set the stage for any future gatherings. Figure 7–13, page 170, shows a sample letter of appreciation to someone who contributed to the success of a meeting.

Other Duties

Immediately after the meeting, you may be responsible for putting the conference room or other facility in order. This task may include returning borrowed audiovisual equipment, straightening chairs, or clearing dishes if refreshments were served.

Figure 7–13
Letter of appreciation.

April 2, 19XX

Mr. Tobias Silver, Coordinator
Duplicating Service Office
103 Corporate Headquarters
P.O. Box 90167
Nashville, TN 37209

Dear Toby,

Thank you so much for getting together all the material for the March 23 sales managers' meeting on such short notice. I know how busy your office is. The efficiency your staff showed was really appreciated.

It's certainly reassuring to know that you can be relied on for special assistance when it's needed.

Sincerely,

James Arnaud

James Arnaud
Vice-President of Sales

jah

If travel expenses or speaker fees are to be paid, plan to complete this task as soon as possible after the meeting ends. Make sure that expense forms and instructions for filling them out are passed out at the meeting's end. Request that they be promptly returned to you for timely processing.

Check with your manager about the immediate follow-up duties you are expected to perform. Experienced co-workers can also provide you with this information.

Meetings at a Distance

Some meetings can be held at a distance through audio and videoconferencing. The telephone-based technology underlying audioconferencing is well established. However, videoconferencing is becoming more common as facilities for use of television increase.

Both technologies substantially reduce the cost of conducting meetings when participants are geographically far apart. Research indicates that such meetings

Conducting a videoconference. *(Photography by Bruce Powell, Courtesy of Ameritech)*

use participants' time more effectively than do face-to-face meetings because participants tend to concentrate on business more and socialize less. Another advantage is that no necessary papers are left behind; each participant has access to his or her own office.

Meetings can also be held via computers linked together. Participants type in messages, which appear on all parties' screens, and responses are transmitted back and forth.

Another method is to use an electronically connected blackboard. When someone writes on the blackboard, the image is transmitted over the telephone lines to television screens at the other participants' locations. While viewing the message, participants can also talk to one another using a teleconference arrangement.

In addition to familiarizing yourself with the technology used, you will have the following responsibilities when you arrange meetings at a distance:

1. Arrange a time when all participants can be at their telephones or in a teleconference setting, working with a conference operator
2. Reserve any special equipment needed, including that needed by the participants
3. Reserve the teleconferencing facility
4. Confirm the meeting, giving special attention to differing time zones

5. Send out an agenda, reports, graphs, and other material in advance by mail, messenger, or facsimile
6. Check with conference operators before the meeting begins
7. Be alert to special needs or problems, such as a participant going off-line during the meeting
8. In addition to taking notes, review the meeting at its conclusion to prepare a summary

While teleconferencing technology in use is generally sound, breakdowns do occur. As you become familiar with the forms in use, your ability to anticipate problems and advise your manager will increase.

Communication Tips

To organize effective meetings and conferences, you must communicate with a number of individuals. The following guidelines can improve your performance of this important task:

- Be sure you understand the purpose of each meeting, who will attend, and what will be covered.
- Confirm and reconfirm all details in writing.
- Recheck arrangements with your manager before all meetings to determine any changes.
- Write down questions or requests that occur during the meeting so that you can note when they were answered or addressed.
- Recheck what must be done after the meeting with your manager(s).

SUMMARY

By organizing the details of meetings according to set procedures, you can help ensure successful meetings. Attention to the "little things"—the details that contribute to an effective event—must be an ongoing concern. Your assistance may be needed regularly, and certainly at times when unexpected difficulties emerge.

Before the meeting,

- Select the day, time, and length.
- Confirm the location.
- Prepare an agenda and all necessary supporting materials.
- Check all last-minute details.

During the meeting,

- Greet visitors.
- Take minutes and provide special assistance when needed.

After the meeting,

- Prepare minutes.
- Note any problems for future reference.
- File minutes and other materials.
- Draft acknowledgments and letters of appreciation.

Key Terms

The following terms appeared in boldface type in this chapter. Do you recall what they mean? For a more complete definition, turn to the glossary beginning on p. 442.

chronological order (p. 164)
minutes (p. 161)
motion (p. 164)
proceedings (p. 167)

Robert's Rules of Order, Newly Revised (p. 161)
verbatim (p. 163)

Discussion Questions

1. The sales manager for whom you work has just received some new and startling instructions from corporate headquarters. She wants to have a meeting of the five branch managers in the state at a motel central to all of them within two weeks. What steps should you take to prepare for this meeting?
2. You have been asked to take the minutes of a monthly managers' meeting. While an agenda is usually prepared and distributed in advance, it is rarely followed. Discussions tend to wander, and conclusions are frequently vague. Therefore, preparing the minutes has become a frustrating job for you. What could you do to make this task easier?
3. The annual staff meeting in June suffered one set of crises after another. Everything that could go wrong did: Materials didn't arrive, copying machines broke down, scheduled speakers' planes arrived late, meeting rooms at the hotel were not arranged as requested, and hot meals were served cold and vice versa. However, a sense of humor and a calm attitude, plus much assistance from hotel staff, airline personnel, and others, enabled you and other participants to survive those four days. Looking back, what can you do to "wrap it up" and benefit from your experience?

Assignments

1. People who regularly plan meetings or conferences have learned how to handle all the details and potential problems associated with them. You could profit from their advice. Select one of the following individuals in your community:

a. The sales manager of a local motel or hotel
b. A restaurant owner who arranges small meetings to large banquets
c. A conference director at a local college
d. An administrative assistant who plans meetings for a corporation
e. A training director for a local business or industry

Use the following questions in interviewing that person (by phone or in person):

a. What information do you consider essential when a client asks you to plan a meeting?
b. How much lead time do you like to have?
c. What are the most common problems that arise?

2. Plan a mock board meeting with your class. Include all the steps involved in planning the meeting, and conduct the meeting according to established agenda.
3. Attend a business meeting of a local professional organization, such as Professional Secretaries International. Prepare a five-minute oral report to the class on what procedures you observed and how effectively the meeting was handled.
4. Review a set of minutes kept by your local college's board of trustees. (These minutes are a matter of public record.) Note the format and order of events.

 Those instructors using *Top Performance: A Decision-Making Simulation for the Office* should consult the *Instructor's Guide* at this point for support material regarding use of the software in the classroom.

Case Study

"Just a small change."

Whenever David Dean hears two of his managers say that, he cringes. Why? They will be asking him to change plans for the upcoming meeting after the arrangements have been made and supposedly finalized. For example, additional people have been invited at the last minute, requiring David to locate a larger facility. Also, fifteen pages of material must be duplicated on the Friday afternoon before the meeting, putting pressure on an already overburdened duplicating department.

The managers consider these changes small. But David sees them differently. Extra time is needed; other responsibilities must be put on hold; new arrangements must be made; and last-minute assistance must be requested. David feels these two managers are insensitive to the extra time and energy change requires, and his irritation could spill over into all his contacts with them.

How could David point out to his managers the difficulties these changes create? What steps could he take in advance to minimize as many last-minute problems as possible?

CHAPTER

8

MAKING TRAVEL ARRANGEMENTS

Chapter Objectives

- To become familiar with the types of assistance required to make complex travel arrangements

- To know how to develop an overall trip plan with your manager and finalize the itinerary closer to the date of departure

- To understand your responsibilities while your manager is away and know who is authorized to make decisions in his or her absence

- To know how to handle post-trip tasks

- To learn procedures for arranging international trips

Examples of Excellence

"Extra questions!" is how Jean Deicher describes her widely applauded method for making detailed travel arrangements. "I keep asking about special rates, possible problems, nicer rooms, larger cars, and better routes."

With this system, Jean organizes business trips that are productive and less painful for the traveler. "I don't worry because Jean anticipates for me," her manager says. For example, for a recent trip Jean checked air routes and found that landing at a major city and then driving to a smaller one would be easier than using a commuter airline for the last leg of the trip. She also found a local hotel with a section for businesspeople. She accomplished all this by asking extra questions.

Experienced office professionals report that making travel arrangements can be enjoyable when you approach it as though you were assembling the pieces in a puzzle. Careful planning and close attention to detail won't make problems disappear, but they will decrease them.

Cost control must also be considered in planning business trips. Travel costs tend to be distributed as follows: air fares, 40 percent; lodging, 23 percent; meals, 15 percent; entertainment, 11 percent; and car rentals, 8 percent. The costs in each area go up regularly and must be carefully controlled.

In this chapter, you will learn how to avoid the difficulties associated with various forms of transportation and how to control costs effectively. Specifically, you will learn:

- Why you will need assistance in making travel arrangements for one or more managers
- What you should do before any trip begins
- How you can assist one or more managers during a trip
- What you should do at the conclusion of a trip
- What special arrangements are needed for international travel

Obtaining Professional Assistance

As an office professional, you are an office management *generalist:* You know how to handle a number of different responsibilities. But making travel arrangements is a *specialist's* job. This task has become so complex that you will need the advice and assistance of experts. If your manager travels regularly, an experienced travel agent who has been recommended by others can be a big help. Travel agents receive fees from airlines, car rental companies, hotels, and train and bus lines. Complete arrangements can be made at no cost to your employer. Experienced agents who are familiar with your manager's preferences can handle all details of a business trip with one phone call from you.

You can expect an effective travel agent to provide the following services:

1. Prepare and submit a tentative itinerary, which your manager can change or adjust, and procure tickets
2. Make all travel, hotel, and sight-seeing arrangements for the entire trip
3. Tell you what documents the traveler needs, such as a passport and birth and health certificates, necessary inoculations, and how to get them
4. Supply traveler's checks and a small amount of currency of the country to be visited for tips and taxi fares, for example, in exchange for American dollars
5. Explain all regulations in the country to be visited, such as restrictions on currency exchange and customs requirements
6. Have a representative of the country meet the traveler on arrival; this person will take care of baggage and guide the traveler through customs
7. Arrange for a rental car for the traveler at the destination
8. Arrange personal and baggage insurance
9. Help the traveler take advantage of money-saving travel rates, such as excursion or group rates
10. Arrange for interesting side trips to points of interest or special events

Even if your manager travels only occasionally, you should rely on the advice of a specific agent rather than an agency. In that case, you are more likely to get personal attention.

In a larger organization, you will make all arrangements through the company's travel department. You should become familiar with the services it provides and the deadlines it requires. If the travel department supports many offices, prepare requests early and clearly for best results.

In some large public and private organizations, managers must follow certain procedures, such as using specific airlines and hotel or motel chains if possible.

These procedures are probably outlined in your organization's administrative manual; you should become familiar with them.

Most organizations set a limit on travel expenses, including hotel or motel expenses, daily meal expenses, and alcohol/bar bills (if covered). They also detail what records must be kept and what credit cards to use. The traveler often must pay for expenses that are not allowed.

As you plan travel for one or more managers, your sense of what each prefers will increase. In fact, you may wish to keep a file on each person's preferences regarding airlines, hotels, and rental car agencies. Because most companies that provide these three services offer bonuses for frequent travelers, your managers may wish to use the same companies regularly. Knowing their preferences will be a great help as you arrange the details of each trip.

Before the Trip

You should develop an overall trip plan with your manager well in advance of any proposed trip. The amount of advance planning necessary will vary depending on time of year, mode of transportation, and destination. For example, flight reservations between a large and small city must be planned well ahead of one involving transportation between two major cities. As a general rule, though, you can think of your planning process as an attempt to match your manager's desires with organizational regulations and available travel alternatives. Your plan will include such things as means of transportation, meeting rooms, hotel reservations, advance mailing arrangements, and car rentals. In preparing your plan, make sure that all activities agree with organizational policy.

After you have collected all the preliminary information, it is time to prepare the itinerary. The **itinerary** describes the overall trip and specifies what will happen each day. Figure 8–1 presents a form you could use to prepare a tentative

By knowing you and your particular needs, your travel agent can help you sort out the various options available in fares and accommodations. *(Courtesy of International Business Machines Corporation)*

itinerary. Because plans may change, fill out the form in pencil initially until you have confirmed all aspects of the trip.

Arranging Transportation

Depending on your manager's travel preferences, your first step will be to check air, rail, or bus schedules. You can do this alone or, if you have a complex trip to plan, with the help of a travel agent. If you work alone, one of your most useful references will be the **Official Airline Guide (OAG),** published by Official Airline Guides, Inc., 2000 Clearwater Drive, Oak Brook, IL 60521. The *OAG* provides flight information by destination, carriers flying into a given city with flight times, flight numbers, and available services. Figure 8–2 explains how to use the *Official Airline Guide*.

Travel agents have access to information about flights and space available on their computers. You can have your travel agent make reservations for the preferred flights, or you can speak directly to the airline's reservation agent.

The *OAG Travel Planner and Hotel/Motel Guide* is another valuable resource. For each destination city, you can find information about the nearest airline service to off-line cities, air taxi services, and transportation to and from the airport. Over 14,000 hotels and motels are listed and rated.

Air and rail schedules are revised periodically. By preparing a list of

Figure 8–1
Travel itinerary. *(Courtesy of Day-Timers)*

TRAVEL ITINERARY

NAME *Pat Kaiser*
TRAVEL DATES *March 11-13*
DESTINATION *Detroit, Michigan*
PURPOSE *To meet with author*

DATE	DEPARTURE TIME	LOCATION	CARRIER, FLIGHT #	DATE	ARRIVAL TIME	LOCATION
3/11	6:35 AM	NY	Northwest 579	3/11	8:20 AM	Detroit
3/13	3:10 PM	Detroit	Northwest 532	3/13	4:50 PM	NY

CAR, LIMOUSINE INFORMATION

AGENCY *Alamo Rent-A-Car, Inc.*   DATE OUT *3/11*   DATE IN *3/13*
ADDRESS
PHONE *1-800-732-3232*   RESERVATION # *30018*

AGENCY   DATE OUT   DATE IN
ADDRESS
PHONE   RESERVATION #

HOTEL INFORMATION

NAME OF HOTEL *Ramada Hotel*   DATE *3/11, 3/12*
ADDRESS *400 Bagley Ave., Detroit, MI 48226*
PHONE *(313) 962-2300*   CONFIRMATION # *50153282*

NAME OF HOTEL   DATE
ADDRESS
PHONE   CONFIRMATION #

©1990, DAY-TIMERS, Inc. ALLENTOWN, PA • STYLE L653 • PRODUCT NO. 90527   PRINTED IN USA

Figure 8–2
How to use the *Official Airline Guide.*

To use the *OAG*, first find your DESTINATION (To) city. It will be found in alphabetical order in large boldface type.

Next, find your ORIGIN (From) city. It will be found in alphabetical order under your DESTINATION city in a slightly smaller boldface type. If you don't find your ORIGIN city listed under your DESTINATION city, there are no direct or connecting flights, and a connecting flight must be constructed.

Having found your ORIGIN city, refer to the direct- or connecting-flight schedule and select the desired flight.

Sample Listing

Category 1	DESTINATION (TO) CITY DATA									
	To **DALLAS/FT. WORTH TEXAS**						**CDT**		**DFW**	
	A—ADS (ADDISON/DALLAS)									
	D—DFW (DALLAS/FT. WORTH)									
	F—FTW (MEACHAM FIELD)									
	L—DAL (LOVE FIELD—DALLAS)									

Category 2 GROUND TRANSPORTATION DATA
ADS—DALLAS 9.0 MI N
DAL—DALLAS 6.0 MI NW
DFW—DALLAS 13.0 MI NW   70 MIN $6 R
FTW—DALLAS 38.0 MI NW
ADS—FT. WORTH 1.0 MI N 5 MIN L RA
DAL—FT. WORTH 42.0 MI NE
DFW—FT. WORTH 17.0 MI E   55 MIN L $6 R
FTW—FT. WORTH 6.0 MI N

Category 3 ORIGIN (FROM) CITY DATA
From **WASHINGTON, D.C.**   **EDT**   **WAS**
D—IAD   N—DCA   B—BWI

Category 4 DIRECT FLIGHT SCHEDULE DATA

X67	7:10a	N	11:00a	D	ML	357	YBM	D9S	S	1
6	7:10a	N	11:00a	D	ML	357	BMK	D9S	S	1
X6	7:11a	D	11:31a	D	AA	447	FYBQM	72S	B	1
	7:26a	N	10:19a	D	AA	487	FYBQM	M80	B	1
	7:40a	N	10:18a	D	AA	671	FYBQM	72S	B	1
	7:50a	D	10:05a	D	BN	103	YBQMK	72S	B	0
	8:05a	N	10:47a	D	DL	461	FYBMV	72S	BS	1
	8:06a	D	10:18a	D	AA	671	FYBQM	72S	B	0
	8:18a	B	10:19a	D	AA	487	FYBQM	M80	B	0
	9:25a	B	11:12a	D	DL	617	FYBMV	72S	B	0
	11:25a	N	3:16p	D	AA	273	FYBQM	72S	*	2
							AA 273 * MEALS–L/SL			

Category 5 CONNECTING FLIGHT SCHEDULE

	6:35a	B	8:08a	ATL	DL	368	FYBMV	72S	B	0
	9:34a	ATL	10:30a	D	DL	101	FYBMV	L10	B	0
X7	7:00a	D	8:05a	MEM	RC	551	CYBMK	D9S	B	0
	8:50a	MEM	10:10a	D	RC	227	CYBMK	D9S	B	0
	7:00a	N	8:05a	STL	TW	95	FYBM	M80	B	0
	8:45a	STL	10:22a	D	AA	7	FYBQM	72S	B	0
	7:00a	N	8:30a	ATL	DL	377	FYBMV	72S	B	0
	9:34a	ATL	10:30a	D	DL	101	FYBMV	L10	B	0

telephone numbers of the most often used air, train, and bus lines, you can easily obtain the latest information from service representatives.

After your manager reviews and approves your tentative itinerary, you can begin confirming reservations. Make your plans very clear to the reservation agent; repeat the preference, and obtain a reservation number or written confirmation if possible. For example, when you make an airline reservation, the reservationist or travel agent will ask for the following information: destination (include preference of airport), date and time of day for departure, class of service, number of people traveling, date and time of day for return, name(s) of the passenger(s), and business and home telephone contacts. Instead of waiting for the agent to ask these questions, you can prepare a statement that includes this information.

In addition, you should ask if meals or snacks are available on the flight. If you can find out the distance from the airport to the hotel and the time required to reach the hotel, especially during rush hour, your manager will be better able to plan meetings after arrival. Also, be sure to find out if you can change or cancel reservations without a penalty.

Most airlines require advanced booking of fourteen to thirty days for discount rates. If the cost of a ticket increases after you have made the reservation but you have not yet purchased the ticket, you will pay the higher fare. Therefore, when you know that the trip is a certainty, it is wise to purchase the ticket to avoid unnecessary additional costs. Some organizations routinely charge all trips to a company credit card that is designed for travel use only.

Airline tickets can be paid for by air travel plan card, major credit card, check, or cash. Because credit card numbers are typically required when making travel arrangements, you might keep a list of your manager's major credit card numbers and their expiration dates on file.

You can arrange for the tickets to be ready at the counter when your manager reaches the airport, or you can have them delivered to your office ahead of time. Keep a list of reservations you have made, including dates, airlines, and flight numbers. Check this information against the actual tickets to be sure they are correct. Figure 8–3 shows what information is included on a round-trip airline ticket. When tickets and other confirmations arrive, put them in the trip folder that the manager will carry.

Arranging Hotel/Motel Accommodations

Similar attention to detail is necessary when making hotel or motel reservations. Most of the large hotel/motel chains and individual first-class hotels have a toll-free number for making reservations. It is best to make reservations directly with a national booking center or the reservation clerk at the hotel. You will need to provide the number of people who will be staying and their names and addresses; days and dates of reservation; number of nights of accommodation needed; and arrival time at the destination city's local time. Also, check how long the room(s) will be held in the event of late arrival. You must include either a request to hold the room for late arrival with an approximate time provided or a deposit ranging from $10 to the full cost of the room for one night. Guarantees always apply to the local time in the city in which the hotel is located.

Figure 8-3

Reading an airline ticket. 1. Passenger; 2. Itinerary (from-to); 3. Airline; 4. Flight number and class of service; 5. Flight date; 6. Local departure time; 7. Status box (indicates reservation is confirmed); 8. Fare type paid; 9. Total cost

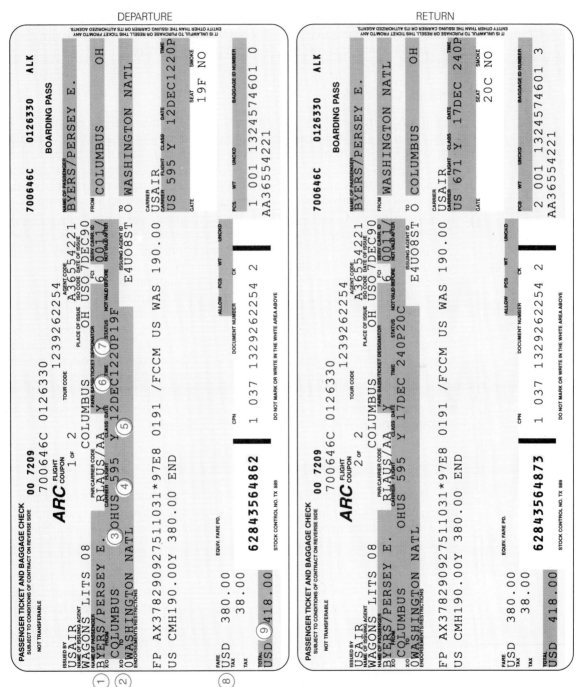

Always inquire about the room rate. You can also check out other options, such as whether the hotel has a conference room or office space, and present them to your manager for a decision. The accessibility of a swimming pool or exercise room may be important to some managers; if so, include this information.

Always ask for a *written confirmation* and a confirmation number. If a room is confirmed and guaranteed, it is the hotel's responsibility to provide the traveler with accommodations, even if overbooking has occurred.

Arranging Car Rental

Another type of reservation you may be asked to make is a car rental. You will need to know the passenger's flight number and date of departure; scheduled arrival at the location where the car is to be made available (if not the same as the point of arrival); name, office address, and telephone number of the car rental operator; date, time, and pickup point of the vehicle (airport or city); and method of payment. As with hotel reservations, it is wise to ask for a confirmation number. Also, ask about the daily rate, mileage costs, discounts, and drop charges, if applicable. A **drop charge** is an extra amount paid if the car is returned to a location other than the pickup point. Your manager may also have to return the car with a full tank of gas or pay a set rate for filling the tank. Usually, renting a car off-site of the airport is cheaper; however, the inconvenience of getting to the car and returning it will be greater.

For car travel, an up-to-date road atlas, such as those published by Rand McNally Corporation, is a necessity, as are state and large-city maps. If your manager is a member of a travel club such as the American Automobile Association (AAA), the club will provide all the necessary travel information, including a tailored trip plan. Reuben H. Donnelly Corporation publishes a directory of rental car services in the United States and abroad. This publication gives agency office locations and pickup points, rates, and mileage charges. The automobile rental companies also publish directories.

Arranging Car, Train, and Bus Travel

Car, train, and bus travel also require special arrangements. In arranging car travel, you need to know if a company, personal, or rental car will be used. A requisition will be needed to obtain a company car or a rental car. You must check what rental car firms the company uses and whether special rates are provided.

When a personal car is used, the traveler is reimbursed depending on the number of miles traveled. Each organization has its own mileage rate. In addition to being familiar with that rate, you should have a list of approved distances to common locations.

Trains are used less often than cars because the number of useful routes has dwindled. In addition to making reservations, you will need to know the class of service, meal and beverage services available, location of the train station and distance from planned appointments, and the train's arrival record.

Bus travel may be used by managers who are unwilling to fly or drive. Again, check schedules and determine how closely the bus line follows them.

Appointment Schedule

After completing the travel arrangements, you should prepare an appointment schedule. For each day, list time, city, address, name of person to be seen, title, organization, and local phone number. If time permits, show the draft to your manager before typing it in its final form. Arrange any necessary correspondence, reports, or memos in a trip folder.

Checking the Office Calendar

Ask your manager what to do about meetings scheduled while he or she is traveling; subscriptions, registrations, or insurance that might be due during the absence; and paychecks issued during the trip. Identify tasks that can be started or completed before the trip or put off until the manager's return. Determine who is authorized to make decisions about certain matters while the manager is absent.

Travel Advances

Securing a **travel advance** is often another part of travel planning. Ask your manager how much is needed and whether cash or traveler's checks are preferred. Allow enough time to secure travel advances.

Many public and private organizations issue credit cards to managers rather than provide cash advances. These cards may include an air travel card and a major all-purpose card such as Visa, MasterCard, or American Express. In addition to the number and expiration date of each card, you should provide each manager with an envelope in which to keep credit card receipts.

Final Itinerary and Materials to Take

The last step is to finalize the itinerary. It should include

1. Departure point—airport, bus, or railroad terminal
2. Day, date, and exact time of departure
3. Flight and reserved seat number
4. Arrival day, date, time (local time at the arrival point), and place
5. Hotel or motel accommodations, with confirmation numbers
6. Appointments and engagements—with whom, where, location of material needed
7. Location of any materials forwarded—to whom sent, how mailed, and when sent
8. Location of tickets
9. Distance from airport to destination
10. Automobile rental arrangements if applicable
11. Dress requirements if any
12. Phone numbers where manager can be reached

Make one copy of the itinerary for your manager, one for the manager's family, and one for your files. Use the appointment schedule and itinerary to check on all items to be taken on the trip. Figure 8–4 outlines a travel checklist. Figure 8–5 shows a sample itinerary that includes all necessary travel information.

At this time, you can organize items your manager will take on the trip. The following checklist will be helpful:

1. All tickets, plus rental car and hotel/motel confirmation
2. One copy of the itinerary
3. Passport and international driver's license if traveling outside the United States
4. Address book
5. Monetary items (traveler's checks, checkbook)
6. Agendas of meetings
7. Business cards and company brochures
8. Copies of correspondence and other material related to the trip
9. Additional material to work on during the trip
10. Paper, pens, notepads
11. Blank, formatted computer disks
12. Personal materials such as medication or eyeglasses

Two days before the trip, make a final check of these and other "take-alongs."

Security Precautions

Your manager should take certain security precautions on trips of all kinds and lengths. High-crime areas of cities should be avoided when making hotel or

Figure 8–4
Travel checklist.

	Completed
1. Travel reservations and confirmations	————
2. Hotel and motel accommodations and confirmations	————
3. Rental car confirmation	————
4. Appointment schedule	————
5. Cash advance	————
6. Travel materials (business cards, relevant correspondence, personal items)	————
7. Final itinerary	————

Additional items for international travel:

1. Confirmation of reservations at least seventy-two hours before departure	————
2. Passports, international certificates of vaccination, and baggage identification labels	————

Figure 8–5
Sample itinerary.

Inez Montoya

Monday, March 23	
3:05 PM CST	Leave Dallas–Ft. Worth, Delta Airlines #224 for Atlanta
5:30 PM EST	Arrive Hartsfield International Airport, Atlanta Reservation made at Marriott Hotel, 5th & Cain Streets
Tuesday, March 24	
9:30 AM	Appointment with Moses Peterson, Public Relations Director Spray-on Plastics 1212 Apple St. (404-555-2277)
11:00 AM	Appointment with Dixie Rusch, Four Seasons Canning, Peachtree Towers, 14th & Peachtree (404-372-6438) Allow 20 minutes by cab from 11:00 appointment to reach the hotel
1:00 PM	Luncheon with Simon Parker and Estelle Latour, Hyatt Regency Clock of Fives Restaurant
4:00 PM	Leave Atlanta, Delta #44 for Chicago O'Hare Airport (snack service on board)
4:30 PM CST	Arrive Chicago

---

motel reservations. On departure at all airports, all travelers and their hand luggage are checked by a metal detector; your manager may need to allow extra time for this procedure. Finally, as mentioned earlier, traveler's checks are safer to carry than cash.

During the Trip

While your manager is away, your office is likely to be quieter. You will have more uninterrupted time to complete or catch up on certain work. To make it easier for the returning manager, prepare a mail digest each day. Sort individual items into material needing immediate attention, material already handled (with an explanation of what was done), and material for information only.

Your manager may prefer to contact the office daily. Your conversations should be short and to the point, using a prepared agenda or list of concerns. There should be time for both you and your manager to ask questions. Your manager may ask you to forward certain mail or documents. For longer trips, the calls can be used to confirm hotel arrangements, check that materials have arrived, reschedule appointments, and handle other business.

Your manager may want to use an office while on a trip to obtain secretarial or other assistance. Travel agents will likely know where such offices are located. The National Association of Secretarial Services at 240 Driftwood Road SE, St. Petersburg, FL 33705 publishes a directory of both bureaus and available services. Most larger airports provide access to these services for a fee. Also, airline clubs make such facilities available to their members.

After the Trip

The period after your manager returns can be hectic, but certain matters will need timely and careful attention. Expense forms should be filled out as soon as possible after the trip. Precision is crucial, because forms filled out incorrectly or incompletely will be returned, which will delay reimbursement. Figure 8–6 contains a completed expense report.

Shortly after the trip ends, you should prepare thank-you and follow-up letters. In addition, gather all materials collected during the trip from your manager; forward them to the appropriate people, or return them to the files. Finally, review the entire trip with your manager to learn what went well, what difficulties were encountered, and what changes need to be made in the future. File these notes where you can easily refer to them the next time you schedule a trip for your manager.

International Travel

Preparing for a trip outside the United States will require some additional work. A travel agent experienced in planning international business trips can be of great assistance, especially in identifying required paperwork, pointing out necessary lead time, and securing reservations. To begin, ask your travel agent or a consulate of the country to be visited about the special requirements imposed on "commercial travelers" as opposed to tourists. Next, compile a list of officers and executives of each firm with which your organization does business in the destination countries. A looseleaf notebook is a convenient place to keep this as well as other relevant information.

Correspondence and Documents

Once you have collected this background material, you can begin writing correspondence for your manager's signature. This might include requests for

Figure 8–6 Expense report.

TRAVELETTER EXPENSE REPORT

WEEK ENDING ___/___/___

NAME _____

TRAVELETTER No. _____

EXPENSE SUMMARY

Odometer Reading - End of Week _____

Odometer Reading - Start of Week _____

Weekly Mileage Total _____

TRAVELORDER No. _____
(PREPRINTED ON CHECK)

DATE CASHED ___/___/___

AMOUNT CASHED $ _____

	DATE	TRAVEL FROM	TO	OVERNIGHT HOTEL	CITY	Auto Gas, Oil, Grease	Auto Repairs, Tires, Etc	Tolls Parking	Car Rental, Personal Car*	Limos, Taxis, Other*	Hotel	Laundry Dry Cleaning	Meals Incl. Tips No.	Amount	ENTER-TAINMENT*	PHONE WIRES POSTAGE*	OTHER TIPS*	MISC.*	TOTAL
S	5/12	COLS	DAYTON	HOLIDAY INN	DAYTON	5 00	—	5 00	PERS.		55 00	—	15	50	7 80	1 75	7 00	1 80	126 85
M	5/13	DAYTON	INDIANAPOLIS	WESTIN	INDIANAPOLIS	—	—	3 50			62 50	—	23 85	16 50		—			106 35
T	5/14	INDIANAPOLIS	COLUMBUS			12 00	—		43 70		—	—	15 27		—		2 00		72 97
W																			
Th																			
F																			
S																			
	TOTAL					27 00		8 50	43 70		117 50	—	54 62		44 30	1 75	4 00	1 80	306 17

*Provide details below or on reverse side.

EXPENSE DETAIL:

CAR RENTALS, PERSONAL CAR, LIMOS, TAXIS, AND OTHER TRANSPORTATION

DATE	EXPLANATION	AMOUNT
5/12	PERSONAL CAR	
PERSONAL CAR MILEAGE 190 @ 23¢	43 70	
	TOTAL	43 70

I hereby certify that this report is a correct statement of my expenses.

Sign ___Jane Lewis___

TELEPHONE, TELEGRAM AND POSTAGE

DATE	EXPLANATION	AMOUNT
5/12	CALL HOME	1 75
	TOTAL	1 75

CHARGE TO:
☐ SALES
☐ SALES MGT.
☐ ADMIN.

CHECKED BY: LG.

APPROVAL: RW

APPROVAL:

LESS: _____ PERSONAL MILES @ $.03

A. TOTAL WEEK EXPENSES	306 17
B. CARRY-OVER LAST REPORT (Line G)	
C. TOTAL ADJUSTED EXPENSES (A + B)	306 17
D. CASH ADVANCES	200 00
E. NET REIMBURSABLE EXPENSES (C - D)	106 17
F. AMOUNT OF TRAVEL ORDER (Up to Traveletter maximum, not to exceed Line E)	106 17

G. CURRENT EXCESS EXPENSES
☐ ON NEXT REPORT (under $50)
☒ ISSUE CHECK ($50 or more)

ACCOUNTING USE ONLY

ACCOUNT NO.	AMOUNT
_____	$ _____
_____	_____
_____	_____
TOTAL	$ _____

EXPENSE DETAIL:

ENTERTAINMENT EXPENSES

DATE	Name of Person and Who He Is	What for? Itemize State whether for lunch, dinner or other entertainment	Reason — Explain fully What RESULTS Accomplished	AMOUNT
5/12	JOHN THOMAS (TEXTBOOK AUTHOR)	DINNER	GO OVER GENERAL OUTLINE OF BOOK	32 80
5/13	LYNN ROBINSON, FREELANCER	LUNCH	TALK ABOUT FREELANCE EDITING	16 50
			TOTAL	49 30

OTHER TIPS

DATE	EXPLANATION	AMOUNT
5/12	BAGGAGE AT AIRPORT	2 00
5/12	BAGGAGE AT AIRPORT	2 00
	TOTAL	4 00

MISCELLANEOUS

DATE	EXPLANATION	AMOUNT
5/12	PURCHASED ADD. LEGAL PAD FOR NOTES	1 80
	TOTAL	1 80

letters of introduction from banks or businesses to their overseas offices. Next, draft letters to the firms your manager hopes to call on; do this at least a month before the trip. Mention travel plans, dates of the proposed stay in each city, local addresses, and purpose of the visit. Follow-up telephone calls to confirm appointments are recommended.

The next step is to assemble necessary travel documents. The most important document is a **passport**. A valid passport is required to enter all European and most other countries except Canada, Mexico, certain Central American countries, Bermuda, and the West Indies. Passport applications can be obtained from travel agents; passport offices in major cities, including Boston, Chicago, Houston, and Los Angeles; or government buildings in your local community such as a courthouse or post office.

Five items are needed for filing an application for a passport with the U.S. State Department Passports Division (Washington, DC 20524):

1. The completed application
2. Evidence of citizenship—a certified birth certificate (considered primary evidence), a baptismal certificate, or naturalization papers
3. Proof of identification—a previously issued U.S. passport or a driver's license with the applicant's signature
4. Two signed identical passport photos taken by a professional photographer within six months of the date of application
5. The passport fee—at this writing, $35 plus an execution of $7 for a total of $42.

It generally takes six weeks to obtain a passport. However, if an unexpected trip abroad comes up and your manager doesn't have a passport, the application can be hand-carried to a passport office and processed in two or three days.

A passport is valid for ten years. It should be signed and carried on the traveler's person, not put in a briefcase or left in a hotel room.

To enter some countries, particularly those in the Middle East, Africa, and Eastern Europe, your manager will need a visa. A **visa** is a permit granted by a foreign government, through a stamped notation in a passport, stating that the bearer may enter the country for a certain purpose and for a specified period of time. Consult a travel agent or consular representative of the country to be visited for current visa requirements and the time needed to get one. The *Congressional Directory* lists the addresses of consular offices.

Certain vaccinations and inoculations may also be necessary. The International Health Regulations adopted by the World Health Organization stipulate that vaccinations against smallpox, cholera, and yellow fever be required to enter a given country. An International Certificate of Vaccination can be obtained from a travel agent, passport office, or local health department. Your manager might also wish to consult his or her personal physician before the trip about inoculations, health precautions while traveling, and prescriptions for appropriate medications to take along.

Customs

Your manager should be familiar with a few simple guidelines regarding U.S. **customs** regulations. In general, U.S. residents are allowed to bring home $400 worth of merchandise duty free from another country. This applies to every member of the individual's family, including children.

You can get information on customs regulations by writing U.S. Customs, P.O. Box 7118, Washington, DC 20044, and asking for the "travel pack." This includes the declaration form your manager will have to fill in upon returning to the United States.

International Flights

International flight arrangements are similar to domestic ones. There are three general classes of service on most flights: first class, business class, and economy or tourist class. Most managers prefer business class because it offers additional room, seating away from tourists, and lower cost than first-class fares. First-class passengers are allowed 88 pounds of non-carry-on luggage; business-class travelers 66 pounds, and tourist-class passengers 44 pounds of luggage.

The flight schedules of international airlines are usually based on the twenty-four-hour clock. Because of time changes, your manager might experience **jet lag** upon arrival at his or her destination. Enough time should be scheduled between arrival and first appointments for necessary rest. Likewise, your manager may experience jet lag on the return trip. Therefore, your manager's schedule should be lighter the first day back in the office. Figure 8–7, page 190, presents a time map of the Western Hemisphere.

Most managers travel abroad by plane. If your manager doesn't wish to fly, consult your travel agent for current information on transatlantic crossings and rates. For a small fee, you can obtain information about freighter crossings from Trav L Tips Freighter Travel Association, 163-09 Depot Road, Flushing, NY 11358.

When traveling within another country or between countries, your manager may elect to go by train because train service overseas is fast, comfortable, and generally economical. Sleeping accommodations must be reserved.

Your manager may also wish to travel in-country by rental car. In that case, a car rental agency can make the necessary arrangements. Because rates vary depending on the city visited, the booklet *The ABC's of European Auto Travel* will be a handy reference. You can obtain it free from Auto Europe, Inc., 1270 Second Avenue, New York, NY 10021. Your manager should carry an American International Driving Permit in addition to a U.S. driver's license. Local AAA offices sell these permits.

Hotel Accommodations

Hotel reservations can be easily handled by a travel agent or the airline. Be sure to specify the type of accommodations and location desired.

Figure 8–7
The twenty-four-hour clock,
Western Hemisphere.

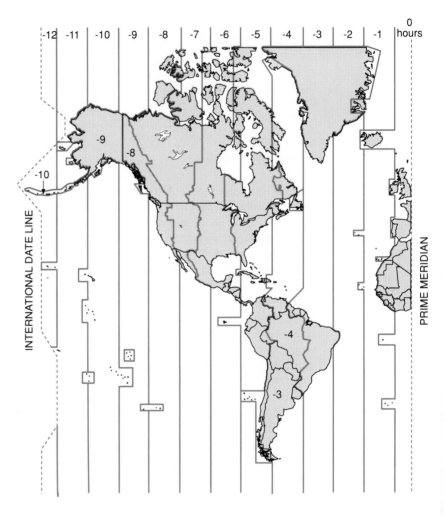

The world is divided into twenty-four time zones, with a one-hour time difference between each zone. Each zone spans 15 longitudinal (north-south) degrees, representing 1/24 of the complete globe.

Each time zone is a certain number of hours plus or minus Greenwich time. Greenwich, called the *prime meridian*, is a section of London, England. It is the beginning point for calculating time. For example, if you travel east of Greenwich, set your watch ahead one hour for each new time zone you enter. When you travel west, set your watch back one hour for each time zone you enter. Keep time differences in mind when making travel arrangements and appointments.

Communication Tips

Planning your manager's trips will require great attention to detail. You must also make these details clear to different individuals. The following communication tips should help you fulfill this responsibility:

- Be sure you understand what your manager wants to accomplish with each business trip.
- Be clear about your manager's preferences regarding airline, hotel, rental car, and so on.
- Put all requests to an in-company or private travel agency in writing, and recheck details with a specific person.
- If changes are necessary, clear them with your manager.
- Add pertinent details to the itinerary so that your manager will be aware of arrangements you have made.

SUMMARY

Planning a trip, regardless of length or complexity, requires careful attention to details. Experienced travel agents can provide valuable assistance with information on the best routes, fares, and accommodations. They can also make the necessary reservations.

Before the trip,

- Develop a temporary itinerary.
- Consult air, rail, or bus schedules and prepare a list of available departure times.
- Make and confirm all reservations.
- Prepare an appointment schedule.
- Check the office calendar.
- Secure a travel advance if necessary.
- Prepare the final itinerary.
- Organize "take-alongs."

During the trip,

- Complete work assigned before your manager left.
- Keep in touch with your manager about business at the office.

After the trip,

- Prepare expense forms.
- Draft thank-you and follow-up letters.

- File materials collected during the trip.
- Review the trip with your manager to pinpoint necessary changes for future trips.

International travel requires certain documents, such as a passport and/or visa; vaccination and inoculation certificates; customs information; and flight, sea, or train arrangements.

Whether travel will be domestic or international, proper advance planning, checks, and rechecks will ensure a successful trip.

Key Terms

The following terms appeared in boldface type in this chapter. Do you recall what they mean? For a more complete definition, turn to the glossary beginning on p. 442.

customs (p. 189)
drop charge (p. 182)
itinerary (p. 177)
jet lag (p. 189)

Official Airline Guide (OAG) (p. 178)
passport (p. 188)
travel advance (p. 183)
visa (p. 188)

Discussion Questions

1. A new office professional has joined your company. He is about to help two managers plan a business trip for the first time. What advice would you give him?
2. When on a business trip, your manager calls in once each day. What items should you discuss with her when she calls?
3. Your manager is about to depart on his first international business trip. He will visit two non-English-speaking countries. A complete itinerary has been planned, all documents assembled, letters to clients written, and other details handled. What else might make him feel comfortable as this important trip draws near?
4. When you call a travel agency, what information should you be prepared to give the agent?
5. When you call a hotel for reservations, what information should you be prepared to give the reservation clerk?
6. What are the differences between a passport and a visa?
7. What points of information should be included in an itinerary?
8. How are travel agencies paid for their services?
9. How would you use an *Official Airline Guide* (see Figure 8–2)? Be prepared to present your explanation to the class.

1. On Monday, one of your managers asks you to make arrangements for a one-day trip to a city three hundred miles away. She will need a hotel room and rental car in addition to confirmed reservations and a departure time that will allow her to meet with three clients in different parts of the city. In sequence, identify what you would do to plan this trip.

2. Two of your managers will be traveling to four cities over a ten-day period, with a weekend break in San Francisco. They will visit Omaha, St. Louis, Seattle, and Los Angeles, in that order. From your location, use an *Official Airline Guide* to plan the route. Allow for two days in each city with a Monday departure, arrival in San Francisco on Friday evening, and return on Friday of the second week.

3. Your manager will be traveling overseas for the first time after a stop in Canada. His itinerary calls for routing from your location to Toronto and on to London, Zurich, and Dhahran, and returning to the United States via Amsterdam. What planning steps would you take to assist your manager with the trip?

4. Your manager had the following problems on a recent trip. How would you prevent such problems in the future?
   a. The rental car agency didn't have the type of car requested.
   b. The room requested couldn't be honored because the previous guest stayed on longer than expected.
   c. The hotel was across town from most of the manager's appointments and the area of the best restaurants.
   d. Your manager had to fly on a small (eighteen-passenger) regional airline.
   e. Two of the three flights were during mealtimes, and the airline offered only snack service.

Those instructors using *Top Performance: A Decision-Making Simulation for the Office* should consult the *Instructor's Guide* at this point for support material regarding use of the software in the classroom.

Case Study

Kay Strahn's manager is a very spontaneous person. He changes his plans unexpectedly and frequently. Altering the times of local meetings, however, is not as serious a problem as disrupting a well-planned trip by throwing in an extra city or eliminating an entire day's appointments. Often his changes appear to have come from a whim rather than from necessity.

Just last week, Kay's manager asked her to change his flight reservations from the following Monday afternoon to Sunday evening—one of the busiest travel periods. Luckily, Kay was able to get him a late connection and a reservation, although not at his preferred hotel. Even more fortunately, the change in flight reservations cost only $25.

In addition to irritating Kay, these abrupt changes are wearing down the patience of her organization's travel department. Her manager's frequent plan changes make it difficult for them to plan his trips effectively. Therefore, the travel people are reluctant to work with Kay.

How can Kay convince her manager to get in the habit of setting up one final itinerary before asking the travel department to make firm reservations? How can she help him do this?

CHAPTER

9

GAINING CONTROL THROUGH TIME AND STRESS MANAGEMENT

Chapter Objectives

- To find out how to manage time and stress effectively

- To learn how to establish priorities

- To know how to establish a regular routine for organizing your day

- To understand the importance of establishing communication checkpoints each day

- To recognize the levels of stress and develop habits that reduce it

Examples of Excellence

Anne Tong works for an attorney who has a large law practice, teaches all across the United States, and owns a substantial amount of real estate. As the senior office professional, Anne works in all three areas and supervises one full-time and one part-time assistant. "Maintaining my 'to do' list, slowing down to review and plan, and getting away at noon are my ways of controlling each hectic day," Anne says.

Anne has identified her major time and stress management activities and, more than likely, relies on other strategies as well. All these methods contribute to her productivity and generally positive attitude. They enable her to stay in control of events.

Why is control so important? After interviewing thousands of professionals in demanding positions throughout the United States, researchers Salvatore Maddi and Suzanne Kobasa have concluded that those who believe they control the events in their lives appear to be more resistant to certain illnesses, such as colds and flu. These individuals not only eat properly, exercise, and get sufficient rest; they also believe that time and stress management are essential daily activities.

By adopting an attitude oriented toward controlling **stress,** you can deal with such pressure-creating events as unexpected deadlines, changing priorities, and work interruptions. By using techniques that let you set priorities, concentrate, and control stress, you can manage each day more successfully.

In this chapter, you will learn the following techniques for increasing your on-the-job control of time and stress:

- How to manage time and avoid unnecessary stress
- How to establish priorities to manage time intelligently
- How to establish a regular routine with one or several managers
- How to concentrate to increase your productivity
- How to develop stress management habits

Test Yourself

Managing time and stress effectively is a skill we all need to develop. Research shows that choosing new techniques that fit in well with those you currently use is important in developing new habits.

The following list of commonly used techniques is divided into those that help you set goals and those that help you control pressure. Select several from each list, write them on an index card, and try them for one week. At the end of each day, stop for a moment to review their effectiveness. If you find that they have helped you get more done with less stress, your willingness to use them regularly will increase.

Techniques for Setting Goals

1. Establish twelve-month, six-month, and three-month goals, and monitor them regularly.
2. Plan for each week; emphasize high-priority assignments first.
3. Develop a schedule for finishing major projects.
4. File the most important papers and throw out the rest.
5. Prepare a daily reminder list of necessary routine tasks; keep it with you.
6. Plan to complete routine tasks in short periods of time.
7. Determine how long it takes to complete important assignments so that you can finish them before the deadline.
8. Divide large projects into smaller, more manageable units.
9. Set and meet deadlines for yourself.
10. Establish which additional activities you will attempt and which you will refuse to get involved in.

Techniques for Controlling Pressure

1. Find time for yourself, even in the middle of busy daily routines.
2. Make others aware of your need for privacy.
3. Pat yourself on the back each day for what you have accomplished.
4. Organize your work area to be comfortable and free of distractions.
5. Learn your company's goals, your supervisor's role in meeting those goals, and the purpose of the work you do.
6. Ask questions when you are confused.
7. Take the initiative to ask your supervisor for more responsibility, if you feel you can handle it.
8. Commit yourself to finishing assignments within a given time frame.
9. Pause to consider whether so-called "urgent" requests are really critical rather than respond automatically.

10. Take time to relax and identify priorities when you feel pressure building.
11. Exercise and develop hobbies to divert your attention from work-related pressures.
12. Think of yourself as a "team member" rather than just an employee.

Now let's examine your selections from the lists. You should have identified three to five techniques that you use regularly or occasionally. Some of your accomplishments can probably be traced to using those methods. For example, a plan that helps you keep better track of assignments may remind you to complete them before the deadlines arrive.

Each day you unconsciously use techniques to set priorities, remember details, limit interruptions, and ease pressure. These techniques are habits that make your life easier and the demands on you more consistent. But to be most effective, the habits you acquired as a child or student generally must be modified when you are employed in the workplace. We will suggest a number of time and stress management techniques specifically designed for office situations. As you read, select those techniques most similar to the ones you already use, for they are more likely to become lasting habits.

Techniques for Daily Control

As an office professional, you assist one or more managers, other office staff, visitors, and telephone callers every day. Because your day may be frequently broken up, you may think that planning and organizing are impossible. Four conditions that lower control and productivity may arise:

- *Task creep*—taking on more work until the assignment load is so heavy that you stagger under its weight.
- *Constant distractions*—they make concentrating on one item for any length of time very difficult and often impossible.
- *Reliance on mythical time*—hoping that more time to get a task completed will become available at a later point.
- *Belief in deadline effectiveness*—a mistaken belief that the best work is done as deadlines near.

These four conditions can combine to make each day more demanding and stressful. For example, an office professional in a hospital is asked to take on an increasing amount of work while other assignments go uncompleted. She feels that saying "no" is impossible and that asking if work can be delayed would be unprofessional. As this task creep continues, the workload steadily increases. The office professional cannot finish one assignment without distraction; her mind wanders to what remains to be done, and valuable time is lost. She expects interruptions, and concentration is impossible as she awaits the next phone call or visitor. Instead of trying to concentrate during the time available, the office professional counts on time that *might* become available—mythical time—and puts off major assignments. But more often than not, that hoped-for time never materializes.

Office professionals who rely on mythical time are often forced to work feverishly at the last minute. In fact, they develop a mistaken belief in deadline effectiveness. These people naturally feel unpleasant pressure each day, and their nervousness increases steadily as the week progresses. By Friday, they are mentally exhausted and can't enjoy the weekend because they anticipate the same hectic pace the following week.

Psychologists who have studied stress point out that individuals who experience regular, uncontrolled stress suffer a form of perpetual discomfort. To avoid this discomfort, they must actively manage time and control the stress that comes with the office professional's job. The techniques discussed in the following sections actually require little time or effort, but they must be used regularly for best results.

Taking Command

By developing a few common-sense habits, you can relieve both time and stress pressures. These habits include establishing a regular time for planning and organizing work into manageable units; developing schedules to complete the work; and setting some guidelines for the types of work that you can perform effectively.

Motivated individuals experience a common time management problem: a reluctance to delegate work to others. If you can show other employees what to do and periodically check their work, offer assistance if questions or difficulties arise, and show appreciation for the help provided, you will find they can provide valuable assistance when you are under pressure. You will then reduce your heavy workload and thus decrease your stress level.

Learning how you work best and organizing your work area accordingly can also help relieve stress. Taking a few minutes out of a stressful situation for personal relaxation and exercise will help you recapture energy.

Another method of taking command is to pause regularly to reflect on both successes and setbacks so that you can learn from each experience. Determine which techniques or procedures helped you succeed. Analyze unpleasant situations to see how you could handle them in the future.

When you have begun to practice these and similar techniques habitually, you will be able to deal with each day more successfully.

Establishing Clear Priorities

If you work with two or more managers, each person may believe that his or her work is more important and should be done first. To avoid becoming confused about priorities, find out which tasks—or individuals—should get priority attention. In some organizations, this information will be clearly outlined for you on the first day of the job. In others, you will have to determine priorities from the attitudes and behaviors of the managers.

Keep stress at a minimum by outlining your schedule. *(Courtesy of International Business Machines Corporation)*

Listening is especially important when discussing priorities with your managers. You should clarify instructions immediately and write them down if they are very detailed.

Following Directions

Inability to follow directions heads the list of complaints managers voice about inexperienced assistants. To follow directions accurately, you must

1. Pay close attention when your manager provides directions and write them down.
2. Ask questions about any confusing steps as soon as they are presented.
3. Summarize what you have been told by saying, "What you want me to do is. . . . " At this point, your manager can correct any misinterpretations.

4. Refer to the written directions while you are working on the assignment. When questions arise, ask your manager for further clarification; don't take the chance of making a mistake and even having to do the assignment over.
5. Review the instructions you were given for completing the assignment. If these instructions will be used again, place them in your procedures manual.

Whether your office is well organized or chaotic, you need to determine priorities for your own well-being. The following methods will help you determine priorities and clarify your responsibilities:

- Use your job description to prepare a general monthly plan that includes all major assignments to be completed during this period.
- Develop a five-day plan on Friday afternoon for the week to come, and share it with your manager for his or her reactions. Figure 9–1 contains a sample weekly plan.
- Ask your manager for a list of assignments that must be completed by the end of the following week.
- Establish regular times to meet with your manager to discuss work flow and related matters.
- Prepare a daily "to do" list. Identify "A" (must do), "B" (need to do but can wait), and "C" (no time demand) priorities. Devote your time to completing the A items before working on the Bs and Cs.
- Keep a record of how much time you have needed to finish certain major recurring assignments, such as monthly reports, payroll forms, or minutes (Figure 9–2). Use this information to prepare monthly and weekly plans. One good way to deal with long-term projects is to set several **mini-deadlines** to meet as the project progresses.
- Shortly after you arrive at the office each day, list the major assignments, or portions of them, that you plan to complete and in what order. Check the list with your manager(s).
- Review what you are able to accomplish each day, and use this as a basis for revising your daily goals.

Figure 9–1
Weekly plan.

Work to Be Finished	Work to Be Started
• Monthly payroll forms	• New files for upcoming sales campaign
• Quarterly sales report narrative and figures	• Decision on photographs for annual report
• New-product sales letter mailing	• Response analysis of sales manager survey
• Board minutes	
• Arrangements for fall sales seminar: hotel, agenda, meals, travel information	

Figure 9–2
Task completion record.

Task	Started	Finished	Time Required
Monthly payroll	3:00 PM	5:30 PM	2½ hours
Sales report	8/20/91	8/23/91	4 hours
Mailing	8/22/91	8/23/91	3 hours
Board minutes	8/27/91	8/29/91	2½ hours
Seminar arrangements	9/2/91	9/9/91	10–12 hours

- List phone calls and contact persons daily. Ask your manager if there are additional calls you should make. If you are placing a call for your manager and the person called is unavailable, find out the best time for a return call. This can prevent "telephone tag," which is not only frustrating but costly and time-consuming.

If used regularly, these techniques will help you organize your day and keep your priorities in order. As a result, you will be able to concentrate better, accomplish more, and feel less pressure.

If your workload remains overwhelming despite all your efforts, consider asking for assistance from co-workers, other units in the organization, or outside agencies that specialize in temporary help.

Tapping the Powers of Concentration

Concentration—the ability to focus on a specific task exclusively—will help you block out distractions. Experienced office professionals report that they have developed the self-discipline necessary for shutting out their surroundings. If you develop the ability to concentrate and use it each day, you will be calmer and more organized because you will use precious time effectively. Figure 9–3 outlines a routine for concentrating.

Figure 9–3
Concentration routine.

1. Identify a task in need of your undivided attention that you wish to complete partially or fully.
2. Organize to complete the task by assembling the necessary material.
3. Relax for a moment before starting, to clear your mind and recapture energy.
4. Visualize doing the task, and imagine its being completed.
5. Tell yourself to start and to keep going until the job is done.

Office professionals who have learned how to concentrate report that the following techniques help them get more done each day:

1. **Visualize** the completed task; that is, imagine how it "looks" and the satisfaction you feel. This will keep your motivation high.
2. Complete similar tasks, such as filing, at the same time. Similarity of tasks, even unpleasant ones, establishes a "flow," that is, a rhythm that leads to more rapid completion of work.
3. Prepare a short list of three to four jobs to be completed in a certain portion of the day, and commit yourself to finishing them.
4. Ask managers and co-workers for "quiet time" so that you can give undivided attention to one task.
5. Find a location away from the principal work area where you can work on an assignment without interruption.
6. Identify work that you are currently putting off, and begin some portion of it now. Segmenting the work into short blocks of time (thirty minutes or less) will help you get started on large projects.
7. When presenting information, work to achieve **first-time understanding**; that is, make sure that listeners hear the information correctly when you initially present it. Figure 9–4 lists guidelines for ensuring first-time understanding.
8. Pause for a moment when the phone rings or a visitor arrives to ask yourself, "What am I doing now?" This will enable you to resume work more quickly once the call is completed or the visitor leaves.

Organizing for Daily Productivity

In addition to clarifying priorities and achieving active concentration, you should establish a clear routine for organizing your day. First, perform certain tasks, such as sorting mail, preparing correspondence, filing, and copying, at approximately the same time each day. Second, list priority tasks that must be completed by the end of each day or at another specific time. Finally, allow time

---

Figure 9–4
Achieving first-time understanding.

1. The speaker and listener are committed to communicating; ideally, they have found a time and a place that make this possible.
2. The speaker indicates the topic that will be covered and the approximate amount of time involved.
3. The speaker presents the points of the discussion clearly, allowing time between each point for questions.
4. If appropriate, the listener repeats major points to be sure they are understood.

for regularly scheduled meetings; working alone on special assignments that require concentrated attention; breaks and lunch; meeting with one or more managers to discuss immediate or upcoming work; exchanging information; addressing problems; and looking back at the day and planning for tomorrow.

In addition, be aware of habits that cause you to waste time. Common time wasters include

- Socializing too often, especially with less motivated co-workers
- Excessively long telephone calls during which you or the caller fails to stick to the point
- Visitors from other offices who drop in for a chat, make themselves at home, and take up several minutes of your time
- Poorly organized desk, cabinet, or file material that forces you to search frantically for what you need
- Starting a task with incomplete instructions so that you need extra time to complete it
- Interruptions that you could avoid by writing notes or scheduling meetings with co-workers or others

Regardless of your efforts, you will waste some time. But you can limit the amount by identifying your own poor habits and working on them. Once you have mastered these techniques, you will be able to control more of your time and use it to complete work steadily and effectively. In addition, managers and co-workers will become aware of those periods during which you need to concentrate.

Gaining Control of Information

Information control is essential to a well-run day. Several experienced office professionals and time management experts offer the following suggestions to help you improve your control of information.

Anticipate communication needs. This is a variation on the "to do" list so widely advocated for busy people. On a desk calendar or notepad, list major speaking/listening tasks or key people with whom you will communicate that day. Check it several times throughout the day to be sure no items are overlooked. If you are on the move a great deal, take the list pad with you.

Set aside time for morning quiet. A recent study completed at the University of New Hampshire points out that individuals who start early each day are more productive. Whether you are an early active worker (a "lark") or a late starter (an "owl"), set aside a moment for thinking before your day begins. Take notes so that you won't have to rely on your memory alone.

Make contact with key people early. Before the rush of activities begins, spend a few minutes with certain key people. In particular, important matters to discuss with your manager(s) should take place at this time, including (1) information needed from you; (2) work you believe must be done by the end of that day; (3) information you need that day; and (4) tasks, events, and assignments that are likely to come up in the next few days.

These meetings should be brief. Before the end of the day, write down a few notes to use as an agenda for the next day's morning meeting. Because these early meetings are often the only time managers and assistants have the opportunity to talk, they are particularly valuable.

Establish communication checkpoints each day. You should establish four brief communication checkpoints during the day—two in the morning and two in the afternoon. They will let you and others slow down and ask, "Is there anything we need to be talking about right now?" In addition to improving communication, these regular checkpoints tend to reduce interruptions. Figure 9–5 suggests specific times for establishing communication checkpoints.

Establish slowdown points each day. Before communicating with others, ask yourself

1. What should I be doing right now?
2. What have I been doing the last two hours? What have my goals been during this time?
3. What should I be doing in the next two hours? What should my goals be during this time?
4. Whom should I talk to during the next two hours to get work accomplished?

Active Stress Management through Identification, Self-Support, and Logical Response

We all experience some stress each day. However, not all stress is harmful. According to University of Chicago psychologist Mihali Czikszentmihalyi, concentration is a form of self-induced and self-controlled stress called **eustress**. Very likely, the hospital assistant referred to earlier in the chapter began her journey up the stress continuum with that mild form of positive stress. But as

Figure 9–5
Communication checkpoints.

1. *First thing in the morning* (5 to 10 minutes): Check the day's priorities.
2. *Mid- to late morning:* See if any work must be completed before lunch.
3. *Early afternoon:* Determine whether priorities have changed; check on work.
4. *Late afternoon:* Review, think ahead, and take pride in what you have accomplished.

pressure mounted, she began to experience more and more unhealthy forms of stress, or **distress**. Figure 9–6 outlines the stages of the stress continuum.

Research shows that individuals who believe they have little control over events in their lives can experience a condition called *learned helplessness*— each time the pressure rises, the person feels more helpless, likely to fail, and battered by forces too strong to control. Overcoming learned helplessness begins with recognizing the causes of pressure. Use the list in Figure 9–7, page 206, to identify the pressures that affect you most often during your day. Once you know the causes of that pressure, you will be better able to manage stress.

Figure 9–6
The stages of stress.

Stress
excitement, high concentration,
determination to succeed

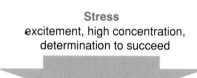

Early Indicators
lowered energy levels, muscular tension, mild gastric
disturbances, heart flutters

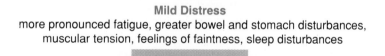

Mild Distress
more pronounced fatigue, greater bowel and stomach disturbances,
muscular tension, feelings of faintness, sleep disturbances

Moderate Distress
loss of interest in formerly pleasurable activities, severe sleep
disturbances, lack of concentration, fear that cannot be pinpointed

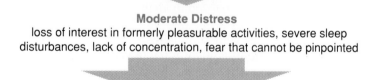

Extreme Distress
extreme fatigue, difficulty in managing all but the simplest tasks,
major gastric disturbances, insomnia, pervasive fear

Panic
pounding heart, gasping, trembling, shivering, sweating,
numbness and tingling in extremities, exhaustion

Figure 9-7
Causes of pressure in the office.

Cause	Level of Control				
	none		some		a lot
1. Changing priorities	1	2	3	4	5
2. Constant interruptions	1	2	3	4	5
3. Continual phone calls	1	2	3	4	5
4. Incomplete instructions from managers	1	2	3	4	5
5. Noisy work environment	1	2	3	4	5
6. Little cooperation from managers and co-workers in completing assignments	1	2	3	4	5
7. Little or no support from managers	1	2	3	4	5
8. Irritable visitors	1	2	3	4	5
9. Inadequate equipment	1	2	3	4	5
10. Unreasonable expectations for amount of work to be done	1	2	3	4	5

By evaluating what you can do about each source of pressure, you will take another step toward improving stress management. Research on stress experienced by office professionals suggests that a lack of information on any work-related subject increases stress. Therefore, if you are confused about an assignment, ask your manager; receiving the information will reduce tension. If you are in a high-pressure job, you should assess your control over stress-producing forces regularly—at least once a week or even daily, if possible. Researchers urge you to identify specific steps you have taken and evaluate your progress. As you see how you have improved your ability to manage stress, you will bolster your confidence.

In addition to identifying the causes of stress, you should make the following relaxation activities part of your daily routine:

1. Make a list of personal and professional accomplishments to remind yourself about successes.
2. Relax on and off the job using suggestions such as those in Figure 9-8.
3. Get regular exercise by participating in an active sport.
4. Develop hobbies or pastimes to take your mind off your work.
5. Watch your energy level and behavior for signs of increasing stress by considering the questions listed in Figure 9-9.

These are just a few examples of ways to bolster your self-confidence and improve your attitude. By adopting those approaches and making certain activities habits, you will reduce your stress level.

Figure 9-8
Relaxation activities.

- During morning and afternoon breaks, get away from your work area.
- At lunchtime, leave the office and do something enjoyable such as reading a book, sitting out in the sun, or going for a walk.
- As the workday ends, collect your thoughts and look back on the day's accomplishments.
- After you get home, take a few minutes to sit quietly, talk with family members, or take a nap.
- In the evening, after household chores are finished, set aside an hour or so to read, watch television, or listen to music.
- Soak in the bathtub, or take an invigorating shower.

Figure 9-9
Self-analysis questions: how pressured are you?

Answer these questions on a regular basis to determine the level of pressure you are experiencing.

1. Do minor problems and disappointments bother you more than they should?

   Yes _____ No _____ Not sure _____

2. Are you finding it hard to get along with people? Are people having trouble getting along with you?

   Yes _____ No _____ Not sure _____

3. Have you found that you're not enjoying the activities you used to, such as watching a sporting event, going to a party, or seeing a movie?

   Yes _____ No _____ Not sure _____

4. Do your anxieties haunt you? Are you unable to shut them out of your mind?

   Yes _____ No _____ Not sure _____

5. Are you now scared of people and situations that never used to bother you?

   Yes _____ No _____ Not sure _____

6. Are you becoming suspicious of people around you, even your friends?

   Yes _____ No _____ Not sure _____

7. Do you feel inadequate, incapable of success as a student, or unlikely to succeed later in your job?

   Yes _____ No _____ Not sure _____

The National Association for Mental Health (NAMH) has worked with a number of individuals in demanding positions. NAMH suggests the following techniques for reducing stress:

- *Ventilate.* Let off steam by talking out problems with trusted individuals such as a member of your immediate family or a long-time friend. According to NAMH, ventilating relieves strain, puts stress in a clearer light, and can lead to rational and realistic solutions to problems.
- *Move away.* Remove yourself physically from the source of the pressure. Even a momentary departure for a drink of water, a brisk walk, or a chat can change your perspective.
- *Sweat away the tension.* Pressure usually starts building inside of you, causing headaches and other psychosomatic symptoms. To some extent, you can "sweat" it out of your system with some physical activity.
- *Move on.* If you run into a roadblock, don't exaggerate its significance by fretting over your inability to get past it. Avoid it for awhile and come back later. According to NAMH research, you'll generally find new strength during the break.
- *Avoid perfectionism.* Many capable individuals tie themselves in knots because they seek "perfection." They expect a great deal of themselves and believe they have failed if they do not accomplish the impossible immediately.
- *Give in.* Don't stand your ground all the time, even when you are completely certain that you are right. Yielding occasionally reduces strain on the nervous system and pays off in better all-round relations.

These six suggestions are starting points. If you identify and record the techniques that work for you, you will be ready for the next stressful situation.

Communication Tips

The following tips are directed toward increasing your control over time and pressure problems:

- Make sure that you and your managers discuss daily and weekly priorities and that you are clear about what must be done.
- If you need to concentrate on your work, ask for quiet time.
- Before starting a new assignment, be sure you understand what is required.
- Communicate by written note or electronic mail so that important messages and their responses are not forgotten.
- Indicate to your manager(s) when you feel pressured by the work to be done, and ask for assistance.
- Communicate problems you are experiencing and suggest solutions. Problem solving is part of the job.

SUMMARY

Office professionals are subject to pressures that can sap energy levels and reduce effectiveness. Those who fail to take control regularly take on too much work, are easily distracted, tend to procrastinate, and believe their best work is done under the pressure of deadlines. To avoid these problems, you should recognize that you can manage time and stress and identify the techniques you now use that work for you.

In addition, you should identify priorities and regularly ask managers for assistance in keeping them clear. By recognizing priorities, you can establish a routine for achieving them. Always remember that the most important work comes first.

It is also important to make concentration a daily habit. Concentrate on one task at a time. Concentration will allow you to get more done with fewer errors and interruptions.

Finally, you should actively manage stress each day. By identifying causes of stress and solutions that work, you can reduce some of the pressure. Relaxation techniques can also ease pressure, as can ventilating and removing yourself from the source of the pressure when appropriate. All of these techniques can make each day calmer and more productive.

Key Terms

The following terms appeared in boldface type in this chapter. Do you recall what they mean? For a more complete definition, turn to the glossary beginning on p. 442.

concentration (p. 201)　　　　　　mini-deadlines (p. 200)
distress (p. 205)　　　　　　　　　stress (p. 195)
eustress (p. 204)　　　　　　　　　visualize (p. 202)
first-time understanding (p. 202)

Discussion Questions

1. In what kinds of situations do you feel under pressure—preparing for examinations or responding in class? How do you cope with them now?
2. What kinds of situations might you face on the job as a beginning or returning office professional that could cause tension and possible stress? What control methods might work best for you?
3. How would you tell your manager about stress you are experiencing for which he or she may be partly responsible?
4. When would it be appropriate for groups of office professionals working together to discuss the tension and stress they feel?
5. The "unexpected" will be a constant in your professional life. What attitude have you developed, or will you work on, to prevent surprises from creating excessive tension?

1. A great deal has been written about understanding and managing stress in your professional and personal lives. Go to your school library and select three or four office management or office publications. Review them for articles on the following subjects:
   a. Stress management
   b. Stress and the use of computers
   c. Time management
   d. Staying healthy
   Identify techniques presented in these articles and share them with the class.

2. Today both public and private organizations are paying more attention to conditions that create stress for employees. Choose an organization in your community, and contact its human resources department to find out what programs and services concerning stress management it provides for employees.

3. Keep a time log for one week. Set three goals at the beginning of each day. Review your day's activities against these goals. Did you accomplish them? If not, why not?

4. Observe how people waste time. Make suggestions on how to avoid these pitfalls.

5. Write a paragraph about one habit you plan to adopt or one you are planning to change to enable you to concentrate more completely.

6. Interview a word processing operator to find out the types of stress he or she encounters (e.g., eyestrain, unexpected equipment breakdowns, pressure to complete documents on a time schedule).

7. How would you begin a discussion with your manager about setting priorities and managing your time so that you will be more productive?

8. List three goals that you want to achieve next month and believe you can accomplish. One of the goals should be related to this class; the other two may concern your other classes, job, health, or personal relationships. Next, list all the things you need to do to achieve the goals you identified. Place the tasks in the logical order in which they should be performed. Set a deadline for completing each task.

Those instructors using *Top Performance: A Decision-Making Simulation for the Office* should consult the *Instructor's Guide* at this point for support material regarding use of the software in the classroom.

Case Study

Cynthia Johnson thought she enjoyed pressure and challenging responsibilities. As a high school student, she worked on the school newspaper and yearbook. She also held part-time positions to have money for clothes and other personal expenses. Cynthia liked to think that she was a well-organized person. Her record of achievements certainly would have attested to that.

Then Cynthia accepted a position as a newsroom assistant at a local television station. The newsroom was chaotic, and the phones rang constantly. Cynthia was always being interrupted by the news director and reporters. The clutter of papers on her desk and the constantly shifting priorities elevated her stress level.

Cynthia's well-intended plans to organize her work evaporated rapidly. She liked the excitement but hated the chaos. Despite frequent compliments on her work, Cynthia left work each day depressed about what she had not accomplished.

Pretend that Cynthia and you have been classmates and friends for a number of years. As she talks about her situation, you can sense the tension she experiences each day. Based on what you have read in this chapter and your own experiences, what advice would you give her? Keep in mind that Cynthia should try to establish some control over each day. Identify three or four logical steps she could take to lessen her level of stress.

UNIT 3

INFORMATION MANAGEMENT

CHAPTER

10

CAPTURING INFORMATION THROUGH DICTATION AND TRANSCRIPTION

Chapter Objectives

- To learn how to work with handwritten drafts and how to handle face-to-face dictation

- To become familiar with the best ways to transcribe material from a variety of dictation equipment

- To know the importance of first-time understanding and immediate rechecking if there are questions

- To know how to help managers use dictation equipment effectively

- To learn how word processing equipment can be used to work with one or more managers

Examples of Excellence

The managers at Test Tech, a firm that assists businesses with personnel evaluation, credit their office manager, Laila Singh, with keeping clients happy. "Laila organizes often jumbled material and turns out clearly written letters, memos, and other items," wrote the president in a bonus recommendation to the board of directors. While Laila wouldn't list information management as a primary duty in a firm with numerous clients and volumes of correspondence, it is a major priority.

Like Laila, you will be involved in transforming ideas into stored data and important communications shared by your managers, co-workers, and customers—even those thousands of miles away. **Information management** is therefore a major responsibility.

In this chapter, you will learn how to

- Effectively support managers who use both face-to-face dictation and handwritten drafts to produce correspondence and other written material
- Choose the best methods of transcribing material from a variety of dictation equipment
- Encourage one or more managers to use dictation equipment as effectively as possible
- Use word processing equipment in coordination with one or more managers

How you capture information will depend on many kinds of technology. Word processing and portable dictating equipment will speed up and simplify your work. But they will also replace some of the interaction between you and your manager.

Managerial Preferences

Managers' preferences for handling correspondence are changing. Nevertheless, a recent survey found that 80 percent of managers still draft their letters in handwriting, 8 percent dictate to an assistant who uses shorthand, 10 percent use dictating equipment, and 2 percent write their letters themselves.

Seventy-five percent of the input into word processing centers is in longhand. However, it is estimated that 100 million dollars is lost each year because of illegible handwriting alone.

In 1990 the average cost of preparing a business letter was $10.85, according to the Chicago-based Dartnell Institute of Business Research, while a letter dictated on a machine cost $8.41.

As desktop computers become more common, managers may do more keyboarding themselves, again reducing contact between them and their assistants. You may do more editing than originating. Because you are likely to support two or more managers, be prepared to deal with handwritten drafts, some machine dictation, and occasionally shorthand.

Traditional Methods of Handling Correspondence

Handwritten Drafts

Handwritten drafts of correspondence are relatively inefficient. Nevertheless, you will receive many letters and memos in this form. Some handwriting will be easy to read, and some will be nearly illegible. To make transcription as efficient and easy as possible, consider asking your manager to

- Indicate whether the document you are preparing is a draft or a final copy
- Print all names, terms, and unusual words
- Flag paragraph and other indentations
- Indicate time of expected completion

Following these tips will make your work easier, and you will be more productive.

Machine Dictation

Your manager will probably use some type of portable or stationary dictating equipment. The advantages of such equipment are (1) less dependence on manager and assistant to originate work; (2) a continuous flow of material, even if the manager is out of the office; and (3) more accurate first drafts. While the technology continues to improve, the two basic forms of dictation equipment—discrete media machines and endless loop systems—remain the same.

Endless loop systems (Figure 10–1a) use multihour loops of magnetic tape that are permanently sealed in a case. Tapes revolve for use and reuse. There are two tape heads in each case, one for recording and one for transcription. These systems can be connected to a one-office system centralized to a word processing center and made accessible to remote or phone-in systems. One important aspect of this system is that a transcriber can start dictation before the originator has finished. In rush situations, this feature is valuable.

Discrete media machines and systems (Figure 10–1b) use a specific, removable recording medium, such as a coated belt, disk, cartridge, or cassette. Each medium can be removed from a dictation or transcription unit, which makes it easy to store and mail. This group includes portable models ranging in size from hand-held to full tape recorders, as well as desktop models too large for easy movement.

In the future, you may be working with computerized dictation systems that use digital technology to convert the human voice into codes stored on a disk.

The foot pedal allows the transcriber to stop and play back confusing portions of a tape or belt as often as necessary. *(Courtesy of Lanier Voice Products)*

Figure 10–1
Dictation media.

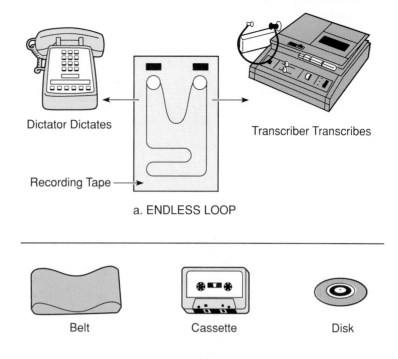

Dictator Dictates

Transcriber Transcribes

Recording Tape

a. ENDLESS LOOP

Belt

Cassette

Disk

b. DISCRETE

Editing will be done using conventional word processing techniques, and information on a disk can be flagged for priority items. This system will also be more secure, because a valid identification code will be needed to gain access. Finally, the same search feature now found in most word processing packages will enable you to find material by subject, dictator, or the source where the dictation originated.

Dictation Tips for Managers

Some managers dictate with great ease and clarity, while others find dictating awkward and are difficult to understand. To make this task easier, ask your manager to

- Outline material in advance to speed dictation and follow the outline when speaking.
- Identify himself or herself and items to be dictated, specifying priority level, special instructions, and especially all rush materials. The manager should include all mechanical details such as number of copies, format, enclosures, and copy receipts.
- Spell out technical terms, names, words that are often misspelled, and any other potentially confusing items. Figure 10–2, page 218, lists words that should be spelled when dictated.

Figure 10–2
Words to spell out when dictating.

accede, exceed	hear, here
accept, except	incidence, incidents
addition, edition	incite, insight
advise, advice	interstate, intrastate
affect, effect	its, it's
allusion, illusion	legislator, legislature
assistants, assistance	loose, lose
bare, bear	material, materiel
brake, break	medal, meddle, metal, mettle
canvas, canvass	miner, minor
cease, seize	ordinance, ordnance
coarse, course	passed, past
cite, sight, site	personal, personnel
complement, compliment	poor, pore, pour
correspondence, correspondents	practical, practicable
council, counsel, consul, console	pray, prey
defer, differ	principal, principle
descent, dissent	quiet, quite
disapprove, disprove	residence, residents
disburse, disperse	respectfully, respectively
eligible, illegible	rite, right, write
era, error	stationary, stationery
finally, finely	their, there, they're
fiscal, physical	through, threw
formally, formerly	whose, who's
forth, fourth	your, you're
has, had, have	

- Dictate figures by digits.
- Include punctuation, paragraphing, and subheads to make the first draft as nearly correct as possible.
- Speak at his or her normal rate and in a clear, natural voice at all times; picturing the reader while dictating will help.
- Listen to the dictation after it is completed to identify any potential problems.
- Be wary of distractions such as gum chewing, pencil tapping, or loud background noises.
- Give reference items such as letters or reports to you in the order dictated.
- Proofread drafts carefully, reading first individual words and then entire sentences.
- Circle or underline corrections in pencil on drafts.

Figure 10–3 outlines methods for developing effective dictation skills.

Figure 10–3
Developing effective dictation skills.

1. Establish a routine.
   a. Set aside a regular time each day for dictation.
   b. Choose a time when transcription will not be rushed.
2. Plan before you dictate.
   a. Prepare a simple outline for each letter to be dictated.
   b. Have everything you will need readily accessible.
   c. Think about what you want to say before dictating.
   d. Visualize the person(s) receiving the information.
3. Organize for excellence.
   a. When dictating to a machine,
      1) Precede instructions with "Operator" or your assistant's name.
      2) Number the letters in order, and refer to them as such.
      3) Use the indication system on the machine to let the transcriber know
         a) The length of the letter
         b) Where you have made corrections
      4) Spell out all first and last names except the most common ones.
      5) Dictate addresses and ZIP codes slowly.
   b. When dictating either to a person or into a machine, prioritize the sequence of items.
      1) Indicate the type of dictation, e.g., memo or letter.
      2) Provide instructions such as the type of paper to be used (e.g., company letterhead), number of copies, to whom, and special instructions such as air mail or enclosures.
      3) Provide guidelines for capitalization, paragraphing, and punctuation.
      4) Emphasize the pronunciation of letters that sound alike.
      5) Pronounce plurals and past tenses with equal emphasis.
      6) Repeat important figures and dates.
      7) Spell out difficult or unusual words after dictating them; then repeat them.
4. Dictate the correspondence.
   a. Speak at a normal rate of speed or slightly slower.
   b. Stay in one spot so your voice level will be consistent.
   c. Use a clear and natural voice.
   d. Speak in phrases, pausing for a breath.
   e. Indicate the type of closure.
5. Check your dictation.
   a. Play back the material to be sure the information is clear.
   b. Provide any written instructions needed to explain specific items.
6. Check the finished transcript.
   a. *Do not sign a letter without reading it first.* Encourage your manager to read all correspondence before signing. Since the person who signs a document is giving approval to the contents, any errors become that person's responsibility.
   b. If enclosures are to accompany the letter, attach them to the finished transcript so that they can be checked before they are inserted into the envelope.

Shorthand Use

Shorthand has contributed greatly to office efficiency for over one hundred years. The Gregg and Pitman symbol systems and some alphabetic systems enable office professionals to write sentences and paragraphs quickly and correctly. If you are to use a shorthand system, the following four steps will help you integrate dictation with your other duties:

1. *Preparation.* Always have the following materials at hand:
   a. A notebook with a rubber band around the "used" pages so you can quickly open it to a clean page (Figure 10–4)
   b. A separate notebook for each manager
   c. At least two pens or pencils to be kept with the notebook at all times
   d. A red or colored pencil to flag, underline, and make special notes
   e. A calendar for meetings and appointments
   f. A special drawer or large folder to hold all items relevant to dictation
2. *Process.* When you are called on to take dictation, follow these steps:
   a. Prepare for action by having someone cover an unattended desk or telephone, and gather all material to be completed. Setting aside a regular

Figure 10–4

Dictation notebook. *(Courtesy of* The Administrative Secretary, *Second Edition, Ruth I. Anderson et al. New York: Gregg Division, McGraw-Hill Book Company, p. 126)*

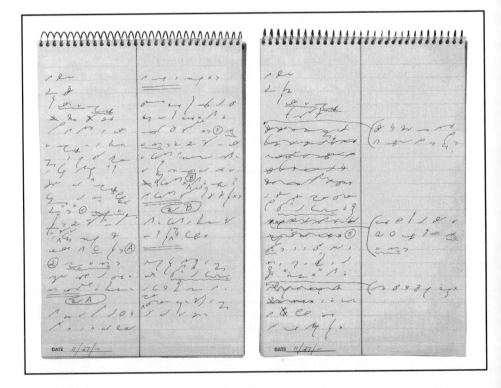

time for dictation will help keep your manager from interrupting your work at inconvenient times.

    b. Emphasize concentration by suggesting that calls and other interruptions be postponed until dictation is over. Spend a moment identifying what needs to be dictated so that both you and your manager will know what should be covered in the session.

    c. Get it right the first time. If the manager is dictating too fast, ask him or her to slow down. Confusing sentences should be restated and technical terms or names spelled out. Extra time spent during dictation will ease the transcription phase.

    d. Agree on procedures. A few minutes spent checking on how to prepare questionable correspondence will be time well spent.

3. *Rechecking.* As soon as all dictation has been completed and you are back at your workstation, review all the material and ask immediately about any confusing marks or omissions.

4. *Refinement.* At this point, make sure that all notes are in order and acceptable. Also, make notes of any difficulties encountered so that you won't forget to mention them to your manager to prevent their recurrence.

Multiple-Manager Dictation

You may be expected to take dictation from more than one manager. In that case, you should establish regular times for each manager, allowing the managers to

---

To aid the person who is dictating, you can repeat the last word or phrase you heard.

work out times when unscheduled dictation is required. A dictation log such as that in Figure 10–5 will be helpful.

Some managers prefer to see what they've dictated in draft form, before the assistant prepares the final copy, to do some editing. Others want dictated letters prepared in final form immediately. Be sure that you understand what each manager prefers.

Keyboard Dictation

In some instances, you will need to take dictation over the phone or at a keyboard. At these times, you should

- Inform the person to whom you are speaking whether you are going to record the conversation
- Give signals to the person speaking by occasionally saying "okay," "yes," or "all right"
- Clarify confusing words; ask any questions you may have, and verify names, addresses, and figures by spelling them again
- Read back short statements, letters, or similar items at the end of the dictation

When you take dictation at the keyboard, the copy will usually be in the form of a rough draft unless it is a form on which data are to be inserted. Ask the person who dictated, the appropriate length of the document so you can set adequate margins and make any other format adjustments. Also, determine whether the copy is to be a rough draft or a "first-time final" (correct on the first entry). This will let you know whether you should take time to proofread and correct errors as they occur. (Of course, you will try to be as accurate as you can even if it is a draft copy.) After you have keyboarded the document, allow the person who dictated to read the copy for additions or corrections.

Transcription

Many managers have their assistants **transcribe** their work, but dictation is also transcribed by people in a word processing center. The dictation is inputted on a floppy or hard disk and reviewed and revised at desktop terminals.

Direct Dictation

You can transcribe dictation directly from your manager more easily and quickly by (1) assembling items to be transcribed in order of their receipt and/or with rush or priority items to be completed first; (2) putting accompanying written material from one belt, disk, or tape with the media in a separate folder; and

Figure 10–5
Dictation log. *(Courtesy of Day-Timers)*

DICTATION LOG

DATE DUE	REF	START	STOP	TO	RE
2/8	L1			JOHN JACOBS	OUTSTANDING BILL
2/9		ORD #1	ORD #10	REESE'S OFFICE SUPPLY	ORDER - 1ST QUARTER
2/9		ORDER 11	ORDER 20	HARRIS OFFICE MACHINES	COPIER SUPPLIES

(3) clearing the work area for transcription so that you have enough room to work and can concentrate on listening.

As you listen to the dictation, concentrate on groups of words, up to sentence length. Listen to as many words as you can remember without having to replay the dictation. Stop the machine but continue to type; as you type the last few words, resume listening. If you can't understand certain words, phrases, or other items, leave a blank in the transcription and write a question mark (?). Read the transcription while listening to the tape (this step can be eliminated with practice). Finally, point out any problems to your manager immediately after completing the transcription assignment.

Read over your notes before typing or entering them. Check names for correct spelling, insert punctuation, note any unclear items, and check for grammatical errors. Also, review the instructions, especially if you are working with the manager for the first time. If the instructions are not clear, ask for clarification immediately and write them down. These steps will speed up transcription time.

When large amounts of dictation must be transcribed, some assistants use an automatic electronic copyholder. This device holds the text upright and has a line guide that moves down the page as the work progresses. This is especially helpful when transcribing from handwritten copy or entering complex tables.

Word Processing Center

If material in its original form—either handwritten or on tape or disk—is sent to a word processing center, you will have to take certain precautions to ensure accuracy. The word processing center's staff processes information from many managers and may not give sufficient attention to any one job. However, the following techniques will ensure that your work proceeds smoothly once it is started.

First, make sure that any potentially confusing material is clarified. Be sure the center knows what material is to be typed, by what day, and in what form.

A word processing center manager can keep track of work flow and the amount of progress made daily.
(Courtesy of Lanier Voice Products)

Figure 10–6 illustrates a work order form you can use for this purpose. Check that names, technical terms, and similar information have been spelled out by the person dictating or written down in a list. Keep backup material readily available for use in reviewing drafts and final manuscripts.

Remember to update mailing lists so that individual correspondence or bulk mailings can be processed quickly and economically. When completed material is returned to you for review, complete the initial proofreading before passing it on to the originator. Then return any previous drafts to the word processing center for final production. Finally, assemble material with enclosures for signature, copying, mailing, and filing.

Depending on your specific responsibilities, you may produce and reuse a number of form letters. **Form letters** can be prepared once, then stored on disk or in the computer's memory and retrieved when needed. They do not need rekeying, which is a great time saver.

Word processing software programs allow you to merge individual paragraphs

Figure 10–6
Word processing work order form.

1. Work originator's initials

   _____

2. Originator's department

   _____

3. Day in _____
4. Time in _____
5. Time due _____
6. Type of work (check one)
   _____ Prerecorded
   _____ Original
   _____ Revision
   _____ a. Stored text
   _____ b. Original work
   _____ Confidential

7. Type of input
   _____ Longhand
   _____ Dictation
   _____ Typed copy
   _____ Statistical data
   _____ Forms
8. Time out _____
   _____ Number of copies
   _____ Job number of the day

into a single letter and insert the inside address, salutation, and date. With the list-merge function in these programs, you can join a form letter with a series of names and produce a form letter for any size group. You or your manager can thus create form letters for recurring correspondence. With a collection of such letters, you can produce correspondence quickly, with fewer errors, and at a lower per-letter cost.

Cooperative Keyboarding

Small computer networks in which a number of personal computers are linked are becoming increasingly common. If your office has this type of system, you will be doing some keyboarding yourself. More often, however, your manager will do his or her own keyboarding and ask you to revise the work—a process called **cooperative keyboarding**.

Some managers now carry portable computers and transmit their keyboarded letters or reports by telephone modem. Their assistants are responsible for preparing drafts, editing, or preparing the documents in their final form.

But don't underestimate the value of a regular typewriter for drafts, short memos, and confidential items such as recommendations or sensitive reports. Your manager will appreciate both the speed and the confidentiality. In particular, he or she may want certain material kept out of a computer file and locked away from unauthorized individuals.

Some organizations have detailed procedures manuals that address the following areas:

- How many copies to make of each item
- How to mark copies sent to others
- How to number correspondence
- How to address envelopes
- How to mark enclosures
- What information is confidential

If you work in a small organization, you may be responsible for developing such procedures.

Communication Tips

The following tips will help you in your information management activities:

- Ask each manager for specific instructions on how correspondence is to be prepared.
- Pay special attention to complex or high-priority assignments and their instructions.
- Ask for clarification if any aspect of an assignment is unclear.
- When assigning work to a co-worker, word processing center, temporary assistant, or outside service, review all instructions; then *pause* and ask for questions.
- Review with your manager(s) procedures for organizing information, solving problems, and improving productivity and quality.

SUMMARY

Information must be transcribed from a variety of sources: handwritten drafts, oral dictation, machine dictation, and computer readouts. In each case, clear procedures should be established to ensure rapid and correct preparation of letters, memos, reports, and other correspondence.

When your manager hand-drafts material, pay particular attention to special instructions and potentially confusing words. When taking dictation, it is important to avoid interruptions, understand what your manager says the first time, and recheck immediately to spot any questions. When you take dictation over the telephone, clarity is more important than speed.

Machine dictation is becoming more common because managers can dictate faster than they can write. The equipment selected should fit the office's operation and the managers' styles.

In some instances, you will send work to a word processing center for completion. A distinct set of procedures should be followed to ensure that material is handled correctly.

Key Terms

The following terms appeared in boldface type in this chapter. Do you recall what they mean? For a more complete definition, turn to the glossary beginning on p. 442.

cooperative keyboarding (p. 225)
discrete media machine (p. 216)
endless loop system (p. 216)

form letter (p. 224)
information management (p. 214)
transcribe (p. 222)

Discussion Questions

1. You have just been assigned to work for three managers in a government agency who have been dictating to an assistant for years. They don't want to even think about new technology. What guidelines would you suggest to them to make your work easier?
2. During face-to-face dictation with one manager, how would you deal with the following tendencies?
   a. Using awkward or run-on sentences
   b. Taking too long to get to the point
   c. Wandering around the room, mumbling, and generally making it difficult to hear what is being said
   d. Dictating ''on the run''
3. You are the assistant to an engineering research unit in a large corporation. One of your duties is to type long letters, progress reports, and proposals for ten engineers. All work is handwritten, and each engineer's handwriting is different. What suggestions for making your work easier could you give them that would be acceptable to all? For example, what could you ask them to do when writing down names or complicated technical terms?
4. As an office professional, what changes to a transcribed document would you be likely to make? Provide specifics related to both the content and the format of a document.
5. Two newly hired managers in your office are great fans of dictation equipment. In addition to their desk models, they have portable units that they carry with them almost all the time. Both tend to dictate in an unpunctuated ''stream of consciousness.'' What steps could you take to (a) improve the clarity and organization of their dictation, (b) make them appreciate the amount of time transcription takes, and (c) encourage them to be more selective in their choice of equipment?
6. You are an administrative aide to a unit of ten managers. Recently your office converted to centralized word processing. Grumbling, dissatisfaction, and complaints about word processing products have become constant. The word processing operators aren't too happy with the managers' dictation techniques. What specific steps can you recommend to make mutual respect and collaboration possible?

Managers and assistants alike are concerned about the potential harm dictation technology can bring to working relationships. Many feel that personal contact will be lost. Nevertheless, this technology is here to stay. This assignment is intended to encourage you to think about how to confront this reality.

Prepare a plan, by yourself or with a group, that includes

a. Specific ways to prevent machine dictation from reducing contact between assistants and managers
b. Ways in which office professionals can continue to assist managers in overall correspondence and written material preparation
c. Ways in which office skills and professionalism can contribute to intelligent use of word processing in general and dictation in particular

The plan should indicate roles that you and others will assume regardless of position. Make communication paramount as you prepare the plan.

Those instructors using *Top Performance: A Decision-Making Simulation for the Office* should consult the *Instructor's Guide* at this point for support material regarding use of the software in the classroom.

Case Study

Janet Weeks believes there is just too much individualism in her small office. Five salespeople plus the manager produce volumes of paper destined for clients and suppliers. Some materials are handwritten; others are dictated into a central transcribing unit. In a few rush or confidential situations, Janet is asked to take a letter in her somewhat rusty shorthand.

Preferences appear to change daily. No two assignments are handled the same way. Sales personnel are creative and want to respond rapidly to clients. The problem obviously is lack of standardization, and the sales manager appears to be the core of the problem. He believes that a small office doesn't need a standardized set of procedures.

What techniques can Janet use to establish some order in the office? How should she implement them? (Keep in mind that old habits die hard.)

CHAPTER

11

PREPARING CORRESPONDENCE AND BUSINESS REPORTS

Chapter Objectives

- To know how to prepare effective letters and memos

- To learn the three basic methods of organizing a message

- To become familiar with various types of letters and short reports

- To learn how to prepare reports

- To learn proofreading techniques

Examples of Excellence

"What would we do without her?" wonder the partners in the law firm of Weiss, Kelley, and Rosen. The person they mean is Estelle Koch, the firm's senior legal secretary. Estelle always sends out clean, impressive documents. In addition to her regular duties, she thoroughly proofreads all outgoing correspondence for correctly spelled names, proper grammar, and consistent and appropriate punctuation. Her commitment to excellence has reflected well on the firm and its personnel.

Correspondence presents a telling image to all who see and read it. Preparing consistently excellent correspondence, one of your major responsibilities, is not complicated. It merely requires careful attention to details and accepted procedures.

In addition to preparing correspondence, you will be required to help make your office reports both readable and understandable. Current word processing technology will make your tasks easier, but good organization, attention to details, and deliberate rather than rushed completion will require your continuing attention.

In this chapter, you will learn

- Seven tests you can apply to written correspondence
- Words and phrases that convey a tone readers will appreciate
- Attention-getting beginnings and endings for correspondence
- How to create clear and brief letters of various kinds
- Proofreading procedures that will eliminate embarrassing errors

- How to complete necessary research and gather relevant information to complete a report
- How to assist managers and co-workers in completing lengthy or complex reports

Guidelines for Preparing Impressive Correspondence

You will be involved in three types of correspondence activities:

1. Preparing and possibly editing letters and memos that were hand or machine drafted by managers
2. Writing letters requested by your manager(s) or composing routine replies
3. Proofreading word-processed material

To ensure that the correspondence you prepare represents your organization well, apply the following seven checkpoints:

1. Is the letter attractive? Readers notice appearance before content. Consider the following:

- Overall appearance (equal margins, clean type, proper placement of letter parts, and attractive letterhead and paper quality)
- Correct spelling and placement of reader's name, title, and address
- Correctly spelled words and accepted grammar
- Correct match of the day of the week and date
- No **typographical errors**
- Correct signature and title line (readers tend to look at the signature line first)
- Well-constructed paragraphs (four lines maximum in the first and last paragraph and eight lines in all others)

2. Is the message complete? To be complete, a message should include as much—and only as much—information as necessary. To decide how much information to include, ask yourself whether the additional material will help the reader understand the message better. When writing a letter, try to anticipate the reader's questions and include the necessary information. When answering a letter, respond to all the reader's questions and provide all items requested.

A useful guide to follow is the **five *W*s and one *H***: **w**ho, **w**hat, **w**here, **w**hen, **w**hy, and **h**ow. Check letters for the following content:

- *who*: Have all the people involved been mentioned?
- *what*: Is the subject clear and stated early in the letter?
- *where*: Is the location, if relevant, included?

- *when:* Are dates and times identified?
- *why:* Is the purpose or reason for the correspondence or activity mentioned?
- *how:* Are all needed procedures or methods clearly specified?

3. *Is the message concise?* A concise message isn't necessarily short, but the length of a message has little to do with its importance. Wordiness irritates people. Long phrases can obscure meanings. Consider the word pairs in Figure 11–1. A simpler word will be understood more easily than a complex one and will also convey a friendly but still businesslike tone.

Before typing correspondence or sending it to a word processing center, read each item. Most managers will appreciate stylistic suggestions, especially if you stress conciseness and a conversational tone. However, be tactful when offering your ideas. Check the letters you compose carefully.

4. *Is your meaning clear?* Keep the reader in mind constantly; make sure the letter is clear on *first reading.* Observe the following elements:

Figure 11–1
Use the simple word.

Simple words are easier to understand and convey a friendly tone.

Instead of	Use
Advise or Inform	Tell
Retain	Keep
Purchase	Buy
Endeavor	Try
Transmit	Send
Terminate	Close or end
Initiate	Begin
Acquire	Get
Commence	Start

Concise letters eliminate unnecessary words.

Instead of	Use
enclosed you will find	enclosed
as soon as possible	soon, immediately, by (date)
contact you by telephone	call or telephone
please do not hesitate to	please
at the present time	now
send it back	send it
small in size	small
absolutely free	free
repeat again	repeat
exactly identical	identical

- Short sentences
- Modifiers (adjectives or adverbs) close to the word being modified ("solid wood posture chairs with built-in padding for managers"; *not* "solid wood posture chairs for managers with built-in padding")
- Listings and tables rather than sentences
- Punctuation to separate ideas
- Active rather than passive voice

5. *Is the tone courteous?* The "you" approach and a positive vocabulary are keys to courtesy. The **"you" approach** simply means thinking of the reader first; this may result in using more second-person than first-person words. You should also avoid beginning sentences with "I." The "you" approach shows your readers that you consider them important people. Figure 11–2 shows what using the "you" approach can contribute to a letter.

Give your letter a friendly **tone** by using the reader's name respectfully in the body of the letter—perhaps at the beginning of a paragraph or in the middle of a sentence. This brings the reader back into the message. It is important, however, not to use the reader's name in a critical or condescending way ("As you undoubtedly know, Mr. Jones . . .").

Please, thank you, and other polite words do not ensure courtesy. If you thank a reader in advance for doing something, he or she might be offended because you have assumed agreement in advance. Showing appreciation is more appropriate after acceptance or action than before.

6. *Is the tone positive?* Positive words improve the tone of your message and are a courtesy to readers. A positive message generally provides more complete information and is also more pleasing to read. Here are two examples:

Negative	Positive
Your document has not been finished.	Your document will be finished tomorrow.
You did not tell us what size you need.	We will be pleased to fill your order as soon as you give us the size.

7. *Are beginnings and endings effective?* The opening and closing paragraphs of your message are sometimes the most difficult to write. Middle paragraphs contain main thoughts or important information. Opening paragraphs must attract and keep the reader's attention, build the tone of the letter, convey sincerity, and seek goodwill. Ending paragraphs should close the letter in a way that will keep the main points fresh in the reader's mind.

Opening. The first paragraph should be no longer than four typewritten lines and state what the letter is about. It should make the reader eager to continue.

Figure 11–2
The "you" approach: which letter is more appealing?

Without the "you" approach:

Dear Ms. Jarman:

The American Business Communication Association's Fifth Annual Awards dinner will be held next Wednesday at 6 PM at the Lincoln Inn.

Our speaker is Peter Churm of Fluorocarbon, one of the nation's top executives. He will share his writing techniques and illustrate many of them.

Plan to attend this valuable informational presentation.

Sincerely,

With the "you" approach:

Dear Ms. Jarman:

You are cordially invited to attend the American Business Communication Association's Fifth Annual Awards dinner next Wednesday at 6 PM at the Lincoln Inn.

This year, you'll be delighted to hear one of the nation's top business executives, Peter Churm of Fluorocarbon. You will learn how today's new writing techniques can improve your business writing.

The planning committee is sure you will be quite pleased with the speaker and his illustrations. Be sure to mark your calendar today.

Sincerely,

Sample openings:

Thank you for your check of $55.

Enclosed are complimentary tickets to our annual home show.

Here are the revised bid figures you requested last week.

Closing. The last paragraph should also be limited to four typewritten lines. Avoid **cliché** endings such as "Do not hesitate to call us"; "If we can be of further service"; "Thank you again for your cooperation."

The last paragraph should be sincere and clear, telling the reader what you want, what you will do, or how much you value his or her goodwill. The best endings are effective and fresh. They are excellent opportunities to tie together the main thrust of your communication.

Sample closings:

Please let me know what you think.

Thank you for your suggestion, Mr. Juarez. We will forward it to our advertising manager.

Letter and Memo Preparation

You can establish the habit of preparing excellent correspondence by using an accepted format for preparing memos and letters.

Business Letter

The letter in Figure 11–3 illustrates the elements of a typical business letter. In the block style, the date is typed or entered flush with the left margin. In organizations that prefer the modified block style, the date is placed at the top center of the page or to the end of the right margin. The remaining parts of a business letter include

- Special on-arrival instructions, such as the attention line
- Inside address
- Attention line (if the letter is addressed to a specific individual or department)
- Salutation
- Subject line (for emphasis)
- Body
- Complimentary closing line
- Signature line
- Reference initials
- Enclosure or attachment notation, if additional materials are being sent
- Copy notation, if copies are being sent (Note that on occasion you will provide a copy for someone not identified to the addressee; "blind copy" notations should be made on the file copy that you keep. Attachments are stapled to the letter, while enclosures are folded separately.)
- Postscripts (to highlight additional information)

Each part of the letter is separated from the part preceding and following it by a double space. Paragraphs in the body are single spaced, with a double space between the paragraphs. Your organization may have established guidelines for margins and spacing; this information is often contained in the office manual.

When letters are two or more pages long, the additional pages are printed on plain paper of the same quality and color as the letterhead used for the first page. The heading on subsequent pages is entered on line 7 from the top of the page and should indicate the recipient, page number, and date. The heading can be entered in block style or horizontal style. Begin the body of the letter three or four lines below the last line of the heading.

As mentioned earlier, many organizations have their own procedures for preparing correspondence. Be sure to become familiar with them and follow them diligently.

Figure 11–3
Elements of a business letter (modified block style).

May 9, 19xx ———————⌐ date

CONFIDENTIAL ————————⌐ special on-arrival directions

Hillcrest Research, Inc.
9005 Harding Road ————————⌐ inside address
Nashville, TN   37205

Attention Ms. Jane Reder ————————⌐ attention line
Dear Ms. Reder: ————————⌐ salutation
SUBJECT: Confidential Report ————————⌐ subject line

⌐ body

Don Chagon asked me to send you a copy of our most recent research study on minority hiring trends. The data has not yet been released, so please treat the material as confidential.

As you can see, many companies report difficulty in finding well-prepared candidates for a variety of entry level positions. A few of the service industries have developed effective ways to locate potential employees, however.

We are interested in your reactions to the report and the method we used to collect information. Please call me when you have read the report and want to discuss it.

Sincerely ————————⌐ closing line

LaVerne Ruez ————————⌐ name
Director of Research ————————⌐ title

XX ————————⌐ reference initials

Enclosure ————————⌐ enclosure notation

c: Ramon DuBois ————————⌐ copy notation

The report will be published in September. ——⌐ postscript

Memos and Other Interorganization Messages

In organizations of all sizes, co-workers communicate in writing for a variety of reasons. Information may be so important or complicated that it must be written. All details may be significant so that an omitted item could cause major problems; confirming arrangements for an important meeting or business trip is one example. Some managers write memos to confirm decisions made at meetings and to report progress.

Today you may find memos on an electronic mail system or in written form. Some electronic mail messages are copied to create a permanent record in case information on a computer hard drive is destroyed.

Managers will handwrite, dictate directly, dictate by machine, or input information on their desk computers. You will normally prepare memos on a form or stationery used for that purpose alone. A specific format is likely to be used for consistency and clarity. The elements of a memo are simple; they include

- A heading that includes the individual(s) receiving the memo, the originator, subject, and date. Figure 11–4 shows three acceptable formats for providing this information.
- The body of the letter, which contains the message, should be typed flush left, single-spaced, with double spacing between paragraphs.
- Special notations at the end of the document may include the initials of the person preparing the document, where additional copies are being sent, an indication of enclosures or attachments, and possibly a numerical and/or letter code used to identify where the document is stored for easy reference.

Many managers travel with a portable computer and modem, enabling them to send and receive memos and other messages. Thus, work is less likely to accumulate. With this equipment, you can keep in touch with your manager and help your manager keep in contact with colleagues and others.

Total Message Organization

You can organize the letters and memos you write or edit according to their purpose and the desired reader response with a simple but effective procedure:

1. Visualize the reader(s).
2. Determine what the reader may want to know, his or her possible reaction, and what actions you want the reader to take.
3. Organize and write the message.
4. Revise the letter to ensure that its organization fits the message and the likely reader(s). Figure 11–5, page 238, charts reader needs or reactions, message, and suggested arrangement based on intent.

Figure 11–4
Memo formats.

STANDARD PUMPS, INCORPORATED

Interoffice Correspondence

Executive Offices   476 Pacific Avenue, Portland, Oregon   97210

To:

From:

Date:

Subject:

STIMSON PRODUCTS CORPORATION

Interoffice Correspondence

490 Main Boulevard   Denver, Colorado   80202   623–6107

To: From: Date:

Subject: File:

DAVIS EQUIPMENT COMPANY

Interoffice Communication

To: Subject:

From: Date:

Figure 11–5

Basic methods of message organization and when to use them.

Direct or Inductive	Indirect or Inductive	Persuasive or Sales (AIDCA Formula)
Main idea	Buffer (something neutral)	Attention (attract favorable attention)
Details or explanations	Reasons	Interest (build interest)
Closing	Refusal	Desire (create desire)
	Buffer (something neutral)	Conviction (get conviction)
		Action (ask for action)

Reader's Needs or Reactions	Message	Letter Arrangement to Use
Favorable, neutral	Good news, pleasant (grant requests, allow an adjustment, provide credit)	Direct or deductive
Unfavorable	Bad news, unpleasantly surprising (refuse requests, credit adjustments, employment, announce incomplete orders)	Indirect or inductive
Interested, but neither pleased nor displeased	Routine, neutral informational (requests, ordering, thanking, congratulating, or expressing condolences)	Direct or deductive
Little initial interest	Persuasive (job application, sales, promotions, suggestions)	Persuasive or sales

Advantages of deductive arrangement:

- First sentence or paragraph is easy to write because it's the main idea and of greatest interest to the reader.
- Reader is in a pleasant frame of mind.
- Time-saving approach for time-pressured managers.

Advantages of inductive arrangement:

- Allows the opportunity to present reasons for having to say no.
- Provides an opportunity to build goodwill by explaining a position and allowing the reader to see why a negative decision was made. (Note: When constructing inductive communications, avoid inappropriate phrases such as "It's against company policy," "you must understand," "you claim"). Avoid words such as hope and trust. Maintain a positive approach; close with a statement about your willingness to serve; do not bring up the problem a second time.

Advantages of persuasive arrangement:

- A modification of the inductive arrangement. Used primarily in sales and sales applications, provides the opportunity to attract attention, present reasons, build goodwill, and generate interest and action.

Paragraph Organization

Analyze each paragraph to make sure it contributes to the letter's overall quality. Use the following procedures:

1. Begin with the point of greatest interest, and follow a priority order.
2. State the problem first; then state the cause, effect, and possible solution.
3. Examine a sequence of events in chronological order, perhaps by date of occurrence.

Routine, Neutral, Informational Messages

Routine, neutral, **informational messages** are easy to prepare, because their intent is clear and simple. Such messages lend themselves best to a direct or **deductive approach** when

- Requesting information, products, services, or merchandise
- Requesting some kind of adjustment
- Ordering merchandise
- Thanking, congratulating, or expressing condolences

In this arrangement, a statement of purpose is followed by the specifics, including the date, and a friendly closing. Figure 11–6 shows a sample **routine message**. Announcements can also be written directly using the who, what, where, when, why, and how approach.

   Goodwill messages are opportunity letters. They aren't always necessary, but they are desirable because they build goodwill. Expressions of sympathy (Figure 11–7, page 240) may not be thought of as goodwill messages, but they do indicate

---

Figure 11–6
Request for information: direct or deductive organization.

Dear Mr. Demmin:

May I have a copy of the investment booklet you mentioned in your June 14 presentation to the Executive Club? — main idea

Last month's Executive Club newsletter included excerpts of your talk and illustrations from the investment booklet. — details

As a potential investor, I would appreciate having a copy of this booklet and any other materials you feel would be of benefit. — closing

Sincerely,

your sensitivity. Examples of goodwill messages are "thank-you's" (Figure 11–8) and congratulatory notes or cards. Goodwill messages must take the "you" approach. They must be sincere and prompt, or they will lose effectiveness. They should be direct, concise, natural, and conversational in tone. In some situations, a handwritten message may be appreciated by the recipient because it indicates a personal interest.

Good-news messages are easy to write because they are positive. The good news should be contained in the first sentence and be followed by details and a pleasant closing (Figure 11–9, page 242).

Form letters, discussed in Chapter 10, are used regularly by public and private organizations for a variety of purposes. A form letter may be customized with the name of the recipient, an order number, and how the request will be handled.

Bad-news messages refuse requests for information, products, services, adjustments, credit, and employment or report incomplete orders (Figure 11–10, page 242). The bad-news message takes planning and organization to help the reader understand why an unfavorable decision was made. This type of message is best presented using an indirect or **inductive approach**, in which you present the reasons first and then state the decision. The bad-news message uses the following format: (1) neutral information; (2) specific facts; (3) a general principle or reason for the refusal; and (4) a neutral statement to maintain goodwill.

Persuasive or **sales messages** build up to the main point. Any request is delayed until the case for granting it can be made. One well-accepted procedure for constructing a persuasive message is the **AIDCA formula**:

- Attract favorable *attention*.
- Build *interest* by introducing the product, service, idea, or plan.
- Create support or *desire* by showing benefits to the reader.
- Build *conviction* in the reader.
- Urge the reader to take *action*.

Figure 11–7
Condolence message.

Dear Mrs. Harren:

You have my sincere sympathy and that of my associates. It's hard to find the right words at a time like this, but we want you to know that Joe was a wonderful person and kind to all of us.

main idea

If there is anything we can do to help you, Mrs. Harren, please let us know.

closing

Sincerely,

Figure 11–8
Thank-you to fellow employee.

```
To:     Pauline Evans
From:   Diane Meyer
Date:   June 29, 1991


Subject: Bradson Contract

Thanks to you, Pauline, we were able to meet          ⎡ main
the deadline on the Bradson contract.                 ⎣ idea

Without your extra effort over the last two
weekends, we would not have been able to
compile all the information needed for the
Bradson contract. Mr. Johnson, president of           ⎤
Bradson, called yesterday to compliment us on         ⎦ details
our professional presentation and our
willingness to put this together on such short
notice.

Thanks again, Pauline. It's a pleasure working        ⎡ closing
with you.                                             ⎣

cc:  C. E. Jones
     R. J. Scann
```

Persuasive letters include job applications, sales and promotion letters, and suggestions to managers. Figure 11–11, page 243, presents a letter using a persuasive arrangement.

Press Releases

In your job, you may have to prepare news releases. Here are some guidelines for making the best impression.

Writing

1. Use journalistic organizational style: who, what, when, where, why, how.
2. Make the heading brief and factual.
3. In the opening paragraph, stress the most unusual aspect of the event, personality, service, or product to gain the reader's attention.
4. Follow with the basic facts, emphasizing the most important ones first.

Figure 11–9
Good-news message.

Dear Mr. Mendez:

Your Order No. 4598 for 12 Model 364 electronic calculators was shipped today. — good news

As soon as we received your letter of April 12, we made an investigation, which showed that we received your order on April 1 and shipped it the same day. Because of an incorrectly addressed shipping label, however, your order was received by the Belmont, Kentucky, store. — explanation

Thank you, Mr. Mendez, for bringing this to our attention. You will receive a 10 percent discount on this order, and we are pleased to have you as a customer. — goodwill closing

Sincerely,

Figure 11–10
Bad-news message.

Dear Mr. Nelson:

Thank you for your check for $350 to cover invoice no. 4780. Prompt payment is always appreciated. — neutral

According to the payment terms listed on your invoice, all orders paid within thirty days of the date of sale are entitled to a 10 percent discount. This policy allows us to pass along savings to our customers. — reasons

Since your purchase of September 21 for $385 was paid on October 27, we cannot allow you to take the 10 percent discount. You can either send a check for $35 in the enclosed self-addressed stamped envelope or instruct us to carry the $35 in your account. — refusal

Mr. Nelson, it has been a pleasure serving you, and we are looking forward to your future orders. — neutral goodwill

Sincerely,

Typing

1. Use special "Press Release" letterhead or 8½″ × 11″, 20-pound paper.
2. Make top and side margins at least one inch wide.
3. Allow a wider bottom margin for editorial changes.
4. Indent paragraphs either five or ten spaces consistently.
5. Double-space the body of the press release.
6. Block information in the upper left-hand corner: Include
   a. Name and title of person sending the release
   b. Company name
   c. Address
   d. Telephone number
7. Enter the release information (e.g., "For Release Tuesday, October 22, 19xx" or "For Immediate Release") double spaced below the address block, on the right-hand side.
8. Add the actual date the material is sent if the material is for immediate release. Place this date in the far upper or lower left-hand corner.
9. If the release is more than one page,
   a. Type the word *more* in the lower right-hand corner of all pages except the last one.
   b. Number all succeeding pages at the top center.
10. Indicate the end of the release with three number symbols typed on a separate line (# # #).
11. If possible, provide a title for the article.

Figure 11–11
Persuasive or sales message.

To: Public Relations Director
From: Coordinator of Conferences and Meetings
Date: April 1, 1991
Subject: Conference Center signs

At Wednesday evening's supervision session, it became evident that the Conference Center is not adequately marked.　　　　attention

Many people mentioned that they weren't sure how to get back to the center or if they were at the right building. As a temporary solution, I have had the physical plant director put up temporary directional signs.　　　　interest

From a public relations viewpoint, you may want to pursue a more permanent solution to this problem.　　　　desire and conviction

You may also want to consider having signs made to be placed on all four exterior walls of the center.　　　　action

Report Preparation

Managers use reports to provide information, to **interpret** facts, and often to make **recommendations**. Reports can be prepared periodically or upon special request from an individual or agency. At the beginning of every report assignment, you and your manager should consider four questions to clarify the purpose of the report:

1. Who will have to be informed about what?
2. How much information will have to be collected, and how should it be organized?
3. What are the clearest and most effective ways to present this information?
4. How can graphics and other visual aids be used to make a point?

Thoughtful answers to all these questions will increase your clarity of purpose and allow you to begin your research confidently.

By categorizing reports, you can quickly identify their purpose. Three categories are commonly used:

1. **Informational:** fact-finding
2. **Examinational** or **interpretive:** fact-finding plus interpreting the facts
3. **Analytical** or **research:** fact-finding and interpreting the facts, plus conclusions and recommendations

You will need to know which of these kinds of reports your manager is expecting. For example, if an informational report is desired, you won't want to provide interpretations or recommendations.

Gathering Information

The term **research** covers the variety of tasks that precede the preparation of reports, letters, speeches, and other formal communications. Research means gathering facts to support opinions or recommendations. The extent of the research required depends on the assignment and can range from checking figures for a price quote in a letter to extensively examining possible solutions to a problem.

Your research is likely to involve

- Gathering data from several offices for a regular monthly, quarterly, or annual report

- Working under pressure to find information needed for a quick answer to a major customer, organizational superior, or board of directors

- Conducting computer-based searches for information from sources within or outside of the organization

- Searching organizational records for pertinent information for a manager preparing a report

- Assisting a manager in preparing a speech by organizing slides, transparencies, graphs, and other visual aids to supplement the presentation

You can organize a system for controlling the amount of information you collect. Too little information will make a report incomplete or a position difficult to defend. Too much information will delay completion and obscure the main point of the report.

The seven organizing steps suggested in this section are designed to help you and your manager collect enough information to support the positions taken in the report. Regardless of the amount of research to be collected, the process is the same. In some cases, you will do much of the information gathering yourself. However, if this task begins to interfere with other responsibilities, you may have to request assistance.

Step 1: Define the "researchable" problem. The first step is to thoroughly understand the problem your research is to address. If you are not sure, check with the person who gave you the assignment; then you can determine what information you need. In some instances, one or two phone calls will provide enough information. In others, you can consult the basic reference texts on your

An employee gathers data for a quarterly report. *(Courtesy of International Business Machines Corporation)*

desk or in the company library to obtain sufficient information. Still other research assignments will require a great deal of time and effort. Figure 11–12 outlines a method for defining the scope and nature of your research.

Step 2: Organize the information collection process. Completing this planning step will make you use the time you spend collecting information to best advantage. The organization process should include

- Identifying specific information you will have to collect and the sources you will use
- Gathering the reference sources
- Preparing a list of questions to ask, such as "Where would I find . . .?" or "How can I locate information about . . .?"
- Setting aside sufficient time to collect and organize the information
- Finding a quiet place to concentrate on collecting the information in an orderly fashion

Although these activities may require some extra time, they will make the time spent collecting data more effective.

Figure 11–12

1. *What do I wish to learn more about?* The advantages and disadvantages of text-editing typewriters.
2. *Why do I wish to learn more about this subject?* To be able to assist my manager in making the best choice in an upcoming purchase.
3. *What do I know already?*
   a. From observation, Model A breaks down more than Models B and C.
   b. From using two models, Model B's keyboard is more comfortable.
   c. From talking with other assistants, Model B has the most useful add-on features.
   d. Summary of the three: Model B has the most advantages and the fewest limitations.
4. *What more would I like to learn? What are the best information sources?*

To Learn	Sources
Model B limitations	Periodicals/other assistants
Training available	Supplier
Cost and payment plans	Supplier

Step 3: Locate sources of information. You will be able to collect factual information more quickly when you have located the best sources in advance. Here are a few sources you will want to consult:

- A manager's office (may include certain kinds of technical material, reports, texts, and other items)
- A central unit or organizational files
- The company library or the public library
- A co-worker who has finished a similar assignment and can tell you where to find the best sources
- Computer-based searches available through libraries, shared databases, and single-organization retrieval systems

As you familiarize yourself with the sources you will need to consult, you will have a clearer idea of how much time to schedule for completing step 4—collecting the data.

Step 4: Collect the data. To reduce the time spent looking for information, make a list of the subject headings or index entries likely to cover the information you need. Then quickly survey

- The tables of contents and indexes of books to find the sections of chapters that contain the information you need
- The tables of contents of magazines or pamphlets
- Card catalogs in libraries for books, pamphlets, and other documents that relate to your topic
- Published indexes such as lists of periodicals and specific books in print

In your office you will find other useful information in files, on desks, and on bookshelves. Past reports, background memos, letters, financial statements, and meeting notes may also be helpful.

Step 5: Record information for easy use and reuse. Be sure to take sufficient time to carefully record your information so that you can use it again if necessary. Clarity and accuracy are essential. The information should be collected and organized so that anyone familiar with the problem can understand it.

Many reports are produced on a regular basis, and basic information along with formats can be stored. This will make revising or updating information easier.

Step 6: "Rough out" the data into the draft report format. Sometimes you will collect more information than you actually need, especially if you have postponed integrating data within the report. When you have basic information on each question or area, stop gathering information for a time and prepare a rough draft of the report for your manager's reaction. Keep in mind the desired outcome as you arrange the data to make the final product as effective as possible.

Step 7: Note items for future use. This step is often omitted because research projects, like crisis situations, are viewed as isolated events. However, you will be prepared to handle comparable future research assignments more easily if you remember to complete three activities at the end of your information-gathering project:

1. Check notes one last time, then put them away in an accessible location should you need them to **validate information.**
2. Identify what you did well or poorly; especially note improvements to suggest to your manager.
3. Record the amount of time the research actually took so in the future you can allocate enough time to do an effective job without unnecessary pressure.

Figure 11–13 reviews the report preparation process. This process can be especially helpful if you are a newly employed office professional.

Research in a Changing Environment

A variety of technological assistance will be available for your data-gathering activities. Desktop terminals will allow easy access to information both near and far. The terminals display the data and then allow you to make copies for reference. Knowing what computer-stored data you need and how to access it quickly and easily will be important for rapid and correct report preparation in the modern office environment.

Figure 11–13
Organizing a report.

1. *Define the researchable problem.* Which of three possible conference sites would be best for our annual three-day all-staff meeting?
2. *Organize the information collection process.*
   a. Call or write to the three sites
   b. Call past users
   c. Talk with meeting planners
3. *Locate sources of information.*
   a. Information on each site, including cost and facilities for planned meeting activities (e.g., meeting rooms with audiovisual equipment, duplicating services, cable television hookup)
   b. Lists of similar groups using the facility
4. *Collect data with the outcome in mind.* Prepare a recommendation on the best site or a comparison of the three.
   a. Focus on costs, facilities, and attractive features
   b. Obtain evaluation from previous users
5. *Record information for easy use and reuse.* Prepare a sheet on each site listing pertinent items:
   a. Cost   d. Distance
   b. Rooms available e. General attractiveness
   c. Other facilities f. Past users' thoughts
6. *Rough out the data into the draft report format.* Prepare a one-page summary of the three choices, and attach for supervisor to examine.
7. *Note items for future use.* Recheck notes, identify future improvements, and record the amount of time the research took. Keep reports on file for use in planning other staff meetings.

A second important technological factor will be computerized transmission of reports. This will increase the need for concise composition and careful targeting (discussed shortly). Graphic portrayal of data in charts, graphs, and tables will also be important.

A third factor that can complicate your research work is the likelihood that you will work for more than one manager. How much assistance will you receive? How will the organization of reports change?

Techniques for Increasing Report Preparation Efficiency

The techniques presented in this section are designed to organize each research assignment according to an appropriate formula to be followed by both you and your manager. Each technique will make organization and detail control easier and help you produce concise, carefully focused writing.

Know Your Audience. You must know your audience and write with them in mind. This technique is called *targeting* and includes several indispensable steps:

1. Focus on the main point.
2. Adjust material, language, and data to the audience.
3. Write simply.
4. Be sure that every point makes sense and is well-supported.
5. Conclude by emphasizing the meaning and importance of what you have said.

Choose the Appropriate Format. Whether your report is short or long, it must follow the appropriate format. *Format* refers to the general physical appearance of a document. This section will describe the formats for the most common types of reports: (1) memorandum reports, (2) letter reports, (3) short reports, and (4) long reports.

Memo reports. Sometimes an interoffice communication must contain more information than the typical short interoffice memo format will accommodate. The memo report contains the same heading and closing as the interoffice memo, but the body follows this format:

1. *Introduction:* A brief overview of the subject matter.
2. *Background:* An explanation of why the report was necessary. This section states the problem under investigation and the procedures followed.
3. *Findings:* The data on which the conclusions will be based.

Mailing lists can be stored, updated, and accessed on the computer. *(Courtesy of International Business Machine Corporation)*

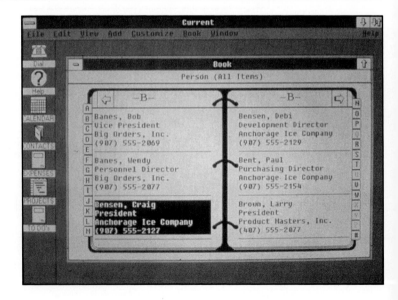

An office manager prepares a chart. *(Courtesy of International Business Machines Corporation)*

4. *Conclusion:* A comprehensive evaluation of the findings that results in new patterns or combinations of information when viewed as a whole.
5. *Recommendation:* The answer to the problem, based on the conclusion(s).

Letter reports. Letter reports are intended for persons outside the organization. Sometimes the content is similar to that in a **memorandum** (commonly called a *memo*), but because it is mailed to someone outside the firm, a letter format is used. Typically, letter reports are one to three pages long, are single spaced with double spacing between paragraphs, and include a date, inside address, salutation, body, complimentary closing, typed signature, and enclosure notations if appropriate.

Short reports. Short reports are prepared for use within the organization or may be sent to persons outside the firm. The problem under study is usually somewhat more complex than one that a memo or letter report could adequately address and thus requires more pages to fully explore. Most short reports are double spaced, with five- or ten-space indentations of paragraphs for easy reading; however, it is acceptable to use single spacing with double spacing between paragraphs. Short reports commonly contain five to ten pages in the body, preceded by a title page.

Long reports. Long reports differ from short reports primarily in length— eleven or more pages. They usually involve problems requiring considerable research that provides substantial amounts of data. Long reports typically use more graphic aids to supplement data than do other types of reports. Because of their length, the contents should be succinctly summarized in an abstract. Other prefatory pages are title page, letter of transmittal, table of contents, and a list of tables or other illustrations (if the document contains more than five). Most long reports are double spaced. Often they are bound, which means leaving a one-and-one-half-inch left margin.

In some companies, formal reports of all kinds must follow a preset format. In that case, you will simply do as you are instructed.

Package Longer Reports. *Packaging* means organizing and designing a report with a view toward image and desired impact. Completeness and a professional appearance are critical elements.

In addition to the body of the document, the following items can be included:

1. Title page containing the title and brief information about the report to aid cataloging and filing. The title you select should be brief and dignified. "Cute" titles give an unprofessional appearance. The title must also be attractively positioned on the page. Titles are usually centered and typed in all capitals or with initial capitals for all important words.
2. Authorizing statements, which show why a report was prepared.
3. Letter of transmittal made out to the person or organization receiving the report.
4. Table of contents indicating what the report contains.
5. Table of illustrations indicating where charts, graphs, tables, and illustrations appear.
6. Synopsis or summary (sometimes called an *abstract*) that presents a preview or review of the entire report in one page or less.
7. Appendix containing supporting material to which the reader can refer, including tables, graphics, letters, forms, and other items relevant to the report.
8. Bibliography identifying sources of material used in the preparation of the report. (Be sure to use a consistent and appropriate guide for the bibliography format.)
9. Index, if the report is very long.

Within the body of the document, you must be careful about your choice and design of subheads and the mechanics of quotations and references.

Subheads. The headings you use in your report will flag the various parts, such as the introduction, findings, or conclusion. But if your report is long and complicated, you may have to create **subheads** to divide the individual sections under each main heading. Make sure your subheads are specific enough to tell the reader at a glance what the section covers.

The use of subheads follows the rules of outlining, presented in the next section: Because subheads divide up a section, there must be two or more. If you have only one subhead in a section, you probably don't need it.

Quotations. If you use someone else's words, you must show whom you are quoting. Even if you footnote the passage, failure to indicate that you are using someone else's words is **plagiarism** and may lead to a lawsuit. It is not sufficient to change just one or two words, either. If the substance of the **quotation** remains the same, it still belongs to someone else. Unless you *completely* rephrase your source material, do not attempt to change it. Quote it exactly (except for certain allowable changes detailed below). There are two ways to do this:

1. *Use quotation marks.* If a quotation is fewer than four typed lines, type it in the body of your text and place quotation marks around it.
2. *Use a block quotation.* If a quotation is four or more lines long, indent it from the left margin (or from both margins), single-space it, and omit quotation marks.

Sometimes you will need to change a quotation slightly because it (1) is too long, (2) contains some reference the reader will not understand, or (3) does not fit grammatically with the material that introduces it. Use ellipses (. . .) to show that you have omitted text. Place brackets ([ ]) around changed or added words.

References. If you use someone else's ideas or data in a report, you must credit that person in some way. Failure to use **references,** like omitting quotation marks or a block indent when presenting words from another source, is plagiarism. In this case, it doesn't matter whether the material is quoted directly or is completely rephrased—it still belongs to someone else.

Every profession—doctors, engineers, English professors, lawyers, psychologists—has its preferred referencing standards. Find out your company's guidelines, and follow them carefully. If your company has not adopted a set of guidelines, you can choose a set from an accepted handbook. The use of a handbook will also help you to be consistent in your writing.

Outline Longer Reports. Outlining is an important part of writing effectively. Although this step may be less important when a writing a one- or two-page report, outlining written material for longer reports is crucial before starting to write a draft.

Outline written material more than three pages long before preparing a draft. Use either a sentence or topic outline to arrange the ideas in a logical order. By putting your material under carefully chosen headings and subheadings, you can test the strength and balance of your presentation and identify any omissions before you begin writing.

Following is the most common format for an outline:

I. Main idea
  A. Subtopic 1
    1. Sub-subtopic 1
    2. Sub-subtopic 2
      a.
      b.
  B. Subtopic 2
    1. Sub-subtopic 1
    2. Sub-subtopic 2
      a.
      b.

There should be two or more subtopics to justify the inclusion of subheadings. As you work with your outline, however, you will probably think of additional subtopics and can add them. Logically, if you want to divide up a section, you must divide it into at least two parts. This rule also holds for the use of subheads, as you will see shortly. In fact, you may want to use the subheadings from the outline subtopics.

Prepare Drafts. Writing becomes somewhat easier if you make a habit of composing drafts of all reports. By taking the time to prepare and polish a draft, you will enable your manager to contribute additional ideas before the report is in final form. Double or triple spacing and wide margins will make the draft easier to edit. The first edit should focus on seven problem areas common to all writing:

- Unusual, unfamiliar, or vague words or terms
- Cold, negative, or inappropriate words or terms
- Lengthy sentences with cumbersome words and phrases
- Excessive repetition of a word or phrase
- Poor transition between sentences or paragraphs
- Omission of facts
- Overuse of passive voice

Systematically Review and Revise. Systematically review and revise your work to sharpen both your argument and your style. Argument revision is best done at the outline stage and stylistic revision at the draft stage.

To review your ideas and points, ask the following questions:

- Is the main point of the report really its central focus, or have you digressed too much?
- Does every subheading of your outline relate directly to its main heading, or should it be placed elsewhere?

- Does each idea flow easily into the next?
- Are there sufficient reasons to support all arguments and opinions?
- Are generalizations backed up by specifics?
- Does your conclusion accurately sum up your argument? Does it tell your readers what they should do, expect, or think on the basis of that argument?

To review style, ask these questions:

- Are your sentences clear and simple?
- Have you used plain, clear words?
- Do verb forms agree in tense and number?
- Are all pronoun antecedents clear?
- Are all words necessary to your argument?
- Are you repeating words or ideas?
- Are your sentences as simple as possible without being repetitive?
- Have you used appropriate transitions between sentences and paragraphs?
- Have you used active voice whenever possible?

You may find it useful to keep both of these checklists available for use in reviewing all kinds of material that have been drafted and are ready for final typing.

Check for Details. Errors in fact or expression can spell disaster for otherwise well-conceptualized and carefully prepared documents. An important last step before marking "complete" on any document includes these three checks:

1. An accuracy check, especially of technical data and numbers
2. A consistency check so that statements or points on one page do not contradict those previously made and the meanings of words do not change from sentence to sentence

Leave a generous amount of white space when working on a rough draft of a report or graph. *(Courtesy of International Business Machines Corporation)*

3. A spelling and punctuation check, with special attention to unfamiliar terminology and commonly misspelled words

When making a consistency check, it is also important to check for "mechanical" consistency. Do you always indent your numbered lists? Are your figure titles printed in all caps, initial caps, or caps at the beginning of each important word? Do all list items end with a period or only those that form complete sentences? If you hyphenate a word on one page, do you hyphenate it on the next? Is a particular term always capitalized?

Be Alert for Common Mistakes. There are some mistakes that everyone is likely to make. Others are unique to the individual manager or the topics being addressed. An office professional alert to both types of mistakes performs a valuable service by catching errors that frequently go undetected. The most common types of errors include improper use of commas and apostrophes; spelling errors resulting from similar-sounding words (*affect/effect, council/counsel, principal/principle*); and suffixes and prefixes applied incorrectly.

Typing the Report

When typing the final draft of the report, use the following guidelines:

1. Observe the rules of good manuscript form.
   a. Use 8½″ × 11″ paper unless instructed otherwise.
   b. Use double spacing (except for quotations four or more lines long, which should be indented and single spaced in a block). Some managers prefer reports to be single-spaced with double spacing between paragraphs; check for preferences.
   c. Leave margins of at least 1 inch at the tops, bottoms, and sides of all pages; a 2-inch top margin on the first page; and, if the report is to be bound, a 1½-inch margin at the left side of all pages.
   d. Prepare at least one additional photocopy. If the document has been stored in a computer, include the file name under which it is located at the end of the report.
   e. Number all pages except the first in the upper right-hand corner (assuming the report is bound at the left side).
2. Use variety in paragraphing. Avoid too many long paragraphs.
3. Be generous in the use of headings (leave plenty of white space around major headings, tables, and other displayed materials). Use parallel construction in the wording of headings.
4. Use **footnotes** to give credit to the ideas of others. Footnotes may be placed at the bottom of each page or at the end of each chapter; in the latter case, they are called **endnotes**.
5. Select tables, charts, graphs, or other illustrative materials used to supplement the writing carefully.
6. Bind the report attractively in a special report folder.

Problems in Preparing Reports

The most basic problem in preparing a report is finding sufficient time to get the job done correctly. When you must scramble frantically to meet a deadline, you are bound to make some type of error. Proper time management (see Chapter 9) is therefore crucial to the successful completion of assignments and to the reduction of needless tension.

Insufficient time often results in lack of clarity. Both you and your manager can be guilty of failing to spell out the importance, intent, or even the major points of a "rush" report. A busy manager doesn't provide the needed information; an equally busy assistant doesn't ask. Planning to take time for questions, outlining, and reviewing can reduce errors and anxiety.

A second problem is the lack of a system—realistic procedures that point out how similar assignments were finished in the past. Specific directions for completing both long and short tasks should be included in a job manual, along with possible problems and sources of assistance. These directions should be updated as new assignments present new problems.

A third problem is failure to follow directions. Local, state, and federal agencies may require specific information presented in defined ways in both reports and proposals. Directions may range from the correct information to include in the cover page to what to include in an appendix. Some requirements will seem logical and others pointless. Nevertheless, all must be followed correctly, or revisions and delays will be required.

Your manager may make errors that you will need to anticipate. The office professional who is alert to these problems provides a valuable aid to management by anticipating and preventing errors.

The Importance of Proofreading

When you have completed all report preparation steps successfully, one important task remains: **proofreading**. If this vital task is not done properly, the report can be a disaster. Proofreading is an essential step in preparing correspondence as well.

Error correction "after the fact" is always more costly and time consuming than careful proofreading during the preparation process. In today's technology-oriented office, proofreading is more important than ever. High-speed message transmissions, for example, like incorrect billings on a computer, tend to "institutionalize" errors. For this reason, a consistent and methodical approach to proofreading is essential.

The proofreading process should provide not only error correction in the present but error prevention for the future. Use your proofreading responsibilities to make yourself aware of mistakes or difficulties that occurred in the document's preparation. Also, try to determine the causes of errors, such as poor-quality dictation; unclear handwriting; insufficient time to do the job right the first time; constant alterations resulting in contradictory statements; and/or last-minute information that had to be squeezed into the report. This will give you the opportunity to acquaint your manager with potential and actual problems, changed procedures, or good habits that should be encouraged.

A Proofreading System

- Proofread documents while they are still in the typewriter or word processor.
- Proofread important documents more than once. Read the first time for grammar and sense. Then read the second time, sometimes backwards (last sentence first), for typographical errors. You might wish to do the second proofreading a day later.
- Don't assume that common parts of a letter are automatically typed correctly. Pay attention to dates, inside addresses, salutations, and signature lines as well as to the body of the letter.
- Check all tables, charts, and other illustrations against the original copy. If the material has been typed across the page, proofread down the columns.
- When proofreading technical material, place a ruler under each line as you scan.
- Have two people proofread complicated and/or very important documents, one reading the final draft and the other checking it against the original copy.
- Always look in the dictionary for spellings of which you're unsure.
- Take an overall look at the document for margins, consistency of capitalization, and placement of headings.
- Protect final copy from smudges or smears by keeping it in a folder with the top page turned over or by placing a blank sheet on top of it.
- Develop a form on which to note corrections. This eliminates the need to make corrections on the final copy.
- Prepare a list of the most commonly used proofreader's marks (see Figure 11–14). Share that list with all users to encourage a common correction "language."
- Make sure your corrections are clear so that you will not introduce new errors.
- Don't try to proofread when you're confused, tired, subject to constant interruptions, or worried about other duties.

SUMMARY

One of your most important responsibilities will be to prepare effective letters and memos. The most important guidelines for ensuring impressive correspondence include

- Attractiveness: Make the reader's first impression favorable.
- Completeness: Fill in the who, what, where, when, why, and how.
- Conciseness: Use simple words; avoid outdated expressions.

Figure 11–14
Proofreader's marks.

Mark	Meaning	Example
≡	Make a capital letter	see her
/	Make a capital letter small	To give him
∧	Insert word	to give him
—	Omit word	to give him
stet	No, don't omit	to give him
\	Omit stroke	too give him
=	Insert a hyphen	full size
#	Insert a space	togive him
⌒	Omit the space	7 p. m.
⊐	Move as indicated	see her
2⊐	Indent ___ spaces	To give him
═	Line up, even up	TO: Mary / So be it
‖	Line up, even up	so be it / so it be
ss ⌈	Use single spacing	
↶	Turn around	
ds ⌈	Use double spacing	to give him / so be it
___	Italicize this	
⋁	Raise above line	EC2
¶	New paragraph	So be it
○	Make into period	see her
◯	Don't abbreviate	Mr. Jones
⌒	Spell it out	5 or 6 apples

- Clarity: Make sure your message will be clear on the first reading.
- Courtesy: Use the "you" approach—think of the reader first.
- Positive tone: Use positive rather than negative words.
- Effective beginnings and endings: Make opening paragraphs capture the reader's attention; use strong endings to close the letter.

The three basic methods of organizing a message are direct or deductive, indirect or inductive, and persuasive or sales. Good-news and routine messages use the direct arrangement; bad-news messages use the indirect format; and persuasive messages use the AIDCA (attention, interest, desire, conviction, action) formula.

You will also be responsible for preparing reports. There are four basic types of reports: memo, letter, short, and long reports. Regardless of the type, all reports require two basic steps.

The first step is identification of purpose. The audience to be addressed and the information they require must be clear to the manager and the assistant alike. Once the purpose of the work is clear, it will be easier to determine the amount of time needed to produce an excellent report.

The second step is research. The research process should be limited to gathering the facts necessary to prepare the report. Seven organizing procedures will help improve efficiency in this area:

1. Define the "researchable" problem.
2. Organize the information collection process.
3. Locate sources of information.
4. Collect data.
5. Record information for easy use and reuse.
6. Rough out the data into the draft report format.
7. Note items for future use.

You can prepare written reports more easily if you follow these rules:

1. Write to a target audience.
2. Choose the appropriate report format.
3. Package longer reports.
4. Outline longer reports.
5. Prepare drafts.
6. Systematically review and revise.
7. Check for details.
8. Be alert to common mistakes.

The final step in both letter and report writing is proofreading—several times. At this point, you can identify consistent mistakes and suggest improvements to your manager. Record both problems and solutions for future reference.

Key Terms

The following terms appeared in boldface type in this chapter. Do you recall what they mean? For a more complete definition, turn to the glossary beginning on p. 442.

AIDCA formula (p. 240)
analytical (research) report (p. 245)
cliché (p. 233)
deductive approach (p. 239)
endnote (p. 256)
examinational (interpretive) report (p. 245)
five *W*s and one *H* (p. 230)
footnote (p. 256)
goodwill message (p. 239)
inductive approach (p. 240)
informational message (p. 239)
informational report (p. 245)
interpret (p. 244)

memorandum (p. 251)
persuasive (sales) message (p. 240)
plagiarism (p. 253)
proofreading (p. 257)
quotation (p. 253)
recommendation (p. 244)
reference (p. 253)
research (p. 245)
routine message (p. 239)
subhead (p. 253)
tone (p. 232)
typographical error (p. 230)
validate (p. 248)
"you" approach (p. 232)

Discussion Questions

1. You are program chairperson for the annual awards banquet of Future Business and Professional Women of America. All of the members want the feature speaker to be Ann Holmes, a local author who has just written a book titled *Workforce Dynamics*. The book is enjoyable to read and contains motivating ideas on how to prepare to succeed in the twenty-first century. Draft a letter to Ms. Holmes using the "you" approach to win her enthusiasm about speaking at the banquet.

2. Your manager has asked you to compose a letter using the block style. The letter will go to Dennis St. John and will include the following information:
   a. The material arrived on schedule.
   b. Two boxes of envelopes were damaged.
   c. The invoice was totaled incorrectly.
   d. One ream of special forms was missing.
   e. Replacements are needed soon.

   How would you arrange this material for easy reading and to obtain quick action? Draft a letter.

3. Indicate what salutation you would use for the following. (Consult a secretarial handbook or one of the references listed on pages 264–266 for guidance.)

   a. Sales Manager
      Johnson Industries
      45 S. National Avenue
      Fond du Lac, WI 54935

   b. Members (all are women)
      City Garden Club
      Sacramento, CA 99734

   c. Mrs. Phyllis Mayfield
      Smith, Jones, & Murphy
      Attorneys-at-Law
      P.O. Box 806
      Huntington, WV 25755

   d. *News Gazette*
      Box 5679
      2300 Adams Avenue
      Dunmore, PA 18509

   e. Mesa Public Schools
      2218 E. Frye Road
      Chandler, AZ 85225
      Attention: Mrs. Cynthia Donaldson

   f. Mr. John Joneway
      3817 Hillsborough Street
      Raleigh, NC 27607
      (Subject: Future Plans)

   g. Mrs. Anabelle Vincente
      617 S.W. 27 Avenue
      Miami, FL 33135

   h. François Boucharde
      33 Rue de la Reine-Marie
      Montreal, Quebec 134U1A2
      (Subject: Case 456)

   i. General Electric
      1228 North State Street
      Jackson, MS 39202-2002
      Attention: Mr. Steve Pate

   j. J. M. Artez Company
      210 N. Main Street
      Hudson, OH 44136
      Attention: Mr. John Plotner

4. Your company prints calendars for home and business use. Your managers regularly want information from public and private agencies to include on the calendars. Most of the information is free; occasionally

there is a small charge or a return stamped envelope must be enclosed. What elements would you include in a form letter? Draft a form letter.

5. You have been invited to a leadership conference in Omaha but can't attend because of class and work responsibilities. How would you politely turn down the organizers of the conference? The conference is held annually, and you want to be invited again. Draft a letter.

6. Six students in your class want to observe the word processing center at the local telephone company office and talk with operators. The manager of the center generally doesn't allow visitors. How would you persuade this manager to allow a visit to the center? Draft a letter.

7. Your manager has agreed to chair a local charitable drive. He wants to appeal to the twenty largest businesses in the city. How would you find out
   a. Their names and locations?
   b. The names of their chief executive officers?
   c. How much they have given to other charities and which ones they favor?

   Consult the list of reference sources on pages 264–266 as a starting point. Be creative in finding places where information may be just a phone call away.

8. A month ago, your managers asked you to look into various word processing systems and write a draft recommendation for purchase. You read information from various vendors. You saw three systems in operation and talked with office professionals who used them. The salespeople for these systems reviewed each system and answered your questions. One system, Excel-Quick, seems best for your office. What outline form would you follow, and what items would you include in the draft recommendation?

9. Security has been a continuing problem in your office because of client traffic and access to the general public. One manager for whom you work has been placed in charge of a group to reduce the theft, vandalism, and general disruption caused by this situation. A good deal of progress has been made, and the manager is to outline a briefing to senior management. Your assistance has been requested. The main points to be made include the following:
   a. Thefts have been reduced by nearly 40 percent since the effort began six months ago.
   b. A three-point control program has been responsible for the success: file locks, a requirement that visitors sign in and out, and strategic placement of security guards.
   c. An educational program is needed for employees to emphasize the importance of continued cooperation.

   Suggest methods for making these three points that will grab and hold the senior managers' attention.

1. Find examples of as many messages or letters as you can that illustrate the goodwill, good-news, and bad-news formats for business letters. (Avoid the persuasive or sales form of letter at this time.) Analyze these communications and make suggestions for needed improvements. Consider both their organization and the seven tests of a good letter. Identify specific changes you believe should be made.

2. The following library research projects are designed to increase your familiarity with the valuable support the library can provide.
   a. Develop a bibliography on one of the following topics, with an equal mix of books published since 1980 and articles in at least three office-related publications published since 1985.
      1) Word processing
      2) Micrographics
      3) Information retrieval
   b. Locate sources of statistical information on the following topics:
      1) Postal rates for sending material to locations in the United States, Canada, and Mexico
      2) Population trends in your state and in surrounding states
      3) Trends in the cost of preparing letters
   c. Find out where biographical information can be obtained on the following:
      1) The current chief executive officers of Xerox, IBM, and ITT
      2) The mayor of your city and governor of your state
   d. Find out where to look for the following miscellaneous data:
      1) Subscription rates to *Business Week, Administrative Management,* and *The Wall Street Journal*
      2) Win and loss records over a five-year period for major league baseball teams
      3) Predictions on employment trends in Michigan for the next two years

3. You are requested to find the following information. Prepare a list of answers and sources of information.
   a. Your manager has this address — 1303 East Oak Street — and needs the phone number. Get the company name and phone number.
   b. What is the address of the national headquarters of Kiwanis International? What is the total membership?
   c. What was the population of New Orleans at the last official census?
   d. Who is the Illinois regional manager of the Interstate Commerce Commission?
   e. What are the total circulation and the advertising rate for color and black-and-white ads in *Fortune*?
   f. What is the annual crude petroleum production of Alaska?
   g. What products are manufactured by A. E. Staley Company, Decatur, Illinois?

h. Who said, "The man who makes no mistakes does not usually make anything?"
i. Owen Tucker used *S.J.* after his name as author of a magazine article. What do those letters stand for?
j. Corporal Carlos J. Oliveros sometimes uses *CPL* in abbreviating his title and sometimes *corp.* Which is right?
k. You work for an automobile agency that sells imported English cars. In the instruction manual for these cars, the word *bonnet* frequently appears. What does this word mean?
l. What do the middle initials stand for in the name *Samuel F. B. Morse?*
m. What state has for its motto *sic semper tyrannis?* What is the meaning of *chacun à son goût?* (In typing foreign words and phrases, be sure to add the accents in pen if the typewriter doesn't have these characters.)
n. Your manager has a phone number (422-1765) and can't remember whose it is. Find the listing.
o. What are your U.S. representative's local and Washington office addresses?
p. Your manager has just ordered one *fanega* of grain from Mexico. How many bushels of grain would that be?
q. Your manager got a letter from Idfu. Where is this city?
r. Who makes Mounds candy bars? What is the company's address?
s. Your manager asks you about a stock listed on the New York Stock Exchange, Wal-Mart. Find the national address of this corporation.
t. Last night your manager saw a television ad for Fargo trucks. What company manufactures Fargo trucks?
u. Your manager asks you to find out the name of the fashion editor of the *Chicago Sun-Times.*
v. Your manager has heard about a magazine called *Australia Now* and wants to subscribe to it. Find the address.
w. Your manager has heard about British Petroleum buying out Standard Oil of Ohio. Locate an article that will give him or her more information about the buyout.
x. Your manager wants to find recent periodical articles about electronic point-of-sale systems. How can you find these articles?

Here are the references you will need to consult to answer these questions:

Who's Who Biographical Directory (Biographies of notable living men and women)

Encyclopedia of Associations

The World Almanac (Contains many pages of statistics and facts, preceded by an excellent index. Covers stock and bond markets; notable events; political and financial statistics of states and cities; statistics on population, farm crops, prices, trade, and commerce; educational data; and information on the postal services)

Statistical Abstract of the United States (Published yearly; provides summary statistics about area and population, vital statistics, education, climate, employment, military affairs, social security, income, prices, banking, transportation, agriculture, forests, fisheries, mining, manufacturers, and related areas)

U.S. Government Manual (The official handbook of the federal government; provides information on the purposes and programs of most government agencies and lists those agencies' top personnel)

Ayer's Dictionary of Newspapers and Periodicals (Provides information such as name of publication, editor, publisher, date established, technical data, and geographic area served in the United States)

The Statesman's Yearbook (Provides factual and statistical information on countries of the world, including type of government, area and population, religion, education, justice, defense, commerce and industry, and finance)

Thomas Register of American Manufacturers (Lists all businesses engaged in wholesale manufacturing)

The Oxford Dictionary of Quotations

Webster's New Collegiate Dictionary

Dictionary of Foreign Phrases and Abbreviations

Dictionary of Foreign Words and Phrases

Acronyms, Initialisms, and Abbreviations Dictionary

Who Was Who in America

The Macmillan Book of Proverbs, Maxims, and Famous Phrases

Trade Names Directory (A guide to common trade names, brand names, product names, coined names, model names, and design names, with addresses of their manufacturers, importers, marketers, or distributors)

Webster's New Geographic Dictionary (A quick-reference source of essential geographical information)

Standard City Directory (Includes buyer's guide and classified business directory, alphabetical directory, street directory of householders and businesses, numerical telephone directory)

Congressional Staff Directory (Publishes the names of staff personnel of members of Congress in Washington and those serving on committees and subcommittees)

For Good Measure (A complete compendium of international weights and measures)

Million Dollar Directory. Dun's Marketing Service, 1990. (Names and addresses of corporations with yearly sales of over one million dollars)

1990 Editor and Publisher International Yearbook (The encyclopedia of the newspaper industry)

The Television Sponsors Product Cross-Reference Directory

Ulrich's International Periodical Directory (A classified list of national and international periodicals)

Reader's Guide to Periodical Literature (Subject and author indexes of periodicals of general interest)

Business Periodical Index
The 1990 Dow Jones–Irwin Business Almanac
The Europa Year Book (1990)

In addition to these directories, you should have one that lists major national and international corporations. Dun & Bradstreet and Standard & Poor's Corporation publish major directories annually.

 Those instructors using *Top Performance: A Decision-Making Simulation for the Office* should consult the *Instructor's Guide* at this point for support material regarding use of the software in the classroom.

Case Study

If ever opposites worked together, it was Ann Burrell and Nina Abruzzi, assistant and manager, respectively. Ann preferred neatness, order, and clarity. Nina resisted all of those conditions; she believed that creativity and spontaneity were hindered by too much rigidity.

The two women genuinely liked each other. Each felt their differences were complementary to some extent. In most areas there was some tension, but eventually they reached satisfactory agreements. Preparing reports was the one exception. It was a constant source of irritation to Ann, who could work well only when she had clear directions to follow. In contrast, too much careful organization and systematic preplanning made Nina feel rushed and restricted.

As in most situations, neither person is completely right or wrong. There are benefits to Ann's organization and Nina's flexibility. A middle ground is desirable, but it will be difficult, and perhaps impossible, to reach.

How might the difficulty these two individuals face be tempered? The initiative will probably have to come from Ann and could take the form of time management suggestions and the complementary use of conflicting styles. (Keep in mind that Ann would have to make these suggestions tactfully and constructively rather than critically.) Based on material presented in this and earlier chapters, What could Ann suggest to Nina concerning the importance of allowing more time to complete reports? When and how should she make these suggestions? How can Ann's organizational tendencies be used to best advantage and still allow for creativity?

CHAPTER
12
COPYING MATERIAL

Chapter Objectives

- To know about the available types of copying equipment

- To learn how to use duplicating equipment and services

- To understand how copying costs can be controlled

- To become familiar with copyright rules

- To learn about types of binding

Examples of Excellence

When the regional manager awarded Lydia Bienvenu a $1,000 bonus, he emphasized that her "plan" would save the office at least $10,000 per year in copier costs. "Lydia learned what copying should be done on our convenience copier and the services our duplicating department offers to produce more impressive-looking material," he added.

In her first full-time position since completing an office management course, Lydia took the time to read instructions on operating the copier and to talk with the service representative. She found out about the convenience copier's capabilities, common user problems, and times when sending material to the duplicating department would be more cost effective. From this information, she developed a plan for duplicating office documents that resulted in a substantial cost reduction.

In a recent television commercial, a harried clerk brings one version after another of a major report to a staff meeting as each manager suggests that different parts be reduced, enlarged, presented in color, or moved to another section. Not long ago, producing copies was difficult and time consuming and fewer options were available. Now that copying has become easier, the amount of paper produced has increased. However, uncontrolled copier use can be a large and recurring cost.

Reprographics—the process of duplicating materials—ranges from relying on a single desktop copier to using a large in-house duplicating department. When reprographics is effectively organized, paper flows smoothly and economically.

In this chapter, you will learn

- Why copying has become easy yet expensive
- What copying equipment will be available to you
- How to use duplicating equipment and services effectively
- Which copier control methods will reduce costs
- What copyright regulations must be followed
- How binding can make documents look more professional

A Rapid Evolution

Throughout the Middle Ages, monks laboriously hand-copied the Bible. When the printing press was invented, only single copies could be printed. As office equipment evolved, office professionals made multiple copies of a letter or memo with carbon paper and had to correct mistakes on every copy. When spirit and stencil duplicators arrived, assistants were able to type a document once and then make several hundred copies. However, the process was messy.

Today's quick, clean photocopying equipment allows offices of all sizes to copy hand- or typewritten documents easily. Each new model offers additional features, such as automatic document feed, two-sided copying, reduction capability, color options, collating, and stapling. But because these machines are simple and fast, many offices make more copies of letters, memos, and reports than are needed. You can help your organization hold down unnecessary costs by keeping up with the changes and advances in reprographic technology and by putting some controls in place.

Basic Copying Equipment

Because photocopying costs have declined and equipment rental agreements are available, most offices have basic photocopiers. These machines may range from small desktop models to large, multioption copiers.

You may also have access to spirit or stencil duplicators. **Spirit duplicators** require a master and a moistening solution to produce copies. The master set

A desktop copier is ideal for small jobs. *(Courtesy of Packard Bell)*

A large-volume copier such as this is suitable for monthly output of 75,000 to 500,000 copies. *(Courtesy of Eastman Kodak)*

consists of a top white sheet and a second sheet of carbon dye. Once the master is prepared, the two sheets are separated and the sheet with the carbon image is attached to the master cylinder of the spirit machine. Blank sheets of paper are moistened in the spirit solution and then pressed against the master. The surface of the moistened paper absorbs a small portion of the carbon dye from the master, and the negative or mirror image on the master becomes a positive image on the sheet of paper. Spirit duplicators are used more for their economy than for the quality of the images they produce.

Stencil duplicators, also known as *mimeograph duplicators,* produce copies from a plastic-coated sheet called a *stencil.* As you type on the stencil sheet, the letters are cut into the plastic coating and create a path through which ink flows. When the stencil is completed, it is mounted on the machine's cylinder. A single-cylinder stencil contains an inking pad. A dual-cylinder stencil is fastened onto an inking screen belt supported by two cylinders. Ink is transferred from the pad or belt through the holes in the stencil and onto the paper, which is pressed against the master. Up to several thousand copies can be run from one stencil. The copies generally look better than those produced on a spirit duplicator.

Spirit and stencil duplicators are somewhat outdated. However, many churches, schools, and service organizations continue to use them.

Some small organizations use **convenience copiers.** These machines are easy to use, but they permit only minimal daily usage, often under five thousand copies per month. Some use coated paper, but newer models reproduce on plain paper. Some convenience copiers are small enough to fit on a desk- or tabletop. Smaller-capacity models make only single copies at a time.

Many large organizations have high-speed copier/duplicators that can print up to one hundred copies at a time. Some models also collate, reduce, **duplex** (print on both sides of a page), and lighten or darken a document. Most have automatic paper-feeding options, and some newer models have color features. Three other convenience features include **interruption,** which enables a job to be stopped temporarily in an emergency; **return-to-position,** which returns all controls to the first position when the job is completed; and a **recirculating document feeder,** which feeds originals from a stack to the exposure glass and brings them back to the feed tray for another copy run of the set.

Today, organizations generally use plain-paper rather than coated-paper copiers. Copies more closely resemble the originals, letterhead stationery can be used, operation is easy, and supplies are readily available.

The control panel contains the keys for selecting a particular job's options and the number of copies to be made. Figure 12–1 shows a typical copier control panel.

You may also have access to special copy machines. **Color copiers** are especially useful for duplicating charts, drawings, maps, and other graphic material. **Fiber optic copiers** are lighter and smaller, require less maintenance, and consume less energy. Fiber optic filaments transmit light to form an image and can produce smaller-size copies. **Intelligent printers** are linked to text-editing typewriters and produce high-quality copies of text on a VDT (video display terminal) screen; you can print as many copies as needed.

This desktop model makes copies on plain paper. *(Courtesy of Canon USA, Inc.)*

Many organizations now have equipment that supplements the work of copiers and duplicators. You might find the following in your word processing center:

- **Headliners** create display type for headlines, subheads, and similar items that require large type, one letter at a time.

This copier can print eighty copies per minute. *(Courtesy of Canon USA, Inc.)*

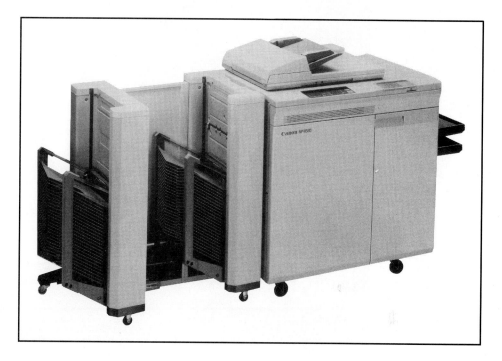

Figure 12–1

Copier control panel. *(Courtesy of Canon USA, Inc.)*

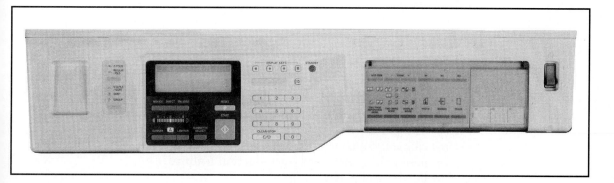

This copier can reproduce documents in full color at twenty-three copies per minute. *(Courtesy of Eastman Kodak)*

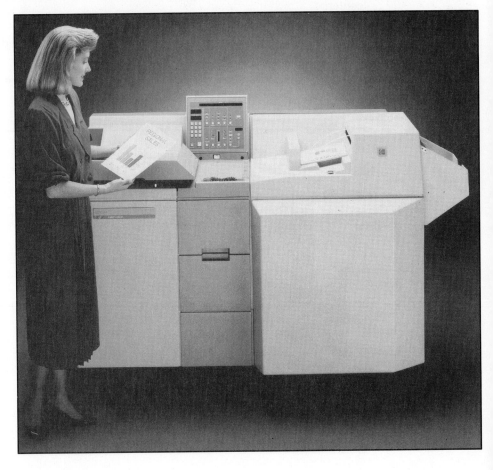

- **Composers** transform typewritten copy into the kind of print found in magazines and newspapers. These machines have a regular typewriter keyboard and allow you to interchange type styles and sizes.
- **Phototypesetters** transform typewritten words into print, with various typefaces and spacing.

Regardless of how sophisticated your organization's copying equipment is, you need answers to the following questions before you make copies:

1. How do you insert originals into the copier and start the copying process?
2. In what ways can you feed documents into the machine automatically?
3. How can you copy on both sides?
4. How can you collate a document?
5. Are there enlargement and/or reduction features?
6. How do you add paper?

7. What problems might you encounter? Is there a designated person who can help (a key operator)?

With experience, you may become a **key operator,** an employee trained to handle certain copying responsibilities. These tasks include changing paper rolls and cassettes, adding paper, adding toner and developer (the liquid needed to make copies), and clearing up paper jams. A representative of the manufacturer or a more experienced employee will show you how to perform these functions. Most machines today allow you to identify problems quickly and easily.

Binding Equipment

Businesses spend significant amounts of time and money to make documents look polished and professional. A final touch that creates a favorable impression is packaging documents with a binding system. The most common systems use spiral binding, velo-binding, and thermal binding. All require special equipment.

Spiral binding uses a plastic comb or a wire thread that fits through machine-punched rectangular holes in the pages you want held together. Pages bound in this way can be easily removed. However, they can be applied to only one document at a time, which makes spiral binding a labor-intensive and relatively expensive process.

Velo-binding has two plastic strips. One strip has teeth that are threaded through the document pages; the other has holes that hold the teeth tightly and keep the pages together. Two disadvantages of velo-binding are that open documents cannot stay flat and alterations are difficult to make once this binding has been applied.

Thermal binding produces a very professional finish; it looks like the binding on books. The pages are placed inside a folder that has a strip of glue along the inside of its spine. A machine binds the pages by melting the glue. Pages bound in this way are held very securely. Also, because this system can bind several documents at a time, substantial time savings can be realized.

Bound documents project a professional image to clients. With a well-designed cover, your bound documents will have greater impact and make an impression that translates into success.

Paper Care

Copying paper should be kept in a location with a stable temperature. Be sure to insert paper in the machine correctly; load it in the "up" position to prevent jamming, and ruffle it to free sticking pages.

Advanced Developments

You are likely to see computer copier/printer connections in many organizations. With computer networks connected to laser printers, you can make a single copy of a letter or memo and/or transmit that document to a printer, where multiple copies can be made at high speed.

Documents can be sent to a printer at distant locations as well. This is especially useful for sending material to teleconferences at multiple sites.

Documents, transparencies, and other material can be stored in a computer's memory. Each can be retrieved to revise items or make additional copies. Vendors and users call the technology *intelligent* or *smart copiers*. Using the same structure as word processing software, you can instruct a copier to personalize letters to one thousand individuals, merge material from several sources, and indicate how to locate a final document. This technology is very expensive and more likely to be found only in the duplicating or reprographic units of large organizations.

Preparing Transparencies

With most copiers, you will be able to prepare **transparencies** for projecting on a screen with an overhead projector. With a transparency, typed or handwritten copy can be placed on a transparent sheet. To prepare transparencies with a copier, you must use a special film prepared for plain-paper copies. You can purchase this film from office supply companies.

Centralized Copying Facilities

Some large organizations have **centralized copying facilities**. These units are equipped with high-speed machines capable of copying large jobs economically.

If a centralized unit is available, you will need to follow certain procedures to take advantage of the services such a facility provides. These include

- Providing material the required number of days in advance to meet your schedule
- Specifying how material is to be prepared, including collating, stapling, or double-sided copying if needed
- Identifying the type of paper to be used
- Supplying the budget account number

Figure 12–2 contains a sample work request form. This form may be used to submit work to a word processing center as well.

Occasionally you will need a rush job. In that case, it is best to ask the head of the copying unit for special help. If you have unexpected rush work beyond the capability of your convenience copier or if the in-house center can't accommodate your request, you may need to use an outside copying service. In all cases, you should prepare **camera-ready copy**—material that can be photographed for reproduction.

Figure 12–2

Sample work request form.

JOB REQUEST			
Title/Description _Business Law_		Job Number/Account Number _0-02-654875-3_	
Work Submitted by: _Paul Conrad_		Date Submitted _1/11/91_	Time Submitted _11:00 a.m._
Telephone _X3650_	Department _Business_	No. of Pages _52_	Date Required _1/13/91_ / Time Required _8:00 a.m._

(Note: Items marked "ASAP" are given LOW priority.)

DESCRIPTION OF WORK

INPUT	OUTPUT	CHARACTER COUNT/MARGINS	TYPE STYLE
( ) Handwritten	(✓) Camera-Ready	_65_	_Times Roman_
(✓) Typewritten	( ) Final Draft		
( ) Dictated	( ) Corrections		
( ) Other_____	( ) Rough Draft		
	( ) Other_____		

PAPER	TYPE SIZE	LINE SPACE	COPIES
( ) Letterhead	( ) 10-pitch	( ) Single	( ) Originals _____
( ) Memorandum	(✓) 12-pitch	( ) 1-1/2	(✓) Photocopy _7_ copies
(✓) Plain Bond	( ) Variable	(✓) Double	(✓) 1-sided
( ) Labels		( ) Triple	( ) 2-sided
( ) Other_____		( ) Other_____	( ) _____

Special Instructions _____
_____

• •

Date/Time Received _1/11/91 - 11:00 a.m._ Date/Time Due Out _1/13/91 - 8 a.m._

Priority Code: ( ) RUSH (Same Day) ( ) Within 24 hours (✓) Within 48 hours

Assigned to: _Kris Patton_   Supervisor/Coordinator's Initials _SnD_

Date/Time Completed _1/13/91 - 8 a.m._ No. Hours _45_

Total Units Produced _59 Pages_   Errors _10_

Work   Acceptable ☑   Unacceptable ☐   Comments: _____
_____

Proofreader's Signoff _ATM_   Supervisor's Signoff _SnD_

A centralized copying facility is likely to offer one or more of the following duplicating processes. **Offset duplication** or **multilith** involves making a master plate of the document to be reproduced. Photographs, typed or handwritten pages, and drawings can be reproduced accurately and economically using offset processes.

Copy Control Methods

Four common problems raise copying costs: nonbusiness, or personal, copying; unnecessary copying of documents that could be reproduced more economically; copying documents when offset printing would be less expensive; and making more copies than are needed.

In some organizations, a central copying facility does all copying and charges every copy to a specific account. Some offices keep logs; however, this isn't a very accurate method.

Certain machines have built-in limits on the number of copies that can be made on each job. Some centers have separate control panels—one for routine use and another for more complicated jobs.

Some copiers provide memory keys, which allow you to program into the machine's memory the two ratios most frequently used to enlarge or reduce documents by a specified percentage; you can then recall these ratios simply by touching the memory key. Another feature gaining in popularity is the automatic production of same-size copies from a stack of originals of varying sizes.

Another method of controlling the use of a copier is to place one person in charge of approving all materials to be duplicated. Individual copy keys (which resemble small plastic cards) can be given to employees with duplicating needs. The copy machine will record the number of copies made with each key. Such monitoring of individual use may discourage employees from making extra copies or copying unauthorized materials.

Before deciding to use a convenience copier or a copier in a centralized facility, you should consider the following:

- If fewer than 50 originals are involved, a convenience copier is the fastest, most cost-effective method.
- When more than 50 originals but fewer than 250 are to be made, a high-speed in-organization copier or one at a private shop is most cost effective.
- When more than 250 originals are involved, an offset method is best; the more copies made, the lower the per-sheet cost.
- For reproduction of lengthy reports, an in-organization duplicating unit, if available, or an outside shop may provide items such as ring binders, laminated cover pages, and colored divider pages.
- If you are to reproduce a lengthy document, consider your time, wear on the machine, and inconvenience to those waiting.

Copyright Regulations

Because you will be responsible for preparing copies of business documents, it is important that you familiarize yourself with what can and cannot be legally copied. **Copyright** is the legal right of authors and artists to protect their work against unauthorized reproduction. The current U.S. copyright law, revised most recently in 1978, follows international standards that extend copyright privileges for fifty years beyond the author's or artist's death. All copyrighted material contains a notice of copyright. This consists of either the word *copyright*, the abbreviation *copr.*, or the symbol V, accompanied by the copyright holder's name and date of publication. Whenever substantial portions of documents protected by copyright are to be copied for distribution, you must obtain the copyright holders' permission. A valuable aid is the Copyright Information Kit, which you can obtain free of charge from the Copyright Office, Library of Congress, Washington, DC 20559.

Communication Tips

It is important to find out the following information to make intelligent choices about photocopying:

- Ask questions about your office's copying procedures and regulations.
- Find out about special features of and possible problems in operating your office's convenience copiers.
- Discuss special requests for copying jobs with the duplicating unit of your organization to determine what services it can offer.
- Ask sales and service representatives about a copier's special features and the care necessary to maintain smooth operation.
- Fill out work request forms correctly the first time so that jobs will be done as desired and on schedule.
- Keep a log of any difficulties encountered, the dates, and how the problems were handled.

SUMMARY

Because copying documents has become easy but expensive, you should select the most economical and effective equipment for each duplicating job. In most offices, you will have access to convenience photocopiers. Some models will have features such as collating, double-sided copying, and reduction.

You may act as a key operator, an employee responsible for copier maintenance tasks such as changing paper and clearing up paper jams. Larger organizations have established in-house duplicating units equipped with high-speed copiers, offset printing equipment, and perhaps spirit and stencil duplicators. Large copying jobs should be sent to these centralized units.

Binding adds a professional finish to documents. Bound documents create greater impact and convey the importance of the material to others.

Paying attention to copy control is always important. Common cost-raising factors include copying for personal use, copying instead of reproducing by more economical methods, and making more copies than are needed. It is also important to heed copyright regulations.

Key Terms

The following terms appeared in boldface type in this chapter. Do you recall what they mean? For a more complete definition, turn to the glossary beginning on p. 442.

camera-ready copy (p. 274)
centralized copying facility (p. 274)
color copier (p. 270)
composer (p. 272)

convenience copier (p. 269)
copyright (p. 276)
duplex (p. 270)
fiber optic copier (p. 270)

headliner (p. 271)
intelligent printer (p. 270)
interruption (p. 270)
key operator (p. 273)
offset duplication (multilith) (p. 275)
phototypesetter (p. 272)
recirculating document feeder (p. 270)
reprographics (p. 267)

return-to-position (p. 270)
spiral binding (p. 273)
spirit duplicator (p. 268)
stencil duplicator (p. 269)
thermal binding (p. 273)
transparency (p. 274)
velo-binding (p. 273)

Discussion Questions

1. Which of the following would you copy in your office? Which would you send to a centralized copying facility?
   a. Confidential salary recommendations on ten employees
   b. Thirty-page annual financial report for a six-person staff meeting
   c. Five-page magazine article going to twenty staff members
   d. Fifty copies of a two-page meeting agenda
2. What special features of a convenience copier or larger machine could help you control the number of copies you make?
3. What steps should you take to use the services of a central duplicating unit to ensure that the output is exactly what you want?
4. How would you respond to a person who asked you to duplicate copyrighted material?
5. Describe how you might report to your manager instances of employees copying material for personal use. What other methods might be used to control excessive copying by employees?
6. How would you describe a good-quality copy? What have you seen on duplicated documents that indicated the preparer didn't take enough time or that the equipment was malfunctioning?

Assignments

1. Develop a copying request form that could be used by the people in your office. This form should provide all the information you need to do the job yourself; if forwarded to a central copying center, it should provide the information they need. The form should meet the preferences of your manager(s).
2. You work in the marketing department of a bank that writes a twenty-four-page annual report. This year your manager wants you to look into dividing the preparation and printing of the report. This assignment will involve three firms. One firm will write the copy; one will typeset and prepare the layout with pictures; and one will print the report. Prepare a list of questions you might ask each firm. (Note: You could also call an advertising agency, describe your project, and ask them for a quote for doing the entire annual report.)

3. Find out the major copier or duplicator vendors in your area. If you were to ask them for a demonstration, what questions would you ask them? Would you want to recommend a vendor yourself, or would you ask a particular person to help you?

 Those instructors using *Top Performance: A Decision-Making Simulation for the Office* should consult the *Instructor's Guide* at this point for support material regarding use of the software in the classroom.

Case Study

In Joy Guardino's office, all copying jobs that require more than five copies per original must go to the central copying unit. This rule was established because many employees were copying large quantities on the convenience copier. Costs went up, and the machine was tied up for long periods.

Joy needs ten copies of a seven-page document. This is a rush job; her manager told her the document must be in that day's mail. Joy's manager is in conference for the rest of the day and doesn't want to be disturbed.

Joy called the copying center to see how fast they could finish the job. They couldn't get to it for twenty-four hours. Joy could do the job herself on one of the firm's small copiers, but that would violate company regulations.

What should Joy do? To whom should she turn since her manager is not available?

CHAPTER
13 FILING

Chapter Objectives

- To know how to prepare material for filing

- To know how to retrieve material

- To understand how to organize files

- To learn how to handle special items

- To obtain an overview of various filing systems

Examples of Excellence

"Did you keep an extra copy of the quarterly report?" Wendell Arnold anxiously asked Lenore Davidoff, his assistant. "I can't find mine, and I need to review it before this afternoon's managers' meeting."

Lenore knew exactly where to go and delivered the report to her manager in moments. She had learned early that being unable to find material creates pressure. Maintaining order was important, because Lenore needed to find material quickly on a regular basis. Although filing was low on Lenore's to-do list, she did a little filing every day. "I can't let the paper control me!" she emphasizes. Her concern is well founded: More than 21 trillion pages of paper are stored in the United States today.

Whether your office has one filing cabinet or one hundred, the rules are the same. Despite the movement toward a paperless society, hardcopy in the form of letters, memos, and reports will always be with us—and being able to find them quickly will always be a priority.

In this chapter, you will learn how to

- Prepare material to be filed
- Retrieve material from files
- Organize filing systems
- Handle special items
- Use alphabetic, subject, geographic, and numeric filing systems

An Efficient Filing Process

You can make filed documents easier to retrieve by following a five-step process before filing them. This process includes inspecting, indexing, coding, sorting, and storing.

Inspecting

Your first step in efficient filing is to **inspect** all documents for a release mark. A **release mark** indicates that the document has been processed and may be filed. It usually appears in the upper left-hand corner in the form of a FILE stamp, the manager's initials, the assistant's initials, a check mark, or some other designation that you and your manager have agreed on. Having a standard release mark, such as an initial with a check mark, on completed documents keeps material that has not yet been answered or processed from being filed unintentionally. You will usually be responsible for establishing the release mark and telling your manager what it means.

Items that will not need a release mark before filing include photocopies of outgoing letters or incoming originals with reply copies attached. However, you should follow your manager's criteria in determining which materials can be filed without a release mark.

During the inspection process, you will need to deal with damaged or irregular materials. This responsibility includes

- Removing items incorrectly stapled or paper-clipped together
- Removing paper clips
- Photocopying or attaching small items to full-size sheets
- Folding and identifying oversize documents to fit the file

Indexing

After you have completed your inspection, you must decide on the name or **caption** under which the document to be filed will be requested. This process is called **indexing**. Once you have learned more about your organization's operations and personnel, and your manager's preferences, indexing will become easier. Some of the more common indexing captions are

- Name on letterhead of incoming correspondence
- Name of organization on outgoing mail
- Name in the signature line of incoming correspondence
- Major subject discussed in the content of incoming or outgoing mail
- Geographic location of incoming or outgoing mail

Coding

The third step involves writing the index name or caption on the document to be filed. One method of **coding** is to underline, check, or circle the caption with a colored pencil. Another is to write the caption in the upper right-hand corner of the document. Coding makes it easier to return material to the correct file.

If you find it necessary to code a document under two or more captions, you can prepare **cross-reference** sheets (Figure 13–1) so that the document can be located regardless of the name under which it is requested. The cross-reference caption should be underlined or written on the original and be followed by an *X*.

Complete the cross-reference sheet by putting the cross-reference caption at the top and filing it. File the original according to the caption listed beneath the word *SEE* on the cross-reference sheet.

Common situations that require cross-referencing include the following:

1. An individual whose first and last names are difficult to distinguish
   Example: filed under *Nelson, Frank*; cross-referenced under *Frank Nelson*
2. A business or special name such as an organization
   Example: filed under *American Association of University Women*; cross-referenced under *AAUW*
3. A university
   Example: filed under *Illinois, University of*; cross-referenced under *University of Illinois*
4. A subject area
   Example: filed under *Automobile Repairs*; cross-referenced under *Pete's Automobile Repairs*

Sorting

The next step in filing is to **sort** items, that is, arrange them in alphabetical order by caption to speed up filing. First, sort materials into small groups such as *A–E*,

Figure 13–1
Cross-reference sheet.

```
Name or Subject                                          DATE

   Martin and Johanssen Law Firm


Regarding

   Correspondence


SEE

   
Name or Subject

   Johanssen and Martin Law Firm
```

F–J, K–O, P–T, and *U–Z.* Second, sort the material within each group. Finally, assemble all the documents in alphabetical sequence and file them.

Storing

The final step in filing is **storing**—placing documents in files. Figure 13–2 offers some suggestions for this process.

Figure 13–2
Filing tips.

1. As you face the file, the left edge of the document should be at the bottom of the folder. This will place the letterhead or top of the document at the left and put it in correct reading position.
2. The most recent correspondence should be on top. When filing newspaper or magazine clippings, be sure to include the name of the publication and the date of the issue.
3. Always lift a folder or guide by the sides, never by the tab. Replace folder labels as soon as they become difficult to read.
4. To save time when filing material, do not remove the folder from the file. Raise the file at one end and rest it on its edge so that about one-third of the file is exposed. The document can be easily inserted and the file returned to its location quickly.
5. Before refiling any folder that has been removed from the files, quickly examine its contents to see if any documents have been lost or items misfiled there.
6. Set aside a definite time each day for filing. Keep records in the file rather than in stacks on desks.
7. Don't allow folders to bulge; this encourages filing errors. When a folder is overfilled, documents extend above the top edge of the back or the folder slips down, making the tab difficult to read. Expand your system by preparing special or individual folders whenever possible or by creasing the lines on the bottom of the folder to increase its capacity.
8. If a particular document was difficult to find, cross-reference or reclassify it to save time the next time it is requested.
9. Don't fill a file drawer to capacity. Leave at least three to four inches of working space in each drawer.
10. Separate records that must be kept on file for long periods of time from those filed for a short time.
11. For safety, close a file drawer immediately after using it and open only one drawer at a time.
12. Use your filing cabinets only for filing, not for storing office supplies and other items. File only vital records in special fire-resistant equipment.
13. Regularly remove inactive records from active files.
14. Be certain to follow, *without variation,* established office procedures for protecting vital records.

File Control

To keep track of filed material and prevent loss and delay, you will have to follow certain procedures.

Charge-out Methods

To ensure that all records are accounted for, especially when several people have access to files, you should use two *charge-out systems*: one to record the removal of individual documents from a folder and one to record the removal of an entire folder. For each procedure, record the same information: (1) a description of the material removed; (2) the name of the person to whom it was issued; (3) the date it was removed; and (4) the date it should be returned.

When an individual document is removed, record this information on a **substitution card** and place the card in the folder exactly where the document was located. When an entire file is removed, record the information on either an out folder or an out guide. An **out folder** holds materials that must be stored when the file is removed. An **out guide** is a marker that shows where the file is to be replaced and records the charge-out information. When you use this system, store materials to be placed in that file separately, to be filed when the original folder is returned.

If your office uses a requisition slip for requesting materials, place a copy of the slip in your tickler file under the due date. If material has been requested for a short time, make a notation on your desk calendar or in a notebook showing what material was removed and who borrowed it. When you return material to the file, be sure to remove the requisition slip from the tickler file or cross out the note on your calendar or notebook.

The charge-out methods you adopt will depend on the number of managers for whom you work, the amount of material removed, the frequency of requests, and the length of time material is kept.

Misfiled Documents

Most filing is done too rapidly, resulting in misfiles of documents and entire files. As a precaution against misfiling, write the correct file heading in the upper right-hand corner of each document, or underline it in colored pencil if it appears in the text, before filing anything.

When a letter, memo, report, or other item has been misfiled, you must begin a *systematic* search. The following steps can help you locate what is missing:

1. Double-check your desk and your manager's desk. Pay special attention to items that are clipped or stapled together. The missing item may have accidentally become attached to something else.
2. Double-check the file folder in which the letter or memo is supposed to be. First, examine the contents of the folder to see whether the document is sandwiched between pages that were clipped or stapled together. Then check the folders immediately in front of and behind the proper one.

3. Look through folders with similar subject headings. *Forbe* may be misfiled under *Ford*, *Benton-Bailey* under *Bailey-Benton*, *Consolidated Insurers* under *Consolidated, Inc.*, and so forth.

4. Check for transposed names. You might have accidentally switched the names on a letter and placed the letter in the wrong folder. For instance, the *Ray Charles* letter you're looking for may have been misfiled under *Ray*.

5. Check related files or cross-referenced listings. For instance, a letter from Acme Suppliers many be filed inside a folder containing Acme's bills or under the name of one of the products it supplies.

6. In a subject file system, look under related subjects. In a numeric file system, look under every possible combination of the numbers. If the correct number is 832, for instance, try 823, 328, 283, 238, and 382.

7. Ask your co-workers. Did anyone borrow the letter and forget to return it? Did someone use the letter and refile it in the wrong file? Be careful not to accuse someone of taking or losing a file.

8. Check your pending, to-be-filed, or tickler system. Your memory may be playing tricks on you—perhaps it was another letter that you filed.

Seven Causes of Misfiles and How to Avoid Them

- *Guide headings are too complex.* Keep them simple!
- *Headings are barely legible.* Type labels in either all caps or initial caps.
- *There are either too many or too few guides.* Use no more than fifteen or no fewer than five guides per drawer.
- *File drawers are overcrowded.* Leave three to four inches of extra space per drawer for expansion and working space.
- *File folders are overcrowded.* Don't let papers ride up; that will cover up the guides.
- *Cross-references are used too infrequently.* Use a standard cross-reference form on colored stock showing the subject of the document, the date, and where it's located in the files.
- *Papers are indexed incorrectly.* Use one of the common indexing captions listed on page 281, if applicable.

Filing Systems

There are four basic filing systems: alphabetic, subject, geographic, and numeric.

Alphabetic System

In an *alphabetic* system, items are filed under the letters *A* through *Z*. To establish an alphabetic file for correspondence, you will need primary guides, special guides, individual name folders, and miscellaneous folders.

Primary guides divide a file into major alphabetical sections. Small organizations may have, for example, only twenty-six sections, while larger organizations may have several primary guides for each letter of the alphabet. For example, *B* may also have guides for *Be*, *Bi*, *Bo*, and *Br*.

This alphabetic standing file is called the Alphascan Folder Filing System. *(Courtesy of the Kardex System)*

Special guides designate folders that are frequently used or subdivide a section.

Individual name folders follow the guides in alphabetical order. When a minimum of five documents have been collected from one correspondent, an individual folder is set up and the documents are filed in chronological order by date, with the most recent date first.

Miscellaneous folders are placed after the last folder in each primary-guide section. These folders contain documents from correspondents who do not have individual folders. Documents are filed alphabetically by the name of the correspondent, with the most recent date first.

Color-coded and plain folders with color-coded labels may be used with any of the filing systems discussed earlier. Color-coding makes filing easier by guiding the reader's eyes to the proper areas. This technique also shortens out-of-file search time, reduces errors, provides a psychological "lift" by brightening the file area, and makes it easier to locate misfiled items.

Subject System

In a *subject* system, documents are classified by subject, rather than by names of individuals or organizations, and then filed alphabetically.

A subject file has two parts: a main file and a relative index or cross-reference. The relative index lists possible captions under which material may be filed.

A typical subject file contains main headings, which may have a number of subheadings; the subheadings may, in turn, have several subdivisions. Subject filing relies on the assistant's ability to determine from the document's content the most accurate subject heading for filing.

Geographic System

In a *geographic* system, files are captioned by location. This system is commonly used by sales organizations, public utilities, national real estate firms, and service organizations such as the Jaycees and Boy Scouts.

Captions for geographic files are arranged alphabetically, usually beginning with the state; the county, city, or town; the company's or individual's name; or the subject. Figure 13–3 provides an example of a geographic file. The state name is on the primary guide and the city or town on the secondary guide.

Like the subject file, the geographic file usually has an alphabetical card index that lists the company's correspondents by name.

Numeric System

In a *numeric* system, items are categorized by assigned numbers that are then cross-indexed with an alphabetically arranged index. This system is often used when there are large numbers of names to be alphabetized. For example, social security and credit card records are more efficiently handled in a numeric file.

Figure 13–3
Geographic filing.

First Position (State and alphabetic guides)	Second Position (Town or city guides)	Third Position (Miscellaneous folders— city or individual)	Fourth Position (Individual folders)
I Illinois	Peoria	Illinois Peoria	Peoria, IL— Porter & Rames
		Illinois Danville	Danville, IL— Wilco Hardware Company
	Danville	Illinois Danville	Danville, IL— Interstate Water Company
		Illinois Chicago	Chicago, IL— Baker Forms, Inc.
	Chicago	Illinois Chicago	Chicago, IL— Ames Chicago Beverage Co.
		Illinois Champaign	Champaign, IL— Southland Corp.
	Champaign	Illinois Champaign	Champaign, IL— Kraft Foods, Inc.

A numeric file has four parts:

1. The *main numeric file* has guides and individual folders with numeric captions. Each correspondent's folder is assigned a number, and the documents are filed in the folder chronologically, with the most recent date in front.
2. The *miscellaneous alphabetic file* contains documents that have not been assigned a numeric file. Guides and individual folders have alphabetic captions.
3. The *alphabetic card index* has individual cards with the name and address of a correspondent (plus other information) and the number assigned to that correspondent.
4. The *register* gives the numbers that names have already been assigned and the numbers still available.

There are several methods of numeric filing. In *consecutive* or *serial number filing*, documents are arranged in consecutive order by number. As the most recent records are assigned the larger numbers, the lower-numbered files tend to have less activity.

In *terminal-digit filing*, the number is divided into pairs of digits and read from right to left. For example, if a court case is filed under number 620312, the number is divided into 62 03 12. The last (or terminal) two digits (12) are the drawer number, the next two digits (03) are the folder number, and the remaining numbers (62) indicate the sequence of the folder. Court case 620312 is filed after 610312 and before 630312.

The advantage of the terminal-digit system is that as new documents are added (such as 620313), they are distributed to a different drawer (13). This keeps most of the filing activity from occurring in a small section of the files.

Triple-digit filing is similar to the terminal-digit system except that the number is broken into two parts: the last three digits and the remaining digits. Thus, court case 620312 would be filed in drawer 312.

Middle-digit filing uses first the third and fourth digits from the right, then the first two digits on the left, and then the last two digits on the right. Court case 620312 would be filed in drawer 03, folder 62, and in the sequence between 11 and 13. Like the terminal-digit system, this system permits a uniform assignment of drawer space.

In *decimal-numeric filing*, subdivisions of a file are created by adding a decimal point, followed by the desired number of subdivisions:

220	Mailing List
220.1	Chamber of Commerce
220.2	Women's Organizations
220.3	Current Customers
220.31	New Account Within Last 6 Months, Current Customer
220.32	New Account Within 1 Year, Current Customer
220.4	New Customer

Duplex-numeric filing permits large numbers of records to be filed because it offers unlimited expansion capacity. The duplex numbers are assigned when they're added to the file. New numbers can be assigned for additional major headings and subdivisions at any time:

5	Sales Materials
5-1	Direct Mail
5-2	Point of Sale
5-3	Publications
5-1 - 1	Direct Mail—Loans
5-1 - 2	Direct Mail—Estate Planning
5-2 - 1	Point of Sale—Banners

The ARMA Rules of Filing

This section presents rules developed by the Association of Records Managers and Administrators, Inc. (ARMA), a nonprofit management association formed in 1975. One of ARMA's missions is to provide guidance on information management. The following guides to file management were designed to improve the consistency with which filing procedures are used, as well as efficiency in completing this task.

The ARMA material is divided into four sections: Simplified Filing Standard Rules, Specific Filing Guidelines, Automated Conversion Guidelines, and Other Indexing Practices. ARMA has chosen to define the filing method as *unit by unit;* the filing unit may be a number, a letter, a word, or any combination of these as stated in the simplified or specific rules section.

SECTION I: Simplified Filing Standard Rules

The following seven rules provide consistency in simplified filing.

1. Alphabetize by arranging files in *unit-by-unit order and alphabetically within each unit.*
2. Each filing unit in a filing segment is to be considered. This includes prepositions, conjunctions, and articles. The only exception is when the word *the* is the first filing unit in a file segment. In this case, *the* is the last filing unit. Spell out all symbols, e.g., &, $, #, and file alphabetically.
3. File "nothing before something." File single unit filing segments before multiple unit filing segments.
4. Ignore all punctuation when alphabetizing. This includes periods, commas, dashes, hyphens, apostrophes, etc. Hyphenated words are considered one unit.
5. Arabic and Roman numbers are filed sequentially before alphabetic characters. All Arabic numerals precede all Roman numerals.
6. Acronyms, abbreviations, and radio and television station call letters are filed as one unit.
7. File under the most commonly used name or title. Cross-reference under other names or titles which might be used in an information request.

These simplified filing standard rules are illustrated in the following applications.

Personal Names

1. Simple Personal Names

Use the last (surname) as the first filing unit. The first name or initial is the second filing unit. Subsequent names or initials are filed as successive units.

As Written	Unit 1	Unit 2	Unit 3	Unit 4
	As Filed			
O. Betty Greene	Greene	O	Betty	
Wm. David Michael Kelly	Kelly	Wm	David	Michael
Julie Tregaskis	Tregaskis	Julie		

2. Personal Names with Prefixes

Surnames which include a prefix are filed as one unit whether the prefix is followed by a space or not. Examples of prefixes are: *D', Da, De, Del, De la, Della, Den, Des, Di, Du, El, Fitz, L', La, Las, Le, Les, Lo, Los, M', Mac, Mc, O', Saint, St., Ste., Te, Ten, Ter, Van, Van de, Van der, Von, Von der.*

As Written	Unit 1	Unit 2	Unit 3
	As Filed		
Dan P. De Leon	DeLeon	Dan	P
Peter J. Leuck	Leuck	Peter	J
Winifred A. LeVan	LeVan	Winifred	A
Warren C. Mace	Mace	Warren	C
S. John MacGregor	MacGregor	S	John
Thomas R. Macy	Macy	Thomas	R
Donna Mc Allister	McAllister	Donna	
John R. Mc Manville	McManville	John	R
Verna Morrison	Morrison	Verna	
Helen Grace M'Peters	MPeters	Helen	Grace
Mary J. Saint Thomas	SaintThomas	Mary	J
Joseph H. St. John	StJohn	Joseph	H
F. P. Van der Linden	VanderLinden	F	P

3. Personal Names with Personal and Professional Titles and Suffixes

Suffixes are not used as filing units except when needed to distinguish between two or more identical names. When *needed*, a suffix is the last filing unit and is filed as written, ignoring punctuation.

As Written	Unit 1	Unit 2	Unit 3	Unit 4
	As Filed			
John J. Johnson, 3rd	Johnson	John	J	3rd
John J. Johnson, II	Johnson	John	J	II
John J. Johnson, C.P.A.	Johnson	John	J	CPA
John J. Johnson, Jr.	Johnson	John	J	Jr
Maj. John J. Johnson	Johnson	John	J	Maj

As Written	As Filed			
	Unit 1	**Unit 2**	**Unit 3**	**Unit 4**
Mayor John J. Johnson	Johnson	John	J	Mayor
John J. Johnson, M.D.	Johnson	John	J	MD
Mr. John J. Johnson	Johnson	John	J	Mr
John J. Johnson Ph. D.	Johnson	John	J	PhD

4. Personal Names Which Are Hyphenated
Ignore the hyphen and file the two words as one unit.

As Written	As Filed	
	Unit 1	**Unit 2**
Mary-Kay deWinter	deWinter	MaryKay
Don Miller	Miller	Don
Peter Winter	Winter	Peter
Kathy Winter-Smith	WinterSmith	Kathy

5. Pseudonyms and Royal and Religious Titles
Pseudonyms are filed as written. Personal names which start with a royal or religious title and are followed by *only* a given name(s) are filed as written.

As Written	As Filed		
	Unit 1	**Unit 2**	**Unit 3**
Dr. Seuss	Dr	Seuss	
Grandma Moses	Grandma	Moses	
Pope John Paul	Pope	John	Paul
Queen Elizabeth II	Queen	Elizabeth	II
Sister Teresa	Sister	Teresa	

6. Foreign Personal Names
If the surname is identifiable, file the name as any other personal name is filed. If there is a question about the surname, use the last name as the first filing unit and make a cross-reference from the first name.

As Written	As Filed		
	Unit 1	**Unit 2**	**Unit 3**
Camillo Benso Cavour	Cavour	Camillo	Benso
Gerard De Geer	DeGeer	Gerard	
	Lim	Yauw	Tijn
	(See Tijn Lim Yauw)		
Sri Mulijono	Sri	Mulijono	
	(See Mulijono Sri)		
Lim Yauw Tijn	Tijn	Lim	Yauw

Note: When corresponding with many people from other countries, refer to *Anglo-American Cataloguing Rules*, Second Edition, for the correct filing procedure.

7. Nicknames

When a person commonly uses a nickname as a first name, file using the nickname. Cross-reference from the given name only if necessary.

As Written	As Filed		
	Unit 1	**Unit 2**	**Unit 3**
	Carter	James	Earl
	(See Carter, Jimmy)		
Jimmy Carter	Carter	Jimmy	
Dizzy Dean	Dean	Dizzy	
	Dean	Jay	Hanna
	(See Dean, Dizzy)		
Betty Hersey	Hersey	Betty	

Business and Organization Names

1. Business and organization names are filed as written according to the *Simplified Standard Rules* and using the business letterhead or trademark as a guide. Names with prefixes follow the example for personal names with prefixes on page 290.

As Written	As Filed			
	Unit 1	**Unit 2**	**Unit 3**	**Unit 4**
1-A Photo Service	1A	Photo	Service	
3M	3M			
XXI Club	XXI	Club		
A-1 Printing Company	A1	Printing	Company	
AAA Travel Agency	AAA	Travel	Agency	
Able Action Plan	Able	Action	Plan	
AFL-CIO	AFLCIO			
American Insurance Co.	American	Insurance	Co	
Amoco	Amoco			
Angleton's of Boise	Angletons	of	Boise	
The Book Shop	Book	Shop	The	
Century 21	Century	21		
Century Cleaners	Century	Cleaners		
CH_2M Hill	CH_2M	Hill		
Child's Play	Childs	Play		
Dr. Spock's Clinic	Dr	Spocks	Clinic	
Ft. Ord Taxi	Ft	Ord	Taxi	
I.B.M.	IBM			
	(Use for International Business Machines Corp)			
	International	Business	Machines	Corp
	(See IBM)			
Mrs. Peter's Computers	Mrs	Peters	Computers	
Mt. Blanc Sound Shop	Mt	Blanc	Sound	Shop
Saint Luke's Hospital	StLukes	Hospital		

As Written	As Filed			
	Unit 1	**Unit 2**	**Unit 3**	**Unit 4**
There's Always Flowers	Theres	Always	Flowers	
Tom Wikon Painting	Tom	Wikon	Painting	
Wagon Works	Wagon	Works		
WGKM Radio Station	WGKM	Radio	Station	

Note: When necessary to ensure information retrieval, cross-reference between acronyms and the complete name.

2. Subsidiaries of businesses will be filed under their own name with a cross-reference to the parent company if needed.

As Written	As Filed			
	Unit 1	**Unit 2**	**Unit 3**	**Unit 4**
	H	J	Heinz	Co
	(for subsidiaries see Ore-Ida Foods Inc Star-Kist Foods Inc Weight Watchers International)			
Ore-Ida Foods, Inc.	OreIda (See also H. J. Heinz Co.)	Foods	Inc	

3. Place names in business names follow the *Simplified Filing Standard Rule* that each word/filing unit is treated as a separate filing unit.

As Written	As Filed			
	Unit 1	**Unit 2**	**Unit 3**	**Unit 4**
Alabama Power and Light	Alabama	Power	and	Light
New Jersey Coliseum	New	Jersey	Coliseum	
Se Valle Publications, Inc.	SeValle	Publications	Inc	
St. Louis Power Company	StLouis	Power	Company	

4. Compass Terms in Business Names
Each word/unit in a filing segment containing compass terms is considered a separate filing unit. If the term includes more than one compass point, treat it as it is written. Establish cross-references as needed.

As Written	As Filed			
	Unit 1	**Unit 2**	**Unit 3**	**Unit 4**
North East Forms Co.	North	East	Forms	Co
North Eastern Microfilm	North	Eastern	Microfilm	
North-East Data Co.	NorthEast	Data	Co	
Northeast Systems	Northeast	Systems		
Northeastern Equipment Co.	Northeastern	Equipment	Co	

Government/Political Designations. When filing government/political material, the name of the major entity is filed first, followed by the *distinctive* name of the department, bureau, etc. This rule covers all government and political divisions, agencies, departments, committees, etc., from the federal to the county/parish, city, district and ward level.

Federal
Prefix with the name of the government and eliminate the department, i.e., Department of the Interior, Department of the Treasury, etc. File titles of the office, service, bureau, etc. by their distinctive names.

United States Government
  Coast Guard
United States Government
  Environmental Protection Agency

United States Government
  Forest Service
United States Government
  Interstate Commerce Commission

State and Local
State, county, parish, city, town, township, and village governments/political divisions are filed by their distinctive names. The words "county of," 'city of," "department of," etc., if needed and as appropriate, are added for clarity and are considered filing units.

Note: If *of* is not part of the official name as written, it is not added.

As Written	As Filed			
	Unit 1	**Unit 2**	**Unit 3**	**Unit 4**
Kane County Department of Public Works	Kane	County	Public	Works
City of Lovelock	Lovelock	City	of	
Nevada Department of Highways	Nevada	Highways	Department	
Washoe County	Washoe	County		

Foreign Governments
The distinctive English name is the first filing unit. If needed, the balance of the formal name of the government forms the next filing unit(s). Divisions, departments, and branches follow in sequential order, reversing the written order where necessary to give the distinctive name precedence in the filing arrangement.

  States, colonies, provinces, cities, and other divisions of foreign governments are filed by their distinctive or official names as spelled in English. Cross-reference written name to official native name where necessary.

As Written	As Filed	
	Unit 1	**Unit 2**
Commonwealth of Australia	Australia	
Bermuda	Bermuda	
South Korea	South	Korea
London, England	London	England

Note: A current copy of *The World Almanac and Book of Facts* is an excellent reference for the translation of foreign names into English and for clarification of relations between governments. Another source is the book *Countries, Dependencies and Areas of Special Sovereignty* published by U.S. Department of Commerce, National Bureau of Standards, Institute for Computer Sciences & Technology, Gaithersburg, MD 20899.

SECTION II: Specific Filing Guidelines

Often, certain organizations correspond with, invoice, etc. specific groups of people or businesses. When this is the case, special filing systems may be developed to aid in the filing and retrieval of records. The following guidelines may be applied. Remember to *document* your decision to ensure *consistency*.

Personal Names. Legal offices only may need to relate the files of both partners of a marriage. If a married woman chooses to maintain her maiden name or connects her maiden name to her husband's surname with a hyphen, file using one spouse's surname and cross-reference from the other spouse's name.

As Written	As Filed			
	Unit 1	Unit 2	Unit 3	Unit 4
Rhonda J. Bluer-Acker	Acker	Rhonda	J	Bluer
	(See Acker Wm Mrs)			
	Acker	Wm	Mrs	
Becki Blake	Blake	Becki		
	(See Peters John J Mrs)			
	Bluer Acker	Rhonda	J	
	(See Acker Wm Mrs)			
	Peters	John	J	Mrs

Business Names. When the same filing segment is applicable to more than one location, filing order is determined by an identifying location. In the case of banks, unions, etc., this location may be a branch, local number, post, etc. For most businesses, it will be an address. When using an address, cities are considered first, followed by states or provinces, street names, house number or building number in that order.

Address Arrangement
When the first units of street names are written as figures, the names are considered in ascending numeric order and placed together before alphabetic street names.

Street names with compass directions are considered as written. Numbers after compass directions are considered before alphabetic names (East 8th, East Main, Franklin, SE Eighth, Southeast Eighth, etc.).

If a filing unit within an address is not necessary for identification, it does not have to be used.

Note: Bracketed numbers refer to the appropriate *Simplified Rule* on page 289.

As Written	As Filed					
	Unit 1	Unit 2	Unit 3	Unit 4	Unit 5	Unit 6
Assoc. of Hotel Employees, Portland, ME [2]	Assoc	of	Hotel	Employees	Portland	ME
Assoc. of Hotel Employees, Portland, OR [2]	Assoc	of	Hotel	Employees	Portland	OR
The Baltimore Sun	Baltimore	Sun	The			
	Benevolent	and	Protective	Order	of	Elks [7]
	(See Elks Club)					
Chamber of Commerce, Phila, PA	Chamber	of	Commerce	Phila	PA	
Springfield Chamber of Commerce, IL	Chamber	of	Commerce	Springfield	IL	
Springfield Chamber of Commerce, MA	Chamber	of	Commerce	Springfield	MA	
Chicago First National Bank Aspin Branch	Chicago	First	National	Bank	Aspin	Branch
Chicago First National Bank Oaks Branch	Chicago	First	National	Bank	Oaks	Branch
College of Idaho	College	of	Idaho			
	College	of	Notre	Dame [7]		
	(See Notre Dame)					
College of Ste. Catherine, Library School	College	of	SteCatherine	Library	School	
Columbia Public Library, Columbia, AL	Columbia	Public	Library	Columbia	AL	
Columbia Public Library, Columbia, MD	Columbia	Public	Library	Columbia	MD	
Elks Club [7]	Elks	Club				
Grinnell College	Grinnell	College				
Insurance Library, Chicago	Insurance	Library	Chicago			
Library of Congress	Library	of	Congress			
Lincoln School, St. Paul, MN	Lincoln	School	StPaul	MN		
Lincoln School, Willmar, MN	Lincoln	School	Willmar	MN		
	Local	125	UAW			
	(See UAW)					
Mary Carter Paints, 3404 3d St., Waco, TX	Mary	Carter	Paints	Waco	3d	

| As Written | As Filed | | | | | |
	Unit 1	Unit 2	Unit 3	Unit 4	Unit 5	Unit 6
Mary Carter Paints, 415 East Main St., Waco, TX	Mary	Carter	Paints	Waco	East	Main
Mary Carter Paints, 210 Main St., Waco, TX	Mary	Carter	Paints	Waco	Main	
Mary L. Carter, Inc., Austin, TX	Mary	L	Carter	Inc.	Austin	
Mary L. Carter, Inc., 414 3d St., Waco, TX	Mary	L	Carter	Inc	Waco	
Motel 6, Reno East [5]	Motel	6	Reno	East		
Motel 6, Reno South	Motel	6	Reno	South		
Motel 6, Reno West	Motel	6	Reno	West		
Motel Idanha	Motel	Idanha				
College of Notre Dame [7]	Notre	Dame				
Readers Digest (CH) [2]	Readers	Digest	CH			
Readers Digest (NY)	Readers	Digest	NY			
The Southwind Motel	Southwind	Motel	The			
St. Joseph's Hospital, Chicago, IL	StJosephs	Hospital	Chicago			
St. Joseph's Hospital, Milwaukee, WI	StJosephs	Hospital	Milwaukee			
UAW Local 52 [7]	UAW	Local	52			
UAW Local 85	UAW	Local	85			
Local 125, UAW	UAW	Local	125			
University of California, Berkeley	University	of	California	Berkeley		
University of California, Riverside	University	of	California	Riverside		
University of Iowa	University	of	Iowa			
VFW Post 45	VFW	Post	45			
VFW Post 121	VFW	Post	121			
The Wall Street Journal	Wall	Street	Journal	The		
YMCA, 1515 1st, Miami, FL	YMCA	Miami	FL			
YMCA, 2101 Ohio, Miami, FL	YMCA	Miami	FL	Ohio		
YMCA, 801 S.W. 1st Ave., Miami, FL	YMCA	Miami	FL	SW	1st	

1. Compass Terms in Scientific Document Filing

Compass terms are frequently applied to technical studies conducted by geographers, geologists, geophysicists, and other scientists studying the earth's surface. To maintain a geographically organized file, the compass term is treated as an adjective and is filed after the name only in *scientific document filing.*

As Written	As Filed		
	Unit 1	Unit 2	Unit 3
Northwest Castle Rock	Castle	Rock	Northwest
South Padre Island	Padre	Island	South
Texas	Texas		
East Texas	Texas	East	
West Texas	Texas	West	
Eastern Williston Basin	Williston	Basin	Eastern

2. Guardians, Receivers, Trustees, and Agents in Legal Files

Guardians, trustees, receivers, and agents act for another person or organization and their names are not indexed. Such guardians, receivers, trustees, and agents may be persons, financial institutions, or companies. *Records are filed by the name of the person or organization for whom the guardian, trustee, receiver, or agent is acting.* For instance, if the Pacific Security National Bank is the trustee for Angela Dixon, a minor, the original records are by the name of Angela Dixon. A cross-reference is made in the name of the guardian, receiver, trustee, or agent to refer the filer to the name of the individual or organization for whom the agent is acting.

As Written	As Filed			
	Unit 1	Unit 2	Unit 3	Unit 4
Brockman & Clapp, Agents	Brockman	and	Clapp	Agents
	(See Rytex Trucking)			
Colfax Webb, Receivers	Colfax	Webb	Receivers	
	(See Samuelson Instrument Co)			
Angela Dixon	Dixon	Angela		
William E. Nadeau	Nadeau	William	E	
Pacific Security National Bank	Pacific	Security	National	Bank
	(See Dixon Angela)			
Rytex Trucking	Rytex	Trucking		
Samuelson Instrument Co.	Samuelson	Instrument	Co	
Forrest W. Work, Guardian	Work	Forrest	W	Guardian
	(See Nadeau William E)			

3. Religious Titles

With numerous files using religious titles, the title may become the last filing unit.

As Written	As Filed		
	Unit 1	**Unit 2**	**Unit 3**
Sister Bernadette	Bernadette	Sister	
Father William Buechner	Buechner	William	Father
Sister Mary Elizabeth	Mary	Elizabeth	Sister
Sister Teresa	Teresa	Sister	

SECTION III: Automated* Conversion Guidelines

This section covers some of the considerations which must be understood to ease the transition from a manual to an automated or electronic, alphabetic filing system. Each automated system has its own peculiarities, so the most important step is to identify a person in the organization who understands both the software and the hardware that will be used. It is important to establish a good communication base with this person. This person should be able to provide the following information:

1. What the hardware/software can do now
2. How much time and cost will be involved if programming is needed for changes in the sort capability
3. If the program changes are going to be cost-effective or if the present sort format needs to be reassessed

Once there is a liaison person to work with, communicate how the alphabetic file is designed and how items should be sorted. Some of the questions which need answering are listed below.

1. When inverting personal names, should prefixes be included with the surname?
2. If prefixes are included with the surname, will the computer read/sort those with spaces between the prefix and the following name differently than those without spaces?
3. What happens with name suffixes? Will the output read *Kearns, Jr. Glenn E.* or *Kearns, Glenn E. Jr.?*
4. Does the computer have a table which converts abbreviations to the full name, i.e., *Wm.* to *William?*
5. What happens when the computer sorts punctuation (hyphens, apostrophes, spaces, periods, etc.) and diacritical marks? Will the result throw the alphabetic sequence out of order?
6. Does the computer sort all Arabic numbers first? How does it sort capital and lower case letters? How are symbols sorted?
7. Should numbers be right justified? If so, how many characters should be planned for and do zeros need to be used to the left of the number itself?

Automated implies hardware, from mainframes to personal computers and word processors.

8. If prepositions, articles, and conjunctions are not to be used as filing units, does the system have a "stop list" which allows the words to be ignored?
9. Is there a limited field size? If so, is it satisfactory to abbreviate government names, i.e., *U.S. Gov.*, or use a truncation/wild card option?
10. Is it advisable to provide two separate name fields for each record: (1) a field for the indexed name to be used primarily for alphabetic sorting and (2) a field for the name as written to be used for printouts on correspondence, directories, labels, etc.?

Before the complete alphabetic file (database) is entered into the automated system, carefully choose a sample of typical filing segments including items which may present filing problems. Have this input sorted and checked to see that the output is as planned. There will probably be more questions at this time. As these problems are solved, *document* the solutions. When the first phase of research is completed, reassess the alphabetic filing needs.

Some inconsistencies can be resolved at the time of data entry. If the information is to be placed on coding sheets to be used by data entry personnel, the coding must be set up in advance to reflect the filing order as it will appear in the database. The coding must be *consistent*. When the information is being input directly from file folders, data entry personnel must be instructed to input the data the way it is to be sorted and printed; e.g., *St.* for *Saint* is always entered *Saint*, or *St.* for *Street* is always entered *Street*.

The time and effort put into preparing the information to be input will pay off in ease of retrieval and usable output.

Automating files can be fun, challenging, frustrating, and rewarding. Think about the fun and rewards when the frustrations are no longer overwhelming.

Other Indexing Practices

The indexing practices described in this section are a collection of some of the more common, inconsistent practices which have been in use over a long period of years. These practices are included only to aid in proper documentation of the rule actually being used. It is important to note that most practices violate the rule of consistency and thus may interfere with the effective filing and retrieval of documents. For ease of reference, these practices are arranged in the same order as the examples for the Simplified Filing Standard Rules. Remember to note and cross-reference which Standard Rule, Specific Rule, or Other Indexing Practice is used in the filing system.

Personal Names
1. Personal Names with Prefixes
a. Where there are a significant number of names starting with a particular prefix, such as *Mc* or *Van*, the prefixes are filed as a separate letter group preceding the other names.

As Written	As Filed		
	Unit 1	Unit 2	Unit 3
David L. De Chambeau	De Chambeau	David	L
Bill R. De La Rosa	De La Rosa	Bill	R
Sally Deaton	Deaton	Sally	
Robert MacCaw	MacCaw	Robert	
John McGiff	McGiff	John	
Peter McGill	McGill	Peter	
Dana Maas	Maas	Dana	
F. P. Van der Linden	Van der Linden	F	P
John Van Hook	Van Hook	John	
Mary Vance	Vance	Mary	

b. When the prefix is separated by a space from the rest of the surname, file each part of the surname separately with the first prefix as the first unit.

As Written	As Filed			
	Unit 1	Unit 2	Unit 3	Unit 4
Dan P. De Leon	De	Leon	Dan	P
Peter J. Leuck	Leuck	Peter	J	
Winifred A. LeVan	LeVan	Winifred	A	
Peter Mac Bride	Mac	Bride	Peter	
Warren C. Mace	Mace	Warren	C	
S. John MacGregor	MacGregor	S	John	
Frank Van der Linden	Van	der	Linden	Frank

c. All *M'*, *Mac*, and *Mc'* surnames which are pronounced "mac" are filed as though they were spelled "mac."

As Written	As Filed		
	Unit 1	Unit 2	Unit 3
Robert M'Caw	M'Caw	Robert	
Warren C. Mace	Mace	Warren	C
John McGiff	McGiff	John	
Peter MacGill	MacGill	Peter	

2. Personal Names with Suffixes

a. Seniority designations, such as *Sr.*, *Junior*, *Jr.*, *2nd*, etc. are considered separate filing units and filed in abbreviated form in numeric sequence when needed for identification (*Sr.* equals 1st, *Jr.* equals 2nd).

As Written	As Filed			
	Unit 1	Unit 2	Unit 3	Unit 4
John J. Johnson Sr.	Johnson	John	J	Sr
John J. Johnson II	Johnson	John	J	II*

*Numbers precede alphabetical equivalent.

As Written	As Filed			
	Unit 1	Unit 2	Unit 3	Unit 4
John J. Johnson Jr.	Johnson	John	J	Jr
John J. Johnson 3rd	Johnson	John	J	3rd

b. Degrees, military ranks, and professional titles which are commonly abbreviated are left in abbreviated form with each segment of the abbreviation filed as a separate unit.

As Written	As Filed				
	Unit 1	Unit 2	Unit 3	Unit 4	Unit 5
John Johnson, C.P.A.	Johnson	John	C	P	A
Dr. John Johnson	Johnson	John	Dr		
Maj. Gen'l John Johnson	Johnson	John	Maj	Gen'l	
Mayor John Johnson	Johnson	John	Mayor		
John Johnson, PhD	Johnson	John	Ph	D	

c. (1) A personal title (Miss, Mr., Mrs., and Ms.) is spelled out and used as the last indexing unit when needed for identification. **(2)** College and university degrees, professional certifications, and military ranks are spelled out and used as the last indexing unit when needed for identification.

As Written	As Filed			
	Unit 1	Unit 2	Unit 3	Unit 4
Miss Marion Brown	Brown	Marion	Miss	
Mr. Marion Brown	Brown	Marion	Mister	
Mrs. Marion Brown	Brown	Marion	Mistress	
Ms. Marion Brown	Brown	Marion	Ms	
Marion Walter Brown	Brown	Marion	Walter	
Captain Marion Walter Brown	Brown	Marion	Walter	Captain
Prof. Marion Walter Brown	Brown	Marion	Walter	Professor

4. Personal Names Which Are Hyphenated

When the surname of an individual is hyphenated, use the last segment of the surname as the first filing unit. The first name or initial is the second filing unit. The first segment of the hyphenated name is the last filing unit.

As Written	As Filed		
	Unit 1	Unit 2	Unit 3
Helen Canizales-Diego	Diego	Helen	Canizales
Patsy Hooper-Ragan	Ragan	Patsy	Hooper
Wm. B. Ragan	Ragan	Wm	B

5. Nicknames

When a person commonly uses a nickname for the first name, find out if the nickname is truly the given name. If a given name is available, file under that name and cross-reference from the nickname.

As Written	As Filed		
	Unit 1	**Unit 2**	**Unit 3**
Dizzy Dean	Dean	Jay	Hanna
	Dean	Dizzy	
	(See Dean Jay Hanna)		
Jimmy Carter	Carter	James	Earl
	Carter	Jimmy	
	(See Carter, James Earl)		
Betty Hersey	Hersey	Betty	

6. Abbreviated Given Names

When a given name is written in an abbreviated form, file it as if it were spelled out.

As Written	As Filed	
	Unit 1	**Unit 2**
Chas. Peterson	Peterson	Charles
Rbt. Peterson	Peterson	Robert
Wm. Peterson	Peterson	William

Business Names

1. Articles, Prepositions, &, Conjunctions

A, an, the, prepositions, &, and conjunctions are disregarded in filing. These words are placed in parentheses to indicate that they are not used in filing.

As Written	As Filed		
	Unit 1	**Unit 2**	**Unit 3**
Garfield for President Club	Garfield (for)	President	Club
Gatzka & Sons, Inc.	Gatzka (&)	Sons	Incorporated
Rain or Shine Apparel	Rain (or)	Shine	Apparel
Top of the Mark	Top (of the)	Mark	
The Watson Plumbing Co.	Watson	Plumbing	Company (The)

2. Individual Names in Company Names

a. When a company name begins with the full name of an individual, file the surname first, then the given name, initials, and the balance of the name. Cross-reference as necessary.

As Written	As Filed			
	Unit 1	**Unit 2**	**Unit 3**	**Unit 4**
Geo. Banta Company, Inc.	Banta	George	Company	Incorporated
F. G. Olendorf Co.	Olendorf	F	G	Company

b. When a company named for an individual(s) becomes so well known that to reverse the names would cause confusion, file as written; cross-reference as necessary.

As Written

	As Written	As Filed		
	Unit 1	**Unit 2**	**Unit 3**	
J. C. Penney	J	C	Penney	
Marshall Field & Co.	Marshall	Field (&)	Company	
Montgomery Ward Co.	Montgomery	Ward	Company	

3. Hyphenated Business Names

a. When two or more initials, words, names, word substitutes, or coined words in a business name are joined by a hyphen, the hyphen is disregarded and each part of the name is considered to be a separate unit. (If a surname and a coined name are used to form a business name, a cross-reference should be prepared.)

b. Articles, prepositions, and conjunctions that are joined to other words by hyphens also follow this rule: Each is a separate unit.

c. When a hyphen joins two parts of a single word, both parts are considered together as one unit. Words of this type often begin with *anti-, bi-, co-, inter-, intra-, mid-, non-, pan-, pre-, re-, self-, trans-, tri-, un-,* and the like.

As Written	As Filed			
	Unit 1	**Unit 2**	**Unit 3**	**Unit 4**
A-C Supply	A	C	Supply	Corporation
A-Jay-Zee Co.	A	Jay	Zee	Company
Anti-Defamation League	Anti-Defamation	League		
Beef-N-Boards Restaurant	Beef	N	Boards	Restaurant
Cams-Smith Drug Store	Cams	Smith	Drug	Store
Co-operative Marketing Co.	Co-operative	Marketing	Company	
Gaslight Drive-in Theater	Gaslight	Drive	In	Theater
Inter-Ocean Insurance Co.	Inter-Ocean	Insurance	Company	
Stedman Serv-Ur-Self	Stedman	Serv	Ur	Self
Trans-Canada Railroad Line	Trans-Canada	Railroad	Line	
Tri-City Transport Co.	Tri-City	Transport	Company	
U-and-I Laundry	U	and	I	Laundry

4. Abbreviated Business Names

a. A business which is known by an abbreviation of its name is filed under the full name of the company. Cross-references are made from the abbreviation if necessary.

As Written	As Filed			
	Unit 1	**Unit 2**	**Unit 3**	**Unit 4**
IBM	International	Business	Machines	Corporation
3M	Minnesota	Mining (and)	Manufacturing	Company
	Three	M		
	(See Minnesota Mining and Manufacturing Company)			

b. When a business name contains an abbreviated word, file the abbreviated word as spoken.

As Written	As Filed		
	Unit 1	Unit 2	Unit 3
Peter's of St. Louis	Peter's (of)	Saint	Louis
Ste. Joan Winery	Sainte	Joan	Winery
W. State Foodland	West	State	Foodland

5. Contractions and Possessives

Alphabetize and file to the apostrophe, then stop. File as if any letters in the unit which follow the apostrophe do not exist.

As Written	As Filed		
	Unit 1	Unit 2	Unit 3
Johnson's Appliance Shop	Johnson('s)	Appliance	Shop
Johnsons Apparel Shop	Johnsons	Apparel	Shop
Johnstons' Service Station	Johnstons'	Service	Station
What's Cookin Restaurant	What('s)	Cookin	Restaurant
Who's Who in America	Who('s)	Who (in)	America

6. Single Letters in Names

Single letters appearing in company names, including radio and television call letters, are treated as separate units even though they may be written together without spaces.

As Written	As Filed				
	Unit 1	Unit 2	Unit 3	Unit 4	Unit 5
ABC Cartage Company	A	B	C	Cartage	Company
K & E Supply Company	K (&)	E	Supply	Company	
KFGT Radio	K	F	G	T	Radio
Triple T Beverage Service	Triple	T	Beverage	Service	
WGNB Television	W	G	N	B	Television

7. Numeric Names

Names containing numbers are filed alphabetically as if the numbers were spoken.

As Written	As Filed			
	Unit 1	Unit 2	Unit 3	Unit 4
1st Ave. Drug Store	First	Avenue	Drug	Store
Four Ply Wood Products	Four	Ply	Wood	Products
Hank's Pewter Shop	Hank's	Pewter	Shop	
Marty's Finger Steaks	Marty's	Finger	Steaks	
Marty's 400 Dolls	Marty's	Four	Hundred	Dolls
914 Club	Nine	Fourteen	Club	
1010 Downing St.	Ten	Ten	Downing	Street

8. Business Names with Compound Place Words

Sometimes business names contain compound place words. These compound place words are filed as one unit.

As Written	As Filed			
	Unit 1	Unit 2	Unit 3	Unit 4
Los Angeles Coliseum	Los Angeles	Coliseum		
The New York Times Company	New York	Times	Company	The
St. Louis Power Company	Saint Louis	Power	Company	

9. Business Names with Compass Terms

Each word in a name containing compass terms is considered a separate filing unit. If the term includes more than one compass point, treat each compass point as a separate word even if written together. Establish permanent cross-references for compass points written as one word (*Northeast, see North East*).

As Written	As Filed			
	Unit 1	Unit 2	Unit 3	Unit 4
North East Dairy Co.	North	East	Dairy	Company
Northeast Farms	North	east	Farms	
Northeastern Gage Co.	North	eastern	Gage	Company
North Eastern Zinc	North	Eastern	Zinc	

10. Subsidiaries and Divisions

Subsidiary companies, divisions and affiliates are filed after the parent company's name. The parent or holding company name is the first filing unit. Insert a cross-reference from the subsidiary, etc. when needed for retrieval. A complete listing of the organizations under the parent or holding company can be inserted in the file for convenience.

As Written	As Filed				
	Unit 1	Unit 2	Unit 3	Unit 4	Unit 5	Unit 6
Crosley Division, Avco Corp.	Avco	Corporation	Crosley	Division		
Delco-Remy Division of General Motors Corporation	General	Motors	Corporation	Delco-Remy	Division (of)	
Electronics Laboratory, General Electric Company	General	Electric	Company	Electronics	Laboratory	

As Written	Unit 1	Unit 2	Unit 3	Unit 4	Unit 5	Unit 6
As Filed						
The Procurement Division, Martin Company	Martin	Company	Procurement	Division (The)		
Remington Rand Division, Sperry Rand Corporation	Sperry	Rand	Corporation	Remington	Rand	Division
Stromberg Carlson, a Div. of General Dynamics Corporation	General	Dynamics	Corporation	Stromberg	Carlson	(A) Division (of)
Vickers Inc. Division of Sperry Rand Corporation	Sperry	Rand	Corporation	Vickers	Incorporated	Division (of)

Government/Political Designations

Federal

a. Departments and agencies of the federal government are indexed under *United States Government*, first by the department title, and then sequentially by order of authority. Alphabetic sequencing begins at the secondary level (the department, bureau, or office).

> United States Government
>   Commerce, Dept. (of)
>   Economic Development Administration
> United States Government
>   Treasury, Dept. (of the)
>   Internal Revenue Service
>   Taxpayer Information
> United States Government
>   Labor, Department (of)
>   Labor Standards, Bureau (of)
>   Occupational Safety, Office (of)

b. Omit government name and file by the principal words in the name of the department and then by bureau or other units necessary for filing purposes.

> Agriculture, Forest Service
> Interior, Mines (Bureau of)
>
> Commerce, International Trade Administration
> Consumer Affairs (Office of)

Notes:

(1) Use the *United States Government Manual* as a guide for names of branches, executive departments, committees, commissions, etc. of the United States Government. **(2)** When a great deal of correspondence is carried on with one branch of the government, set aside a special section of the files for these records. File the agencies and offices alphabetically within the special section.

Military

File camps, forts, arsenals, bases, stations, depots, etc., after the prefix "United States Government."

United States Government
　Camp Edwards
United States Government
　Caven Point Terminal
United States Government
　Fort Sam Houston
United States Government
　Hawthorne Ammunition Depot

Equipment and Supplies

Filing Equipment

Filing equipment has improved in design and now offers office professionals and centralized filing departments a wide variety of choices. Three important considerations in the selection of filing equipment are available space, protection of records, and ease of retrieval.

Correspondence Files. Correspondence files are available in several types. The *vertical file* offers a two-, three-, four-, and five-drawer capacity. Each drawer holds about 60 to 70 pounds and is 26 to 30 inches deep. The most active files should be stored in the middle drawers, because there they are most accessible with the least amount of effort.

The *lateral file* contains lateral pull-out drawers. (The term *lateral* is somewhat misleading, because this equipment is vertical.) The drawers remain closed until pulled out, which makes them neater looking than open-shelf files. One advantage of this equipment is that the pull-out drawers require less space to access than a vertical file does. Another is that the user can see the contents of the entire pulled-out drawer rather than just a portion, which is often the case with a vertical drawer.

The *open-shelf file* looks more like an open bookcase than the more traditional vertical file. Folders used to hold documents are placed on the shelves in an upright position, with the tabs projecting from the side. Colored folders are often used to identify various kinds of files; this makes it easier to access and return folders to the correct spot. Open-shelf files use less space, reduce filing and retrieval time, and cost less to install. They are available for more than one user

A lateral file makes a neat appearance. *(Courtesy of Westinghouse Furniture)*

at a time and usually extend much higher than vertical filing cabinets; in fact, some extend from the floor to the ceiling and hold many more folders than cabinets would.

Mobile Power Equipment. Mobile filing equipment allows files or file shelves to be moved horizontally or vertically. This equipment requires less floor space than vertical and open-shelf files.

Movable-aisle shelves are open shelves clustered in groups of four or five and mounted on rollers or tracks. You can create an aisle by moving one set of shelves to the right or left. This equipment makes it difficult for several employees to access files in different locations, because when one aisle is open, all the others are closed.

Vertical mechanical shelves imitate a ferris wheel, with the shelves balanced to land horizontally while revolving vertically. This system can accommodate only one user at a time, but it brings the file to the user rather than vice versa. No doubt you are familiar with the desktop rotary file containing names and addresses. The same concept applies to vertical mechanical shelves except that the folders are placed upright on the shelves. This equipment is very heavy and is usually compressed into a small area; therefore, make sure the floor can withstand the weight.

Movable-aisle shelves.
(Courtesy of Gillotte Company)

Computer printout files are available as open-shelf files or as cabinets on wheels. *Circular rotary files* are based on a carousel concept.

Horizontal mechanical shelves are open-shelf files that revolve on electrical conveyors until the shelf on which the document resides reaches the user. Then it stops to allow removal of the material.

Card files are available in several types and serve different purposes:

- Rotary card files—used for limited amounts of information within easy reach
- Box files—used for storage
- Vertical card files
- Visible card files—used for inventories, personnel records, and accounting records
- Tub files—movable from one location to another
- Motorized filing equipment—allows operator to bring cards or folders within easy access by pushing a button

The three most common sizes are 3″ × 5″, 4″ × 6″, and 5″ × 8″.

Filing Supplies

You will be responsible for learning about the different types of filing supplies available. Any office supply company can provide a wide assortment of filing supplies to help you manage records.

Guides. Divider **guides** support folders upright and separate the filing space in drawers or on shelves into labeled categories, which makes it easier to file and retrieve documents. They are usually made of pressboard and have tabs in different positions. The widths of guide tabs and file folder tabs range from a full tab to one-fifth-cut tabs. A *tab cut* refers to the length of the tab extension located at the top of the folder.

Circular rotary file. Instead of moving vertically in a ferris wheel position, the folders are stacked upright on shelves that move in a circle horizontally. These shelves are available in various widths. This system can accommodate only one user at a time, but its placement can be useful if one person files or retrieves most of the records. *(Courtesy of Pollack)*

Divider guides make filing and document retrieval easier. *(Courtesy of Esselte Pendaflex Corporation)*

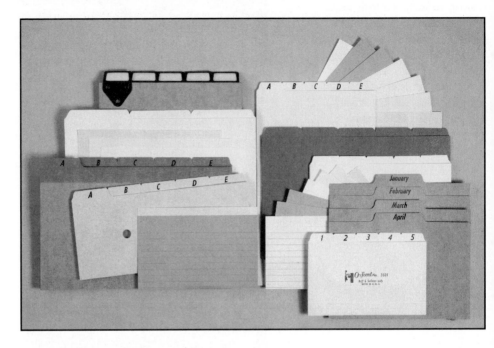

Out guides, as discussed earlier, are inserted when a folder is removed from the files. Constructed of heavy paper, an out guide provides space to record the name of the person who took the file, the date and time the folder was removed, and the anticipated return time. When the folder is returned and filed, the out guide is removed and can be used the next time material is checked out.

File Folders. File folders keep loose documents together. Manila folders are the most frequently used. Other folders are made of plastic, kraft, pressboard, and polyethylene. File folders come in various sizes, weights, and colors, with various tab cuts. Bellows or expansion folders are scored at the bottom, which allows them to expand slightly when they become full.

Hanging Files. *Hanging* or *suspended files* are used in many offices. These files have a metal strip at the top mounted on a metal frame that is placed on both sides of the file drawer or shelf. They resemble a hammock or blanket fold and do not touch the bottom of the drawer or shelf. A manila folder is inserted in the hanging file, which is constructed of heavy but flexible material to prevent folders from sagging.

Other File Drawer Supplies. Other filing supplies include folder labels, available in a variety of colors; colored signals for the top edges of folders and guides for their classification; and cross-reference sheets. Because of the wide variety of materials available, a filing supply catalog is a handy reference.

SUMMARY

Information is well managed when a set of filing procedures is established and followed. The procedures should take into account what managers need to complete their work and what items should be kept, routed, or thrown out immediately. The final test of the adequacy of your filing system is how quickly you can locate needed documents. By following a plan, you will improve your "finding average."

A five-step procedure for filing includes (1) inspecting, (2) indexing, (3) coding, (4) sorting, and (5) storing.

Charge-out records should be maintained for keeping track of material removed from files. A misfiled item can be located by following a set of steps to determine what happened to it.

Most offices use one of four basic filing systems. The alphabetic system is the most common because it is the most easily understood; the other systems are subject, geographic, and numeric systems.

The filing rules developed by ARMA can also be followed to improve the consistency with which files are managed. ARMA has developed Simplified Filing Standard Rules, Specific Filing Guidelines, Automated Conversion Guidelines, and Other Indexing Practices.

Special equipment and supplies are available to make filing simpler. Cabinets, files, and guides can be purchased in different sizes and colors. Catalogs describe and illustrate the various products available to help you select the ones best suited for your organization.

Key Terms

The following terms appeared in boldface type in this chapter. Do you recall what they mean? For a more complete definition, turn to the glossary beginning on p. 442.

captions (p. 281)
code (p. 281)
cross-reference (p. 282)
guide (p. 311)
index (p. 281)
inspect (p. 281)
out folder (p. 284)

out guide (p. 284)
pseudonym (p. 291)
release mark (p. 281)
sort (p. 282)
store (p. 283)
substitution card (p. 284)

Discussion Questions

1. You have been working for a small company since it opened five years ago and are well acquainted with its policies and activities. The owner is out of town for a few weeks, so you decide this would be a good time to clean out the overflowing files. How would you proceed, and why?
   a. Throw out every paper in the file that is more than six months old.
   b. Order storage cabinets and transfer all material more than six months old, keeping only the most current in the active files.
   c. Set up a list of guidelines for retention based on company usage of types of material. Dispose of all unneeded papers regardless of date; transfer to storage any important but unused material; suggest more secure facilities for vital documents.
   d. Separate all the papers you think should be removed from the current files; store them in boxes for the owner to go through at a later time.
   e. Set up suggested guidelines and a retention plan but do nothing further until your plan can be looked over, discussed, and approved by the owner.
2. You notice several large piles of paper on your manager's worktable and decide to see what is accumulating. All are reports that she has received from various departments and other managers. Most contain routine information. Some are computer printouts. You watch the piles grow and the dust gather day by day and finally decide to do something about it. Which of the following methods would you use, and why?
   a. Dump them all in the wastebasket to be recycled.
   b. Sort them according to department or topic and file them to get them out of the way.
   c. Suggest to your manager that those records could be eliminated since they are only gathering dust.
   d. Suggest to your manager that she dispose of them one way or another.
   e. Ignore them.

3. Your manager has read the morning mail and put it back on your desk to attend to. What would you do with the following?
   a. Notice of a meeting
   b. Cover letter accompanying a requested brochure
   c. Contract for a new client
   d. Advertising letter and brochure for office supplies
   e. Reply to a request for information from a client
   f. Minutes of a committee meeting for a community organization
   g. Request for advertising material that has already been sent
   h. Informational notice to all employees
   i. Replies for attendance at a luncheon meeting next week
   j. Thank-you letter
4. In going through the files, you find the following materials. Classify each according to whether it should be filed indefinitely, is temporarily important, or should be destroyed.
   a. Correspondence for an ongoing project
   b. Articles of Incorporation
   c. Contracts with freelance writers
   d. General correspondence on closed matters
   e. Outdated job descriptions
   f. Rough draft of an operating manual printed last year
   g. Financial statements
   h. Outdated price lists and catalogs
   i. Current advertising brochures
   j. General notices to all employees
5. What habits lead to poor records and information storage practices? What eventually can happen to your office's operations as a result of these procedures?

Exercises

1. Rearrange the following in correct order assuming a simple alphabetic system.
   a. Stake's Feed Company
   b. Antoine Salmon, Jr.
   c. Jane Strakes
   d. Scheller Glass Company
   e. St. Roberts Church
   f. S. & Q. Shoe Store
   g. Stein-Adelman Furs, Inc.
   h. San Carlos Rest Home
   i. Oak Street Garage
   j. South City Auto Supplies
2. Indicate which of the following pairs would come first, and why.
   a. John McMurthy; Homer MacNulty
   b. All-State Pavers; Charles Allenbury

    c. Marian Van de Vost; Merle Vancleeter
    d. Katrina Powers; Kermit Power's Vending Company
    e. 18th Street Garage; 8th Avenue Shoe Shop
    f. Merwin Fitz Ryan; Fitzgerald Market
    g. George Halsted; George H. Halsted
    h. St. Louis Terminal Company; San Francisco Hotel
3. Rearrange the following in correct order assuming a geographic system.
    a. Carthage, Illinois
    b. Evansville, Indiana
    c. Fargo, North Dakota
    d. Butte, Montana
    e. Rhode Island
    f. Jane's Catering
       900 North Edwards
       Memphis, Tennessee
    g. The Citizens Bank
       2 West Oak
       Bowling Green, Kentucky
    h. Small Business Development Center
       208 Main
       Reno, Nevada

Assignments

1. In groups of two or three, visit one of the following organizations to obtain information on their filing procedures: law office, hospital or clinic, manufacturing firm, or insurance agency. Ask the office manager or a senior office professional the following questions:
    a. Is material coded before it is filed?
    b. What type of filing system is in use? Alphabetic? ARMA? Other?
    c. Are all files decentralized? Which, if any, are centralized?
    d. Is a file retention schedule followed? When are files cleaned?
    e. How are files charged out? What records are kept so files can be easily located?
    Present brief reports of what you learned.
2. Review several recent issues of office management publications and prepare a list of filing systems, equipment, and related items now available. Pick out interesting or unusual features that could make filing easier.
3. Set up a list of classmates in a manual file using the ARMA filing rules. Make a similar list combining your family and friends.

Those instructors using *Top Performance: A Decision-Making Simulation for the Office* should consult the *Instructor's Guide* at this point for support material regarding use of the software in the classroom.

Case Study

Helen See loves working for the vice-president of administration at RPM/ Bamco, one of the fastest growing producers of hospital measurement equipment in the country. Nearly one hundred office, sales, and production personnel work in a new facility. But the new building is already too small. Endless boxes of equipment are stacked next to office supplies.

Helen began a filing system last year. But work was so rushed that she ended up cramming items into the few cabinets available. Now some files are lost and stacks of to-be-filed items are still in boxes.

One Saturday morning, Helen began a review of the files and boxes. She found quite a collection, including, among other things, miscellaneous papers, payroll records, income tax returns, advertising layouts, contracts, job applications, and purchase orders. The chaos seemed overwhelming, but she knew that some order must emerge. She also believed that RPM/Bamco management would support and finance a logical plan, including hiring personnel to assist her.

Helen's work won't slow down enough to allow a lot of uninterrupted time to set up the needed files. Can you help her work out a plan that takes into account the company's needs and her own responsibilities? The plan should include methods for keeping the proposed system in top operating condition.

CHAPTER

14

MANAGING RECORDS

Chapter Objectives

- To know why offices need records management

- To learn different ways to manage records

- To find out how to analyze an office's records management system

- To realize the importance of office professionals in records management

- To understand the importance of periodically reviewing a records management system for possible changes

Examples of Excellence

"Backup file or archive?" Ann Demorest asked the caller when she requested that the records of a sales campaign be retrieved. "These records are on my backup disks," she said. "I keep them handy for requests like these."

To avoid overloading her computer's hard-disk memory, Ann regularly puts some information onto individual disks. She has access to hundreds of files in active storage, all of them easy to retrieve and use. Another group of files are in archives, or "inactive storage," in her computer network's centralized memory. Retrieving these records takes a bit longer, but all are coded and on a menu, so they are easy to locate.

In addition to her many other duties, Ann manages information. She has numerous files stored in the manner described in Chapter 13. One small metal cabinet contains the microforms of old but still important documents stored in a bank vault.

Although the terms *information* and *records* are used interchangeably, information indicates the value organizations place on stored material; it is the data essential for daily operation. Most organizations would have a difficult time surviving without information, but it is becoming increasingly difficult to capture, organize, and store it so that it will be available when needed.

At one time, experts predicted that the "office of the future," with all its electronic bells and whistles, would be "paperless." People assumed that because computers allow for easy transmission and screen reading, hardcopies would no longer be needed. Computers will definitely eliminate some paper, but there will be plenty left. By the year 2000, some businesses will still need a space equivalent to all of the office space in Pittsburgh to file the 120 billion sheets of new paper they will generate each year.[1]

Most office professionals use a three-part system to keep track of the great volume of information for which they are responsible. First, some information is kept in folders in filing cabinets or desk drawers. Second, micrographics technology is applied for storing large numbers of documents, such as historical records, for extended periods. Third, the use of electronic filing is growing rapidly. Today information is often stored on computer disks with a filing system for easy reference. This approach requires a well-thought-out filing method to permit easy access to and retrieval of documents. Coding systems in particular aid in locating materials quickly.

In this chapter, you will learn

- Why every office need a records management system
- Various systems for managing records
- How to analyze your office's records management system
- The contributions office professionals make to records management

Why Offices Need a Records Management System

Handling office paperwork is very time consuming and costly. If records are not carefully stored, businesses tend to

- Make duplicate copies out of fear that the originals will be lost
- Buy additional filing cabinets or additional memory to store records
- Create piles of material to be reviewed before throwing out what has become irrelevant
- Keep more records than necessary because no systematic method for destroying records that are no longer useful has been established

Studies of information use consistently point out how rarely material in files is used. For example, 70 percent of documents one year old are never reviewed again. Only 60 percent of material less than a year old is checked.

Obviously there are exceptions to these statistics. Financial and personnel records are checked regularly. Contracts and other agreements must be stored where they can be easily found. Ongoing reports or projects need to be close at hand.

As you saw in Chapter 13, the potential for misfiling documents is great. The more material kept, the greater the likelihood of misplacing or losing items. Research indicates that about one out of twenty documents placed in a file drawer is misfiled.

[1]Wohl Associated, *The Wall Street Journal*, June 4, 1990.

By learning about your office's recordkeeping procedures and applying some effective techniques for records management, you will make an important contribution to your organization.

How Records Are Managed

To manage records effectively, you first need to learn the recordkeeping systems of your manager and the office in general. If these systems differ, you may need to make some changes in one or the other.

As you learned in Chapter 13, all filing systems use an alphabetic or numeric index or a combination of the two. The principles for filing information in a manual system are often the same as those in a computer system. Let's review each of the three filing systems used in offices today.

Manual Filing Systems

Manual filing systems, the oldest of the three types of systems, generally work well when the business uses a low volume of information. When the amount of information needed increases, however, a manual system can quickly become overburdened. First, regular filing of documents is put off. Then piles of items to be sorted, labeled, and stored accumulate. Often the response to this situation is to buy more filing cabinets.

Some managers establish their own separate sets of files to have ready access to important information. Records may be stored in a manager's private group of files, the office's files, or both. Thus, the same materials are filed in several places. This takes up expensive space and requires additional time for locating lost items.

Technology has effectively addressed some of the problems of manual filing systems. However, this does not mean that manual filing systems have been replaced. Actually, technology should be used to *enhance* manual filing systems. Most offices continue to use a manual system for some of their recordkeeping activities.

Micrographics Filing Systems

Important original documents and frequently used file folders are often kept in a file drawer or cabinet. However, **micrographics filing systems** have made it possible to reduce the number of file drawers and cabinets and still allow access to all the documents previously stored there.

Micrographics is based on the principle of miniaturization. This technology provides such efficient reductions of printed documents that complete books can stored on a single "page" of 6″ × 4″ film. Today micrographics represents a total information system, from filming to filing and retrieval.

Banks, libraries, government agencies, newspaper publishers, and other organizations concerned with large volumes of records now routinely use microfilm-based systems. All types of documents, from invoices to personnel files, are successfully microfilmed and microfiched. The use of micrographics reduces document storage needs, and allows records to be kept indefinitely and retrieved quickly.

Microfilm. **Microfilm** is the oldest and the most economical form of this technology. Information is recorded on film and can be viewed on a microfilm reader (Figure 14–1). Microfilm is generally best suited for large volumes of sequentially numbered documents that are retrieved infrequently.

Microfilm generally uses roll film in reels, cartridges, or cassettes. Reels are manually loaded and must be rewound before being used again. Cartridges are easily tucked in a holder on the reader. Cassettes, which have a continuous loop of film, are also loaded in a holder on the reader and are easy to use. On some viewing equipment the image can be rotated or small sections of the document enlarged for better viewing. Full-color microfilm is available, but it is expensive.

In many organizations, documents are microfilmed and assigned an eleven-digit number. The first five digits indicate the date and roll number, and the remaining six indicate the position on the roll. This system ensures accessibility.

Figure 14–1

Microfilm reader. Back issues of numerous magazines and newspapers are among the types of items that can be viewed on a microfilm reader. *(Courtesy of Minolta)*

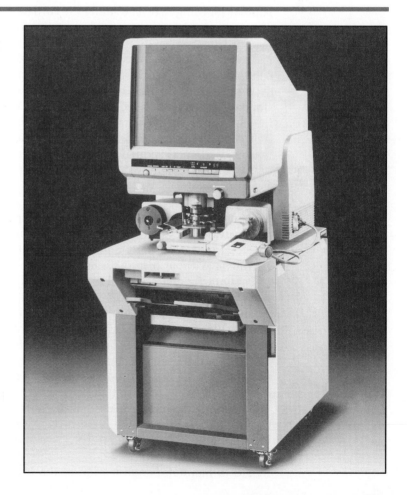

Before microfilming any record, consider these questions:

1. How long will documents be kept? Records kept from one to fifteen years or permanently, and used periodically should be microfilmed.
2. In what condition is the material? Records that show signs of wear, such as yellowing, should be stored on microfilm.
3. How clear is the document? Blurred material and colors will not show up well. Also, defects will be magnified.
4. How will the microfilm material be used? Individuals can read documents easily, but groups of more than three will have difficulty.
5. How many individuals will use the microfilm? Infrequent users may find locating records difficult and then misfile them.

Aperture Cards. Aperture cards are paper cards that have a piece of film mounted in an opening on the right-hand side. Each card usually holds one image, but it can also hold a filmstrip with two or three images. The top of the card carries a line of identifying information for filing purposes.

Aperture cards are generally used for engineering-type drawings and are also popular for filing X-rays. Usually the cards are filed and retrieved manually. The filing space on an aperture card is around five times that available on microfilm.

Microfiche. Microfiche is a sheet of film with microrecords stored in rows and columns on a card. A large number of documents (currently in the thousands, depending on document size and the amount of reduction) can be stored on a standard-size single sheet of 4″ × 6″ film. Microfiche is suitable for documents that are retrieved frequently and widely distributed. It is also easy to mail.

It is possible to store pieces of microfiche in microfilm jackets for individual images or a small sequence of images. The jackets are open-ended plastic- or card-stock carriers in which individual film frames can be inserted and updated at any time.

Computer Output Microfilm (COM). Computer output microfilm (COM) is a more advanced system of records management. This technology uses magnetic tape as input, translates data into readable language, and then microfilms a document without printing a hardcopy.

Computer-aided retrieval (CAR) is used with COM. This process speeds up retrieval of microfilmed documents using a computerized, key-word-indexed database. The computer will automatically index all films, and the user can later request the computer to locate the filmed records. Most records can be located within fifteen seconds. After the film is loaded onto a reader, the computer guides it to the exact location desired. The document can then be displayed on the reader screen. If desired, a paper copy of the document can be made.

Sometimes records are used in a court of law. The Uniform Photographic Copies of Business and Public Records as Evidence Act of 1951 allows records to be admissible if (1) the microrecord was made from an original document in the regular course of business; (2) the microrecord was photographed from an entire record to facilitate identification of the original document; and (3) the microrecord is legible enough to constitute an accurate representation of the original record. To use such records, you must maintain logs to verify the accuracy of the microfilming process.

Electronic Filing Systems

Although floppy-disk or diskette sizes vary and the lack of standardized equipment sometimes results in compatibility problems, many companies now rely heavily on **electronic filing systems**. One diskette can record information that would occupy fifteen or more file folders. Today, storage cases for diskettes have replaced filing cabinets (Figure 14–2). Keeping the "files" current is easy because information can be quickly added, deleted, or changed.

The same careful attention in managing records is needed when using an electronic filing system as is required with a manual system. Each document must be accurately labeled and a system developed for easy access. Some offices keep a list of the contents with the disks. Such a list can save a great deal of locating time if it is kept up to date.

You can store groups of floppy disks in file boxes with alphabetical or numerical tabs. Some disks can be stored in protective jackets and their contents listed on the outside. Be sure to remove the disk from its jacket before writing on the jacket so you do not damage the disk.

Other electronic storage media include magnetic tapes (which are decreasing in use as more advanced technology appears); hard disks with much greater capacity and faster access; and optical disks. Hard-disk storage is becoming more common in all types of computer systems—from desktop personal computers to computer networks. Hard disks can store much more data; one hard-disk drive can hold the contents of fifteen floppy disks. Also, hard disks let you retrieve information more quickly.

With electronic filing, you will truly be managing information. Detailed data on customers, for example, can be kept, updated, and sorted in numerous ways.

Figure 14–2
Diskette storage cases. Storage cases save desktop space and keep diskettes clean and well organized. *(Courtesy of Curtis Manufacturing Company, Inc.)*

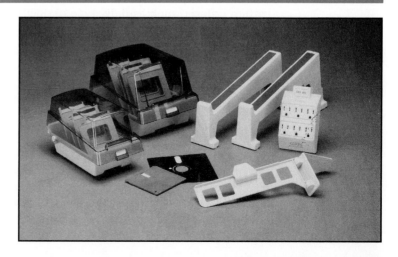

With **sorting,** you can produce lists of customers in specific locations categorized by ZIP codes or by the ages of the account. You will be able to search these files rapidly, expand them as needed, maintain their security with passwords or codes, and prepare hardcopy quickly.

One obvious disadvantage of electronic filing is that if the system breaks down, you will not have access to data. If the hard drive is destroyed, data will be lost. Experienced users therefore emphasize the importance of backing up data on diskettes or tape. *Backing up* means making a second copy of all material on your hard disk in case the first copy is lost or damaged.

CD-ROM. Compact disks with read-only memory (CD-ROMs) are becoming viable for business. This technology is an outgrowth of the popular compact audiodisk systems that produce near-perfect sound. CD-ROMs are laser disks that carry data (instead of music) in previously unheard-of quantities. For example, one CD-ROM 4.72 inches in diameter can store all the data from 1,500 to 1,800 traditional floppy disks, about 50 four-drawer vertical files, or 250,000 pages of text. A CD-ROM system hooks up to a standard personal computer and is suitable for information that does not change.

Organizationwide Computer System. An organization-wide computer system can bring together information from a variety of documents to form a new one. For example, suppose your manager requests you to prepare a report that requires you to collect certain data. Instead of having to make phone calls to get information or collect several documents from a manual file or a diskette, you send messages by computer to various offices and ask that the information be transmitted to your computer. Or you may decide to directly access from your computer the database on which the information is stored. After you have completed the report, you can restore or delete the data. To use this procedure, you must know how to "call up" the data. Generally, you will be able to use various commands to obtain the data you need.

Technology will continue to expand the capability of computers, and costs will continue to decrease. For example, recently available software will allow you to track specific documents or information on an individual by entering certain criteria, such as date, type of document, or general subject.

Keeping Records

Most organizations keep records either in a single location or close to where individual employees work. Each system has its advantages and disadvantages.

Centralized System

In a **centralized system,** all records are kept in one location and the authority and responsibility for maintaining them are in the hands of one person. A centralized system is usually more cost-effective, because there are more controls over it; thus, fewer records are lost. Because most records are located in one place, equipment and space can be used more efficiently. Also, this system reduces the need for duplicate records.

On the other hand, the records in a centralized system are less accessible to users. Also, confidentiality of records may be difficult to preserve because documents may be accessible to several employees unless other security arrangements are made. For this reason, some companies prefer to keep confidential records in specific employees' offices.

Decentralized System

In a **decentralized system,** no one person is placed in charge. Each work area is responsible for keeping its own records, and employees in that area usually share the recordkeeping function.

The lack of a designated person in charge, however, can be a disadvantage. Because no one individual feels primarily responsible, updating records and other tasks may suffer. Many organizations solve this problem by using a combination of centralized and decentralized systems: "Neutral" files are stored in a centralized place with one person in charge, while confidential materials are kept in designated offices.

Analyzing Your Records Management System

As an office professional, you will have few opportunities to set up a new records management system. Most likely, you will "inherit" a system that is unlikely to change fundamentally. It's important that you learn your organization's **retention and disposal procedures**—methods for determining which records are kept and which are discarded. If you believe that modifications are needed, take the following steps:

1. Carefully review the records management system. Then prepare a list that identifies
   a. Format of records kept—paper, microfilm, floppy disk, hard disk
   b. Types of records kept, especially those to be kept indefinitely
   c. Location of active and inactive files, particularly those essential to the organization's operation
2. List the materials that are kept, such as correspondence, reports, personnel records, and financial forms. Also, find out how long each item is kept and when material can be thrown out.
3. Learn what methods are used to identify records that are no longer useful and to destroy outdated, confidential material.
4. Discuss with your manager and experienced co-workers any problems related to locating specific records.
5. Assemble a list of files less than a year old, both hardcopy and computer stored. Identify those that are still considered active.

Figure 14–3, page 326, outlines a typical record retention schedule.

Usually your manager, co-workers, and you will clean out filing cabinets at certain times each year. To avoid throwing out material that should be kept, ask your manager to approve the removal of records that appear to be of lasting value. Also, check active files for duplicate copies and other unneeded material. Destroy confidential information properly: by shredding it or tearing it up completely.

Your Role in Records Management

The ultimate goal of any records management program is to deliver a filed document or other information to a person at the desired time and location, in the form requested, and at a reasonable cost.

Figure 14-3
Record retention schedule.

This is only a rough guide and requires adjustment to specific needs and statutory requirements. Legal counsel is advisable before putting a record retention schedule into effect.

Retain Indefinitely

- Audit reports and financial statements
- Cancelled checks for taxes, capital purchases, important contracts
- Capital stock and bond records
- Cash books
- Contracts and leases in force
- Copyrights, patents, trademark registrations
- Corporation charter, minute books, and bylaws
- Correspondence on legal and tax matters
- Deeds, mortgages, easements, appraisals, and other property records
- General ledgers and journals
- Insurance records
- Tax returns and work papers, including records to support carrybacks and carryovers

Retain Seven to Eight Years

- Other cancelled checks
- Vouchers for payments to vendors, employees, etc.
- Inventories
- Payroll records, including time sheets
- Expense reports
- Payables and receivables ledgers
- Expired contracts and leases
- Purchase orders
- Invoices and other sales records
- Plant cost ledgers

Retain Six Years

- Monthly trial balances
- Employee withholding tax statements
- Employee disability benefits records

Retain Three Years

- Personnel files on terminated employees
- Bank reconciliations
- Petty-cash vouchers
- Expired insurance policies with no residual values

Retain Two Years

- General correspondence
- Requisitions

You are likely to be involved in all four phases of records management: (1) creation, (2) active use, (3) inactive storage, and (4) final disposition. Your responsibility at each stage is to ensure that any record can be found easily.

Creation

During the creation phase, you may prepare a letter or memo or organize a lengthy document. Often you will use portions of existing letters to compose form letters more quickly. Once you have completed and sent items, file all paper copies. Experienced office professionals suggest filing items at least once every other day to avoid buildup. At this time, you can quickly check files for duplicate or potentially confusing items.

Often you will prepare a document using your computer. When it is completed, you will "save" it in a new or established file. You should establish some type of coding system to allow quick retrieval. Nothing is as frustrating as knowing that you have stored a document in your computer and having no idea where it is stored.

File Naming for Electronic Filing. Currently there is no standard method of naming files. Each organization should develop a consistent system for naming documents as they are originated, updated, or requested. Some word processing equipment will automatically assign a number to each document. This number is then used as part of the coding system.

One method is to name a document by using a *character position scheme*. With this method, each character position is assigned either an alphabetic or a numeric code that the user will understand. For example, a simple code might have the following elements:

Position Number	Data
1	File classification
	(T) Tax
	(A) Auditing
	(C) Consulting
2	Subclassification
	(P) Private
	(G) Government
3	Month: (0–12)
	(O) October
	(N) November
	(D) December
4	Year: (0–9) (6) 1986
	(5) 1995
5	Client ID: (a–z)
6	Client ID: (a–z)
7	Creator ID: (A–Z)
8	Open position: (O)

In this format, a file named TG96rvMO would give the user the following information: It contains tax information (T) for the government (G); it was created in September (9), 1986 (6), for a client (rv) by Mary Brown (M); a position is still open (O), too. This file name could be typed at the bottom of the document to indicate where the document was filed.

Another file-naming method uses descriptive alphabetic abbreviations of the document, such as EXAM1 (Examination 1), PROJB (Project B), or JOB8 (Job 8).

Most software packages allow limited space (six to eight letter or number combinations) for naming a file; thus, providing a name that will be recognizable in the future may be challenging. This method may prove difficult if other users need to access the files, because they will not know the file names unless you keep a list.

Active Use

During the active-use phase of a document's life cycle, the document must be readily accessible to a user. The length of time specified varies from one organization to another; a rule of thumb is that documents should be accessible for reference two or three times a month. To ensure that documents can be found easily and quickly,

- Return files to their proper locations.
- Review documents to see that they are in chronological order.
- Throw out unneeded duplicate items.
- File material as soon as possible after it has been marked or checked by your manager.

With your manager, establish guidelines for determining when documents should pass from the active-use phase to the next phase: inactive storage.

Inactive Storage

To determine when a record should be transferred from an active to an inactive status, develop a records retention schedule. This schedule should list all documents (or categories of documents) and identify when and how to dispose of each (see Figure 14–3, page 326). After a trial schedule has been prepared, the company's attorney and representative of top management should review it. These individuals are in the best position to determine which items must be kept and which can be destroyed.

A similar procedure should be followed with documents filed electronically. Electronic records filed in computer memory or other media can become expensive to maintain. On the other hand, take care not to delete any records that will be needed in the future. One way to reduce the number of files on a hard disk is to periodically clear it and keep important documents on floppy disks as backup to hardcopy.

It may be appropriate to destroy some records after the active-use phase. Others will enter the inactive-storage phase in a less used and less expensive area.

Final Disposition

In the final-disposition phase, records that have fulfilled their purpose may be destroyed. Typically only about 1 percent of all records in an organization need to be filed permanently. However, because these are critical records, special care must be taken to ensure that they are kept properly.

Communication Tips

The following tips will help you perform your records management duties effectively:

- Ask your manager to identify records used daily or weekly.
- Find out from your manager and others which materials are used monthly or bimonthly.
- Show your manager any proposed changes in the records management system for review and approval.
- Determine from your manager which documents can be kept and which can be thrown out.
- Determine which records should be on microfilm.
- Periodically review the records management system to determine whether changes are needed.

SUMMARY

Efficient records management is essential to the smooth running of a business. In this Information Age, the need for quick retrieval of documents continues to grow. This may be your responsibility.

A records management system plays a vital role in office productivity. The goal of a records management system is to allow quick and easy retrieval of documents. To make this possible, you should learn when it is appropriate to use manual, micrographic (microfilm, microfiche, COM, CAM), and electronic (floppy-disk and hard-disk) filing systems.

When analyzing your office's records management system, you determine the storage methods used, materials kept and used frequently, identification methods, and disposal procedures. Special care is needed when disposing of confidential records.

Because increasing numbers of documents are being stored in computer memory, you need to develop uncomplicated methods for identifying electronically filed documents.

You will likely be involved in all four phases of records management: creation (documents are prepared), active-use (documents must be kept accessible for reference), inactive storage (documents move from active to inactive status), and final disposition (documents of no further use are destroyed).

Key Terms

The following terms appeared in boldface type in this chapter. Do you recall what they mean? For a more complete definition, turn to the glossary beginning on p. 442.

aperture card (p. 322)
centralized system (p. 324)
compact disk read-only memory
(CD-ROM) (p. 324)
computer-aided retrieval (CAR)
(p. 322)
computer output microfilm (COM)
(p. 322)
decentralized system (p. 325)

electronic filing system (p. 323)
manual filing system (p. 320)
microfiche (p. 322)
microfilm (p. 321)
micrographics filing system (p. 320)
retention and disposal procedures
(p. 325)
sorting (p. 324)

Discussion Questions

1. Your manager has asked you to convert to microfiche certain information, now kept as paper files, for a trial period. Which of the following would you suggest for testing the value of this method? (Your manager is "technology shy" and will have to be convinced that this innovation won't reduce accessibility of needed records.)
   a. Meeting log for a large project in operation for the past year and likely to continue
   b. Financial records for the past five years
   c. Organizational procedures manual, especially sections dealing with cost verification
   d. Correspondence related to an OSHA complaint concerning plant safety
   Explain how microfiche would be useful and convenient for the item you choose.
2. You are an assistant to three accountants in a small accounting firm in your community. The firm has a mix of correspondence, financial statements, copies of IRS forms, and manuals. Given the kinds of records the accountants are likely to keep, what advantages would a micrographics system provide? What records should be kept on microfilm for both cost and security reasons?
3. What would you include in a list of guides to security for computer-stored and micrographically stored records? Design your guides so that both managers and part-time personnel can use them easily.
4. What magazines would you check for information on the state-of-the-art in micrographics and pending developments of interest and possible value to your office?
5. As an office professional, what will be your major responsibilities in the operation, maintenance, and expansion of a micrographics filing system?

Be creative in your thinking, remembering that managers will rely on your professional ability in this area as in others.

6. One of the first things you notice in your new job is that the files are in chaos. Many materials are misfiled, file drawers are overcrowded, there is no room for new file cabinets, some materials in the folders are not filed chronologically, and many documents are over ten years old. You learn that all materials over three years old can be transferred to the central files. Make a list of procedures you'll need to ask about to ensure an efficient records management system.

Assignments

1. Identify three organizations such as a school district office, accounting firm, or manufacturing plant. Develop a short list of questions to ask someone in each organization about how records are managed. These questions should deal with how much and what kind of technology is used, if they have a centralized or decentralized system, who manages records, any problems they can identify, and anticipated changes. After gathering responses from these organizations, prepare a short report on similarities, differences, and degrees of reliance on technology.

2. Go to your local library and look up an article on micrographics in a periodical stored on microfilm. View the article on the reader and make a copy of it, if possible. Identify any problems you encountered using microfilm. Was reading the document difficult? How much time do you think you would spend reviewing documents kept in this manner?

Those instructors using *Top Performance: A Decision-Making Simulation for the Office* should consult the *Instructor's Guide* at this point for support material regarding use of the software in the classroom.

Case Study

J. M. Wheeling opened a small gift shop. Through hard work and good management, his business prospered and expanded to include many new items. Wheeling's inventory now numbers in the thousands and has become increasingly difficult to control even though he has six full-time and ten part-time employees.

Wheeling had read several articles about the use of micrographics and computer systems to maintain inventory records. As he considered these alternatives, he asked himself the following questions:

1. Would a micrographics or a computerized filing system better help me in my business?
2. How would I go about converting my records with each system?
3. What types of equipment and training would each system require?

How can Wheeling use the alternatives of micrographics and computerized filing systems to manage the records of his expanding business? Review the material in this chapter and Chapter 2 on computer use to develop your responses.

UNIT 4

BUILDING YOUR COMPETENCE

CHAPTER

15 HANDLING FINANCES

Chapter Objectives

- To learn the specific procedures required for financial control

- To learn to manage an office petty-cash fund and checking account

- To understand the procedures to follow with computer-based accounts

- To learn to manage credit cards

- To understand which financial records to keep and why

Examples of Excellence

"That's why your account shows a deficit," Diane Boucek told the new manager, who was puzzled about the monthly statement's figures and the minus sign in front of the total balance available. "The middle column shows expense," she added.

Having worked in a large government bureaucracy, Diane knew how to interpret complex financial statements. By attending training sessions, calling the business office, and asking co-workers, she had developed valuable financial management expertise.

In addition to interpreting statements, Diane shows co-workers how to fill out forms properly and alerts managers to potential account problems. Although she rarely handles cash or checks directly, Diane and many of her colleagues play a significant role in the management of their organization's finances.

Through a quick review, Diane and the manager were able to pinpoint how certain purchases had exceeded monthly income. Diane also outlined the key points of the report so that the manager could easily interpret it without her assistance.

Today, both public and private organizations have strict procedures for handling their own or other people's money. As an office professional, you will have to know and follow those procedures, whether the amount is $20 or $20,000. Your close attention to all aspects of financial transactions will be especially important.

In this chapter you will learn the details of managing a variety of financial responsibilities, including

- Why financial control requires specific procedures
- How to manage an office petty-cash fund and checking account
- What procedures to follow with computer-based accounts
- How to pay bills
- How to manage credit cards
- Which financial records to keep and why

Managing Money Today

Managing money has always been important in both public and private organizations. You will need to pay careful attention to details and develop simple but effective financial management procedures for several reasons.

First, today there is a widespread emphasis on cost control: Managers stress cutting back, purchasing less-expensive items, and reimbursing only legitimate expenses.

Second, consistent and careful auditing is extremely important in today's business world. Auditors may be employees of your organization or representatives of a firm hired to check past statements and determine whether both organizational and government regulations are being followed. They will ask for records such as receipts, bills, monthly statements, and cancelled checks, and those items must be readily available for inspection. Also the federal or state government may request proof of transactions for tax verification purposes.

Third, most transactions today are computerized. You may need to fill out forms that initiate a purchase, payment, travel advance, or cash deposited in a checking account and enter the information on your desktop terminal. To do this correctly, you will have to follow specific directions: The correct boxes must be checked and the total account number entered along with the account title and information justifying the transaction. Errors slow down important transactions and lead to lengthy delays and missed deadlines.

For these reasons you must carefully check all details, review all work, and keep complete records. The following sections focus on procedures for managing specific financial responsibilities.

Checking Accounts

You may be in charge of an office checking account, especially if you work in a relatively small organization such as a law office, architectural firm, or insurance agency. This account will likely be a regular business checking account, which requires no minimum balance and pays no interest on the balance maintained. You should know the type of checking account used and the requirements for its use. When you have questions, your organization's financial institution will readily assist you.

Your manager will need to make four decisions regarding the office checking account:

1. What bills will be paid and when
2. How deposits will be made
3. How much cash will be kept in the account at any given time
4. Who will reconcile statements and address any problems that arise

Deposits

You will deposit checks or cash with a deposit slip each time you put money into the account. In some organizations, deposits are made each day; in others, deposits are held until a certain dollar amount is reached.

To ensure that you make deposits correctly, you will need the following information:

- Name and address of the account as it is listed in the bank's records
- Account number, printed in magnetic ink along the bottom of the check
- Date of deposit
- List of denominations in which cash is being deposited
- List of checks to be deposited

All checks must be endorsed. It is suggested that each check be listed by its ABA transit number. This is the multidigit number assigned by the American Bankers Association and located on the front of the check, just beneath the check number. It is used to identify the specific bank on which the check is drawn so that the check will be returned to that bank. If the check is drawn on the bank to which the deposit is being made, record the name of the person writing the check.

If there is a large number of coins, sort them by denomination and put them in coin wrappers (supplied by the bank). Identify the account name on each roll. To save time, many businesses bring their loose coins to the bank and have them sorted by machine. If there are only a few coins, put them in a sealed envelope. Stack bills according to denomination, face up in the same direction, and put them in bill wrappers (also supplied by the bank). Identify the account name on each wrapper.

Endorsements

To be deposited, a check must be endorsed by the *payee*—the person or company to whom the check is written. The endorsement is made by the payee or a representative of the payee in handwriting or with a rubber stamp. If the payee's name is written incorrectly on the face of the check, the check should be endorsed twice: first as it is written on the face of the check and then as the account name appears in the bank's records. There are three basic types of endorsement: blank, restrictive, and full (Figure 15–1).

A *blank endorsement* is simply the payee's signature. This type of endorsement should be used only when you're at the bank and plan to deposit the check immediately. Because the check is payable to the bearer, anyone who has possession of it can cash it.

Figure 15–1
Check endorsements.

Blank Endorsement

Thomas B. Anderson

Restrictive Endorsement

For deposit only in account XXXX

Full Endorsement

*Paid to the order of:
Ace Vending Company
Thomas B. Anderson*

ENDORSE CHECK HERE

X *Thomas B. Anderson*

DO NOT SIGN/WRITE/STAMP BELOW THIS LINE
FOR FINANCIAL INSTITUTION USE ONLY

A *restrictive endorsement* limits the use of the check to the purpose stated in the endorsement, for example, "for deposit only in account XXXX." This form of endorsement should be used when checks will be sent to the bank by mail.

A *full endorsement* includes both the name and signature of the payee. With this type of endorsement, only the payee can endorse the check.

Recent regulations governing banking procedures require that endorsements be written in a designated space on the reverse side of the check. Most newly printed checks specify exactly where to place endorsements.

Writing Checks

For the checks you write to be legal, they must be written in ink, *not* in pencil. Also, you must provide the following: check number, current date, payee, amount (both in numbers and written out), and signature (Figure 15–2, page 340).

Magnetic ink character recognition (MICR) numbers preprinted at the bottom left-hand corners of all checks represent the routing symbol, the bank's transit number, and the depositor's account number. These numbers are read by optical character recognition (OCR) equipment. When the check is presented to the bank, the amount and date are added in magnetic ink below the MICR numbers.

If you make a mistake in writing a check, do not erase or cross out the error. Instead, write *void* both on the front of the check and next to the check number

Figure 15–2
Parts of a check.

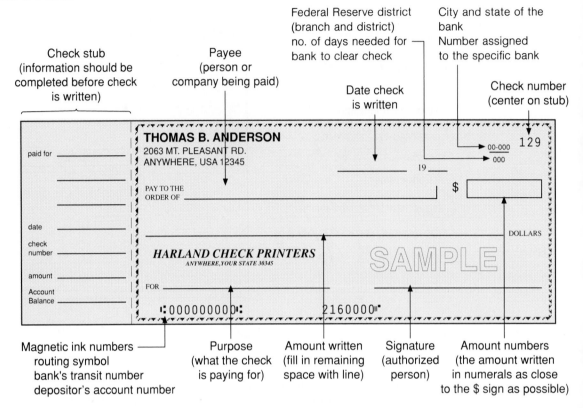

Check stub
(information should be
completed before check
is written)

Payee
(person or
company being paid)

Federal Reserve district
(branch and district)
no. of days needed for
bank to clear check

City and state of the
bank
Number assigned
to the specific bank

Date check
is written

Check number
(center on stub)

THOMAS B. ANDERSON
2063 MT. PLEASANT RD.
ANYWHERE, USA 12345

129
00-000
000

paid for

19

PAY TO THE
ORDER OF

$

date

DOLLARS

check
number

HARLAND CHECK PRINTERS
ANYWHERE, YOUR STATE 30345

SAMPLE

amount

FOR

Account
Balance

⑆000000000⑆   2160000⑈

Magnetic ink numbers
routing symbol
bank's transit number
depositor's account number

Purpose
(what the check
is paying for)

Amount written
(fill in remaining
space with line)

Signature
(authorized
person)

Amount numbers
(the amount written
in numerals as close
to the $ sign as possible)

Note: Review subtraction of check amount from balance. Errors at
this point make reconciling errors on bank statements difficult.

in the register or stub, and write a new check. Be sure to keep voided checks for
your records.

Stopping Payment on a Check

A *stop-payment order* is used when (1) a check for an incorrect amount has been
written; (2) the payor has issued a check by mistake; and (3) a check has
apparently been lost or stolen. To stop payment on a check, you must go to the
bank and complete a form giving the account number, amount of the check,
check number, and name of the person or organization to whom the check was
written. Banks typically charge $10 to $15 to stop payment on a check.

Voucher Checks

Many organizations use printed **voucher** checks (Figure 15–3). The top portion is
the check itself; the bottom portion gives the details of the payment. A check stub

is not required with a voucher check. A record of both the check and the voucher is kept and compared against monthly account balances.

You may be asked to "walk a voucher check through" to speed up payment, particularly if you work in a large organization. In this case, a check request is prepared and taken directly to the accounts payable office. The check is usually issued in one or two days rather than the three to four weeks required for regular processing.

Reconciliation

Another of your checking account management tasks will be to **reconcile** monthly bank statements with cancelled checks and with your records. The

Figure 15–3
Voucher check.

THOMAS B. ANDERSON
123 ANYWHERE ST.
USA, MO   12345

N̲O̲   101

9-5678
1234

January 28, 19 *91*

PAY TO THE
ORDER OF *University Bookstore* $ *88.25*

Eighty-eight and $\frac{25}{100}$ ————————— DOLLARS

HARLAND BANK & TRUST
YOUR TOWN, YOUR STATE

SAMPLE-VOID

Thomas B. Anderson

⑉0000101⑉ ⑉0123456781⑉ 123⑉4567⑉

M · W · V · HARLAND NO. 802

DETACH AND RETAIN THIS STATEMENT
THE ATTACHED CHECK IS IN PAYMENT OF ITEMS DESCRIBED BELOW. IF NOT CORRECT PLEASE NOTIFY US PROMPTLY. NO RECEIPT DESIRED.

THOMAS B. ANDERSON

DATE	DESCRIPTION	AMOUNT
1/28/91	*University Bookstore: books for accounting, business law, and office procedures courses*	*$88.25*

bank statement (Figure 15–4) shows the date and amount of each check paid, deposits made, and bank fees such as service charges. It also shows the balance at the end of the period. This balance will likely differ from the checkbook balance, because some checks will not have been paid and deposits made after the end of the period will not show on the statement. The reverse side of the statement contains a form that you can use for reconciliation. Figure 15–5 explains the reconciliation process.

If the adjusted balances of your bank statement and checkbook do not agree, ask yourself the following questions:

1. Did you enter the amount of each check correctly?
2. Do the amounts of deposits entered in your checkbook agree with those shown on the statement?

Figure 15–4
Bank statement.

STATE FINANCIAL BANK
201 Third Avenue
Tuscon, AZ 85701

STATEMENT OF YOUR ACCOUNT

PERIOD ENDING: July 23, 19—

ACCOUNT 00–12658

Raul Garza
11849 Cactus Drive
Tucson, AZ 85701

POSTING DATE	BALANCE FORWARD
June 28, 19—	96.50

CHECKS		CODE	DEPOSITS	CODE		BALANCE
			221.14		July 10, 19—	317.64
111	125.00				July 13, 19—	192.64
110	35.76				July 14, 19—	156.88
112	10.00				July 21, 19—	146.88
	0.80	SC			July 23, 19—	146.08

BAL. FORWD.	CHECKS	DEPOSITS	ITEMS ENCL.	TOTAL DEBITS	TOTAL CREDITS	SC	NEW BALANCE
96.50	3	1	3	171.56	221.14	.80	146.08

3. Did you deduct all checks written from your checkbook balance?
4. Did you deduct all bank charges from your checkbook balance?
5. Did you carry the correct balance forward from one checkbook stub to the next?
6. Did you check all additions and subtractions in your checkbook?
7. Did you review last month's reconciliation to make sure any differences were corrected?

When you locate the error, note on the stub where it occurred and that you've made the correction. Then, after the last stub entry, make the correction and note the stub number on which it occurred. In the stub register after the last

Figure 15–5
Reconciliation procedure.

1. Add to the checkbook balance any deposits made but not yet recorded in the checkbook and deduct any service charge or special fees. This figure is your *adjusted checkbook* balance. $3,465.00

2. Forward the ending balance on the bank statement to the reconciliation form. $1,501.10

3. Add the deposits that have been recorded in your checkbook but are not on the bank statement. $4,321.00

4. Add total of deposits (#3) to statement balance (#2) for *subtotal*. $5,822.10

5. Put cancelled checks in order by number or date of issue.

6. Check amount of each cancelled check with amount listed on bank statement (optional).

7. Compare returned checks with the checkbook stub or register. If the check amount agrees, check it off.

8. List on the reconciliation form the check number of all checks not marked or circled on the stubs or in the register. Total the outstanding checks and enter them on line 8. $2,357.10

9. Subtract the total outstanding checks (line 8) from the *subtotal* for the adjusted bank statement balance (line 4). $3,465.00

10. Line 9 is the true balance of your account and should agree with line 1, your adjusted checkbook balance. When the figures agree, the amount is reconciled. If they do not agree, a careful verification of figures should be made.

| CHECK(S) OUTSTANDING (Issued by you but not yet indicated as paid on any statement). ||
CHECK NUMBER	AMOUNT
2734	$ 37.50
2745	400.00
2751	9.85
2754	11.12
2755	18.75
2756	126.14
2757	75.00
2758	46.50
2759	245.79
2760	69.00
2761	1317.45
TOTAL	$2357.10

entry covered by the bank statement, write the date and note that the account is now reconciled.

Review all depositing, check-writing, and reconciling procedures with your manager periodically to determine whether any changes are needed. If so, record the revisions in your job manual.

As you've seen, careful attention to details at all stages of the checking account management process is essential. Experienced office professionals suggest that you will make fewer errors if you find a quiet place in which to do this work. They also recommend keeping current records of deposits and checks written at all times.

Computer-Based Accounts

You are more likely to be responsible for computer-based accounts than for bank checking accounts. You may be required to enter information directly into a computer or record information on forms to be processed by your organization's business unit. Your office may have several accounts involving multiple transactions, such as executive travel, office supplies, special projects, and customer billings. As in the case of individual credit card accounts, there will be multiple-digit identification numbers, each with a special purpose. Figure 15–6 shows a form used at a university to record expenses.

To use computer-based accounting systems, you will have to follow specific procedures. Deadlines and time needed to complete transactions are important factors in computer-based accounts: when amounts must be entered to be computed on an account balance; how long it takes for a check to be drawn; the amount of time between identification and correction of an error. If forms are used, a record of all transactions will be created automatically. When data are entered directly into the computer, you must remember to keep your own record of charges against the account (Figure 15–7, page 346). Also, be aware of the amount of time between when funds are obligated and when they may be drawn from an account; careful recordkeeping will reduce the possibility of overspending.

Your organization may operate accounts on monies from local, state, or federal government agencies. Each agency requires different procedures for handling transactions, especially in what is and is not allowed. Because those accounts will be audited periodically, you must take special care to follow required procedures and to check with a government officer responsible for such accounts if you believe any exceptions are needed. Again, accurate recordkeeping is essential.

Attention to details is especially important when handling computer-based accounts. Here are some typical problems:

- Amounts assigned to the wrong accounts
- Loss of supporting data needed for check requests
- Incorrect codes entered, causing the computer to reject amounts to be paid in or paid out

Figure 15–6
Expense report.

Sample of July through September

Account Number	Working Title	July	Aug.	Sept.
321	World Heritage Museum	0	0	0
1302	Carolyn R. Carson	6	1	20
9438	MBS	0	479	45
10105	Summer Session	823	664	1854
10257	Statewide Programming	0	0	46
10265	CEPS Duplicating	109	17	66
11140	CEPS Administration	2262	1303	4981
11141	Program Development	460	512	515
11142	CEPS Marketing	3105	3436	1063
11145	CEPS Correspondence	0	70	1140
11387	EXM CLS State GEN	0	283	861
12167	International Affairs State	136	26	56

- Transactions that need to be redone because a procedural change was forgotten (even though corrections can be made, the time required to do so can be considerable)

Electronic Banking

Increasingly, organizations have begun to transfer funds electronically instead of by check. Computers and related technology have made **electronic fund transfers (EFTs)** very common. EFTs move money from one account to another within the same bank or among different banks and within or among cities or countries. The details of these transfers are specific to each organization. In

Figure 15–7
Account log.

Account Number 00–73–01–401		
Description	**Amount**	**Account Balance**
		2,407.19
1. Kaler travel voucher	93.12	2,314.91
011742 7/22/XX		
2. Caudillo travel voucher	101.17	2,212.84
011750 7/26/XX		
3. Ink travel voucher	36.50	2,176.34
011762 7/29/XX		

general, EFTs require entering correct account numbers and providing clear descriptions of what is to be done.

Some EFT services you are likely to encounter include

- *Automatic teller machines,* which perform a wide variety of banking services—from deposits to withdrawals and payments using a plastic identification card—twenty-four hours a day
- *Regular direct deposits* of payroll or government checks or withdrawals from various accounts to pay recurring bills
- *Bank-by-phone* service, after preauthorizing a bank or other financial institution to pay bills or transfer funds regularly or whenever you call and request a funds transfer
- *Point-of-sale* transfers of cash between a buyer's account and a seller's account using a special identification card to authorize the transaction

Each time you complete a transaction through an EFT, the transaction will be listed on your monthly statement. If you find an error, you have sixty days from the date the error occurred to notify the bank; after that point, the bank has no further responsibility. It is therefore important that you learn the provisions of the agreement when you purchase the EFT service.

Special Payment Methods

In addition to writing checks against your organization's account, you may be required to use one or more of the following payment methods:

1. **Cashier's check** or **bank money order.** This type of check is drawn on the bank's funds. You pay the amount of the check and a service fee. Usually the bank teller prepares the check to the purchaser or another designated person.

You use these forms of payment when you wish to demonstrate that money has already been withdrawn from an account so that the person or organization receiving it will, for example, send out an order more rapidly.

2. **Certified check.** This form of check indicates that the amount has been deducted from the check writer's account. The check is stamped *certified*, meaning that it is guaranteed by the bank.

3. **Bank draft.** This type of check is drawn by one bank against funds deposited to its account in another bank. Bank drafts are commonly purchased for making remittances in places where a bank check is more readily accepted than a check written by an individual or where the payee has requested that the transaction occur in the town or city where his or her place of business is located. One situation in which a bank draft is used is when sending checks overseas; the payor and payee may not know each other and thus want an established bank to manage the transaction.

4. **Commercial draft.** This is an order to a bank from the maker of the order to pay a third party.

5. **Sight draft.** This type of draft is payable upon presentation. With a sight draft, an order for merchandise, such as a large supply of computers, would be released to the buyer.

6. **Time draft.** This type of draft gives the purchaser more time to make payment. When the seller accepts the draft, the order will be delivered.

As a first step in handling these procedures properly, you should learn when to use each of these special payment forms. You should also find out how they have been prepared in the past, as well as any special problems encountered. Keep samples of correctly filled-out forms or copies of previous transactions in your job manual, and update them as necessary; some forms change regularly based on government regulations. If you have questions about any of these forms of payment, consult your bank, someone in the business department of your organization, or another knowledgeable person.

Petty-Cash Fund

You may also be responsible for managing a petty-cash fund. A **petty-cash fund** is a small amount of money kept for the purchase of small items needed immediately, such as stamps, batteries, or items not kept in stock. Petty-cash funds usually contain enough money to meet office needs for about one month—typically $200 or less in a business firm, and about $50 in a government agency or nonprofit organization. It is recommended that only one person have access to the petty-cash fund.

If the petty-cash fund is your responsibility, you will need to maintain careful control over expenditures. First, keep the cash and completed vouchers in a box or envelope in a locked desk drawer, file, or office safe. Balance the petty-cash records at least once a week. Next, prepare a petty-cash voucher, or receipt, for each expenditure. The voucher should show the amount paid, the date, to whom the payment was made, the purpose of the payment, the expense category to which the payment will be charged, and the signature or initials of the person authorizing payment. Some organizations also require the signature or initials of the person receiving payment. In some cases, you will charge another account after giving an employee cash for a purchase. Write the amount to be charged on the voucher. Keep the petty-cash vouchers along with the cash in a secure place.

Third, be sure to maintain accurate petty-cash records. To do this, use a petty-cash book, distribution sheet, or large envelope. For each payment from the petty-cash fund, enter the date, amount, voucher number, and explanation in the petty-cash records. The total of the expenditures plus the amount of cash on hand should equal the original amount of the petty-cash fund.

Fourth, replenish the petty-cash fund as needed to keep an adequate supply of cash on hand. In some organizations, petty cash is replenished at a set time, for instance, when only one-fourth of the original amount of cash is on hand. In others, replenishment is left to the judgment of the person in charge of the fund.

Request the amount needed to restore the petty-cash fund to the original amount, unless you have been authorized to decrease or increase the fund. Along with the request for cash, submit any records required by the accounting department. Before you release the vouchers, make a copy of them for your files. If you keep a petty-cash book, submit a petty-cash report.

Finally, cash the check for the petty-cash fund and enter the amount and date in the "received" column of the petty-cash record. If you are using a new cash distribution envelope, transfer the balance to the "received" column and then enter the amount.

Follow these precautions in managing the petty-cash fund:

1. Check that all requests for cash are for a legitimate purpose (a petty-cash fund is not intended for personal emergencies).
2. Make sure all vouchers are signed before giving out any money.
3. Keep vouchers and money in a secure place, such as a locked steel box that is stored overnight in a locked drawer.
4. If a discrepancy occurs, immediately inform your manager and begin a careful check of records.

Paying Bills

As your competence in managing office finances increases, you may be asked to pay bills. This is especially likely to occur in a small, private organization such as a law office, insurance company, or single-owner business. Whether you are to pay one or several bills, follow these procedures to perform this important task correctly:

1. Verify all items on a bill, and check the totals to ensure they are correct.
2. Fill in the check stub with information about the bill.

3. On the bill write the date, check number, and amount paid.
4. Tear off the invoice or statement stub, and attach it to the check and remittance envelope.
5. Present the bills to your manager for approval and signature.

Also, verify when a payment is due, the amount due (if only a partial payment is required), and whether deductions for early payment are possible. File paid bills for easy retrieval; depending on the quantity, they can be stored in a single file folder or by month in several file folders.

Credit Cards

Credit cards have replaced cash and checks in many aspects of business life because of their convenience and often high credit lines. Many private and some public organizations provide managers with

- One or more major all-purpose or travel/entertainment credit cards: Visa, MasterCard, Discover, American Express, Diner's Club, Carte Blanche
- An air travel card
- One or more rental car and/or gasoline company cards
- One or more hotel chain, airline, or special entertainment cards or keys (such as for an airline club at an airport)

It is essential that credit cards be protected. If a card is lost or stolen, the issuing bank must be notified immediately. When the loss or theft is reported within two days, the cardholder is responsible for only $50 charged against it; after two days, the cardholder can be liable for as much as $500.

In larger organizations, a central office usually distributes credit cards and handles renewals. If you work for a smaller organization, you may be responsible for renewing credit cards.

To manage credit cards effectively, you need four basic pieces of information: (1) account numbers, (2) expiration dates, (3) terms and amounts of liability, and (4) numbers to call in the event of loss or theft. Keep three sets of this information: one for yourself, one for your manager at the office, and one for your manager at his or her home.

Formerly, credit card companies sent verification copies of signed charge receipts along with the monthly statement; today they usually provide only a list or photocopies of the receipts. Therefore, be sure to collect all charge slips from your manager. When your manager prepares for a trip, provide an envelope for those slips and put it with other documents to be carried. Collect all charge slips immediately after the trip. Reconcile the slips with the monthly statement before you pay the bill. If an error has occurred, contact the credit card company immediately.

Records to Keep and How to Keep Them

Because of reporting requirements of government agencies, particularly the Internal Revenue Service, the following items must be kept complete and current:

- Personnel and tax records—some should be kept for at least three years, others for seven years. An accountant or a representative of the Internal Revenue Service can provide you with a list of records that must be kept and information on how long to keep them.
- Balance sheets and profit-and-loss statements should be maintained for a minimum of seven years.
- Yearly tax items, such as deductions, expense forms, and interest payments, are necessary for accountants and auditors.
- Records of all expenses related to publicly funded activities should be kept available for public scrutiny, potential audit, and review.

Some firms have procedures for retaining certain financial records not necessarily required by law. These items might include invoices for sales of a particular product or to a certain number of firms; budget-planning documents that may be needed for future reference; and financial proposals that were turned down but could be resubmitted.

Inventory Records

Inventory records list all of the business's physical assets, such as equipment and furniture. Organizations maintain inventory records for general-information purposes; to document depreciation of equipment; and as evidence for insurance claims in the event of loss by fire or theft. For each property item, the inventory record typically includes a description of the item, date of purchase, purchase price, and estimated trade-in or sale value. In some organizations, each item has an identification tag and number. An etched-in identification number or symbol on small, easily removable items may be especially useful for deterring theft.

Insurance Records

Insurance records are lists of policies kept by the business. Insurance policies may include life insurance; health and accident coverage; special travel coverage, including use of company cars; general or specialized property insurance; and malpractice insurance in the case of physicians, attorneys, and certain other professionals.

If you work in a large organization, you may keep a single log of policies in effect for individual managers and for the office as a whole. For each policy, the insurance log should contain the policy number, date on which the policy took effect, expiration date, name of the insurance company, and kind of insurance. In a smaller organization, you may be responsible for paying premiums and/or recording changes in coverage. Information to be recorded would include the dates on which policy premiums are to be paid; amount due for each payment; grace period (number of days after a premium is due allowed for payment without penalty); and significant coverage changes, such as increases in deductible rates.

You can keep the insurance log in a tickler file or on a single sheet. In addition, individual managers should carry insurance information with their daily calendars in case of accidents away from home or the office. It is also advisable that managers maintain an up-to-date insurance record at home.

Keep insurance policies in a safe but accessible location, such as a safe deposit box at a bank, an office safe, or a locked file cabinet. Place policies in individual pockets on a folder, with information about the policy written on the outside.

Obtaining accurate insurance information quickly is important when (1) filing claims, especially in an emergency; (2) preparing tax materials to verify that policies being deducted are truly in force; and (3) reviewing the organization's insurance coverage to determine whether it is still adequate and whether changes in insurance companies should be made.

General Financial Records

General financial records cover a number of areas depending on the size of the organization. Such records typically contain the following information:

- Stocks and bonds held by individual managers or the organization, including date purchased, number of shares, number of certificates, purchase price, and date sold; similar information is kept for securities issued by the organization
- Real estate holdings of individual managers or the organization, including property deeds, mortgage payment information, and associated expenses
- Trusts or other restricted funds kept as certificates of deposit or for special activities or individuals

Like insurance records, general financial records must be kept up-to-date, accessible, and safe.

Payroll Information

Payroll information and related requirements (e.g., social security, health care, retirement, and tax deductions) are strictly governed by state and federal laws. In large organizations, the payroll process is usually centralized and specific procedures are in place. In a small organization, you may be responsible for writing employee paychecks as well as checks for other purposes. You may also have to prepare payroll information for a bank or other financial service organization that writes checks for small businesses and organizations.

Payroll information must be recorded accurately and should be kept confidential. Necessary information related to payroll includes

- Employees' social security numbers
- Withholding forms for local, state, and federal tax purposes
- FICA and unemployment compensation materials
- Payroll deductions made for health and related insurance
- Time records, either computerized or maintained on forms that individual employees keep, sign, and turn in

Figure 15–8 contains a sample employee information form. In this case, you are likely to prepare information for the payroll department. You may also have to keep time cards or records, along with deductions for meals, equipment, or uniforms, perhaps on a computer. In addition, be prepared to answer employees' questions about payroll deductions and other calculations.

Requirements for reporting payroll information change periodically. Therefore, it's wise to locate sources of up-to-date information both inside and outside your organization. Obvious sources are the local Internal Revenue Service office and offices of local, county, and state taxing bodies. Each of these sources regularly publish basic information and regulation changes. Your organization's financial institution can also provide useful payroll information.

Tax Records

Keeping clear and accurate records will make preparation of all tax forms easier. It will also increase the chances for a positive outcome should your organization undergo a tax audit. Effective tax record organization involves three basic steps:

1. Learning the items managers will likely report on income tax forms, especially deductions
2. Accumulating relevant information regularly during the year, especially documents necessary to support deductions
3. Providing information to managers and accountants in the clearest and most timely manner possible

Keep documents for individual years separate; put all information and completed forms for a given year into one file. Records to be kept include

- All taxable income (from wages; commissions; dividends; interest; capital and other financial gains; and income from royalties, rent, fees, and other sources)
- Deductions allowed by federal law (legitimate business expenses; family-related expenses such as for education, child care, and hospitalization; real estate, state, and local income taxes; charitable contributions; contributions to individual retirement accounts; business expenses such as travel and dues paid to professional organizations; and losses of all kinds)

Figure 15–8
Employee information form.

```
                          EMPLOYEE INFORMATION FORM
  NEW HIRE  _____                                        CHANGE  _____

  DIVISION NAME                                           LOCATION
  ASSIGNED BY PAYROLL
  FILE NUMBER                                             PREPARED BY

                        I.  PERSONAL INFORMATION (PER)

  SOCIAL SECURITY NUMBER

  *(1)      EMPLOYEE NAME:  _____ , _____ , _____
                           Last                First               M.I.
  *(3)      ADDRESS LINE 1:
  *(4)      ADDRESS LINE 2:
  *(5)      CITY:
  *(6)      STATE:                                    *(7) ZIP CODE:
  *(8)      PHONE AREA CD:                            *(9) PHONE NUMBER:
  *(10)     GENDER:                                   *(12) RACE:
  *(13)     EEO OCCUP CAT:

                          II.  PAY INFORMATION (PAY)

  *(1)      BI-WEEKLY RATE 1:                          *(13) JOB COST:
  *(2)      EFFECTIVE DATE:                            *(15) HIRE DATE:
  *(3)      HOURLY RATE 2:                             *(17) BIRTH DATE:
  *(5)      BI-WEEKLY STD HRS:                         *(19) CHECK MAILED TO:
  *(8)      HOME DEPARTMENT:                           *(26) COST CENTER P/R:

                          III.  TAX INFORMATION (TAX)

  (1)       MARITAL STATUS:

                    POST FROM ATTACHED W-4 - FOR PAYROLL USE ONLY:

  (2)       STATE 1:                                   EXEMPTIONS:
  (3)       CITY 1:                                    FEDERAL:
  (4)       SUI/SDI:                                   STATE:
  (5)       STATE 2:                                   CITY:
  (6)       CITY 2:

                    IV.  PERSONNEL REPORTING SYSTEM (PRI)

  *(11)     EDUCATIONAL LEVEL:
  *(19)     ACTUAL MARITAL STATUS:
  *(22)     STATUS:
  *(23)     HIRING SOURCE:
  *(25)     ANNUAL SALARY:
  *(27)     TITLE OF PRESENT POSITION:
  *(26)     JOB CODE NUMBER:

                              V.  COMMENTS



                          VI.  PAY HISTORY FILE (PR2)

  *  SALARY LEVEL:
  AUTHORIZATION SIGNATURE:
  EXECUTIVE APPROVAL SIGNATURE:
  (*)  INFORMATION TO BE ENTERED BY PREPARER
```

Tax laws at all government levels change regularly. For up-to-date information on required tax records, consult the same sources cited in the preceding section on payroll information.

Organizing and Presenting Financial Information

Managers often must present financial information to groups both inside and outside the organization. Senior management, investors, auditors, and the general public all study detailed income statements, budgets, and running totals of assets and liabilities with great care.

Preliminary and final profit-and-loss statements and status reports on individual accounts are usually prepared monthly or, in some cases, weekly. Figure 15–9 shows a basic *balance sheet* for a small business. The balance sheet shows *assets* (what the organization holds and owns) and *liabilities* (what the organization owes); the difference between assets and liabilities is the organization's *net worth*. You may be responsible for preparing balance sheets using information supplied by an accountant.

An *income statement* (Figure 15–10, page 357) shows how much the organization has earned (e.g., income) or spent (e.g., expenses) over a specified period of time. An excess of income over expenses is a *profit*; when expenses exceed income, a *loss* has occurred.

You may be responsible for reconciling balance sheets, income statements, and other documents with an office record of transactions or other supporting material. When errors are identified, it will be your job to report them to the central budget office to ensure that corrections can be made.

Managers now use computer graphics to present financial information. *(Courtesy of International Business Machines Corporation)*

Figure 15–9
Basic balance sheet for a small business.

ALLIANCE PUBLISHING COMPANY
1991 budget by product area
BALANCE SHEET
($000's omitted)
December 31, 1991

ASSETS

Cash	$ 41,732	
Intercompany cash	123	$ 41,855
Accounts & Notes Receivable:		
Gross receivables	$137,642	
Reserves	3,411	
Net A/R & N/R		134,231
Inventory		
Gross	$108,172	
Obsolescense reserves	$186	
LIFO reserves	250	436
Net inventory		107,736
Prepaid Expenses		1,416
Total Current Assets		$295,238
Prepublication Costs:		
Gross	$ 74,610	
Accumulated amortization	1,784	
Net prepub costs		72,826
Property, Plant & Equipment:		
Gross	$297,636	
Accumulated depreciation	104,392	
Net P, P & E		193,244
Goodwill & Intangibles:		
Gross	$ 43,000	
Accumulated amortization	33,000	
Net goodwill/intangibles		10,000
Other non-current assets		25,000
TOTAL ASSETS		$596,308

Continued on page 356

You may also be required to draft budget requests for various units in your organization and prepare information for senior management on expenditures for proposed projects. To complete such assignments accurately, you must carefully follow procedures and allow enough time for checking and rechecking.

Figure 15–9 Continued

LIABILITIES AND NET WORTH

Current Liabilities:

Accounts payable	$ 3,692	
Accrued wages payable	541	
Taxes payable	1,020	
Current portion of long-term debt	5,000	
Total Current Liabilities		$ 10,253

Long-term liabilities

8% 20-year convertible debentures		205,000
TOTAL LIABILITIES		$215,253

Net Worth

Preferred stock $100 par, 5% noncumulative, convertible, 200,000 shares issued	$ 20,000	
Paid-in capital in excess of par	9,000	
Common stock $100 par, 1,000,000 shares issued	100,000	
Paid-in capital in excess of par	75,000	
Retained earnings	177,055	
TOTAL NET WORTH		381,055
TOTAL LIABILITIES & NET WORTH		$596,308

When you have to complete multiple calculations involving rows of numbers, following a few simple procedures will help you avoid costly errors. First, estimate how long preparation and execution will take so that you can allow enough time to do the assignment correctly the first time. Second, find a location where you can concentrate without interruptions and distractions.

Before you begin, recheck figures if any are not clear. If columns are to be totaled or other computations are involved, make a final accuracy check to eliminate the need to redo the calculations. Obtain proofreading assistance: Have one person read the original copy out loud, while a second person checks the finished document. If you are working on a computer, spreadsheet software will provide mathematical checks for you.

Spreadsheet programs will allow you to develop a variety of worksheets that display various types of information in columns. This format will make review and comparison easier. With this software you can also produce total figures, make changes in one entry that will be reflected in the total of an entire column of figures, and set up your own formats for organizing information. The spreadsheet shown in Figure 15–11, page 358, provides a detailed summary of the financial status of a complicated educational program.

Figure 15–10
An income statement.

ALLIANCE PUBLISHING COMPANY
1991 budget by product area
INCOME STATEMENT (PARTIAL)
($000's omitted)
December 31, 1991

REVENUE

Domestic sales		$12,362	
International sales		784	
Total gross sales			$13,146
Other revenue—external			72
Total revenue			$13,218

COST OF SALES

Paper, printing & binding		$ 2,147	
Other cost of sales			
LIFO provisions	$250		
Freight in	82		
Prov for inventory W/O	74		
Other mfg expenses	161		
Volume rebates	191		
Contract costs	33		
Cash discount on paper	93		
Paper freight	109		
Total O.C.O.S.		993	
Royalties		1,024	
Total cost of sales		$ 4,164	
Amort of prepub costs		1,784	5,948
Operating margin			$ 7,270

Unethical Behavior

We have all heard stories about how funds have been mishandled in both public and private organizations. In some cases, office professionals have been implicated in stealing from employers. The amounts involved range from less than $10 to thousands of dollars. Some unethical money-related activities include

- "Padding" expense vouchers
- Preparing unauthorized checks for individuals or groups
- Allowing petty cash to be used for personal purposes
- Falsifying financial records

Figure 15–11
Part of a complex spreadsheet for a university.

Summer Tuition Options by the Credit Hour

		Summer '89 Base		A $97/hr.		B $88/hr.		C $83/hr.		D $102 +$80/hr.	
Hours	Enrollment	Rate	Revenue	Rate	Revenue	Rate	Revenue	Rate	Revenue	Rate	Revenue
0	370	102	$37,832	97	$35,890	88	$32,560	83	$30,710	102	$37,740
1	27	204	$5,521	97	$2,619	88	$2,376	83	$2,241	182	$4,914
2	80	204	$16,360	194	$15,520	176	$14,080	166	$13,280	262	$20,960
3	624	394	$246,011	291	$181,584	264	$164,736	249	$155,376	342	$213,408
4	517	394	$203,827	388	$200,596	352	$181,984	332	$171,644	422	$218,174
5	265	394	$104,476	485	$128,525	440	$116,600	415	$109,975	502	$133,030
6	895	584	$522,680	582	$520,890	528	$472,560	498	$445,710	582	$520,890
7	515	584	$300,760	679	$349,685	616	$317,240	581	$299,215	662	$340,930
8	295	584	$172,280	776	$228,920	704	$207,680	664	$195,880	742	$218,890
9	246	584	$143,664	873	$214,758	792	$194,832	747	$183,762	822	$202,212
10	119	584	$69,496	970	$115,430	880	$104,720	830	$98,770	902	$107,338
11	34	584	$19,856	1067	$36,278	968	$32,912	913	$31,042	982	$33,388
12	40	584	$23,360	1164	$46,560	1056	$42,240	996	$39,840	1062	$42,480
			$1,866,123		$2,077,255		$1,884,520		$1,777,445		$2,094,354 $2,123,954*

Additional revenue
per 100 students $48,900 $43,650 $49,600 $37,350 $46,200
*Total tuition with "0" credit at the same rate as "1" credit

You may observe co-workers and even managers participating in these and other activities. It would be unrealistic to expect to be applauded every time you "blow the whistle." In some instances, you will need a great deal of courage to report the unethical conduct of others. Unfortunately, many office professionals have been forced to quit their jobs because of circumstances such as these.

If you work in a large organization, you may be able to report misdeeds to an audit unit or similar operation. Your confidentiality will be protected in those cases. It is unlikely that you will ever be placed in such a position, however. Most of those with whom you work will likely be honest and law abiding.

As an office professional, you may be responsible for several financial management activities, ranging from petty cash to credit cards. All of these responsibilities will require careful attention to details and checking and rechecking of all transactions. Record all financially related procedures in your job manual, review them regularly, and update them as necessary.

Your areas of responsibility may include

- Checking accounts and other forms of payment
- Computer-based accounts
- Petty-cash fund
- Bill payment
- Credit cards
- Financial records

All of these activities will require you to keep correct and complete records for your organization and/or individual managers. The types of records you may be responsible for include personnel, taxes, inventory, insurance, payroll, and general financial records.

Finally, you may have to assist managers in preparing financial information for reports, budgets, and proposals. These activities will require as much attention to details as managing petty cash and writing checks.

Key Terms

The following terms appeared in boldface type in this chapter. Do you recall what they mean? For a more complete definition, turn to the glossary beginning on p. 442.

bank draft (p. 347)	insurance records (p. 350)
cashier's check (bank money order) (p. 346)	petty cash fund (p.347)
	reconcile (p. 341)
certified check (p. 347)	sight draft (p.347)
commercial draft (p.347)	time draft (p.347)
electronic fund transfer (EFT) (p. 345)	voucher (p. 340)
inventory records (p. 350)	

Discussion Questions

1. What procedures should you follow to replenish a petty-cash fund?
2. Name three methods of endorsing a check. When might you use each?
3. How do you think electronic fund transfers will affect your financial responsibilities?
4. What steps should you take to manage credit card transactions?
5. What procedures should you follow to manage computer-based accounts effectively?
6. Why do you think it is important to maintain confidentiality about payroll records?

7. What types of taxes are deducted from an employee's gross pay?
8. Describe the steps in reconciling (balancing) a bank statement.

Assignments

1. In the past, your office's petty-cash fund has been used for postage, small office supplies, "treats," flowers, and coffee. Now, however, your organization's accountants have requested two changes: All supplies are to be ordered centrally, and mileage for short trips by sales representatives and others is to be paid for in cash. The accountants believe that these changes will increase the amount of money in the petty-cash fund.
   a. How can you change the habit of three assistants and ten managers of running to the petty-cash box to buy "emergency" supplies?
   b. What procedure(s) could you establish to verify trips made and mileage reimbursed?
2. You prepared a deposit of nearly $1,000 in checks from customers and arranged for a messenger to deliver the deposit to the bank. The messenger returned and reported that the checks were stolen on the way to the bank.
   a. How would you deal with this problem? Be sure to consider the messenger, bank, customers, and any creditors who were to be paid out of funds from that deposit.
   b. How would you avoid this problem in the future?
3. For several weeks, the accounting office has been refusing to pay what they claim is an incompletely documented bill for a major printing job. Because the material was not completed on schedule, there was no time to ask for competitive bids, which the organization requires. The entire office is responsible for the mishap. Now a bill of over $3,000 must be paid, the accounting department must be satisfied, and the office's image must be protected. What would you do?
4. Each of the following situations involves the transfer of monies from one point to another. What could go wrong in each instance? What extra precautions could you take?
   a. A $500 electronic transfer from a manager's personal checking account to a correspondent bank in Mexico City for use by the manager's son, who is vacationing there
   b. An international money order, to be paid in German marks, that must be received by noon Monday (it is now Friday morning)
   c. An authorization made by telephone to a computer to release funds in the organization's checking account to pay three bills
5. Your manager's wallet was stolen while she was on vacation. In it were four credit cards that she regularly uses on business trips: air travel, American Express, Avis Rent-A-Car, and Shell. She called you less than two hours after she discovered the theft and wants you to notify each credit card company and obtain new cards. What steps would you take, and in what order?

Those instructors using *Top Performance: A Decision-Making Simulation for the Office* should consult the *Instructor's Guide* at this point for support material regarding use of the software in the classroom.

Case Study

Sandra Johnson feels she has been put in the middle, between the company's accountants and the seven engineers in her office. The engineers dislike all the "red tape" and refuse to follow proper procedures for purchase requests, payments to be made, and expense accounts to be paid. They rely on Sandra to take care of the paperwork, but she is getting tired of doing this. She gets handwritten notes—sometimes barely legible—with requests to pay certain bills.

The chief engineer seems too busy to be bothered about Sandra's problem; he too has little patience with all the documentation associated with financial transactions. The accountants are equally difficult. They haul out procedure books and clearly point out why rules must be followed. Sometimes Sandra understands their explanations, sometimes not. She agrees with the engineers some of the time and with the accountants on other occasions.

Imagine that you work in another office of the same company and have become friendly with Sandra. She asks you for advice about realistic alternatives in this situation. What would you suggest she consider to solve a problem that puts her squarely in the middle of two very different opinions?

CHAPTER
16

SUPERVISING

Chapter Objectives

- To learn what people and tasks you are likely to supervise

- To recognize problems you may encounter in a supervisory role

- To develop the qualities of an effective supervisor, learning techniques for building cooperation and motivation

- To learn effective planning and delegation techniques, and proven instructional strategies

Examples of Excellence

"Can you handle United Way collections for the unit this fall? You can pick one person in each department to help you."

"From now on, I'd like you to distribute work to the two word processing assistants. Please check what they have done before giving it to me or the assistant managers for signature."

"The regional sales meeting will be the largest we've ever had. Give as much time as you need to coordinating it. I'll get you a temporary assistant to help with the details."

"We need one person to be responsible for the monthly report. You're the only one who really knows how to put it together. If you need help, tell me!"

As you gain experience and demonstrate competence, your manager is likely to have you supervise tasks and people on a temporary or permanent basis. These responsibilities will be challenging and rewarding. If you perform them well, these opportunities can greatly enhance your professional career.

Office professionals who are positioned between managers and co-workers are often asked to take responsibility but given little authority. In such a situation, you will need to rely on persuasion and diplomacy to get things done, especially if co-workers challenge your authority.

In this chapter, you will learn

- The people and tasks you are likely to supervise
- Problems you may encounter in a supervisory role
- Qualities that will help you become an effective supervisor
- Effective planning and delegation of work

- Instructional methods
- Techniques for building cooperation and motivation
- Development and maintenance of a supervisory style

A Challenging Mix

Every supervisory assignment, from coordinating a major meeting to collecting for a leading charity drive, is unique. Some duties will require you to supervise employees in all phases of their work. Others will involve requesting assistance, monitoring the work of a temporary employee, or obtaining information from several individuals.

In most cases, you will be supervising very few employees. As senior assistant in a department or small business, for example, you may assign work to clerks or word processing operators. As an experienced office professional, you may explain procedures to a new employee and perhaps guide his or her other work for four to six weeks. On occasion you may be responsible for the work of part-time or temporary employees.

Explaining assignments, providing clear instructions, answering questions, and evaluating completed work will be part of your supervisory role. Depending on how your office is organized, one or more office professionals may assist you. They will report to you rather than to your manager. In addition to completing your own work, you will be responsible for their output. You will need to set aside enough time to supervise and complete your other duties.

Often you will be responsible for large assignments, temporary projects, major events, and emergency situations. Your manager will identify you as the person

Establish standards for each task so that the person you are supervising has a clear picture of the final product before starting. *(Courtesy of International Business Machine Corporation)*

who will see that a special assignment is finished on time and up to standard. Assistance may be provided, offered, or left up to you to request. You will need to obtain cooperation from many people and departments and motivate them to provide timely information and help.

Your manager may also direct you to complete portions of tasks that he or she has just been assigned, such as a report, financial statement, proposal, or presentation. Your regular duties during this period will most likely continue, but others in the office may be selected to assist you with the completion of the work.

If your manager gives you **responsibility** but not **authority,** you will need a great deal of tact and sensitivity to gain the support essential for completing any assignment. Even though you will be in charge of the task, the people whose cooperation you need will report to different managers. They may feel you are imposing on their time and refuse to cooperate.

Supervising the completion of an assignment requires coordination, attention to details, and continuous follow-up. You will have to hold meetings, write out instructions, discuss assignments, ask managers to provide information, and keep several concerned parties informed of overall progress. If you supervise in a situation in which you have little authority, you must concentrate on defining what is expected, applying subtle pressure to ensure completion of the assignment, and showing appreciation to those who help.

Problems to Anticipate

Whether you supervise people or tasks, your supervisory duties will be *in addition* to your regular assignments. It should be easier to integrate permanent responsibility for one or two assistants than to juggle one or more temporary projects, especially those with unexpected and firm deadlines. Many office professionals report that short-term and intensive pressure is often more difficult to handle than predictable pressure on a continuing basis.

The potential size of your supervisory load is a second problem to consider. According to the principle of **span of control,** you should supervise only as many subordinates as you can handle effectively. Try to limit the number of people and tasks you take on to two or three. As you add a new person or assignment to your supervisory duties, you will increase the potential for task creep discussed in Chapter 9.

Unity of command, another supervisory principle, presents the third problem: No one can be expected to serve two masters. In some cases, the people you supervise directly may be given other assignments and/or conflicting instructions by your manager. In such situations, you will need to establish open lines of communication with your manager to determine priority of tasks and correct procedures. You will also need flexibility to make schedule and procedural changes in a professional manner.

A potentially greater problem involves obtaining help from co-workers and those who report to different managers. If your request is of low priority to them, they may not provide the assistance or information you need from them. In such cases, you will need to give them frequent but tactful reminders. Obviously, establishing a rapport with co-workers will be helpful, as will showing empathy for their already heavy workloads. When they do give you the assistance or information, make sure to demonstrate your appreciation.

In addition to these problems, you will likely experience ones common to all supervisors. The following problems may be even more difficult because you will still be an assistant rather than a manager:

- *Inability to accept criticism.* "You have not done this letter properly" could produce an assortment of reactions: hostility, hurt feelings, resistance to your authority, reluctance to redo, outright refusal, and even complaints to your manager. As an assistant, you will need to develop tactful ways to make those you supervise aware of their mistakes. As you explain why the task was not carried out properly, focus on the *task* rather than on their performance of it.
- *Resistance to assignments.* "That's a terrible job! Why do I have to do it?" Clearing out files, cleaning, taking inventory, making a special trip to the post office, or unpacking supplies are all unappealing jobs to some people. The successful manager finds ways to make such tasks less monotonous by using humor, assigning two or more people to do them, and/or interspersing the drudgery with more fulfilling assignments.
- *Attempts to take advantage of your goodwill.* The people you supervise may come in late, take longer than allowed for breaks or lunch, make personal calls, or fake illness to get time off. Some may work slowly in an effort to do as little as possible. In such situations, you will need to be firm but be careful not to show emotion.
- *Refusal to help out.* "That's not my job!" is an all too familiar statement. The employee who sticks with a narrow definition of "the job" may feel justified in refusing to help out, even when others are scurrying to finish the assignment. As a supervisor aware of the "total" picture, you may have to explain the disadvantages of this negative position. For example, you might point out that those who help out usually are themselves helped when they become overloaded with work.

Be wary of neat formulas or simple methods designed to solve these or other problems. Each person you supervise, project you handle, or crisis you face will be unique. You can and should learn from the past by talking with more experienced office professionals, observing their actions, and, most of all, using your common sense and intelligence. Keeping a written record of situations you handled well and those you managed poorly will help you remember important details. The procedures manual described in Chapter 3 is a good place to store this information.

Qualities to Cultivate

To be a successful supervisor, you must strengthen your professional attitude, as discussed in Chapter 1. Be aware that certain situations can be disruptive to the work atmosphere and must be dealt with decisively:

- If you become too friendly with co-workers, your ability to supervise can diminish. Extensive socializing in particular can weaken your authority and leave you open to embarrassing challenges.
- You may be criticized for supervising too aggressively or too passively. Indeed, negative rumors about why you were given this additional responsibility may circulate.
- Uneven motivation among employees in the same unit or office can cause some people to work very hard while others do as little as possible.
- Co-workers of different generations, sexes, or nationalities may not get along. Male subordinates may resent female supervisors. Hostilities such as these may hinder performance of the assignment.
- One or more managers may make unrealistic demands, such as impossible deadlines, on the office staff and refuse to discuss the problems with assistants.

These five situations are but a sample of what you are likely to encounter. However, there are some strategies you can use to diminish these problems:

1. Obtain reliable information. If one or more people are involved, listen to all concerned; try to sort out fact from opinion or impression before taking action.
2. Define the conflict so that the specific issue is clear to you. The simple question "What is bothering you?" can begin the process of communication and understanding.
3. Try to convince subordinates that the problem can be solved with joint effort. "How can we resolve the problem?" is a useful approach to take.
4. Focus attention on solutions and be willing to compromise. Write down ideas, negotiate openly and honestly, praise others' good suggestions, and look for solutions that everyone can accept.
5. Develop friendly relationships with all your subordinates, but maintain some distance to keep your position of authority clear.

A second important supervisory quality is confidence. You have already demonstrated supervisory ability in various ways—by instructing new employees, directing completion of a special assignment, or chairing an in-office charitable drive, for example. Your confidence will transfer to your subordinates, and the result will be a team committed to helping you accomplish your objectives.

Third, you should cultivate a realistic perspective about how much you will be able to accomplish. No matter how experienced you become, some employees and assignments will remain difficult to handle. Both will take extra time and obviously reduce what you can accomplish.

Still another important quality is determination to avoid being intimidated by others. For example, if a co-worker fails to redo a poorly done task, he or she may be challenging you. How you respond will vary from situation to situation. In many instances, you will have to establish a position and stick to it. With a firm commitment to completing assignments properly, you will be less likely to give in or be intimidated by an uncooperative person.

Obviously, given the variables involved in any supervisory position, you must learn to tolerate uncertainty. Often there will be no clear-cut right or wrong. Rules and precedents will help, but what will really count is your own sound judgment, self-confidence, and determination to make the best decision possible in an imperfect situation.

Finally, you must develop high standards of conduct and performance. You should set a good example in all areas of your professional life, emphasizing punctuality, attendance, confidentiality, and honesty. You can then legitimately expect others to act the same way.

As your professionalism and supervisory experience increase, you will develop a mental picture of how to perform in this role. You will see yourself effectively communicating with subordinates—giving appropriate compliments and tactful criticisms—while maintaining enough distance to be credible. This self-image will be an important guide in future supervisory tasks and will serve as a role model for others.

Organize to Supervise

Effective supervision is rarely an accident. Those able to accomplish work by supervising others who do it usually do the following:

- Plan precisely what tasks each person will perform and by what day and time. Sometimes only a day's activities will need to be outlined; other assignments may require much more time to finish. Figure 16–1, page 368, shows a work chart used to assign duties to three assistants.
- Establish standards for each task so the person doing it will have a clear picture of the final product before starting. Your procedures manual will be an excellent source of performance guidelines, as will examples of letters, memos, and reports.
- Assign specific duties to each person after describing in complete detail what is to be done and when it must be finished. If you explain carefully and thoroughly the first time, you will avoid the need to explain again.
- Check on your subordinates' progress to see if any problems have developed, answer questions, compliment, and prod those who appear to be falling behind in their work. As subordinates become more experienced, less daily contact will be necessary.

Studies on effective supervision point out how important the habit of regular **follow-up** is to you and your subordinates. Following up will allow you to observe what others are doing, ask about progress, and provide speedy correction

Figure 16–1
Work assignment chart.

		Week of January 13			
	Monday	**Tuesday**	**Wednesday**	**Thursday**	**Friday**
Cindy	Type 30 letters	Clean out files for 1988	Clean out files for 1988	Type Herbert's letters	Sort and route week's mail (nonurgent) to department
Anne	Type 30 letters	Type Harmon report	Filing for last quarter 1990	Filing for last quarter 1990	Help Cindy with mail requests
Herbert	Work on Harmon report	Pay bills for December	Answer January correspondence	Financial forecast, 1993	Financial forecast, 1993

when you spot an error. This habit is particularly important when one or more co-workers are involved in a task with a firm deadline. If you check regularly, you can identify possible problems, shift assignments around, and obtain other needed assistance. Figure 16–2 shows a weekly record of follow-up work.

If you feel confident about your subordinates' progress, you will be less likely to retain work you should delegate to others. As part of your planning, identify what you alone must do. Then delegate carefully. Holding on to work that should be delegated or allowing those assigned a task to give it back incomplete are two pressure-producing problems. Proper delegation will allow you to use time more effectively, give attention to priorities in your own work, and supervise more efficiently. To become a habit, delegation requires that you

- Know what you must do and identify additional tasks that co-workers, temporary staff, and others can do
- Organize what will be assigned so that those doing the work will complete it satisfactorily
- Follow up and check on progress to avoid any difficulties that may hinder completion
- Concentrate on your own work without thinking about what your subordinates are doing

The Instructional Dimension of Supervision

Every person who supervises also instructs. Those who do it well are likely to delegate more willingly, develop employees' abilities more fully, and become more accomplished in their own work. Supervisors who instruct effectively are very familiar with the work to be done and have a clear mental picture of the final product, especially the quality level expected. They also remember

Figure 16–2
Follow-up form.

	Project	Date Due	Daily Status	Need Assistance	Available for Assistance
	Week of _____ March 11 _____				
John	Financial report— 1st quarter	4/2	Figures done for January	Someone to help with February's figures	No
Karen	100 letters to be typed for Tom Jackson	3/15	20 letters per day	No	Yes
Sue	Sorting mail for 10 people Cleaning out files for 1988	3/15 N/A	Ongoing About 1 drawer per day	No	Yes
Alice	Paying and filing bills for February	3/31	Should finish first half on Friday, 3/15	Will let you know by 3/13	No
Lynn	Filing for February	3/15	A–F Mon. G–L Tues. M–P Weds. Q–S Thurs. T–Z Fri.	No	Yes

difficulties they experienced when they first learned a task and as a result are more sensitive to those they are instructing. They demonstrate such sensitivity, for example, by pointing out potential problems and by indicating that mistakes can and do occur.

Complete preparation is very important for excellent instruction. Effective supervisors plan what they will say and demonstrate, prepare notes, and practice in advance. They are also likely to develop written materials that can be used as a reminder after an instruction session.

A goal of each instruction session is for all employees to understand how to do the task. Again, achieving that goal requires planning. Effective supervisors pick the best time and a location that will have few distractions. They allow enough time for questions, repeating points, and practice, if appropriate. Finally, after the instruction session supervisors check on what employees have learned and how well they understand the task. Correcting, encouraging, and complimenting as appropriate are part of this follow-up.

By following these steps, you can avoid the **shortcut trap** many supervisors experience. This occurs after they have been doing a particular task for a period of time and have discovered how to do it faster by taking shortcuts. Regardless of

Being able to delegate work effectively reduces the pressure supervisors often face. *(Courtesy of International Business Machines Corporation)*

what you now do, you must give a person doing a task for the first time a full explanation.

Effective instructors generally use the following procedures when explaining assignments:

1. Begin with a statement of purpose, including what the employees will learn, the length of the instructional session, and some words of encouragement.
2. Present the new information, often with a demonstration and handouts that outline points to be covered.
3. Review all the information, allowing time for questions and clarification.
4. Pause to encourage questions. This helps draw out people who may be reluctant to interrupt the presentation.
5. If appropriate, ask employees to do some aspect of the task just explained; this will help boost their confidence.
6. Summarize all the points covered, emphasizing their willingness to help those experiencing difficulty.

You can use the preceding approach in a short (fifteen- to twenty-minute) training session. As your experience and expertise grow, you will become involved in many informal training activities. Some of the best training occurs in unstructured ways. Here are four examples of common informal training situations.

A recently hired co-worker asks a question, and the supervisor takes the time to explain both how to do the job and why attention to detail is so important. The supervisor points out that incorrectly filled-out forms are returned to be corrected, substantially slowing down processing.

A supervisor discovers a useful feature of a newly purchased software program and stops to explain its use to three co-workers. The explanation lasts less than five minutes, and the supervisor offers to help others who have questions after they try out the feature.

A memo describing a revised procedure is circulated among personnel. One supervisor reads it and discovers that two important changes in procedure have been made. The supervisor mentions this to her co-workers, and they discuss how the changes will be handled.

A newly hired assistant has to use the copying machine for the first time. His supervisor spends ten minutes showing him the basic copying features, common problems, and whom to contact if problems with the copier arise.

These four examples illustrate the wide variety of informal training that goes on in offices every day. Explanations, responses to questions, reminders, analyses of how to handle problems, and reviews of procedures are training activities. Consider these informal training procedures, which are similar to what many organizations follow to emphasize the importance of safety procedures. Once or twice every month, fifteen to twenty minutes are spent on some aspect of safety. Employees are reminded about what must be done on a regular basis. Research points out that accident rates are substantially lower in organizations that use this form of safety training.

As an office professional who may supervise, your training responsibilities are likely to include helping others use computer hardware and software more productively. Typically, you will be showing one or more co-workers how to use a single software feature and helping them understand how to complete a task. Common topics include how to transfer files; how to find a lost file; what desktop publishing features can be used to prepare written materials; procedures for creating special forms and/or spreadsheets; and when and how to make copies of information on a hard drive or a disk.

The same form of ongoing, informal training addresses telephone use, copying procedures, facsimile operation, organizing teleconferences using technology, and overall equipment care. As a newly employed office professional, you should find more experienced individuals with the expertise and patience to explain and train. Later on in your career, you could become that person.

Typical Supervisory Duties

As an office professional, you may be responsible for supervising temporary employees supplied by an agency, student interns, and outside groups hired to work on major projects. To best use these individuals' or groups' energy and time, you should develop a system for managing their work. Such a system might include the following:

1. *Determine need.* First, decide what should be delegated. Next, clearly define the task, preferably in writing. Also, identify all the steps to be completed, and provide samples of finished work for comparison.
2. *Estimate time needed.* When possible, determine how much time will be required to finish a task. Add 20 percent to your time estimate as a "cushion."
3. *Contact and schedule assistance.* After obtaining approval from your manager or others in the office, contact outside services with your request. Keep records of any potential problems in scheduling for use in future planning.

4. *Organize for completion.* Before the person who will do the work arrives, prepare the material to be completed, provide the necessary supplies, and check the equipment to be used.
5. *Explain the assignment.* As soon as the person is ready to begin, explain the assignment step by step.
6. *Check on performance.* In addition to answering questions or responding to problems, set aside time to observe how the work is being completed. Or review a partially completed assignment, correct obvious errors, and ask if the person is encountering any problems. Through this contact, you can determine if more or less time is needed.

In addition to evaluating others' work, you should evaluate yourself. Take a few minutes after each instruction session to identify your strengths and weaknesses. You might also ask those you are directing for reactions and suggestions. Experience will increase your confidence and improve your instructional ability.

Instructing New Employees

One of your more important duties will be to help new employees begin with sound information and direction. In addition to the suggestions made earlier, consider the following methods designed to promote the idea of "first-time understanding" (see the discussion of time management in Chapter 9):

1. Before showing how to complete an assignment or task, explain why it must be done.
2. Always explain each step first before demonstrating it.
3. Demonstrate slowly, if possible.
4. Repeat a function at least twice when you demonstrate.
5. Let the employee try the procedure before going on to the next step.
6. Ask if there are questions before moving on to the next step.
7. Demonstrate the step again, this time at full speed, so the employee can see what he or she will be doing after the instruction session is over.
8. Use the "buddy" system when you explain a manual process such as assembling copies of a report; that is, work side by side with the employee.
9. Do not allow anyone to interrupt an explanation except in an emergency.
10. Follow through. Don't simply show employees the process and then leave them on their own. Check back with them, and let them know how they are doing.

Teamwork, Cooperation, and Motivation

You will accomplish more if you encourage some degree of team spirit, cooperation, and motivation. None of these qualities will appear automatically; all will require work to develop. Following are proven methods that, by themselves or in combination, will increase your chances of success:

It is important to explain each project step by step to a new employee. *(Courtesy of Esselte Pendaflex Corporation)*

- Recognition of both consistent and special effort is a proven way to foster positive attitudes. Compliment individuals privately, or make a point of saluting them at staff meetings. Written commendations in personnel files, financial awards, and "perks" such as extra vacation days or paid convention registration are examples of more extensive rewards. However, make sure rewards fall within company guidelines.
- Your willing cooperation and regular assistance are important indicators to employees. When you step in to help, your subordinates are more likely to do so themselves when the need arises.
- Emphasize special talents to build individuals' pride. Employees so recognized are likely to volunteer those talents and teach others.
- Through **employee ownership** of tasks, you will increase participation in completing both routine and special duties. When employees can decide, for example, how the work is to be done or how to solve a problem, their involvement and motivation will increase.

As you gain experience, you will learn additional ways to build teamwork, cooperation, and motivation.

Handling Changes

As a supervisor, you will have to suggest changes as well as take the lead in accepting required changes. To minimize the disruption a change is likely to cause, take time to understand how the change will affect each person and, in particular, what new material or procedures have to be learned. You should also determine how those you supervise can be trained to handle a change so they will be more competent, confident, and less fearful of change. In addition, you and your manager will have to decide how much time to give employees to master a change before it becomes part of routine operations. Finally, as you observe employees at work, you can decide what additional training and support will be needed to increase familiarity with the change.

In addition, you should anticipate resistance from employees used to old and established ways of doing their work. By involving them in planning for the change, you may be able to eliminate their resistance.

Obviously, you will encounter some changes that must be accepted with no questions. In those instances, you can explain that these changes are an inevitable part of working in any organization. Emphasize to subordinates the need to learn to work with the changes and not waste energy on what can't be altered.

Evaluation and Constructive Criticism

In your supervisory role, you may be called on to **evaluate** individual performance and, when appropriate, provide **constructive criticism**. Supervisors at all levels agree that this is one of their most important—and difficult—responsibilities.

You should develop a system for consistently evaluating performance and providing constructive criticism. Complete and consistently maintained records are an essential part of any evaluation system. They will enable you to track employee performance. Then, if an employee needs to be disciplined or terminated, there will records documenting why such action is to be taken.

1. *Know your responsibilities.* Be sure your manager has identified those whom you will be evaluating and given you the authority as well as the responsibility to do so. In addition, you should use an approved evaluation form or standard set of questions when conducting a performance evaluation.
2. *Indicate when the evaluation will be completed.* Tell the employee(s) when you will complete the evaluation and what the process will involve.
3. *Carefully complete your portion of the evaluation.* Remember that written comments become part of an employee's permanent record. Be sure you have examples and specifics to back up all your statements. Figure 16–3 illustrates a common evaluation form.
4. *Provide constructive criticism.* Look for ways to show an individual where improvements can be made and how to go about this process. When combined with positive comments, constructive criticism demonstrates support for the individual.

You may also have to evaluate performance on a situation-by-situation basis. The same consistency a formal evaluation requires will be necessary. Also, be sure to document in writing your own and the employee's comments for future reference.

Figure 16–3
Employee evaluation form.

Performance Appraisal

Employee _____   Title _____

Department _____   Date of Hire _____

Eff. Date of Increase _____   Next Review Date _____

For those which apply, indicate how position performance is affected by strengths or weaknesses, and how the latter might be overcome.

Peformance level definitions: 5 = Top Performance; Clearly exceeds expectations for position, operates at sustained top performance. **4 = High Performance;** Meets all and exceeds some expectations for position, operates at continuous level of high performance. **3 = Effective Performance;** Competent in all aspects of position, maintains acceptable and effective level of performance. **2 = Limited Performance;** Limited performance in requirements of position. **1 = Unsatisfactory;** Unable to perform to minimum position requirements.

Performance of Assigned Tasks
Quantity of Work: Volume of work which the employee produces in relation to maximum which could be expected.
Comments: Circle one: (1) (2) (3) (4) (5)

Quality of work: Degree to which work reflects completeness, thoroughness, job insight, accuracy and neatness. Consider errors made and supervision required.   Circle one: (1) (2) (3) (4) (5)
Comments:

Understanding of Job
Job Knowledge: Degree of job "know how" and grasp of job's scope. Describe training completed and additional training needed.   Circle one: (1) (2) (3) (4) (5)
Comments:

Job Comprehension: Comprehension of the position as it relates to the organization as a whole.
Comments: Circle one: (1) (2) (3) (4) (5)

Judgment
Degree of maturity, discretion, insight, reasoning, and understanding demonstrated in actions taken and decisions made by employee.   Circle one: (1) (2) (3) (4) (5)
Comments:

Dependability
Degree that employee can be relied on to get job done in timely manner. Measure of employee's enthusiasm in accepting assignment, plus readiness to accept and initiative in seeking out additional duties.   Circle one: (1) (2) (3) (4) (5)
Comments:

Continued on page 376

Figure 16–3 Continued

Cooperation

Degree teamwork, give and take, harmony and willingness are displayed in job performance. Consider attitude toward the company, department, work, and associates. Circle one: (1) (2) (3) (4) (5)

Comments:

Overall Performance Summary

Comment on the overall performance on assigned duties and responsibilities:

Summary Rating

This summary is not determined by finding the numerical average of previous categories. It should be based on the individual results, job responsibilities, performance factors, and impact on results of the department or division.

Unsatisfactory	Limited Performance	Effective Performance	High Performance	Top Performance
(1)	(2)	(3)	(4)	(5)

Promotability/Personal Development

Is the employee ready for promotion or additional responsibility? Does the performance demonstrate growth and development in knowledge and capability?

Employee Reaction

What specific suggestions for change in responsibility or method of working does the employee feel warranted, based on the performance evaluation?

Goals and Objectives

To be accomplished during the next performance review period.

Initiated by Human Resources: _____   Employee's Signature _____

Manager's Signature _____ Date: _____   Manager of Human Resources _____

Your Supervisory Style

How you supervise will be determined, to a great extent, by how you were supervised. Both positive and negative experiences will have an impact. As you gain experience, try to remember both the good and the bad. This is an important way to mold your attitude.

Watching, analyzing, and talking with experienced and effective office professionals who have supervisory roles can be extremely valuable. With assistance and determination, you will begin to develop your own unique supervisory style. It will incorporate what you have learned from others and what your own personality brings to your role. As your responsibilities grow and change, your supervisory methods must change also. The more people you direct, the more you must delegate.

As an office professional, you will supervise within the limits set by your organization and/or your individual manager(s). Be sure you understand what those limits are.

Communication Tips

Use the following suggestions to increase your supervisory skill:

- Be sure you understand your supervisory responsibilities and the limits of your authority.
- Visualize beforehand how you will delegate work to specific individuals and the words you will use to do this.
- Watch the eyes as well as the "body language" of those to whom you delegate work.
- Listen carefully to questions asked for clarification; respond with special attention to achieving first-time understanding.
- Pause and think before responding when you are angry, frustrated, or tired.

SUMMARY

As your experience increases, you may have opportunities to supervise people and tasks. Supervision can be a challenging task, however, when responsibility is given without the necessary authority.

Problems you are likely to encounter include integrating supervision with your other duties, keeping your supervisory load manageable, dealing with conflicting authority, and working with employees who report to other managers. You may also encounter subordinates who are unwilling or unable to accept criticism, resist assignments, attempt to take advantage of your goodwill, and/or refuse to help out.

Qualities you should seek to develop in yourself are a professional attitude, confidence, patience as your supervisory skill develops, and realistic expectations of how much you can accomplish in your supervisory role. From these qualities will emerge high standards of conduct and performance.

An effective supervisory process will contribute to your success. Establishing standards, providing clear instructions, assigning specific duties, and following up on employee progress are parts of the process. Instructing carefully and completely is also important. Building teamwork, cooperation, and motivation will be an ongoing challenge that can be aided by techniques such as recognition and employee ownership of tasks.

Your supervisory style will be based on your own experiences with being supervised, assistance from effective office professionals, managerial support, and your unique personal qualities.

The following terms appeared in boldface type in this chapter. Do you recall what they mean? For a more complete definition, turn to the glossary beginning on p. 442.

authority (p. 364)
constructive criticism (p. 374)
employee ownership (p. 373)
evaluation (p. 374)
follow-up (p. 367)

responsibility (p. 364)
shortcut trap (p. 369)
span of control (p. 364)
unity of command (p. 364)

Discussion Questions

1. Your manager has asked you to head the company's annual campaign that supports many community agencies. In recent years the number of employees contributing to the campaign has been decreasing. If your leadership is to be respected, what support should you have from this manager?
2. Review the supervisory opportunities mentioned in this chapter. Which most appeal to you now? Why? How and when would you seek the opportunity to demonstrate your supervisory ability?
3. A temporary employee several years older than you will be keyboarding an important technical report. Exact specifications must be followed. Any questions regarding figures, unusual words, or graphs must be checked in advance. A firm deadline must be met. Outline how you would instruct this person.
4. This chapter contained a series of steps to follow when instructing others. How would you use those steps in one of the following situations?
   a. Showing a new employee how to answer the telephone
   b. Identifying and emphasizing procedures for correct use of letter styles and salutations
   c. Explaining office ground rules (e.g., starting and finishing times, break times, and correct ways to address personnel) to a new employee
5. A newly hired assistant habitually records messages in a hard-to-read and often incomplete manner. Your manager has asked you to remind this person that office procedure requires the message taker to print the caller's name, telephone number, exact message, time of call, and request for action. The assistant has interpreted your past suggestions as criticisms of his overall ability. How can you make him see the suggestions as positive and potentially helpful?
6. As a supervisor, you may need to control costs by closely watching overtime, shortening lunch hours, and using other measures. Describe how you might communicate these necessary but unpopular policies to your subordinates.

7. How can your responsibilities as an office professional help you in becoming a supervisor? What can you do in your current job to win recognition by management?

Assignments

1. In groups of two or three, develop solutions you would use in the following situations in which you are the office professional in charge. Explain when and where you would meet with the person and what you would say.
   a. A recently hired assistant's work area is always messy, and he consistently has trouble locating items.
   b. An experienced employee constantly asks questions instead of trying to find the answer on her own.
   c. An insecure employee with proven abilities needs constant reassurance that he is doing good work.
   d. An experienced assistant who greets the public becomes curt at times, especially late in the day.
2. Review past issues of office management and secretarial magazines available in your school library for case studies of both effective and ineffective supervision. As you read these articles, prepare a list of information on the following:
   a. Supervising situations likely to be encountered
   b. Necessary supervisory qualities
   c. Delegation methods used
   d. Instructional approaches used
   e. Motivational methods used
   Prepare a list of specific suggestions from each area.
3. You have been working in your office for five years and are now responsible for supervising an employee recently transferred to your department. You will be asking her to take over your monthly computer reports so that you can take on new responsibilities. How will you make her feel comfortable and eager to learn how to do this task? Describe specific steps.

Those instructors using *Top Performance: A Decision-Making Simulation for the Office* should consult the *Instructor's Guide* at this point for support material regarding use of the software in the classroom.

Case Study

Carol Beber's patience is wearing thin. As assistant to the district marketing manager, she is responsible for obtaining sales information from the regional offices at the end of each month. Of the five offices, three cooperate well and generally get the information in on time. Two offices, however, are an ongoing problem. In one, the assistant is too timid to ask the sales personnel to keep records up to date; she also gets little support from her manager. Carol periodically asks her manager to call that person's manager and ask for more cooperation, but that cooperation—when it comes—is only temporary. In the other office, the assistant never responds to Carol's requests for information in a timely manner. Usually the information comes in too late to be of value. This assistant is always pleasant to Carol, and her refusal to cooperate is a mystery.

Suggest an approach Carol might use in both situations. Remember that Carol's manager has been unsuccessful in dealing with one of the offices. Carol must cooperate with personnel in these offices on a regular basis. What help could her manager provide? What other assistance could Carol obtain? What additional strategies might work?

CHAPTER

17

FINDING YOUR POSITION

Chapter Objectives

- To learn to identify and evaluate available positions
- To learn how to prepare for job interviews
- To develop the ability to start off right in a new position
- To learn to establish successful working relationships with one or more managers
- To develop career goals, with managerial support for your professional development

Examples of Excellance

Within two weeks, everyone regarded Esther Kim as a regular. She fit in well, and all personnel commented on how much she had contributed so soon after starting. But although it seemed that Esther began her new position with little effort, a great deal of planning had contributed to her excellent start. After a careful search for an appropriate position, she had selected the organization and the type of unit she wanted to join. She wanted to work in an office where there would be opportunities to learn and to take on more responsibilities. Her new employer was known to provide both.

As with all important activities, Esther had carefully chosen her new employer. Two friends who worked there had encouraged her to apply, citing the positive atmosphere and excellent working conditions. Esther had listened to them, but she also asked others in the community, gathered information from the company itself, and developed a comparison list of possible employers. These activities made her want to apply for and obtain a desirable position.

As either a generalist or a specialist, you will have many opportunities. Now that you know what these roles involve and how to handle the wide assortment of tasks they require, it is time to learn the best way to find the job you want. In this chapter, you will learn how to

- Identify and evaluate available positions
- Prepare for job interviews
- Start off right in your new position

- Establish a foundation for successful working relationships with one or more managers
- Develop career goals
- Obtain managerial support for your personal growth and development

National Employment Trends

As you begin to think about the kind of position you want, you should consider where opportunities exist now. This section presents information about the public and private organizations that are experiencing the most growth, their locations, their needs for office professionals, and the types of responsibilities and salary you can expect if you work for them.

Economic reports emphasize that the fastest growing sector of America is occurring among small businesses employing from five people to one thousand or more. These businesses are involved in the production of goods and/or the delivery of services.

In your own community, you will find that many of the small, locally owned **franchises** or nationally owned businesses serve distinct groups. Day care centers, cleaning services, and health care organizations, for example, thrive because they do what their customers lack the time, interest, or ability to do themselves.

Growth has also occurred in government at the local, state, and federal levels. Certain agencies that deal with education, health services, housing, and public works improvements have increased in size because of the growing needs in these areas.

As the U.S. population continues to age and individuals live longer, the number of public and private organizations providing services to this sector will continue to increase.

Manufacturing firms are showing signs of rejuvenation. Areas of the United States that once were characterized by partially or fully closed plants are now prospering again. This is due in part to the areas in which American technology and expertise dominate, including production of computer equipment, pharmaceuticals, and specialized medical equipment.

Conditions will vary from community to community. As you know, certain types of business and industry are concentrated in specific parts of the country. For example, you will find manufacturing "belts" or communities clustered in several states: western Ohio through eastern Pennsylvania is one example. Similar clusters exist in parts of Illinois, Indiana, and Michigan. California is the home of many computer development companies, while Florida is known for its leisure-related industries.

Despite the diversity among potential employers, however, you will find some similarity in what they are looking for in office professionals. Those qualities include

- Potential stability in the position
- Computer literacy—the ability to use basic software programs capable of performing word processing, data management, and manipulation of figures

- Knowledge of the employing organization, its products and services, and its basic operating structure and procedures
- An ability to work with the employer's "public," either face to face or by phone
- Language sensitivity—using correct grammar, good manners, and humor when appropriate

In addition to these common qualities, each employer may have special needs. They may be presented to you during your interview or when you begin work. In some cases, you will have to discover them through experience.

Potential Employers

You will probably work for one of four major types of organizations. In this section, you will learn what these are and how to obtain additional information.

Public employers, including agencies of local, state, and federal government, is one possibility. At the federal level, for example, your manager might be the supervisor of a group of employees, such as the head of environmental research for the Corps of Engineers, a unit of the Department of Defense. As a government employee, you will become part of the **Civil Service System** in your state or at the federal level. The Civil Service System protects employees from **indiscriminate dismissal** after an initial **probationary period,** after which your position will be relatively secure (except for large-scale layoffs in times of extreme budget reductions).

In the federal service, you can apply for positions throughout the country and overseas. As an employee of any government unit, you will participate in a pension plan as well as make contributions to social security. Health and other fringe benefits can also be attractive.

Publicly supported educational institutions such as elementary and secondary school systems, community colleges, and four-year/graduate universities operate in the same manner as other government agencies. Opportunities for advancement exist, along with fairly regular salary increases, pension plans, and benefits.

Not-for-profit agencies, such as some hospitals and nursing homes, museums, charities, and foundations, comprise another large group of employers. You may work for a staff member of a large charity such as the Red Cross or United Way and support several staff members, or you may work for a smaller agency. Benefits and salaries will likely vary with the size of the agency.

Large private organizations, such as a major manufacturing plant, a national insurance company, or a chain of retail stores will have well-developed operating procedures. There may be opportunities to transfer to another location as well as attractive pensions and other benefits. You may receive bonuses or other gifts depending on how the organization performed during the year. Some companies offer employees the opportunity to buy stock.

Small businesses usually have the least developed personnel procedures. In a small business, you may be involved in many different tasks. Especially in newly opened businesses, few staff are employed and everyone focuses on the priorities of the moment.

Selecting an Employer

Obviously, there is wide diversity among individual employers. When deciding which firm is most attractive to you, consider the following questions:

1. What does the organization do? Will you be challenged or interested in that type of work?
2. What type of work will you be doing on a regular basis? How many individuals will you work with?
3. What opportunities will you have to increase your responsibilities, learn, and increase your expertise in a variety of areas?
4. How well will you be paid in comparison with other employers? If lower, what will compensate for that level? If higher, what special demands will exist?
5. Are there any special pressures associated with working in this organization?
6. What are the organization's fringe benefits, vacation policy, and other services available to all employees?
7. How far will you live from work? How easy will it be to get to work each day? How costly?
8. Will wardrobe demands require you to spend a great deal on clothes? Will eating lunch be especially costly?
9. How are the employees treated?

Types of Career Opportunities

A **specialist** generally commands a higher salary. You can specialize by taking courses, completing a special program, or learning on the job. On the other hand, certain positions require a generalist—someone who can handle a wide variety of jobs necessary to make an office run smoothly. This section presents the major opportunities for generalists and specialists.

Opportunities for Generalists

As a **generalist,** you will be expected to perform most of the required office tasks. The people for whom office professionals work are concerned with obtaining, controlling, and using information. As new procedures are needed or new technology is introduced into your office, you will need to make the necessary transitions with ease and confidence. Someone who possesses the general skills needed in most offices can provide the type of support managers require.

Employment opportunities abound for generalists who have a wide array of skills at their fingertips. Typical titles for these positions include *secretary, executive secretary, administrative assistant, executive assistant,* and *administrative secretary.* Although the titles may differ, these professionals need to possess outstanding skills in typewriting/keyboarding, organizing, communicating face to face or by telephone, managing records, and working with others. In actual numbers, there are probably more office positions available for people with generalist skills than for those with specialized training.

As a generalist, you may wish to join a local chapter of **Professional Secretaries International (PSI),** an association formed to further the education and development of office professionals. PSI chapters provide their members with continuing education programs vital in keeping up to date. In addition, PSI holds state, regional, and national conferences that encourage professionalism. Through affiliation with PSI, you can also prepare to become a **Certified Professional Secretary (CPS),** which involves studying six areas of business practice before taking a two-day **CPS examination.** Those areas are (1) behavioral science in business, (2) business law, (3) economics and management, (4) accounting, (5) office administration and communication, and (6) office technology. Those who pass the examination can put the highly respected *CPS* title after their names.

Opportunities for Specialists

Office professionals often move from a generalist position to one requiring special knowledge and skills. All the skills a generalist needs will be helpful to anyone making this change. This section discusses the most common areas of specialization.

Legal Secretaries. A high demand exists for office professionals in the legal profession. **Legal secretaries** need a thorough general education, knowledge of the law, excellent typewriting and shorthand skills, and impeccable command of the English language.

Legal secretaries also need to understand legal terms such as *deposition, temporary restraining order,* and *injunction.* Attention to all details and commitment to accuracy are important not only in preparing legal documents but in scheduling appointments, maintaining court calendars, keeping current on billing clients, and staying aware of critical deadlines.

To become a *Professional Legal Secretary,* a designation certifying excellence, you must pass the rigorous certification examination that the National Association of Legal Secretaries (NALS) sponsors and administers. To take the examination, you must hold membership in the NALS, have five or more years' work experience as a legal secretary, and provide letters of recommendation, one of which must be from a member of the American Bar Association.

Medical Secretaries. In addition to working in doctors' or dentists' offices, **medical secretaries** work in hospitals, clinics, public health agencies, and pharmaceutical firms as well as research laboratories and foundations, medical departments in large corporations, and medical publishing companies. All of these positions require secretaries with highly specialized medical knowledge and skills.

The skills required will vary from one job to another in the medical field. If you are employed in a hospital, for example, your job may involve the extensive recordkeeping and paperwork completion so vital in the health field today. You may have little contact with patients. However, if you work in a clinic or for one or two dentists or doctors, a large part of your work will focus on patient interaction.

Certification is available through the American Association of Medical Assistants, a professional organization for people employed in the health care field. The certification examination has three categories that test medical terminology, basic anatomy and physiology, psychology, and medical law and ethics, as well as oral and written communication, accounting, insurance, administrative procedures, and clinical procedures and medications.

Word Processing Specialists. In some larger organizations, office professionals become **word processing specialists**. Those with experience and demonstrated skill will manage word processing centers. In this position, an experienced individual coordinates the entering of information, trains others to use software programs, and works directly with managers to schedule the completion of major projects.

As a word processing specialist, you may be the only person in the firm to use word processing equipment, and you may be expected to do a variety of additional work as well, such as answering the telephone and filing. Or you may be employed along with two or three other word processing specialists in a specific division of a company, such as the engineering department.

In a word processing *center*, on the other hand, there will be more office support personnel devoting their total energies to processing written information in the form of business letters and reports. They will work for all the members of the firm and usually be organized to accommodate work on a first-come, first-served basis.

Technical Assistants. The increasing number of public and private organizations with a scientific, research, or technical focus has led to a similar increase in the number of support personnel. In particular, **technical assistants** work with computer programmers, chemists, engineers, or scientists, handling general office management responsibilities as well as technically related work.

Technical assistants collect and organize scientific articles, papers, and similar information needed for a manager's work. They also help prepare reports and papers, following precise guidelines and a set format. They may also check proposals against specifications set by a client or agency supporting a research project, for example. A strong mathematics and science background is helpful.

Educational Secretaries. Office professionals often choose a position in an educational environment because they enjoy working with young people.

Schools are usually centrally located, and work hours often coincide with the length of the school day, enabling office professionals with school-age children to leave work when their children go home.

A prime requirement for an **educational secretary** is adeptness at meeting and assisting the public. The ability to communicate clearly is essential. Also important is the ability to adapt to the active, ever-changing environment in which the educational secretary assists not only the school administration but parents, students, salespeople, and others while completing ongoing duties.

Many educational secretaries belong to the National Association of Educational Office Personnel (NAEOP). NAEOP is a national educational and professional association; through membership you can participate in their Professional Standards Program. Local chapters meet regularly.

On Your Own

If being your own boss appeals to you, especially setting hours that allow you to pursue other responsibilities, you may consider becoming a public stenographer or a temporary service secretary.

Public stenographers work in large hotels and motels, at some airports, and at major conferences or conventions. Preparing letters and short reports for individual clients is a major part of their work. Public stenographers charge a fee to each client, usually based on the length and complexity of the document prepared.

Temporary service secretaries assist businesses for short periods. After passing a typing or word processing proficiency test and a grammar/spelling test, a secretary is placed on the list of those to be called. Assignments can be as short as one day or as long as a month or more. The agency arranging the assignment pays the secretary an hourly fee. Because temporary employment provides experience in a variety of jobs, this option can be beneficial for beginning office professionals who have not yet decided what they like to do best.

Worldwide Opportunities for Office Professionals

If you are interested in living and working outside the United States, you will find that office professionals are in as much demand in other countries as they are here. Not only do overseas-based organizations need office professionals, but many large American corporations provide similar employment opportunities in their international branches.

Your opportunities are even greater if you can speak or write in other languages. Not only will your abilities widen the number of countries in which you will feel comfortable, but companies often give top priority to people with bilingual communication skills. The U.S. government is one of the largest employers of office professionals overseas. In some of these jobs, expertise in a second language is required, while in others good English skills are enough. For information concerning requirements, contact the United States Department of State, Washington, D.C., or your U.S. senator or representative.

The advertisements in Figure 17–1 demonstrate how an available position is described. Depending on the size of the ad, specific details will be given, including (1) unit to which you will be assigned, (2) nature of responsibilities, (3) background required, (4) salary level and benefits, (5) deadline for application, and (6) person to contact for an application or interview.

Decisions about Direction

Developing your professional **goals** won't be easy. Those who do develop goals have learned to say *yes* to a few selected activities and *no* to many more. Each day these individuals identify small but significant achievements that will make those goals a reality, and they manage their time well to accomplish them.

Here are some typical questions to ask when trying to develop your professional goals:

- How much money do you really need to consider yourself successful?
- What kind of work do you really want to do?
- What type of environment do you want? An **environment** consists of two parts: work setting and geographic area.
- What are your social needs and those of your family? A basic career decision addresses the balance between one's job and one's personal life.
- What kind of family life do you want? The answer to this question, when combined with the preceding one, determines how a person wishes to lead his or her life.
- How much prestige do you need?
- How much security do you need?
- What kind of personality do you have? Are you outgoing or quiet? How aggressive are you? How comfortable would you be supervising others?

Only when you have a clear understanding of your own needs and a definite plan for the future will you be able to decide what to do as each job opportunity arises.

Planning and Accomplishments

Making New Year's resolutions is one way to establish goals, objectives, and priorities. Such resolutions are often difficult to achieve, however, because they consist of unrelated wants or aspirations. A yearly plan, on the other hand, establishes a system for making those resolutions a reality.

Your plan should resemble clay rather than cement: It should be firm but flexible. You can mold, shape, and reshape it as time and personality warrant. Basically, the plan should consist of five parts:

1. *A set of goals.* Begin with a broad statement describing the personal achievements you wish to accomplish in your lifetime. Next, identify a sequence of

Figure 17–1
Sample want ads.

2230 Help Wanted/Clerical/Secretarial

AAAAAAAAAAAA   All Fees Paid

SECRETARY

$19,000–$22,000

Reorganization leaves NEW PRESIDENT needing your EXEC. SEC'Y skills. This dynamic company is in a RECESSION-PROOF INDUSTRY. You must have a high level of confidence and enjoy work. To become a part of this team, call NANCY at 555-3200. OFFICEMATES.

2230 Help Wanted/Clerical/Secretarial

RECEPTIONIST

We have an immediate need for a friendly person who has experience with a multiline switchboard and has knowledge of different word processing systems. If you think you can handle the fast-paced sales environment and love working with people, call for a personal interview. We offer competitive wages and benefits. Prove yourself, and there is unlimited potential to grow. Call the HUMAN RESOURCES DEPT. AT 555-0002 ASAP.
NO AGENCIES, PLEASE.

---

intermediate, more narrowly focused goals to cover periods of, say, two years, six months, or two months. Figure 17–2, page 390, contains a goal-setting exercise you may wish to complete.

2. *Educational decisions.* Select educational programs that will contribute to your goal achievement. These could include

   a. Attending classes in a specialized area such as word processing, business writing, or computer technology.

   b. Completing an associate degree at a two-year college, or a bachelor's degree or beyond, while working or during a leave of absence. Many courses are held on evenings or weekends. Some colleges offer credit for life experience, which can shorten the time required to obtain a degree.

   c. Participating in various one-time or short-term seminars, workshops, and programs such as those an employing organization, association, or educational firm might sponsor.

3. *A conscious search for useful experience.* Learn from others by

   a. Identifying those who have successfully done what you want to achieve.

   b. Asking for an opportunity to learn new procedures and skills in your current position.

   c. Listening, looking, and, when appropriate, asking *how* and *why* questions from knowledgeable people.

   d. Joining a professional organization to meet new people and to learn through active participation.

4. *Independent study.* Read regularly, listen to tapes, or use videocassettes to stay current; this can be easier than attending a seminar or enrolling in a course. Read a few selected publications each week or month. Your employer may subscribe to a number of these publications; you can simply add your name to the routing list. The public library is a valuable source for such information.

5. *A sensitivity to weakness.* Simply put, look for areas in which you need further growth. Identifying specific ways to improve is a sign of strength. As you select

Figure 17–2
Goal-setting exercise.

List your seven most important goals, including work, family, and personal goals. This is extremely important, so take some time to do it:

1. _____

2. _____

3. _____

4. _____

5. _____

6. _____

7. _____

these areas, your goals will continually change and your self-improvement will be a source of great satisfaction. Many companies have every supervisor complete a performance evaluation for employees in the unit, noting areas that need improvement. These observations can serve as a starting point for directing your self-improvement efforts.

Continuing Your Education

A clear goal achievement plan will help you select appropriate **continuing education programs**. As a busy professional, you must become a shrewd consumer of educational programs for all of the reasons cited earlier, plus one more: the need to recognize education as an investment of your time, money, and energy. Each of these resources is in limited quantities and is not to be squandered. Inflation means that the dollar buys less. This is as true with education as it is with food or housing. Figure 17–3 contains a series of questions you might ask when considering a continuing education program.

Subjects of Lasting Value

Many diverse subjects are available to an office professional interested in continuing education. As you add subjects of interest to you, take care to avoid educational fads. Following are some suggested subject areas:

1. *Basic computer operations* is a must because computer technology is so widespread today.

Figure 17–3

Selecting a continuing education activity.

	Yes	No
Part I		
A. Are the areas mentioned in the brochure important concerns to you in your present or future job?	___	___
B. Does the program offer workable solutions to your problems?	___	___
C. Do the speaker's credentials indicate that he or she is an expert in the program's subject?	___	___

Part II

Continue with Part II only if you have answered *yes* to questions A, B, and C.

Brochure

1. Does the bulk of the agenda (outline) appeal to you?	___	___
2. Will your employer give you time off to attend?	___	___
3. Will your job be covered by a substitute?	___	___
4. Will you earn applicable credit toward a degree or promotion by attending this program?	___	___
5. Does the brochure list recommendations from participants along with their names and addresses?	___	___
6. Are "hands-on" participation exercises included in the agenda?	___	___

Recommendation

7. Do you know a past participant in this program who recommends that you attend?	___	___

Speaker

8. Is the speaker an educator, practitioner, or author of a successful book on the program's subject?	___	___
9. Is the speaker addressing a new topic that you have never heard him or her speak on? (Speakers tend to repeat their messages.)	___	___

Sponsor

10. Is the sponsor a recognized university, college, or professional organization?	___	___
11. Have you ever benefited from another program offered by this sponsor?	___	___
12. Has this program been offered before? (Sponsors will repeat successful, well-attended programs.)	___	___

Location

13. Will the program be convenient for you to reach?	___	___
14. Will you be able to attend the entire program? (Multiple-day programs build on materials presented from the first day on.)	___	___
15. If you need to spend a night away from home, will accommodations be suitable?	___	___

Cost

16. Will your employer pay your registration fee?	___	___
17. Will you get your time's and money's worth out of this program?	___	___

Part II Totals	Yes	No
	___	___

If in Part II you answered *yes* to 13 to 17 questions, you should attend; 9 to 12 questions, maybe you should attend; 0 to 8 questions, wait and evaluate the next program offered.

2. *Software program operation* is helpful in understanding the usefulness of various software programs.
3. *Speed reading* is an investment course. If you are in a position that requires you to read a variety of reports and documents, speed reading will be beneficial.
4. *Stress control* is the kind of educational program worth an annual investment of your time.
5. *Public speaking* courses provide another useful educational experience: learning how to talk to others comfortably and well.
6. *Business writing* sharpens a fundamental skill.
7. *Business English* focuses on grammar, punctuation, and spelling rules.
8. *Basic management skills* include such areas as decision making, problem solving, delegation, and staff training.

In addition to taking formal courses, you can learn by reading articles or books dealing with various aspects of office operations. More experienced co-workers can give you guidance and support as you begin work and make position changes. Managers can also help further your growth and development.

Another way to develop yourself professionally is to study for and take the Certified Professional Secretary examination discussed earlier. Community and four-year colleges frequently offer classes that review the topics covered in the CPS examination. Earning the CPS certification is an achievement that most managers value highly.

Joining a professional organization can also provide you with opportunities to grow. Accepting a leadership role in the organization will help develop your skills in working with others to achieve the organization's goals. You will learn to feel at ease and confident in leading a business or committee meeting. Such confidence-building experiences are invaluable for anyone who wants to advance professionally. In addition, professional associations often provide valuable networking relationships.

Managerial Support

A manager who is aware of your long-term and immediate plans to continue your education will often be willing to provide suggestions and growth opportunities by giving you time to learn more, financial assistance to attend a course or program, or even a recommendation for a promotion. A well-prepared plan will signal your discipline and determination to most managers. While some managers may be skeptical or even resistant, most will be willing to help as much as possible.

Your plan should identify not only when it would be professionally desirable to leave a position but when it wouldn't. It is important to avoid premature job hopping because of the real or imagined benefits of a new position. It is also important to part amicably with your present manager: A favorable recommendation is an extremely valuable professional tool. With your plan as a guide, you can evaluate each available position according to its relevance and the growth opportunities it will provide.

Your plan will become especially valuable because it will enable supportive managers and colleagues to advise you on the best decision to make. As your opportunities for career advancement grow, you can set the stage for a graceful and amicable departure from your present position by following these steps:

- Let your manager(s) know that you have a professional development plan, which means you may leave at some point to accept a new position.
- Regularly discuss opportunities you are considering with your manager (if you feel comfortable doing so), and listen to advice on what each offers.
- Maintain an impeccable work record so that your manager will be willing to write a supportive recommendation for a position you seek.
- If you accept a new job, leave your present one on a positive note, expressing appreciation for what you have gained from your current position.

All these suggestions will help you feel more confident and more in control of most situations. You will no longer need to respond quickly and without careful thought; rather, you will be able to coolly assess each situation and apply the knowledge you have acquired to make a sound decision. And one good decision begets another—success breeds success.

A Successful Job Search

Throughout this book, we have emphasized a positive attitude and professional behavior. Exhibiting these qualities will be extremely important as you search for a position that you hope to hold for a substantial length of time. It will also be important to follow an effective job search process, which begins by gathering useful information.

Gathering Information

Perhaps the best way to begin gathering information for a successful job search is to ask friends, family members, and acquaintances how they found their jobs. Talk to individuals at different stages of their careers, including one or two people who recently began a new job. In particular, learn how they prepared for their interviews and what they think made the best impression on their prospective employers.

You can also consult your college or school placement office for assistance. They can show you how to develop a list of prospects and what approach to use when making contacts.

In some areas, you will find state or locally run employment agencies. These agencies can also assist in your job search, including testing and interview preparation. To receive their ongoing assistance, you must remain on their active list. Staying in touch with them is important.

Private employment agencies are another option. Many of these agencies help employers recruit qualified candidates. All maintain a list of available positions in a given area. Private employment agencies' experience and expertise can decrease the time and effort required to obtain a position.

Take care in selecting an employment agency. Employers usually pay agencies a portion of the fees for their services, but applicants often must pay a fee as well. Fees may range from one to two weeks' salary to a percentage of the first month's pay.

You might want to prepare a "business card" that lists your name, address, and telephone number along with "position desired." In addition, you might add two or three words that you believe accurately describe you. Present this card to anyone you think might know of a job, or place it on a bulletin board for high visibility.

Also, consult classified advertisements in local newspapers as well as those from cities or locations in which you wish to work. Once you have identified three or four interesting positions,

1. Show the ads to an experienced person and ask for reactions.
2. Discuss the ads with your college placement officer or one of your instructors to obtain a "second opinion" on the advantages and limitations of each available position.
3. Call the employer advertising the position to try to solicit more specific information about it. If you get vague answers about what is expected on the job, be cautious.
4. Consider visiting potential employers in person. Make an appointment to talk with human resources staff and ask them what qualities and preparation impress them when interviewing candidates for office positions.

These steps will help you determine precisely what type of preparation you will need to obtain the job you want. In particular, you will be better able to direct your attention to a few potential employers rather than to several. You can then prepare a résumé tailored to those employers' needs and preferences.

Preparing a Résumé

Your **résumé** should make a strong and honest case for you and your accomplishments. It should tell potential employers that you are intelligent, well organized, and professional. Ideally, it should explain the specifics of your background and experience without the need for additional explanation. Organization, accuracy, neatness, and clarity are critical.

As you prepare your résumé, put yourself in the position of the potential employer, who may see hundreds of résumés every year. The résumés that stand out have been put together with great thought. They build the best possible case for the applicant. Employers don't want a puffed-up picture, but they do want to know something about an applicant's past, present, and future. The résumé also provides an opportunity to display your attention to detail.

Your résumé should contain the following items:

Talking with a human resources staff member is a good way to get information about a prospective employer. *(Courtesy of International Business Machines Corporation)*

Personal data. At one time it was necessary to include height, weight, marital status, and number of children on a résumé. Now only your name, address (temporary or permanent), and telephone number(s) are required. You can volunteer other information if you think it will be useful to an employer, but you are not required to do so. Also, remember that a résumé must be brief, so avoid any irrelevant material.

Educational background. Begin with your most recent educational experience. Identify schools attended and degrees received, with relevant dates, subjects related to the job sought, skills acquired, and special training courses completed. List your transcription, typing, and shorthand dictation speeds. Also, mention what office equipment and software you know how to use.

When sending résumés before you've graduated, remember to use the future tense to describe your latest educational experiences ("Will graduate with an Associate of Applied Science degree, Legal Secretarial Major, May 1991"). To emphasize coursework related to a specific job, you can add a special section under Education called "Educational Highlights." This will give you the opportunity to list selected courses or educational honors received. Specific course names and numbers are not necessary.

Work experience. Be complete. Make a chronological list of all full-time or part-time positions that show relevant experience, with the most recent first.

Include the dates of employment, employer, job held, responsibilities, and immediate supervisor's name and address. Don't provide excessive detail, but list enough information so that a quick reading will tell the human resources staff and the prospective employer what you have accomplished.

Describe your responsibilities in terms of results, such as "prepared weekly payroll for sixteen employees." Be honest in the description; skillful potential employers will always call to check on applicants and obtain a picture of what they did. If you resigned or were terminated from a job, say so. Be candid about experiences that didn't work out, and tell what you learned from them. Your employer can always find out from previous employers what you may have left out, so it is best not to be evasive.

In regard to education and work experience, you should list the category you wish to emphasize first. If you have more education than work experience, list education first. If you have more related work experience than education, list work experience first.

Uniqueness. Your special accomplishments show that you are a unique person. If you have held an office in one or more school clubs and societies, achieved academic honors, or served your community, tell your potential employer. Depending on the agency or organization to which you are applying, this information can be very helpful. For example, the presidency of a school association indicates leadership ability, volunteer work shows a willingness to assist others; involvement with various clubs and societies demonstrates an interest in working with others. This section of the résumé is thus an opportunity to highlight your successes and reveal important information about you.

Interests and hobbies may also be included if they set you apart from other applicants. Interviewers often break the tension of an interview by asking about them.

References. There are two possible ways to provide job **references**. First, you can provide several names, including those who know your performance in school, in the community, and on the job. The references should be listed in an easy-to-use format and include name, address, title, company, and telephone number. If you want to list a long-time acquaintance as a character reference, note this in parentheses. Be sure to request permission before using anyone's name as a reference. Figure 17–4 contains a sample letter requesting use of a reference.

Second, you can indicate that references are available on request. With this approach, however, prospective employers must take the extra step of asking you the names of your references. Instead of doing this, they may just write or call the listed references of other applicants.

Objectives. This category should be placed at the beginning of the résumé. We mention it at this point to encourage you to reflect on the document already prepared before you form your objectives. Employers are impressed with individuals who have thought about future directions and identified what they

Figure 17–4
Request for a reference.

410 Western Ave.
Albany, NY 12203
March 4, 19XX

Mrs. Ruth Seyler
Admissions Office Manager
St. Mary's Hospital
100 Van Rensselaer Blvd.
Albany, NY 12204

Dear Mrs. Seyler:

May I use your name as a reference when applying for secretarial positions? As you know, my two-year degree program at Rensselaer Community College ends in May.

I am especially interested in positions in which my word processing training can be used. Could you mention my work with that equipment while at St. Mary's?

Any help you give will be appreciated. I will call next week to confirm your permission.

Sincerely,

Alice A. Woods

Alice A. Woods

want to achieve professionally. Your statement of objectives can also include some idea of the skills you wish to acquire and indicate why a particular position interests you.

Miscellaneous information. You can also indicate your salary preference, time of availability, and other relevant factors such as willingness to travel. Generally, however, applicants provide these items at the interview rather than on the résumé.

Format. Résumés should be typed on one side of a page and, in most instances, limited to two pages. Figures 17–5 and 17–6 illustrate two résumé formats. The résumé in Figure 17–5, pages 398–99, focuses on career objectives; the one in Figure 17–6, page 400, called a *functional résumé*, emphasizes skills over work experience. The functional format may be more appropriate if you are returning to work after a long absence.

Figure 17–5
Career objective résumé.

Mary R. Jones
1020 Tropical Blvd.
Sanford, FL 32774
Telephone: (407) 555-1390

CAREER OBJECTIVE	An administrative assistant's position in a large manufacturing firm, with opportunities to use and increase my experience with word processing technology.
EDUCATION 1989–1991	Seminole Community College, 100 Weldon Blvd., Sanford, FL 32773. To be graduated with an Associate of Applied Science degree, Secretarial Major, May 1991.
1985–1989	Sanford High School, 10 Ocean St., Sanford, FL 32775. Diploma, college preparatory major, graduated 11th in a class of 130.
EDUCATION HIGHLIGHTS	Seminole Community College (average in major business courses is 4.2 out of a possible 5.0.)
	Typewriting, 3 semesters; Business Mathematics/Shorthand, 3 semesters; Word Processing Applications/Accounting, 2 semesters; Principles of Management; Business Correspondence; Records Management; Administrative Office Systems and Procedures; Introduction to Business
	Working knowledge of microcomputer software: WordPerfect 5.0, Lotus 1-2-3, dBASE IV, Excel, Filemaker 4.0; shorthand, 100 wpm; word processing equipment; typing, 65 wpm

WORK EXPERIENCE

8/89–5/91	Work-study student, part-time, 15 hours per week, Seminole Community College, 100 Weldon Blvd., Sanford, FL 32773 Duties: typing, filing, answering the telephone, scheduling counselor's appointments with students, taking dictation, and handling the general secretarial duties with minimum supervision. Supervisor: Mr. Joseph Dodds, Office of Student Services. Telephone: (407) 555-1450, Ext.286
1/88–1/89	Sales clerk, part-time, 20 hours per week, during vacations and holidays, at Robert's On-The-Square, Sanford, FL 32773. Duties: helped customers, checked merchandise in from stockroom, priced goods, maintained inventory records, operated cash register. Supervisor: Mrs. Audrey Johnson, Head Buyer, Women's Department, Robert's On-The-Square Telephone: (407) 555-6251
2/87–7/87	Stenographer, part-time, 10 hours per week, First Bank of Florida, 15 West Main Street, Sanford, FL 32775. Duties: typed reports and forms, took dictation and transcribed letters for a number of executives, and assisted in preparation of minutes of the Bank's board meetings. Supervisor: Mrs. Joan Smith, Office Manager Telephone: (407) 555-6174
ACTIVITIES AND HONORS	Dean's List (grade point average of 4.5), Seminole Community College, 1989 President's List (grade point average of 5.0), Seminole Community College, 1990 Business and Professional Women's Club Scholarship,1989 Attended 15th Annual Seminar, Seminole Chapter, Professional Secretaries International
INTERESTS AND HOBBIES	Future Secretaries of America, 1988–1989, President, 1988; Pom Pom Squad, 1987–1989; playing piano, softball, gardening, bike riding.

Continued on page 399

Figure 17–5 **Continued**

PERSONAL INFORMATION	Mrs. R. Jones 611 West Main Street Sanford, FL 32773	Telephone: (407) 555-0064
REFERENCES	Mr. Jose Rivera 1632 North Washington Sanford, FL 32774 (Character reference) Telephone: 555-3230	Mr. Joseph Dodds, Director, Student Services Seminole Community College 100 Weldon Blvd. Sanford, FL 32773 (Former supervisor) Telephone: (407) 555-1450, Ext. 286 Home: (407) 555-1171
	Mrs. Arlene Videa Business Department Seminole Community College 100 Weldon Blvd. Sanford, FL 32775 Telephone: (407) 323-1450, Ext. 317	Mrs. Jean Smith Office Manager First Bank of Florida 15 West Main Street Sanford, FL 32775 Telephone: (407) 555-6174

Mary R. Jones
Signature Line

May 6, 1991
Date

Once your résumé is prepared, you can proceed to the next step: writing letters of application to obtain interviews.

Writing Application Letters

Your **application letter** should follow the basic outline of a persuasive or sales letter. It should emphasize what you can do. Its purpose is to get you an interview. For the best effect, use the AIDCA (attention, interest, desire, conviction, action) formula described in Chapter 11:

1. Capture the reader's favorable *attention* by establishing a uniquely personal beginning. Ask a question, make a statement about the company, or tell how you learned about the job, and indicate that you are applying for a position. Do not be gimmicky or "cute." Also, avoid overusing the pronoun I or giving it too much emphasis. Make sure that the appearance of your letter creates a favorable first impression.
2. Create *interest* by highlighting your background so that it complements the position you wish to fill. Use an introduction similar to one of those presented in Figure 17–7, page 401. Remember that a well-written introductory sentence encourages readers to continue.
3. Develop *desire* by presenting your education, work experience, and abilities in a way that will motivate the prospective employer to read your résumé.

Figure 17–6
Functional résumé.

Leah Madison
309 Eighth Street
Aiken, SC 29801
(803) 555-6851

Career Objective: A secretarial position in which I can utilize the following personal qualities.

Self-Motivation: Did a needs assessment for and organized Meals-On-Wheels program for senior citizens of the Champaign–Urbana area.

After two years, expanded the Meals-On-Wheels Program to Champaign County.

After my father died, I took care of two younger brothers and ran the household while my mother went to work.

Persuasiveness: Convinced United Way staff, church officials, and county social agencies to cooperate in Meals-On-Wheels program.

Used secretarial skills to plan and coordinate a one-year anniversary dinner for the program participants.

Resourcefulness: Kept Meals-On-Wheels program funded through application for a senior citizen grant program.

Organized a group of volunteer social agency volunteers to promote the new program of Meals-on-Wheels.

Education: University of South Carolina, Aiken Campus, Associate of Applied Science degree, Secretarial Studies, Aiken, SC 29801.

References:	Mrs. Diane Becker	Mrs. Julie Martin
	Community Service Director	Business Instructor
	203 West Springfield	University of South Carolina,
	Aiken, SC 29801	Aiken Campus
	(803) 555-1011	Aiken, SC 29801
		(803) 555-6851

4. Establish *conviction* by emphasizing that you would be an excellent employee, have a clear understanding of your responsibilities, and possess the necessary skills and abilities to do the job well.
5. Ask for *action* in the last paragraph by requesting an interview and indicating how the prospective employer can contact you. Use an ending similar to one of those presented in Figure 17–8, page 402.

When answering an advertisement, cover all the points mentioned in the ad in the order in which they are listed. This will show that you are thorough and can meet all requirements.

If possible, address the letter to an individual rather than to the human

Figure 17–7
Sample introductory paragraphs in job application letters.

Dear Mr. Harms:

A recent advertisement in the *Decatur Herald* indicated that you have several secretarial openings. I am finishing a two-year office procedures course and want to apply for a position.

Dear Mr. Harms:

For several years, I have been interested in moving to the Atlanta area. In June, I will be finishing a two-year administrative office systems program and am interested in obtaining an office position in your company.

Dear Mr. Harms:

Elizabeth Riggins, one of my business instructors, reported to our class that your organization has openings for several assistants. I would like to apply for one of those positions.

Dear Mr. Harms:

A recent issue of the *Atlanta Constitution* indicated that you will be hiring office assistants in April. I will be visiting Atlanta on April 6–7 and would like to arrange for an interview.

Dear Mr. Harms:

If you are looking for someone who has had extensive office experience and is willing to work hard to serve your firm, I believe I can prove to you that I can be an excellent assistant to the sales manager.

---

resources manager or the head of the department to which you are applying. If you must call the company's switchboard to get the person's name (be sure to double-check the spelling!) and title, do so. This step will make a strong positive impression on the reader.

Excellent letters create mental pictures. In this case, you will want the reader to visualize a capable and positive individual. As you write, concentrate on creating that impression. Figure 17–9, page 403, contains a sample application letter written with that intent.

Completing the Application Form

If you obtain an interview, the potential employer will probably ask you to fill out an **application form**. This form will represent you in a different light than that in the résumé and application letter. It must be completed legibly and accurately while you wait for the interview, and it is an extremely important part of your self-presentation package.

Figure 17–8
Sample ending paragraphs in job application letters.

> May I have an appointment for a personal interview? You can telephone me at (312) 555-1010.
>
> I am planning to be in Atlanta on August 23 and 24. May I see you on either of those dates?
>
> You can reach me at (312) 555-1010 any day after 4:00 PM. I hope that I may have the privilege of a personal interview at your convenience.
>
> May I have a personal interview? I can be reached by telephone at (312) 555-1010.
>
> May I have the opportunity to come in to talk with you? Since I am in class until 4 PM each day, perhaps you would prefer to write me. If you wish to telephone me after 4 PM, my number is (312) 555-1010.

Your completed application form should emphasize your professionalism and ability to follow directions. To accomplish this, read the form through before proceeding, and fill it out slowly and methodically. If you are uncertain about how to spell a word, use another one (it is advisable to carry a pocket dictionary with you). When a question isn't clear, ask the person who provided the form. Be very careful not to supply incorrect information.

Follow all directions carefully. If you are told to print, *print*—don't write. Fill in every blank. If a question does not apply to you, print *not applicable* or *N/A*; this will show that you have read the question. Finally, proofread the completed form slowly and thoroughly before handing it in. Make sure you have made no errors.

Now you are ready for the interview: the point at which you translate all the favorable impressions created by your résumé, application letter, and application form into a job offer.

The Interview

Effective interviewers are often extremely skilled in determining strengths and weaknesses by means of deceptively simple questions. You will meet many different kinds of interviewers, and each will have a personal style and unique expectations. It is impossible to anticipate everything that might come up in an interview, but there are a few guidelines that will generally produce a favorable impression.

If you are interviewing with a large organization, there will be two steps to the process. The first will involve meeting the human resources staff for a basic

Figure 17–9
Application letter.

3000 Vine Street
Spokane, WA 99209
March 4, 1991

Mr. Kenneth A. Harms
Personnel Director
Hyland Company
1813 East Voorhees
Spokane, WA 99207

Dear Mr. Harms:

The Placement Office of Community Colleges of Spokane indicated that you have secretarial positions available. I would like to apply for one of the positions in the engineering division.

For the past two years, while I've been working toward my degree, I have been employed by a small technical manufacturing firm. I've gained valuable secretarial experience. Last fall, when our class toured the Hyland plant, the work being done looked especially interesting.

In May of this year, I will receive my Associate's degree in secretarial studies. Details of my education and work experience are given on the enclosed résumé. I feel my related work experience and secretarial skills are tailor-made for this position. May I have an opportunity to discuss my qualifications with you further at your convenience? I can be reached after 3:30 PM at 555-2657.

Sincerely,

Arlene A. Woods

Arlene A. Woods
Enclosure

introduction to the organization and a few preliminary questions. You may take a computer use, typing, transcription, or dictation test at that time. It is wise to bring along any supplementary materials you need to perform well on these examinations. You will likely be informed about what to bring along in advance.

The second—and more important interview—will be with the individual who may be your supervisor. That interview can take up to an hour depending on how much information the individual wants to obtain from you and how thorough an interviewer he or she is. Come prepared to perform well on both interviews.

Dos and Don'ts of Interviewing

Do	Don't
• Speak in a pleasant voice	• Carry your coat into the interview
• Make eye contact	• Sit down until invited
• Sit up straight	• Smoke or chew gum
• Be courteous to everyone you meet	• Say too much or too little
• Thank the interviewer	• Interrupt the interviewer

Here are some tips for making a favorable impression at the interview. First, *arrive early and be prepared*. Know the time and place of the interview, and arrive ten to fifteen minutes earlier. Those few extra minutes will help you settle your nerves and give you a cushion against possible delays. Make sure you have any material that might be requested, such as a résumé, school record, letters of reference, and any aids needed to take pre-employment tests.

Second, as part of preparing for the interview, *organize questions in advance*. Prepare questions that you want the interviewer to answer before the interview. Background research on the organization will help you develop questions that deal with the mission of the organization, the type of work you might be doing, and the employer's expectations for an office professional's performance.

Third, at the interview *look, listen, and then respond to questions*. How you do this will demonstrate your method of working with a manager. Answer questions clearly and intelligently. Don't rush answers so that your words come out in a confused jumble. Avoid irritating expressions such as "you know" and "you know what I mean." Smile and be friendly rather than distant. A smile in response to a question or comment is a further indication of how you might behave on the job.

Finally, *obtain all the information needed by the time the interview is over*. It's a good idea to take along a notepad or index cards for brief notations. You may want to find out about such details as where you will work, length of the workday, opportunities to continue your education, and benefits provided. Most interviewers will be impressed by the advance preparation made in answering questions. Figure 17–10 lists some questions interviewers commonly ask.

The interviewer may ask you certain questions that are irrelevant to your performance and that can even cause embarrassment for both of you. It is extremely important to decide in advance how you will answer such questions if they arise. You should, however, try to determine the intent of the question, if possible. For example, a chatty, friendly interviewer might ask you about your children just to put you at ease or to find an excuse to pull out his or her children's pictures. If you respond with a snippy refusal to discuss the matter, you will not only set a bad tone for the interview but also offend the interviewer. In this case, it is probably best to answer the question in the spirit in which it was asked.

Figure 17-10
Questions commonly asked during an interview.

1. What was your most important accomplishment during your school years?
2. Which subjects did you like best? Why?
3. What was your poorest subject in school? Why?
4. Why are you considering giving up your current job/position?
5. What do you like best about your job?
6. If you could have made improvements in your job, what would they have been?
7. How would you describe the best person who ever worked for you or with you?
8. What is it about people that annoys you the most?
9. What has been the most interesting job or project you've been responsible for?
10. Describe emergencies in some of your jobs for which you had to reschedule your time.
11. Tell me what you consider your strengths to be.
12. What about your weaknesses?
13. What can you offer us that someone else cannot?
14. How long do you think it would take you to make a positive contribution to our organization?
15. Why are you interested in working for us?
16. What position and salary do you expect to hold in five years?
17. What other positions are you considering?
18. How would you like our company to help you in your career if you work here?
19. What about the position under discussion interests you the least? What interests you the most?
20. Do you like to work individually or as part of a team? Why?
21. Do you supervise people well? Give an example.
22. What do you think your co-workers think of you?
23. To date, what have been your two most important career accomplishments?
24. What is the minimum salary you would accept?

There are certain questions that are legally restricted or prohibited altogether (see Figure 17-11, page 406). Remember that you not obligated to answer "taboo" questions.

If you feel that a question is improper (even if legal), you should politely indicate that you would prefer not to answer it. By choosing this course of action you may lose your chance for the job, but you probably would not be happy working there anyway. Be especially wary of anyone who seems too preoccupied with the details of your personal life.

Finally, if you feel that any of the questions in the interview were asked with the intent to discriminate, you can contact the nearest Equal Employment Opportunity Commission office. However, this action is usually unsatisfactory because it is difficult to prove and can be time consuming to pursue.

Figure 17–11
Forbidden questions/areas and suggested responses.

Federal law prohibits discrimination on the basis of race, color, national origin, religion, sex, age, and, in many cases, physical or mental handicaps. It is therefore illegal to ask certain questions or comment on certain areas.

1. *Race* or *color* cannot be mentioned or requested on an application form, nor can information on height and weight. You also are not required to provide a photograph with the application.

2. *National origin* cannot be mentioned unless it relates to a position with an organization promoting a particular national heritage. U.S. citizenship can be determined. If one is not a U.S. citizen, the interviewer can ask if the interviewee has the legal right to remain and work in the United States.

3. *Religion* or *creed* is exempt except when you are being interviewed by a religious organization. An interviewee can volunteer information about religion if it relates to the position—such as days or times when the applicant could not work—but the interviewer cannot ask the applicant about this.

4. *Sex* and *marital status* are completely off limits, including questions about spouse's occupation, children, and child care arrangements.

5. *Age* can be determined in only two areas—under 18 or over 70—because of special laws governing employment of people in these age groups.

6. *Handicaps* can be addressed indirectly. Once a prospective employer has described the requirements of the job, an applicant can be asked if there are any physical or mental impairments that would prevent him or her from performing the job.

7. *Credit record* and *type of residence* (house or apartment) cannot be addressed.

8. Information on whether you have ever been arrested or served a jail term cannot be requested unless the position requires security clearance.

9. Armed forces service can be discussed, but you cannot be asked about the experience, especially the type of discharge you received.

Note: Employers with affirmative action programs invite applicants who are minority members, handicapped, veterans, and others in special circumstances. However, the information must be volunteered because the potential employer cannot ask. Only contractors with the federal government are mandated to have affirmative action programs, but many more public and private organizations have these programs.

> ## Communication Tips
>
> The following tips will help ensure that your job interview is successful:
>
> - Prepare a list of points to make about your background and interests and questions you want to ask at the interview.
> - Introduce yourself to the interviewer clearly and confidently. If the interviewer offers a handshake, quickly extend your hand, grasp the interviewer's hand *firmly,* and shake it. Don't offer a limp, "dead fish" handshake.
> - Pause before responding to each question. If the question is unclear, ask that it be repeated or clarified.
> - Answer each question concisely—in two or three sentences.
> - Write down answers to questions you ask.
> - Concentrate on demonstrating your overall professionalism and your interest in the position.

Follow-up to the Interview

It is always good form to thank your interviewer. A **post-interview letter** reinforces your application for the job. It shows that you have effective written communication skills, good manners, and a high level of interest in the position. Figure 17–12, page 408, contains a post-interview letter that communicates these qualities.

A brief letter to organizations that offered you a position is also appropriate. You should thank them for the interview and indicate that you chose another employer. This courtesy will build goodwill with a company or individual that may prove valuable later.

Starting Your New Position

If the position you sought is offered and you accept it, you may think there are no more hurdles. However, you still have to make an effective beginning. The first few days of your new job should be filled with communication between you and your manager. You should follow certain steps to establish guidelines and set a precedent for honest and clear communication. Your new manager should help you make a good adjustment and make his or her expectations clear. If you make no comments or raise no questions, your manager may assume that you already understand everything. Figure 17–13, page 409, identifies steps that you and your manager can take to ensure that communication and understanding won't be taken for granted.

Some people fit into an organization almost magically, as though they have always been there. Most people, however, require an initial period of a controlled pace to allow easy adjustment. Be especially sensitive if your manager is working with an assistant (you) for the first time.

Figure 17–12
Post-interview letter.

Douglas Highfill
Mid South Construction
P.O. Box 1227
Mobile, AL 36608

Dear Mr. Highfill:

Thank you for your time and the consideration you showed me during my interview on Tuesday, April 3.

The tour of your facilities was both interesting and informative, and the time you took to explain the separate functions of the departments shows that your company is a concerned employer.

I am very interested in the executive secretarial position and hope to hear from you soon.

Sincerely,

Julie Hodges

Julie Hodges

Most managers receive no training on how to work effectively with assistants and other support personnel. Some have a natural instinct for establishing sound working relationships, while others require assistance from an office professional in identifying the kinds of support available.

Your first days in your new position will give you a valuable opportunity to evaluate the unique characteristics of your new manager(s) and colleagues. The following five steps may help as you start out:

1. Be conscious of your image, attire, and behavior.
2. Look at and listen to a manager carefully, taking notes on information and suggestions provided.
3. Ask for a limited amount of information during those first days. Learn only what you need to carry out assignments.
4. Identify someone who is willing to provide advice, help, and support, especially an individual whose work can serve as a model.
5. Pay particular attention to doing work excellently—establish a performance standard that will win you respect.

Figure 17–13
Building a team.

Manager	New Assistant
1. Explains own responsibilities	1. Lists responsibilities of manager, checks understanding, and gets sense of priorities
2. Defines assistant's duties and responsibilities	2. Checks understanding of duties and priorities and points out which duties are new and may take some adjustment
3. Sets a specific time for questions each day or indicates willingness to answer questions	3. Organizes questions to make best use of the time when they can be asked
4. Presents material for assistant to read to gain a background and feel for the office (names, telephone numbers, regular appointments, and so on)	4. Familiarizes self with materials, files, and asks questions about them; takes and is given time to do this
5. Asks about assignments and work pace to determine if too much or too little	5. Responds honestly concerning pace and work so manager knows what has been done

Follow-up

1. Assesses production and quality level	1. Notes assignments and areas where manager's supervision and assignments could be improved
2. Provides regular compliments and suggestions to assistant	2. Provides regular compliments and suggestions to manager
3. Immediately corrects any deviance from the norm in hours or work production	3. Takes criticism gracefully but points out reasons for breaking rule, if legitimate
4. Provides information on activities to keep assistant current	4. Reads, keeps alert, and asks questions or indicates a willingness to become involved in other areas
5. Both hold a short conference on mutual progress in developing a team	

In all situations, be sensitive to your manager's work style and pace and try to accommodate it. Second, provide factual information when asked but avoid gossip. Finally, avoid comparing your manager with any previous person who has held the manager's position or with a former employer. You can provide information on past supervisors when asked, but even then you must be tactful and discreet.

Today many assistants work for several managers. If you are in this situation, you should take the time to ascertain each manager's support needs and rules acceptable to all managers; and take time to discuss how well assisting several managers is working out.

If you make an impressive beginning, the chances are great that you will become a valuable and effective assistant to your employer.

It is important to find a fellow employee who is willing to help during the first few days in a new job. *(Courtesy of International Business Machines Corporation)*

SUMMARY

Many options are open today to students preparing for the office professions. However, when there are options, choices must be made. These choices should be determined on the basis of interest, aptitude, and opportunities available.

Continuing education is a necessity as procedures and technology continue to change and grow. Your motivation to find the time for professional growth will increase if you identify professional goals and establish a plan to meet them. Income level, type of position, and preferred work environment are three variables to consider in defining your goals. Goals should be consistent with personal obligations.

Your manager's support will be important. You may need time, financial assistance, and encouragement. Your manager's support will also be valuable when you decide to leave your present position.

Obtaining a desirable position is usually the result of good preparation. That preparation first involves developing a thorough, clear, and honest résumé. A well-written letter of application sets the stage for an interview, in which you can present yourself in the best possible light. Some background information about the potential employer will make the interview more productive, and your preparation and interest will impress the interviewer.

Once you have secured the position, you should begin building a healthy working relationship with one or more managers through a series of specific steps. Be conscious of each manager's style, pace, and attitude. With such sensitivity, the beginning days and weeks on your new job should progress smoothly.

Key Terms

The following terms appeared in boldface type in this chapter. Do you recall what they mean? For a more complete definition, turn to the glossary beginning on p. 442.

application form (p. 401)
application letter (p. 399)
Certified Professional Secretary
   (p. 385)
CPS examination (p. 385)
Civil Service System (p. 383)
continuing education program (p. 390)
educational secretary (p. 387)
environment (p. 388)
franchise (p. 382)
generalist (p. 384)
goal (p. 388)
indiscriminate dismissal (p. 383)
legal secretary (p. 385)

medical secretary (p. 385)
not-for-profit agency (p. 383)
post-interview letter (p. 407)
probationary period (p. 383)
Professional Secretaries International
   (PSI) (p. 385)
public stenographer (p. 387)
reference (p. 396)
résumé (p. 394)
specialist (p. 384)
technical assistant (p. 386)
temporary service secretary (p. 387)
word processing specialist (p. 386)

Discussion Questions

1. Contrast the advantages of working in an urban area of over 100,000 persons versus a small community of fewer than 10,000 inhabitants.
2. What characteristics and aptitudes would be required to be effective in the following specialist roles: legal, medical, educational, and word processing? Do you have a special interest in any of these areas? If so, why?
3. What type of individual is best suited to work in the following generalist roles: finance, insurance, real estate, manufacturing, and temporary service? Do you have an interest and aptitude in these areas? What opportunities are available to you locally? Which ones appear most interesting?
4. What, if any, aspects of a temporary service position appeal to you? In what situations would you pursue one of these positions?
5. What informal continuing education opportunities can be of great value to a newly employed assistant?
6. How would you let more experienced co-workers know that you would like to learn from them?
7. In what specific ways could you let your co-workers and manager know about the value of a continuing education program?

8. If you had a choice of managers, with what type of person would you choose to work? Describe some of his or her qualities.
9. What organizations in your community would be most and least desirable employers to you? Why? Be prepared to share your reasons with the class.
10. Whom would you use as references? Why?
11. What sections would you include in your résumé? In what order? Why?

Assignments

1. Describe a job you find appealing. Write down the size and kind of organization, part of the country in which you would like to locate, and size and kind of community that is most attractive to you now.
2. Select two contrasting offices to visit, such as a physician's office/branch office of a national manufacturing firm or a local government office/radio or television station. Compare (a) the size and type of organization, (b) title of the managers supported by administrative assistants, (c) number of managers supported by one assistant, (d) titles used in the clerical area, (e) salary ranges (if that information is available), and (f) type of office environment.
3. Review the office jobs available in the want ads of your local newspaper. Find out what organizations are hiring, what titles are used, what are identified specialized skills, and what salary ranges are available.
4. Review catalogs and course descriptions from continuing education sponsors in your community to develop a list of courses that might be of interest and value to you. Divide this list into those providing technical information (such as use of computer software) and those emphasizing development of human relations skills (such as an introduction to supervision). Pick the two or three courses that sound the most valuable. Why do you think they would be valuable?
5. Using the guide to résumé preparation and the sample résumés in this chapter, prepare a résumé to present to a prospective employer. In addition, prepare an accompanying application letter.
6. Prepare a letter to the director of human resources of A. R. Brown, a multinational Cleveland corporation. Include the following information:
   a. You plan to visit Cleveland and would like to be interviewed for a possible position.
   b. You have a special interest in international sales and wish to be considered for an opening in an overseas office.
   c. You have certain experience potentially of interest to this company. Ask the director of human resources to refer to your résumé.
7. While planning a vacation trip to Los Angeles, you decide to apply to ABC Television in Hollywood for an interview. Prepare an enthusiastic letter that will encourage the human resources staff to find time to interview you.

8. Your request for an interview at ABC Television in Assignment 7 was granted. Prepare a list of four or five questions to ask when being interviewed. Your goal is to create a good impression as well as obtain useful information about ABC Television.

 Those instructors using *Top Performance: A Decision-Making Simulation for the Office* should consult the *Instructor's Guide* at this point for support material regarding use of the software in the classroom.

Case Study

Everything leading up to the job interview went smoothly. The organization was known for its staff support; office professionals were encouraged to enroll in courses and attend professional development seminars. The corporate headquarters building was attractive. Work areas were designed to promote employee comfort and productivity.

The Human Resources office staff made Diane Bueler feel welcome. Her test scores were good. The office professionals in the office in which she might work seemed open, pleasant, and happy that a new person would be joining their staff.

Diane's interview had begun well—and then hit the snag. If hired, Diane would work for the two assistant directors of marketing. These individuals decided to conduct a joint interview. They asked Diane about her experience, interest in the organization, and professional aspirations. Diane was impressed with them and excited about the work they described.

Then one of the directors noticed Diane's engagement ring. In an effort to be sociable, he began to ask questions about Diane's fiancé, marriage plans, and related issues—all in a genuinely friendly way. Diane knew these questions were off limits, but she really wanted the job. Should she have answered these questions? What should she have said, given the position's appeal and her positive feelings about the organization?

APPENDIX

A GRAMMAR REVIEW

Grammatical Survival Kit

This section covers essential grammatical terminology, common grammatical errors, and fundamental rules of punctuation. Please supplement this brief survey with a good secretarial handbook.

Essential Grammatical Terminology

The following review of terms will help you understand the mechanics of the English sentence, which is the first step in becoming a competent wordsmith.

adjective: a word that modifies (i.e., describes or qualifies) a noun, pronoun, or other noun substitute.

> Look at the *pretty* rose.
> The girl was *lovely*.

adjective clause: a group of words, containing both a subject and a predicate, that acts as an adjective.

> I like a book *that is exciting*.

See also **clause**.

adverb: a word that modifies a verb, verbal, adjective, or adverb.

> I would *really* like an interesting job. (verb)
> *Happily* singing, the children skipped rope. (verbal)
> Let's find a *more* tactful way to approach him. (adjective)
> Let's approach him *more* tactfully. (adverb)

adverb clause: a group of words, containing both a subject and a predicate, that acts as an adverb.

> She wants to lie down *because she has a headache*.

See also **clause**.

agreement: correspondence in number between subject and verb and between pronoun and antecedent.

> *James and Jenny want* to go home. (subject-verb agreement)
> James would go home if *he* could. (pronoun-antecedent agreement)

antecedent: a word or group of words to which a pronoun refers.

> *James* will stay home if *he* can.

appositive: a noun or noun substitute that acts as an adjective by qualifying, describing, or identifying the noun or noun substitute immediately preceding it.

> Phillip, *my brother*, is terribly lazy.
> Alfred *the Great* was the first king of England.

article (*a*, *an*, *the*): articles act as adjectives or determiners and immediately precede the words they modify.

auxiliary verb: a helping verb used with a main verb or verbal to indicate tense, voice, and mood.

> He *has* written a book.
> If he *were* to write a book, he *would* make a fortune.
> The book *has been* written.

case: the grammatical function of a word in relation to the other words in the sentence. In nouns, case is indicated only in the possessive form.

> *Beth's* book is lost.

In most pronouns, case is indicated in the possessive form (*mine, yours, his, her, their, its, whose*), the subjective form (*I, he, she, they, who*), and the objective form (*me, him, her, them, whom*).

clause: a group of words containing a subject and a predicate. A **dependent clause** acts as a part of speech in relation to the rest of the sentence in which it appears.

He went to the store *because he was hungry.* (dependent clause acts as an adverb)

A **main clause** can stand on its own as a sentence.

He went to the store because he was hungry.

See also **adjective clause, adverb clause, noun clause,** and **sentence**.

conjunction: a word that indicates the relationship between two or more words or word groups. A **coordinating conjunction** implies equality among the parts.

He wants to go, *but* he is too shy. (connects two main clauses)

A **subordinating conjunction** implies inequality or subordination and often introduces a dependent clause.

He wants to go *although* he is afraid.

conjunctive adverb: an adverb used to separate two main clauses. (Note: You must separate all main clauses that do not have a coordinating conjunction [see **conjunction**] with a semicolon or a period, even when there is a conjunctive adverb.)

He wants to go; *however,* he is shy.
He wants to go. *However,* he is shy.

interjection: an exclamation such as *Wow!* or *Oh!*

modifier: a word that defines, describes, or qualifies another word.

mood: the intent or purpose of the sentence as expressed in the form of the verb. **Indicative mood** indicates a direct statement or question.

I *am going* out.

Imperative mood indicates a command.

Go home.

Subjunctive mood indicates a statement of wish, possibility, or hypothesis.

If I *were* her assistant . . .

It is also used in *that* clauses to indicate a recommendation or request.

She insisted that he redo the memo.

Finally, it is used in some special expressions, such as "come what may."

nonrestrictive: not necessary to the meaning of the sentence. A nonrestrictive word, phrase, or clause requires commas or parentheses to set it off. Never use *that* to introduce a nonrestrictive clause; use *which* instead.

This is an excellent product, *which retails at $5.97.*

The librarian, *who is away from her desk momentarily,* will be able to answer your question.

noun: a word that names something, such as a person, place, thing, idea, or action.

James believes in *discipline.* He never allows his *dog* on the *furniture.*

noun clause: a dependent clause that acts as a noun.

Whatever you want is fine with me.

See also **clause**.

number: the singularity or plurality of a verb.

object: a noun, pronoun, or other noun substitute that is acted on by a verb, verbal, or preposition.

I saw *him* give the *hammer* to Jim.
To *him,* everything is easy.

person: the classification of a pronoun into one of three groups: **first person** (*I, we*), **second person** (*you*), and **third person** (*he, she, it, they*).

phrase: a group of words that lack a subject, predicate, or both but act together as any one of the parts of speech.

Jacob and I wanted to come along. (noun phrase)
We went *to the opera.* (prepositional phrase)

possessive: a noun or noun substitute that acts as a modifier indicating ownership.

That is *Elaine's* puppy. Don't take away *its* bone!

predicate: the part of a sentence that indicates what the subject does or what is done to the subject.

Evelyn *is applying for the position.*
Rebecca *will be hired.*

preposition: a word that indicates the relation of its object to the rest of the sentence.

Let's go *with* him.
Find him *before* it's too late.

pronoun: a noun substitute. **Personal pronouns** include *I, me, you, he, they,* etc. **Demonstrative pronouns** include *this* and *that.* **Relative pronouns,** such as *who* and *which,* introduce dependent clauses. **Interrogative pronouns,** such as *who* and *which,* introduce questions. **Indefinite pronouns** include *each, someone, everybody, nobody,* and the like. **Reflexive pronouns** add the suffix *self* to an existing pronoun, as in *himself.*

restrictive: necessary to the meaning of the sentence. Restrictive words, phrases, and clauses are never set off by commas. Don't use *which* to introduce restrictive clauses; use *that* instead.

This is the man *whom I met yesterday.*
Here is the book *that I was telling you about.*

sentence: a group of words that contains both a subject and a predicate and does not depend on any other group of words as a dependent clause does.

subject: the word, phrase, or clause that rules a verb. It may act or be acted on.

Bill is going home.
Amy is being sent home.

tense: the "time" of a verb in relation to the rest of the sentence.

I *am* here.
He *was* here.

verb: a word of action, being, or feeling that has tense, mood, and voice. A **transitive verb** takes an object.

Put that paper down here.

An **intransitive verb** does not take an object.

Why don't you *lie* down for awhile?

A **verb of being** takes a complement, which can be an adjective ("you look *nice*") or a noun ("It is *I*"). A noun complement is always in the subjective case; do not, for example, use "it is *me.*"

verbal: a verblike word that has tense, voice, and mood and can take an object. However, it acts as a substitute for another part of speech. **Gerunds** act as nouns.

Running is great fun.

Participles are used as modifiers.

Daydreaming, he bumped into the door.

Infinitives can be used as either nouns or modifiers; they are distinguished from other verbals by the use of *to.*

To help others has been my lifelong ambition.

voice: the quality of activity in a verb. **Active voice** indicates that the subject is acting.

I *am going* home.

Passive voice indicates that the subject is being acted on.

I *am being sent* home.

The Rules of Grammar

The rules of grammar are perfectly logical and quite easy to remember once you have learned the principles behind them.

1. All verbs must agree with their subjects in number. Few people are likely to say, "I are a college student" or "Jim and Bob is coming to dinner." But there are times when subject-verb agreement is not as easy as it seems. For example,
a. When two or more subjects are joined by *or, either . . . or, nor,* or *neither . . . nor,* the verb agrees with the final item.

Incorrect: Either James or Ellen are going to babysit.

Correct: Either James or Ellen is going to babysit.

b. When the subject is a collective noun, like *family, team,* or *jury,* it is usually singular and takes a singular verb.

The jury is unanimous.

My family is coming to visit.

It is technically correct, however, to make a collective noun plural when its activity indicates division, internal competition, or disagreement.

The jury are arguing among themselves.

This sounds peculiar to most readers, however, so it is generally better to say, "The members of the jury are arguing among themselves" and thus avoid the problem.

c. When the subject is followed by a prepositional phrase, the verb must still agree with the subject, *not* the object, of the preposition.

The sack of potatoes is heavy.

A number of forms is required.

The second example probably sounds wrong to you. That's because most people ignore words like *number* and *variety* when they appear as subjects and instead make their verbs agree with the object of the preposition ("A number of forms are required"). To avoid this problem, it is better to substitute *numerous* or *many* for *a number of* and *various* for *a variety of.*

d. When the subject is an indefinite pronoun (*everyone, someone, everybody, each*), the verb must be singular.

Everybody is happy.

2. Pronouns must agree with their antecedents in number. As with subject-verb agreement, you are likely to make mistakes only in certain situations, such as the following:

a. When two or more antecedents are joined by *or, either . . . or, nor,* or *neither . . . nor,* the pronoun refers to the final item.

Neither the truck nor the car is going to win its race.

b. Pronouns like *everyone, nobody, everybody, each, anyone, either, one,* and *someone* are singular and can be referred to only by another singular pronoun.

Everyone must remain in his seat.

If your organization condemns the use of the generic pronoun (*he, him, his*) as "sexist," either use *his or her* or change the antecedent to a plural and use *they, them,* or *their.*

Everyone must remain in his or her seat.

All participants must remain in their seats.

It is never permissible to say "Everyone must remain in their seats."

c. When the antecedent is followed by a prepositional phrase, the pronoun must agree with the antecedent, *not* with the object of the preposition.

Each of the managers is involved in the decision-making process.

d. Collective antecedents can be singular or plural depending on the nature of their activity. Ordinarily, collectives are singular.

The jury is taking its time arriving at a consensus.

They can, however, be correctly used as plurals:

The jury are taking their seats.

If the latter example sounds strange to you, you may prefer to use

The members of the jury are taking their seats.

3. A complete sentence must contain at least one main clause. A phrase or dependent clause is never sufficient.

Incorrect: He is going skydiving. Which I consider foolhardy.

Correct: He is going skydiving, which I consider foolhardy.

The first example is incorrect because the final statement is a dependent clause and cannot be written as though it were a sentence.

4. When there are two main clauses in a sentence, they must be separated by a coordinating conjunction (*and, but, or, nor*),

a semicolon, or a colon. (See the section on punctuation rules to find out when to use a colon instead of a semicolon.)

> *Incorrect:* I am going to the store, he is going home. (This is called a *comma splice.*)
>
> *Correct:* I am going to the store, but he is going home.

Do not confuse conjunctive adverbs (*however, therefore, then, thus*) with coordinating conjunctions.

> *Incorrect:* I am going to the store, however, he is going home.
>
> *Correct:* I am going to the store; however, he is going home.

5. All modifiers must be placed where it will be clear what they modify. Watch out for modifiers that seem to refer to two things at once.

> *Unclear:* Although this is not a popular course, really, it is very useful.
>
> *Clear:* Although this is not a popular course, it is really very useful.

Also, be alert for modifiers that refer to the wrong thing.

> *Incorrect:* When out of order, place a note on the machine.
>
> *Correct:* When the machine is out of order, place a note on it.

6. Nouns and pronouns must be used in the proper case. Nouns can be either subjective or possessive (*James, James's; girl, girl's*); personal, relative, and interrogative pronouns can be subjective, objective, and possessive (*he, him, his, who, whom, whose*). Most people handle the rules of case easily, but confusion may arise in some instances.

a. To make a noun possessive, add the possessive inflection (either an apostrophe alone or an apostrophe with an *s*) to the end of the subjective form. Many people mistakenly "borrow" the *s* from a plural like *boys* or even from a singular like *James* and place the apostrophe before it, creating *boy's* rather than *boys'* or *Jame's* rather than *James's*. (See the section on punctuation rules to find out

when you can leave off the possessive *s* in a plural possessive noun.)

b. Gerunds (participles acting as nouns) or gerund phrases are introduced by possessive nouns or pronouns. This rule rarely presents a problem with a simple gerund, as in "I dislike his dancing." But errors may occur when a gerund phrase is involved.

> *Incorrect:* I dislike James dancing with Janet.
>
> *Correct:* I dislike James's dancing with Janet.

To see the difference, simply ask yourself, "Do I dislike James or the fact that James is dancing with Janet?"

c. The case of the relative pronouns *who/ whom* and *whoever/whomever* is determined by their placement in the clause they introduce. *Whom* is the proper objective form of *who*. To determine whether the *whos* and *whoms* are subjects or objects, restate the dependent clause as a main clause with a personal pronoun in place of the relative one. (See figure A–1.)

d. The case of pronouns that follow the conjunctions *than* and *as* depends on whether the pronoun is being compared to the subject or to the object of the sentence.

> He likes Jane as much as I. (i.e., "as much as I like Jane")
>
> He likes Jane as much as me. (i.e., "as much as he likes me")

e. The complement of a verb of being must be in the subjective case. Verbs of being do not take objects.

> *Incorrect:* It is me.
>
> *Correct:* It is I.

7. All items in a series—even if there are only two—must be grammatically parallel. For example, in a series of items in which two elements are relative clauses and one is a participial phrase, the sentence is unparallel.

> *Incorrect:* We are learning how to fill out tax forms, document our deductions, and preparing for an audit.

Relative Pronoun	Personal Pronoun
This is the man whom I met last night.	I met him last night.
This is the man who I believe will run for Congress.	I believe he will run for Congress.
I will vote for whomever I like.	I like him.
I will go to the prom with whoever asks me.	He asks me.

Correct: We are learning how to file our tax returns, document our deductions, and prepare for an audit.

8. Verbs must follow a correct sequence of tense.

a. Verbs must show the proper relation to one another in time.

When I received my trophy, I was very proud.

When one action occurs before another, the tense of the prior action must be further back in time than the tense of the more recent event.

I had been waiting for an hour when the doctor arrived.

b. Present infinitives express action simultaneous with or later than the main verb.

I would have liked [in the past] to see that movie [at that time].

I would like [now] to see that movie [later].

Present perfect infinitives express action prior to the main verb.

I would like [now] to have seen that movie [in the past].

Do not say, "I would have liked to have seen that movie."

9. The subjunctive mood can be used only to indicate actions believed to be contrary to fact. If you believe that some day you will become president, you may say,

When I am [indicative mood] president, I will veto that bill.

But if you have no reasonable expectation of becoming president, you say,

If I were [subjunctive] president, I would veto that bill.

When using the subjunctive mood, be sure to follow the correct sequence of tenses.

If I had been president [at some previous time], I would have vetoed that bill.

The Rules of Punctuation

Each punctuation mark is directly related to some grammatical unit in the sentence. The rules of punctuation are really simple and logical when you think of them in this way.

Period (.)

1. Periods mark the end of a declarative or mildly imperative sentence.

I am going to the park.

Go to the park.

Be careful to use periods, *not* question marks, to mark the end of declarative sentences that refer to, but do not ask, a question.

Incorrect: She asked me how tall am I?

Correct: She asked me how tall I am.

2. Periods mark the ends of abbreviations such as *Mr., Mrs., Ms., Dr.,* and so on. Periods are omitted in abbreviations of organizations, countries, agencies, and honorary titles following names, such as *UN, USSR, PhD, AID, BA.* Style books differ on the allowable exceptions, so it is best to consult one when in doubt.

Ellipsis (. . .). Ellipses (singular *ellipsis*) indicate a missing portion of text. For example, if you wish to leave something out of a quotation, you must use ellipses to flag the omission.

Full version: The reviewer thought our play was "a very good production."

Shortened version: The reviewer thought our play was "a . . . good production."

If ellipses fall at the end of a sentence, they are followed by a period—four dots in all. Ellipses across an entire line indicate the omission of a paragraph.

Question Mark (?). Question marks indicate the end of an interrogative sentence. They are never used to mark the end of a declarative sentence that refers to, but does not ask, a question.

Incorrect: I asked if you were going with him?

Correct: I asked if you were going with him.

Exclamation Point (!). Exclamation points are used to mark the end of declarative or imperative sentences or simple exclamations that are meant to convey great excitement.

Wow! You won the sweepstakes!

Use exclamation points as sparingly as possible.

Colon (:). Colons introduce words or groups of words that define or restate other words or groups of words in the same grammatical form.

In this chapter, I will discuss the following grammatical terms: parallelism, modification, and agreement.

He is a true outdoors enthusiast: He tracks, shoots, and lives off the land like a mountaineer.

Do not use colons to separate an object from its verb or preposition or to separate the parts of an infinitive, even if you are introducing a list.

Incorrect: My objectives are: to learn to type 90 words per minute, to memorize all the common word divisions, and to learn all my computer codes.

To use a colon, you must alter the construction of the sentence.

I have several objectives: to learn to type 90 words per minute, to memorize all the common word divisions, and to learn all my computer codes.

Dash (—). Dashes are commonly used in place of colons to introduce single-word appositives, redefinitions, or amplifications.

I have only one thing on my mind—food.

Dashes also set off parenthetical elements that are not closely related, either in meaning or structure, to the rest of the sentence in which they appear.

Last Tuesday evening—what a night that was!—we all danced till dawn.

In informal writing, dashes are often used in place of colons even when introducing larger constructions. Colons are generally considered more formal.

Semicolon (;)

1. Semicolons separate two or more main clauses that are not already separated by a comma and a coordinating conjunction (*and, but, or, for, nor, yet*) or by a colon.

I am a writer; my brother is a carpenter.

You can't use a colon here because the second clause does not define, amplify, or expand the first. Main clauses joined by *however, therefore, thus, then, nevertheless,* and the like require semicolons.

I am going into business; therefore, I am working on an MBA.

(See item 2 in the section on commas.)

2. Semicolons separate items in a list in which one or more individual items already contain commas.

I am a writer, editor, and consultant; a homemaker and parent; and an enthusiastic amateur violinist.

An item can also be a main clause.

I am a writer, editor, and consultant; my brother is a carpenter; and my sister is an opera singer.

Comma (,)

1. Commas separate items in a series.

My hobbies include swimming, reading, and hiking.

Commas can also separate items in a series joined with a coordinating conjunction (*and, but, for, nor, yet, so, or*) when there are no commas in the individual items.

Our omelettes come with pepper and onion, bacon and cheddar, and ham and swiss.

Use a coordinating conjunction before the final item in a list even when the individual items contain coordinating conjunctions.

We have invited Bill Davis, Paula Adams, and Jim and Marge Bettmann.

The final element in a list ending in *etc.* is *etc.*, which means "and other things."

2. Commas separate main clauses joined with a coordinating conjunction.

Bill Thompson broke his leg in the collision, and his wife received minor bruises.

Don't confuse conjunctive adverbs (*however*, etc.) with coordinating conjunctions; main clauses joined by conjunctive adverbs must be separated with a semicolon.

3. Commas separate coordinate adjectives not linked by coordinating conjunctions. *Coordinate adjectives* are similar in quality and degree of specificity.

Incorrect: Grandmother left me a delicate, translucent porcelain vase.

Correct: Grandmother left me a delicate, translucent porcelain vase.

4. Commas separate contrasting elements when confusion could otherwise result.

We are here to learn, not to socialize.

Commas are not used to separate double predicates, except to mark a contrast.

Incorrect: Bill was in a train wreck, and lived to tell the tale.

Correct: Bill was in a train wreck and lived to tell the tale.

Correct: Bill was in a train wreck, but lived to tell the tale.

In the last example above, the comma is acceptable because it marks a contrast; it is optional, however. Also, commas are usually omitted in short, straightforward phrases ("poor but proud").

5. Commas set off *nonrestrictive* words, phrases, and clauses, that is, modifiers that are not essential to the meaning of the words they modify and could be removed from the sentence without changing the meaning. You must use your judgment in deciding what is or is not nonrestrictive. For example, if you are showing someone how to cash a check at a bank that has only one teller, you say,

Go see the teller, who is on your far right.

The *who* clause is nonrestrictive here because it makes no difference to your listener's understanding of the word *teller*. But if you are showing someone how to cash a check in a bank with several tellers, you say,

Go see the teller who is on your far right.

In this case, the *who* clause is necessary to avoid confusion.

6. Commas set off other short parenthetical elements, such as interjections, apostrophes, transitions, and asides, that are closely related in meaning and structure to the rest of the sentence in which they appear.

The fault, dear Brutus, is not in our stars, but in ourselves.

Dashes and parentheses can also be used to set off parenthetical elements, but they indicate a much greater separation between items. (See the sections on dashes and parentheses for further information.)

7. Commas follow introductory phrases, transitions, clauses, and interjections.

> In the event of a national emergency, you will be advised where to tune in your radio.
>
> Nonetheless, I beg to differ with my opponent.

Modern style books generally consider commas after very short introductory elements to be optional as long as there is no possibility of confusion.

> In 1984, Ronald Reagan won by a substantial majority.

Never omit the comma when the introductory element ends in a verb.

> Before I had a chance to think, Sara had gone.

Likewise, use a comma when the introductory element ends in a preposition.

> If you're ready to dig in, the potatoes are terrific.

8. Commas set off state names following city names, years following month and day, and honorary titles following names.

> I have lived in Kansas City, Kansas, all my life.
>
> On March 8, 1989, we received a summons from the IRS.
>
> James Fields, Ph.D., will speak at our dinner.

Note: A comma is optional with just a month and year; for example, both "March 1989" and "March, 1989" would be correct.

Parentheses ( ). Parentheses set off parenthetical elements that are not closely related, in either structure or meaning, to the sentence in which they appear.

> My professor's article (PMLA, 1980) has had a great influence on me.
>
> The money collected in the fund drive (most of it ours) greatly exceeded expectations.

Quotation Marks (" . . . ", ' . . . ')

1. Double quotation marks (" . . . ") set off direct quotations.

> James said, "I don't see how I can do it."

Quotation marks are *not* used to set off indirect statements.

> James said that he didn't know how he would do it.

2. When periods or commas appear at the end of a quotation, they go inside the quotation mark.

> My roommate angrily remarked, "We've had enough noise from the people upstairs."
>
> "But I'm afraid to talk to them about it," I replied.

3. When colons and semicolons appear at the end of a quotation, they go outside the quotation mark.

> The director said, "We have important goals to meet"; . . .

4. When question marks and exclamation points appear at the end of a quotation they may go either inside or outside the quotation marks depending on whether they are part of the quotation alone or part of the entire sentence in which the quotation is included.

> What do you suppose James meant when he said, "I know what you're up to"?
>
> James asked, "What are you up to?"
>
> Susan ordered, "Now let's all get moving!"

5. Double quotation marks set off titles of short works such as magazine articles, chapters in books, song titles, and pamphlets.

> The fifth chapter of Richardson's *Principles of Office Management* is called "Supervisory Skills."

See the section on underlining for more information.

6. Double quotation marks set off words used ironically.

> So these are your so-called "best" shoes.

They are also used to set off words used as words.

The word "reek" is derived from an Old English word meaning "to rise."

In the latter case, however, underlining or italics is often preferable to avoid a cluttered appearance.

7. Single quotation marks (' . . . ') set off direct quotations within other direct quotations.

> My son cried, "But Daddy, Mommy said, 'Have some chocolates if you want them!'"

Be sure to close up the double quotations after the singles and to punctuate appropriately.

Underlining and Italics

1. Underlining is generally used on typewriter or word processing systems that do not have italics or boldface. You should substitute one of the latter if your system has these capabilities. Nevertheless, we will use the term *underlining* for convenience.

2. Underlining is used to place emphasis.

> This is the <u>last</u> time I intend to speak to him about his tardiness!

3. Underlining is often used in place of quotation marks to set off words used in a special sense.

> The word <u>reek</u> is derived from the Old English word meaning <u>to rise</u>.

As mentioned earlier, underlining is preferable when quotation marks would create a cluttered appearance on the page.

4. Underlining sets off major titles such as books and periodicals.

> Last night I stayed up late to finish <u>A Tale of Two Cities</u>.

Slash (/). The slash or virgule indicates a choice between equal options.

> Did Anthony pass/fail the intermediate calculus course?

Hyphen (-)

1. The hyphen indicates that a word is divided at the end of a line of type and continued on the following line.
   a. Words are divided by syllable. When in doubt, consult a dictionary.
   b. Hyphenated words are divided only at the hyphen (*co-workers*, not *co-work-ers*).
   c. Words are divided after the prefix and before the suffix (*pre-destination*; *predestina-tion*).
   d. Words are divided between two vowels that are pronounced separately (*cori-ander*).
   e. Words are divided after a one-syllable vowel in the middle of a word (*ere-mite*). For better readability, it is best to avoid word division whenever possible.

2. Do *not* divide (a) a one-syllable word; (b) a word of five or fewer letters; (c) proper nouns, dates, numbers, titles, abbreviations, contractions, and titles; (d) the last word on a page; or (e) words that appear on more than two consecutive lines.

3. Don't separate only one or two letters from the rest of a word (*atheist*, not *a-theist*).

4. Hyphens join words that are meant to be considered as a single unit but not as a single word. Examples are compounds containing prefixes such as *self* (*self-conscious*), *cross* (*cross-country*), and *vice* (*vice-president*); compounds with certain suffixes (*president-elect*); fractions (*one-half*); equal noun + noun compounds (*city-state*); and noun + participle compounds (*market-driven economy*). Note, however, that there are exceptions (e.g., *viceroy*, *crosswise*), so check a dictionary or style manual if you're not sure.

5. Hyphens are used primarily to avoid confusion. For instance, if you wrote, "He has high quality consciousness," it would be unclear whether *quality* belongs with *high* or with *consciousness*. Use common sense to determine when hyphens are likely to be re-

quired, and check a dictionary or style handbook if in doubt.

Rules of Spelling

A dictionary and a good memory are your best safeguards against spelling errors, so when in doubt look it up, write it down, and memorize it. There are, however, a few general rules that can help save you dictionary time if you use them properly—and always remember to watch out for exceptions.

1. Place *i* before *e* (*yield*) except after *c* (*receive*) or when sounded like an *a* (*eight*).

2. Drop the silent *e* from the end of a word when you add a suffix beginning with a vowel (*type, typing*) except when the word ends in *ce* or *ge* (*courage, courageous*) or is used to prevent confusion (*die, died*). Do not drop the silent *e* from the end of a word when you add a suffix beginning with a consonant (*spite, spiteful*).

3. Change the final *y* to an *i* when you add a suffix that doesn't end in *i* (*happy, happiness*). Don't change the final *y* to an *i* when you add a suffix that begins with *i* (*carry, carrying*) or when the *y* is preceded by a vowel (*convey, conveyance*). Finally, don't drop the final *y* from words of one syllable when adding *ly* or *ness* (*spry, spryly, spryness*). There are exceptions to this one (e.g., *day, daily*), so be careful.

4. Retain a double letter created by adding a prefix or suffix (*book, bookkeeper*), including vowels (*ski, skiing*).

5. Double a final consonant preceded by a vowel when adding a suffix that begins with a vowel or a *y* (*dog, doggy; swim, swimming*) except when the accent is not on the last syllable (*benefit, benefited*). Don't double a final consonant preceded by more than one vowel, even when adding a suffix that begins with a vowel or a *y* (*rail, railing*). Also, don't double a final consonant when adding a suf-

fix that begins with a consonant (*ship, shipment*). Finally, don't double a final consonant preceded by another consonant when adding a suffix of any kind (*parch, parchment*).

Rules of Capitalization

Capitalization is used to indicate the special status of a particular word either because of its meaning or due to its function in a sentence. The following categories require capitalization.

1. The first word of a sentence

   The birds are singing.

2. The first word of a quotation following an introduction, such as "he said"

   He said, "Leave me alone."

3. The first word of the salutation or complimentary close of a letter

   Dear Mr. Smith:
   Very sincerely yours,

4. Proper nouns and adjectives (John Smith is English), but not words derived from them (french fries)

5. Titles preceding a name (Professor Jones; *but* Bill Jones is a professor)

6. Names of holidays (Veterans' Day)

7. All words in the titles of books, articles, plays, poems, and songs except for prepositions, conjunctions, and articles (*Crime and Punishment; How to Succeed in Business without Really Trying*). Any word that begins or ends a title should be capitalized (*The Ills That Flesh Is Heir To*).

8. Standard and popular names of geographic regions and features (the South), but not directions (I am going south)

9. Names of buildings, parks, and streets (Union Terminal, Central Park, Fifth Avenue)

10. Names of the "supreme being," sacred books, religious figures, and religious denominations (God, the Bible, the Virgin Mary, Roman Catholicism)

11. Names of historical periods, events, and documents (Restoration, War of the Roses, Constitution)

12. Names of political parties and government entities (Democratic party, Congress, Department of Health and Human Services)

13. Trademarks (Pepsi-Cola, Quaker Oats, Kleenex)

14. Names of ships, trains, airplanes, and spacecraft (*HMS Bounty*, Orient Express, Air Force One, Voyager II). Note that names of ships are usually underlined or italicized.

Commonly Used Abbreviations

Perhaps the most useful rule of abbreviation is to avoid abbreviating unless tradition demands it. There is some disagreement among authorities over when to use periods with abbreviations. We give the most modern guidelines here, but the most important guideline is consistency: Choose the style manual that best suits your organization, and then follow it.

1. Titles that commonly precede a name (*Mr., Mrs., Ms.,* and *Dr.*). *Miss* is, of course, not an abbreviation. Don't abbreviate less common titles (*Professor, Senator*). It is permissible, however, to abbreviate *Honorable* (*Hon.*) and *Reverend* (*Rev.*).

2. Titles that follow a name (*John Jones, PhD; William Race, Jr.*). Note that the modern trend is to dispense with periods in honorary titles following names (*PhD*) but not seniority titles (*Jr., Sr.*).

3. Well-known organizations (IBM, UN, FBI), including universities commonly known by

their abbreviations (UCLA, CCNY). Do not use periods.

4. Countries commonly known by their abbreviations, but only when used as an adjective before a noun (the U.S. Constitution; *but* life in the United States). Always abbreviate *USSR* (no periods here).

5. Ship designations (*HMS Bounty*). No periods.

6. Commonly abbreviated terms (*etc., et al., i.e., c.o.d.*). These terms should be in lowercase letters and include a period after each abbreviated word. Note that *et* is the Latin word for *and* and therefore is not abbreviated. Do not confuse *i.e.* and *e.g.*; *i.e.* means *that is,* and *e.g.* means *for example.* It is unnecessary to italicize Latin abbreviations, although this was commonly done in the past. There is disagreement over *a.m.* and *p.m.*. Some publishers use lowercase, some uppercase, and some small capitals; some omit the periods and some include them. The important thing is to choose one form and stick to it. Upper- and lowercase forms take periods; small-capital form does not.

7. Do not space between periods within an abbreviation, and do not place an extra period after an abbreviation that ends a sentence.

Contractions

1. Unlike abbreviations, contractions always contain an apostrophe to indicate where letters were omitted. The use of single-word contractions is generally limited to business forms and tables. Some common single-word contractions follow:

ack'd (acknowledged)

ass't (assistant)

gov't (government)

nat'l (national)

rec't (receipt)

sec'y (secretary)

dep't (department)

'90 (1990)

2. A second kind of contraction occurs with verb forms. An apostrophe indicates where letters have been omitted when two words are combined. The use of verb contractions is generally limited to informal business writing. A sampling of commonly used verb contractions follows:

aren't (are not)

didn't (did not)

doesn't (does not)

don't (do not)

hasn't (has not)

she's (she is)

I'll (I will)

isn't (is not)

it's (it is)

let's (let us)

I've (I have)

that's (that is)

there's (there is)

they're (they are)

wasn't (was not)

we'll (we will)

who's (who is)

won't (will not)

wouldn't (would not)

you're (you are)

Irregular Verbs

Many verbs do not form their parts in the usual manner. These irregular verbs take a variety of forms, and the forms are listed in the dictionary after the present form of the verb. A list of parts for commonly used irregular verbs follows:

arise	arose	arisen
become	became	become
begin	began	begun
bite	bit	bitten
blow	blew	blown
break	broke	broken
bring	brought	brought
burst	burst	burst
buy	bought	bought
catch	caught	caught
choose	chose	chosen
come	came	come
dig	dug	dug
do	did	done
draw	drew	drawn
drink	drank	drunk
drive	drove	driven
eat	ate	eaten
fall	fell	fallen
fight	fought	fought
fly	flew	flown
forget	forgot	forgotten
forgive	forgave	forgiven
freeze	froze	frozen
get	got	got
give	gave	given
go	went	gone
grow	grew	grown
hang	hung	hung
hide	hid	hidden
know	knew	known
lay	laid	laid
lead	led	led
leave	left	left
lend	lent	lent
lie	lay	lain
lose	lost	lost
make	made	made
pay	paid	paid
ride	rode	ridden

ring	rang	rung
rise	rose	risen
run	ran	run
see	saw	seen
set	set	set
shake	shook	shaken
shrink	shrank	shrunk
sing	sang	sung
sink	sank	sunk
sit	sat	sat
speak	spoke	spoken
spring	sprang	sprung
steal	stole	stolen
strike	struck	struck
swear	swore	sworn
swim	swam	swum
take	took	taken
tear	tore	torn
throw	threw	thrown
wear	wore	worn
write	wrote	written

Commonly Misused and Confused Words

a while/awhile

a while (used as a noun meaning "a short time"): He will be here in a while.

awhile (used as an adverb meaning "a short time"): He left awhile ago.

accede/exceed

accede (to agree or consent): I will accede to your wishes.

exceed (to surpass a limit): Many accidents occur when people exceed the speed limit.

accept/except

accept (to take or receive): Yes, I will be glad to accept your check.

except (to leave out or exclude): All orders have been delivered except Mr. Reed's.

access/excess

access (admittance or approachability): Everyone in the office should have access to the files.

excess (beyond ordinary limits; a surplus): At the end of the day, all excess materials should be stored.

ad/add

ad (abbreviated form of *advertisement*): We filled most of our personnel needs by running an ad in the local newspaper.

add (to increase by uniting or joining): The new computer will add to the efficiency of the office staff.

adapt/adept/adopt

adapt (to adjust or modify): We must adapt ourselves to new situations.

adept (skilled): She is very adept at taking and transcribing dictation.

adopt (to take and follow as one's own): We will adopt Mrs. Williams's proposal.

addition/edition

addition (the process of uniting or joining): The addition of more floor space is necessary to meet the increased production quotas.

edition (a particular version of printed material): Only the second edition of this book is available now.

advice/advise

advice (a suggestion, opinion, or recommendation): He would have avoided the problem if he had followed our advice.

advise (to counsel or recommend): We had to advise her not to sign the contract in its present form.

affect/effect

affect (to influence or change): Large pay raises throughout the country will affect the rate of inflation.

effect (verb—to bring about or accomplish): Our government plans to effect a change in the rate of inflation by tightening bank credits.

effect (noun—a result or consequence): Inflation usually has a negative effect on our economy.

allude/elude

allude (to mention or refer to): I allude to the fact that the popularity of small cars has increased in recent years.

elude (to evade or escape): The halfback was

able to elude his pursuers through fancy footwork.

allusion/delusion/illusion

allusion (an indirect reference): John made allusions to Mr. Reed's apparent laziness.

delusion (a false belief): He was under the delusion that no one liked him.

illusion (a false image or misconception): We were all under the illusion that the new equipment would enable us to reduce our office staff.

among/between

among (refers to more than two persons or things): Distribute the supplies equally among the three departments.

between (refers to two persons or things): The final selection for the position is between Ms. McCreery and Mr. Muha.

amount/number

amount (indicates mass items that cannot be counted and singular nouns): A great amount of food was wasted because of the power failure.

number (indicates items that can be counted and plural nouns): A number of errors appear in this letter.

appraise/apprise

appraise (to estimate): Before the merger, we hired an outside firm to appraise our assets.

apprise (to inform or notify): I will apprise Janet of the situation and obtain her reaction.

as/like

as (used as a conjunction at the beginning of a clause): I will get the material to you by Friday as I promised.

like (used when the sentence requires a preposition): I have never met anyone like him.

ascent/assent

ascent (rising or going up): The recent ascent of stock market prices is an encouraging sign.

assent (to agree or admit as true): Everyone at the meeting will surely assent to the plan.

assure/ensure/insure

assure (to promise; to make a positive declaration): I assure you that the loan will be paid back on time.

ensure (to secure or make certain): The loan will ensure the completion of the project.

insure (to protect against loss): We insure all our facilities against earthquake damage.

beside/besides

beside (by the side of): Please put the new file beside the one in the corner.

besides (in addition to): Who else besides Ms. Graham was awarded a bonus?

biannual/biennial

biannual (occurring twice a year): The biannual meeting of the stockholders will be held next week.

biennial (occurring once every two years): The biennial meeting of the society was cancelled this year.

can/may

can (the ability to do something): Pauline can type and take dictation.

may (permission): Yes, you may take a day's vacation tomorrow.

capital/capitol

capital (noun—a city in which the official seat of government is located): The capital of Wisconsin is Madison.

capital (noun—the wealth of an individual of firm): Much of our capital is tied up in equipment.

capital (adjective—a crime punishable by death): Treason in many countries is a capital crime.

capital (adjective—foremost in importance): Her suggestion for improving our credit system was a capital idea.

capitol (noun—a building used by the U.S. Congress; a building in which a state legislature convenes): The tour of the capitol was very interesting.

cite/sight/site

cite (to quote or mention): He can cite many authorities who have studied the problem.

sight (to see or take aim; a view): The hills above our home are a beautiful sight in the spring.

site (a location): This is a perfect site for the housing project.

coarse/course

coarse (rough texture): This material is too coarse for our use.

course (a particular direction or route; part of a meal; a unit of learning): We are now committed to a course of action that we hope will solve the problem.

complement/compliment

complement (to complete or make perfect): The color of the trim will complement the color of the walls.

compliment (to praise or flatter): Mr. Rose complimented me on the job I did.

conscience/conscious

conscience (the faculty of knowing right from wrong): In the last analysis, it was his conscience that made him release the funds.

conscious (aware or mentally alert): Yes, we are conscious of the fact that a new product similar to ours is on the market.

continual/continuous

continual (regular or frequent in occurrence): These continual telephone calls are disrupting my regular routine.

continuous (without interruption or cessation): His continuous humming was disturbing everyone in the office.

council/counsel

council (a governing body): We will present the proposal to the council in the morning.

counsel (to give advice; advice): He received good counsel from his advisors.

decent/descent/dissent

decent (in good taste; proper): The decent thing would have been for the salesperson to apologize.

descent (movement downward): The view of the city was breathtaking as the plane started its descent into the airport.

dissent (difference or disagreement): There was no dissent among the council members concerning the resolution to expand our parking facilities.

defer/differ

defer (to put off or delay): They decided to defer the project until next spring.

differ (to vary or disagree): Doctors differ in their opinions as to the best treatment for this particular virus.

device/devise

device (an invention or mechanism): The device worked perfectly during the demonstration.

devise (to think out or plan): It was not easy to devise an overtime plan that would be equitable for everyone.

dew/do/due

dew (drops of moisture): The heavy morning dew caused her to delay the flight.

do (to perform or bring about): We must do everything possible to ship the order by June 17.

due (immediately payable): All payments are due by the 10th of each month.

disapprove/disprove

disapprove (to withhold approval): The boss will disapprove any plan that is not properly justified.

disprove (to prove false): We must disprove the rumor that we are cutting back production next month.

elicit/illicit

elicit (to draw out or bring forth): The speaker had a difficult time trying to elicit responses from the audience.

illicit (unlawful): He was cited for illicit business practices.

emigrate/immigrate

emigrate (to move to another country): Many Cubans decided to emigrate to the United States after Castro came to power.

immigrate (to enter a country): The United States welcomed those Cubans who immigrated after Castro came to power.

eminent/imminent

eminent (prominent; distinguished): Mr. Mendez is an eminent authority on labor relations.

imminent (impending; likely to occur): There is imminent danger of equipment breakdown unless periodic service checks are made.

envelop/envelope
envelop (to wrap, surround, or conceal): The chief said his men would envelop the fire by morning.
envelope (a container for a letter): Please send me your answer in the return envelope provided for your convenience.

explicit/implicit
explicit (expressed clearly): The letter gives explicit instructions for assembling the new machine.
implicit (implied): By reading between the lines, you can detect an implicit appeal for additional funds.

farther/further
farther (a great distance): The trip to the plant is farther than I thought.
further (additional; to help forward): Refer to my July 8 memo for further details.

formally/formerly
formally (in a formal manner): At our next meeting, you will be formally initiated into the organization.
formerly (in the past): She was formerly the president of a large community college.

former/latter
former (first of two things or belonging to an earlier time): As a former employee, Grace Noonan is always welcome at our yearly company picnic.
latter (second of two things or nearer to the end): Of the two proposals the latter one seems more workable than the former one.

forth/fourth
forth (forward): The speaker asked that his illustrations be brought forth.
fourth (a numeric term): The fourth member of our group never arrived.

good/well
good (an adjective that describes a noun or pronoun): Mr. Collins writes good letters.
well (an adverb that describes a verb, an ad-

jective, or another adverb; a person's well-being and health): Miss Farley takes dictation very well./My secretary did not look well today.

he/him/himself
he (the subject of a clause or a pronoun complement): He is the one I interviewed for the job./It was he who asked for an appointment.
him (a direct object, indirect object, or object of a preposition): The president asked him to head the project./Mrs. Roberts gave him the results of the study yesterday./The choice is between you and him.
himself (a reflexive pronoun used to emphasize a noun or as an object): He had to see for himself what the problem was.

The same rules apply to other pronouns (*she/her/herself, I/me/myself*).

hear/here
hear (to perceive by the ear): Yes, I can hear you clearly.
here (in this place or at this point): Install the telephone here.

holy/wholly
holy (sacred): This place is considered holy by some people.
wholly (completely): Do you agree wholly with the committee's recommendations?

imply/infer
imply (to suggest without stating): Does that statement imply that I have made a mistake?
infer (to reach a conclusion): I cannot comment for fear people will infer the wrong thing.

incidence/incidents
incidence (occurrence): There has never been an incidence of theft within the company.
incidents (events or episodes): Four incidents occurred in which injuries resulted from faulty equipment.

incite/insight
incite (to urge on or provoke): The speaker attempted to incite the audience to take action.
insight (keen understanding): His insight into the situation prevented a serious problem.

indigenous/indigent/indignant

indigenous (native to a particular region): I believe this metal is indigenous only to the Northwest.

indigent (poor; needy): My parents were indigent farmers.

indignant (angry): You should learn how to deal with indignant customers.

interstate/intrastate

interstate (between states): Our company is now involved in interstate commerce.

intrastate (within a state): This firm is concerned primarily with intrastate product sales.

its/it's

its (possessive form of *it*): The company had its stockholders' meeting last week.

it's (contraction of *it is*): It's a fact that our office is first in sales.

later/latter

later (after the expected time): The shipment arrived later than we had anticipated.

latter (the second thing of two things): Your latter suggestion is more likely to be adopted.

lay/lie

lay (to put or place; a transitive verb that needs an object to complete its meaning): Please lay the message on my desk.

lie (to recline; an intransitive verb that takes no object): May I lie down?

lean/lien

lean (to rest against; to be inclined toward): I believe the employees lean toward the first contract proposal.

lien (a legal right or claim to property): If he refuses to pay, we will be forced to obtain a lien on the property.

leased/least

leased (rented for a specified time period): The building has been leased for three years.

least (smallest; slightest; lowest): This month we had the least profit for this year.

lessee/lesser/lessor

lessee (one to whom a lease is given): As specified in the lease agreement, the lessee is responsible for the maintenance of the property.

lesser (smaller or less important): Although the decision was not wholly satisfactory, it was the lesser of the two evils.

lessor (one who grants a lease): The lessor is usually responsible for paying the utility costs of leased property.

lessen/lesson

lessen (to make smaller): She recommended that we lessen our efforts in the manufacturing area.

lesson (a unit of study; something from which one learns): The experience was a good lesson in how miscommunication can cause problems.

local/locale

local (limited to a particular district): Only persons living in the local area were interviewed.

locale (a particular location): This property is an ideal locale for the new plant.

moral/morale

moral (pertaining to right and wrong; ethical): She made the decision on a moral rather than a practical basis.

morale (a mental condition): The announcement of a pay raise boosted employees' morale.

overdo/overdue

overdo (to exaggerate): Exercise is healthful if one does not overdo it.

overdue (late): Your payment is fifteen days overdue.

pair/pare/pear

pair (two of a kind; made of two corresponding parts): I bought her a pair of gloves for her birthday.

pare (to reduce in size): I hope you can pare this budget at least 15 percent.

pear (fruit): He always eats a pear for breakfast.

passed/past

passed (past tense or past participle of *pass*, meaning "to go by" or "circulate"): She passed around the announcement to everyone in the office.

past (gone by or ended): Our weak profit picture is all in the past.

patience/patients

patience (calm perseverance): It took great patience on her part to type the report without error.

patients (people undergoing medical treatment): I am one of Dr. Taylor's patients.

persecute/prosecute

persecute (to harass persistently): He wouldn't hesitate to persecute a colleague if doing so would be to his advantage.

prosecute (to start legal proceedings against someone): We are not sure whether or not the district attorney will prosecute the case.

personal/personnel

personal (private; individual): She is his personal assistant.

personnel (employees): All personnel are requested to work overtime until the inventory has been completed.

precede/proceed

precede (to go before): Mrs. Andrews' presentation will precede the main speaker's address.

proceed (to go forward or continue): Please proceed with your analysis of the financial statements.

principal/principle

principal (noun—a capital sum; a school official): Both the principal and the interest on the balance of the loan are due next month./ As principal of Lindberg High School, Mrs. Brereton was proud that so many of its students continued on to college.

principal (adjective—highest in importance): The principal reason we changed our promotion procedures was to encourage our employees to upgrade themselves within the company.

principle (an accepted rule of action; a basic truth or belief): Her knowledge of accounting principles is questionable./Our country was founded on the principle that all people are created equal.

propose/purpose

propose (to suggest): I propose that we borrow the money for the new equipment.

purpose (a desired result): The purpose of this meeting is to discuss ways to increase sales.

quiet/quite

quiet (peaceful; free from noise): The quiet operation of this typewriter is one of its main sales features.

quite (completely or actually): The salespeople seem quite satisfied with the new commission plan.

raise/rise

raise (to lift something up, increase in amount, gather together, or bring into existence; a transitive verb that needs an object to complete its meaning): Please do not raise your voice.

rise (to go up or increase in value; an intransitive verb that does not take an object): One should rise when the judge enters the courtroom.

reality/realty

reality (that which is real): Our problem began when the manager would not face reality in negotiating with the employees.

realty (real estate): The last realty company that tried to sell my property couldn't find an interested buyer.

respectfully/respectively

respectfully (used in the body or complimentary close of a letter to show high regard or respect for the reader): We respectfully submit that the contract calls for all work to be completed by April 1.

respectively (each in turn): Janice Jackson, Al Turnbull, and Gary Woods won first, second, and third prizes, respectively.

rote/rout/route

rote (mechanical or repetitious learning): All of us had to learn the multiplication tables by rote.

rout (a disorderly assembly or flight): The game turned into a rout after the opposing team scored 30 points in the first quarter.

route (a course taken in traveling from one point to another): Most of our delivery routes had to be changed after they were studied by efficiency experts.

scene/seen

scene (a place of an occurrence; an exhibition of anger): The police arrived at the scene shortly after the guard telephoned them.

seen (past participle of *to see*): The customer was not served because he was not seen.

set/sit

set (to place or make solid; a transitive verb that generally needs an object to complete its meaning): Please set the book on my desk.

sit (to be seated or occupy a seat; an intransitive verb that takes no object): Sit here, Ms. Brown./I sat for an hour awaiting his return.

sew/so/sow

sew (to fasten by stitches with thread): I can't find anyone to sew a button on my coat.

so (in a way indicated; to that degree; therefore): She was so upset over the incident that she accidentally tore the paper.

sow (to plant seed): This machine can sow more seed than a dozen farmhands.

shall/will

shall (used in formal writing when the first person is used or in first-person questions when the answer is up to the interlocutor's discretion.): I shall give your request the utmost consideration.

will (used with all three persons except in formal writing): They will finish the project on time unless they run into bad weather.

shone/shown

shone (past tense of *shine*): If the flashing red lights had shone through the fog, the accident might have been avoided.

shown (past participle of *show*): The filmstrip displaying our new products has been shown to the salespeople.

should/would

should (used in formal writing when the first person is used; also used to indicate a desirable course of action): We should like you to return the completed application by Friday./You should go home early.

would (used with all three persons except in formal writing): She would be happy to work overtime if the report isn't finished.

some/somewhat

some (an adjective or subject complement meaning "an unknown amount"): The report revealed that we will have to make some changes when we move to the new facility.

somewhat (an adverb meaning "to some degree"): Most people feel our proposed budget is somewhat optimistic.

staid/stayed

staid (sedate; composed): A more staid individual is needed to fill this position.

stayed (past tense and past participle of *stay*): She stayed long after closing time to finish the report.

statue/stature/statute

statue (a carved or molded image of someone or something): Meet me in front of the statue of Lincoln.

stature (the height of an object; status gained by attainment): She is a person of great stature within the community.

statute (law enacted by legislature): There is a statute in this state that prohibits gambling in any form.

sure/surely

sure (an adjective or subject complement meaning *certain* or *positive*): Nancy was sure she had made the right decision.

surely (an adverb meaning *certainly* or *undoubtedly*): The employees believed they would surely get a raise this year.

than/then

than (a conjunction used to show comparison): Miss Espinoza had more experience than I in writing contract proposals.

then (an adverb meaning "at that time"): After a letter is typed, it should then be proofread carefully before it is removed from the typewriter.

that/which

that (introduces a restrictive or essential subordinate clause): Mr. Sparks said that this order must be shipped today.

which (introduces a nonrestrictive or nonessential subordinate clause): The security people recommend we acquire a watchdog, which would be kept inside the plant at night.

their/there/they're

their (possessive form of *they*): It was their recommendation that we install the new computer system.

there (at that place or at that point): Please be there promptly at ten o'clock in the morning.

they're (contraction of *they are*): Although most of the assistants are new employees, they're quite familiar with our operations.

them/they

them (a direct object, indirect object, or object of a preposition): I asked them to please wait outside.

they (subject of a clause or a pronoun complement): They are meeting this afternoon.

threw/through

threw (past tense of *throw:*): Mr. Hardy accidentally threw away the report on equipment purchases.

through (in one end and out the other; over the surface of; the end of; during the period of; as a consequence of): It will be a pleasure to give you a tour through the plant.

to/too/two

to (a preposition; the sign of an infinitive): She wanted to see for herself the condition of the plant cafeteria.

too (an adverb meaning "also" or "to an excessive extent"): I was there too./Because the office was too noisy, I had a difficult time hearing you on the telephone.

two (a number): There was too much work for the two of us to finish by five o'clock.

us/we

us (a direct object, indirect object, or object of a preposition): The vice-president took us on a tour of the plant.

we (the subject of a clause or a pronoun complement): We have to catch a plane at 3 PM.

vain/vane/vein

vain (unduly proud or conceited): Tom would be more popular with his fellow workers if he weren't so vain.

vane (a thin plate used to show wind direction): The weather vane indicated that the wind was coming from a westward direction.

vein (a tubular vessel that carries blood to the heart): She had difficulty finding a vein from which to obtain a blood sample.

vary/very

vary (to change): The new office manager said she would not request us to vary any procedures at the present time.

very (extremely): These figures are very difficult to type accurately.

weather/whether

weather (the state of the atmosphere; to bear up against): We are glad to learn that you were able to weather the high rate of employee turnover during the summer.

whether (an introduction of alternatives): We will not know until next week whether or not our company will be awarded the contracts.

who/whom (whoever/whomever)

who (the subject of a subordinate clause or a pronoun complement): I was the one who asked you to attend./Give it to whoever wants it.

whom (a direct object, indirect object, or object of a preposition): Whom have you hired as my assistant?/Give it to whomever you please.

who's/whose

who's (a contraction of *who is*): Please let me know who's taking over for her during August.

whose (possessive form of *who*): He is the employee whose position was eliminated.

The Treatment of Numbers

To make a document look professional, it is important to be consistent in the treatment of numbers. These are the guidelines commonly used in published works.

1. Write out (a) numbers from one to nine; (b) round numbers; (c) any of the above followed by the words *hundred* and *thousand*.

   five hundred; seven thousand

2. In nonscientific text, use arabic numerals for all numbers not covered by rule 1.

   357; 999; 12,946

3. Use only arabic numerals for technical data or for numbers followed by an abbreviation.

   5 km; 16 bytes

4. Use arabic numerals for numbers preceding the words *million* and *billion*.

   56 million; 110 billion

5. Use arabic numerals for numbers representing percentages.

   5 percent; 29%

Note: Spell out the word *percent* in nonscientific text.

6. Follow rule 1 for common measurements.

   We had to walk four miles to school.

7. Write out common fractions in nonscientific text.

   one-half; two-thirds

8. Use arabic numerals in a range of numbers including fractions.

   Our living room is 11½ by 20 feet.

9. Write out numbers that begin a sentence.

   Nine hundred twenty people packed the auditorium.

10. Treat numbers the same if used together in a sentence.

   There were 580 ballots in the box, but 6 were blank.

11. Use a comma to separate each group of three digits in a number. Do not type a space after the commas.

   1,492 (except in years—e.g., 1492—or technical data); 10,978; 1,497,282

12. Hyphenate numerators and denominators in fractions unless there is already a hyphen in one of the numbers.

   one-third; one twenty-seventh

13. Hyphenate any two words that make up a single number between 21 and 99.

   twenty-seven; two hundred fifty-five

14. Abbreviate the second number in a range in the following ways: (a) less than 100—do not abbreviate (20–35); (b) 100 or multiples of 100—do not abbreviate (310–319); (c) 101–109 or multiples of this range—use changed part only (101–9, 1,602–3); (d) 110–199 or multiples of this range—use two digits or more as needed (112–24, 310–947); (e) if three or more digits change in a four-digit number, do not abbreviate (1,176–1,832).

15. Write out ordinals.

   Ours was the ninety-fifth car in the parking lot.

APPENDIX

B

LETTER STYLES

Modified Block Style—Standard Punctuation

April 10, 19XX

Villageview Industries, Inc.
9005 North Oak Street
Portland, ME 04101

Ladies and Gentlemen:

Subject: Business Letters

Mr. Joe Cravens asked me to send you a copy of our newly compiled report, Modern Elements in Business Letters. This report illustrates many of the special elements that may be used in today's business letters.

The purpose of these special elements is to improve the efficiency of correspondence. They are presented in this letter even though the chance of using all of them in a single letter is quite remote.

There are variations to the style presented here. For example, the subject line may be blocked, indented to match the paragraph indentations, or centered. Attention lines, however, are preferably typed at the left margin. The postscript is typed in the same style as the paragraphs.

A good typist understands the functions of these elements and knows how and when to use them. I believe you will find the enclosed report interesting and useful.

Sincerely yours,

Johnathan Stears

Jonathan Stears
Office Manager

JS:jh

Enclosure

c: Sandy Stone

January 24, 19XX

Mr. Michael J. Anderson
Anderson & Associates
1600 North Vermilion
Rockdale, IL 60436

Dear Mr. Anderson

For your firm's correspondence, I would recommend using the block-style letter.

This letter is an example of one that has been typed in block style. All lines, including the date, begin at the left margin. Because it requires no indentations, this style saves time.

Many companies today are using the same margins for all letters to save time. Also, the dateline is generally typed double spaced below the letterhead, and the spacing between the date and inside address varies so that the entire letter is attractively placed on the page. If you have any further questions about letter styles, please let me know.

Sincerely

Jean Wood

Jean Wood
Consultant

JW/jh

AMS Style Letter

In the style used by the American Management Society (AMS), a subject line rather than a salutation is used, and there is no complimentary closing.

June 12, 19XX

Mrs. Jane St. Pierre, Manager
The Pioneer Company
P.O. Box 2000
Ft. Worth, TX 76116

AMS Simplified Style

To type a simplified style letter in the AMS style, the Administrative Management Society recommends following these steps:

1. Use block format.
2. Omit the salutation and the complimentary close.
3. Include a subject heading and type it in ALL CAPS, with a triple space below the address; triple space from the subject line to the first line of the body.
4. Type enumerated items at the left margin; indent unnumbered items five spaces.
5. Type the writer's name and title in ALL CAPS on the fourth line space below the last line of the letter body.
6. Type the reference initials (typist's only) a double space below the writer's name.

The AMS simplified letter style has been recommended for a number of years but is no longer widely used.

Simplified Letter

This style uses the following elements:

1. No salutation
2. First line of body begins a double space after last line of inside address
3. No closing; signature line begins four line spaces (three blank lines) down from first line of last paragraph
4. Reference initials in lowercase, a double space below title line

---

February 3, 19XX

Mrs. Vicki Kibler, Chairperson
Department of Administration—Office Management
Cherry Hill College
8700 South Walnut Avenue
Chicago, IL 60617

I accept your invitation to conduct a seminar during the Third Annual Professional Accountants' International Conference on Saturday, April 3.

To help me prepare for my presentation, could you let me know the number you expect to participate in the workshop? Also, could you let me know the names of eight assistants who would most likely be in attendance at the workshop? I want to use their names in a segment of the program.

Janet A. Dean
Educational Consultant

wk

TO: All Communication Processors
FROM: Pam Wymer, Director
DATE: January 3, 19XX
SUBJECT: Company Correspondence

Within a company, correspondence is frequently typed on interoffice forms, either half or full sheets, depending on the length of the message. Company letterhead is also used. The four parts of the heading are TO, FROM, DATE, and SUBJECT. The following points describe the features of an interoffice memo:

1. Space twice after printed headings to set the left margin stop for typing the heading items and the body. If you're typing the heading, the heading items and body usually have a one-inch left margin. Set the right margin stop an equal distance from the right edge, usually one inch.
2. The full address, salutation, complimentary close, and signature are omitted.
3. Personal titles are usually omitted from the memo heading. They are included on the envelope.
4. Triple space between the headings and the message. Single space the paragraphs, but double space between them.
5. Reference initials, enclosure notation, and carbon copy notation are included.

Special-colored or sized envelopes are usually used for interoffice memos. Type the addressee's name, personal title, and business title or name of department for the address. Type COMPANY MAIL (in all capitals) in the postage location.

xx

c: Deanna Lloyd, Administrative Assistant to the President

Alternative style for a memo heading:

DACC
Danville Area Community College

TO: SUBJECT:
FROM: DATE:

---

1. If the letter is addressed to a specific person, use that person's name:
   Dear Mr. (Miss, Mrs., Ms., Dr., etc.) Jones:

2. If the letter is addressed to an organization, use

Ladies and Gentlemen:

3. If the organization has all women members, use

Ladies (*preferred*); Mesdames

4. If the addressee is a high-level dignitary, use the appropriate salutation:

Mr. President (*or* Dear President Bush)
Your Eminence (*or* Dear Cardinal Smith)

5. If you are addressing a form letter, use a general title:

Dear Customer; Dear Friend

6. If the letter is addressed to a title (e.g., Fashion Editor or Sales Manager) and there is no way you can learn that person's name, use

Dear Fashion Editor; Dear Sir; Dear Sales Manager

Do *not* use "Dear Personnel Director" or "Dear Madam."

7. If you know the name of the addressee but aren't sure of the addressee's sex, eliminate the courtesy title.

Dear J. E. Jacobson; Dear Marion Parker

8. If a woman's preference for *Miss, Mrs.,* or *Ms.* is unknown, omit the courtesy title.

Dear Ruth Jones

APPENDIX

C PROFESSIONAL ASSOCIATIONS

Several professional associations are available to you. Many of them have local chapters in major cities. Membership can provide valuable contacts and a way to keep current on the latest hardware and software in your profession.

Following are the names, addresses, and telephone numbers of the national associations. They will be able to tell you where the local chapter nearest to you is located.

American Association of Medical Assistants (AAMA)
20 N. Wacker Drive, Suite 1575
Chicago, IL 60606
(312) 899-1500

Executive Women International (EWI)
Spring Run Executive Plaza
965 East 4800 South, Suite 1
Salt Lake City, UT 84117
(801) 263-3296

National Association of Executive Secretaries (NAES)
900 South Washington Street, Suite G-13
Falls Church, VA 22046
(703) 237-8616

National Association of Legal Secretaries (NALS)
2250 E. 73rd Street, Suite 550
Tulsa, OK 74136
(918) 493-3540

National Association of Educational Office Personnel (NAEOP)
7223 Lee Highway, Suite 301
Falls Church, VA 22046
(703) 533-0810

Professional Secretaries International (PSI)
301 E. Armour Boulevard
Kansas City, MO 64111
(816) 891-6600

Society of Architectural Administrators
11225 S. E. 6th Street, Building C, Suite 200
Bellevue, WA, 98004
(206) 453-1523

GLOSSARY

AIDCA formula   An accepted system for composing letters based on attention, interest, desire, conviction, and action.

analytical (research) report   A report that uses fact finding and interpreting the facts, plus conclusions and recommendations.

annotate   To add explanatory comments, notes, or questions on a letter or other document.

aperture card   A microform document storage form consisting of a card with pieces of film mounted in openings.

application form   A form that is completed before an interview; background information basically describes education and experience.

application letter   A letter sent to indicate interest in a position and request an interview.

appointment calendar software   A software package used by an office professional and one or more managers to establish appointments and have a permanent record of them.

attribute   A characteristic or quality.

authority   The power to control, enforce, or direct.

bank draft   An order to a bank to pay a third party.

bar codes   Printed lines on an envelope that are read by an optical character reader to speed mail delivery.

bubble memory   Computer memory composed of small magnetic domains, or "bubbles." It is predicted that bubble memory will replace disk storage.

call forwarding   A feature that allows an individual to touch a number and then the extension to which all calls are to be forwarded.

call waiting   A telephone feature that indicates with a click that a second call is waiting while the first call is in progress.

camera-ready copy   Material that is ready to be printed.

captions   Titles at the head of a chapter, file, or page.

cashier's check (bank money order)   A check drawn on a bank and immediately cashable by the designated payee.

cathode ray tube (CRT)   An output unit with a TV-like screen used to display information from a computer.

centralized copying facility   A copying unit that is equipped with high-speed machines and serves many units within an organization.

centralized system   A records management system in which all records are kept in one location.

442

central processing unit (CPU) The main section of the computer, containing the memory, arithmetic/logical, and control units.

certificate of mailing A document accompanying domestic and international mail that proves the item was sent.

certified check A draft that shows that the amount of the check has been deducted from the check writer's account.

certified mail An additional option for first-class mail that ensures delivery of contracts, bids, and similar documents.

Certified Professional Secretary (CPS) An individual who has passed a series of comprehensive tests, developed by Professional Secretaries International, that cover all aspects of an office professional's work.

chronological file A collection of details on difficult activities, with attention to how they can be better handled in the future.

chronological order Arranged in the order in which events occur.

Civil Service System An organization to which appointed government officials at the local, state, and national levels belong.

cliché An expression that uses outdated or overused statements.

code To arrange material using a system or set of rules.

collect-on-delivery (COD) A service that requires the addressee to pay up to $400 upon delivery of an order or item.

color copier A copier that prints in one or more colors.

commercial draft An order to a bank from the maker of the order to pay a third party.

compact disk read-only memory (CD-ROM) A laser disk that stores large quantities of data.

composer A device used to transform typewritten copy into print.

computer-aided retrieval (CAR) A feature of storage software that speeds up retrieval of documents.

computer output microfilm (COM) An output technique that records output from a computer as microscopic images on roll or sheet film.

concentration The ability to focus on one task at a time or to apply great attention.

confirmation copy A written copy of a telegram or mailgram message made after receipt of the original.

consistency The ability to act in a clear and relatively predictable way despite changing conditions.

constructive criticism Specific suggestions for improvement provided by a supervisor to an employee.

continuing education program A formal course aimed at improving one's professional skills.

convenience copier A copier that is small, easy to use, and equipped to perform a minimal number of functions.

cooperative keyboarding A keyboarding process used when one or more managers and an assistant are part of a computer network. The manager originates the document, and the assistant does the revision.

copyright The legal right of authors and artists to protect their works against unauthorized reproduction.

CPS examination A comprehensive examination, conducted annually by Professional Secretaries International, that covers many areas of office operations; those who pass earn the CPS designation.

crisis file A collection of correspondence for a defined time period (one to six months) organized for staff review and sometimes used as a backup for a lost document.

cross-reference To list a document in two or more locations so that it can be found regardless of how it is requested.

cursor control A feature that allows the user to move the cursor blip in all directions on the screen to indicate position. Usually a blinking or nonblinking cursor can be selected.

customs Duties or taxes paid to the U.S. government on items brought in from another country.

daisy wheel printer A letter-quality impact printer consisting of a type element—which resembles the structure of a flower that contains raised characters on each petal—that strikes the paper through an inked ribbon.

database management package A software package that manages the storage and retrieval of records in a database. Most database management packages have prewritten routines designed to make the casual user as effective as a computer programmer in manipulating data and printing reports.

date/time stamp An automatic or hand-held stamp used to register the date and time a document was received.

decentralized system A records management system in which each work area is responsible for keeping its own records.

dedicated (stand-alone) word processor A computer capable of performing only word processing functions.

deductive approach An approach to writing that begins with recommendations or conclusions, followed by specific facts to support them.

desktop publishing software A software package that contains preprogrammed routines for performing functions usually performed by a typesetter. A typical package allows the user to print graphics, as well as an assortment of type fonts, in the same document.

diplomacy The ability to deal with others in a tactful manner; speaking and acting properly at appropriate times.

Directory Assistance An operator service that provides telephone numbers. To obtain a number outside your area code, dial 1–area code–555-1212.

discrete media machine A recording machine that uses a medium such as a coated belt, disk, cartridge, or cassette.

discretion The quality of being careful about what one does and says, particularly in relation to confidential or sensitive matters.

disk drive An electromechanical device that records information and plays it back from a magnetic disk.

disk storage A method of storing information on individual disks.

distress Great pain, pressure, or anxiety.

domestic mail Mail of all classes sent to addresses within the United States.

dot-matrix printer An impact printer that uses a movable print head containing small pins that produce small dots when struck against the ribbon and paper; these dots form characters to be printed.

drop charge An extra amount paid if a rental car is returned to a location other than the pickup point.

duplex To copy on both sides of a page.

educational secretary An office professional who specializes in working in elementary, secondary, or post-secondary schools.

electronic filing system A computer-based filing system that stores documents in the hard drives of individual workstations or the memory of a centralized computer system.

electronic fund transfer (EFT) The transfer of funds by computer.

electronic mail software A software package that allows the user to send messages in the form of letters and memos to other personal computers connected in a network.

electronic notebook A portable, battery-powered laptop microcomputer complete with screen, keyboard, and internal data storage. It contains several user packages, including a word processor, spreadsheet, and appointment calendar, permanently stored in the CPU's memory chips.

electronic typewriter A typewriter that performs a variety of word processing functions and contains a limited memory.

empathy The ability to put oneself in another's situation to better understand that person.

employee ownership A strategy for increasing employees' interest and concern about an assignment or project by giving them some decision-making authority about the steps to be taken to complete the task.

endless loop system A dictation system that uses multihour loops of magnetic tape in a sealed case; found largely in centralized word processing units.

endnote A footnote presented in a list at the end of a chapter or report.

environment A combination of work setting and geographic area.

ergonomics The science of designing machines, operations, and work environments to best meet employees' needs.

ethics A system of morals.

eustress A form of self-stress that enables an individual to concentrate with high levels of energy and motivation.

evaluation The process of examining very carefully, in this case the job performance of an individual employee.

examinational (interpretive) report A report that stresses fact finding plus interpretation of the facts.

express mail A service offered by the U.S. Postal Service that designates one of four guaranteed overnight and one-day delivery services: Next Day Service, Express Mail Custom Designed Service, International Express Mail, and Express Mail Same Day Service.

facsimile transmission (fax) or **transfax** A method for sending written messages, pictures, or drawings over the telephone.

fiber optic copier A copier that uses fiber optic filaments in the reproduction process.

filing Storing information on magnetic media, disks, cards, tape, microfilm, or microfiche as a file for future retrieval.

first-class mail Mail that is sealed or closed against postal inspection; must weigh 12 ounces or less and fall into one of several specified categories.

first-time understanding The ability to master the essence of information or an instruction the first time it is presented.

five *W*s and one *H* Organizing principles based on *who, what, when, where, why,* and *how.*

floppy disk An oxide-coated plastic disk commonly used on personal computers; it stores data as magnetic spots.

follow-up The practice of checking up on individuals to ensure that work is being done correctly and on time.

footnote A note falling at the bottom of a page showing the complete source of material quoted in a report or publication.

form letter A letter that is prepared once, stored, revised on occasion, and reused repeatedly. Orders, standard refusals, or letters of appreciation are three common examples of documents that lend themselves to the preparation of a form letter.

fourth-class mail All mailable material weighing 16 ounces or less and not included in first-, second-, or third-class mail.

franchise A local outlet for a regional or national group of businesses, such as those selling food and those providing quick-copy services.

general-delivery mail Mail addressed to individuals in care of the general-delivery window of a post office in the destination city.

generalist An office professional who has a broad background and can perform a variety of assignments in most office situations.

goal The professional objectives one hopes to reach.

goodwill message A message used to build goodwill with an individual or organization.

graphics package A software package that produces graphic output such as line graphs, pie charts, and bar graphs.

guide Information that provides clear directions.

hard disk An oxide-coated metal platter sealed in a dust-free housing; it stores data as magnetic spots.

hardware Computer equipment used in data processing (as opposed to software programs).

headliner A device used to create display type.

impact printer A printer that transfers images onto paper with a mechanism that strikes the paper, ribbon, and character simultaneously.

index To list items in a specific order.

indiscriminate dismissal Incorrect, inappropriate, or ambiguous methods for terminating employees.

inductive approach An approach to writing that begins with the background for the problem and logically proceeds by presenting the procedures, then the data, and finally a summary of recommendations.

informational message A message intended to provide directions, guidance, or other specific material.

informational report A report that provides fact finding only.

information management The process of moving information from the initial preparation stage through revision to production, distribution, and storage.

information management software Typically, a database management package with specialized programs designed to accumulate, sort, select, and summarize data, creating information needed in planning, directing, and controlling a business organization.

inspect   To examine a document before filing.

insurance records   Records containing information about insurance policies held by an organization.

insured mail   Mail for which additional protection has been purchased.

intelligent printer   A printing device linked to a text-editing typewriter.

International Access Codes   Codes used to dial overseas calls (011 for station-to-station calls and 01 for calls requiring operator assistance).

interpret   To explain the meaning of concepts, ideas, or statements.

interruption   A feature that allows the user to stop copying temporarily to accommodate an emergency or a change in plans.

inventory records   Records containing information about all physical assets owned by an organization.

jet lag   An upset of the "body clock," characterized by fatigue, caused by traveling in a jet plane through several time zones.

job manual   A guide containing a brief but complete explanation of office duties, procedures, and important details.

keyboard   A device used to enter and manipulate information.

key operator   A person trained to handle copier responsibilities such as changing paper and correcting paper jams.

legal secretary   An office professional prepared to support one or more attorneys after receiving specialized training in law office operations.

letter-quality printer   A printer that produces printed characters that are fully formed, solid, and easy to read.

light pen   An input device used to write directly on the display screen or to read special characters printed on paper or tags.

local area network (LAN)   A communications network that covers a limited geographic area. A LAN is privately owned and administered and used mostly for internal transfer of information within a business. It is normally housed within a single building or adjacent group of buildings and transmits data at a high speed.

loyalty   The quality of being faithful to an individual, organization, or cause.

magnetic tape   Oxide-coated tape used to store data as electronic impulses.

mailgram   A message sent electronically by Western Union and guaranteed to be delivered in the next day's U.S. mail.

manual filing system   The traditional method of storing individual paper documents in folders and cabinets.

measured service   A method of charging for service that counts each call made.

medical secretary   An office professional prepared to support physicians and other health care professionals after receiving specialized training in this area.

memorandum   A written statement sent to another person(s) within the organization.

memory aids   Calendars, files, and other devices that enable you to keep track of the schedules of one or more managers and details of a variety of projects.

memory typewriter   A typewriter with an expanded memory; can perform a variety of word processing functions.

metered postage   Postage placed on letters and other pieces of mail using an automatic postage meter.

microchip   A single-unit computer about the size of a matchbox.

microcomputer   A computer that is smaller, has a lower memory capacity, and operates at lower speeds than a mainframe computer; also called a *personal computer*.

microfiche   A sheet of film with microrecords stored in rows and columns on a card.

microfiche film card   A card that holds sheet film, which stores information from computer output microfilm.

microfilm   A storage medium that stores documents in a reduced size.

micrographics filing system   A system that miniaturizes documents to enable a large number to be stored in a small area.

mini-deadline   A deadline set in advance of the final one, designed to motivate a person to begin a major assignment earlier.

minutes   A written summary of what occurred at a meeting.

mix/match/merge/sort   A software function that allows an operator to prepare bulk mailings to multiple addresses.

modem   A device that changes digital data to an analog signal and back again, allowing messages to be sent between two computers.

money order   A certificate purchased at any post office that transfers money from one person or business to another.

monitor   Synonym for *cathode ray tube (CRT)* display.

motion   A formal recommendation or suggestion made in a meeting that is then recorded, discussed, possibly amended, and approved or disapproved.

mouse   A small, lightweight device that the user moves across a flat surface to control the movement of the cursor and select menu options.

nonimpact printer   A printer that uses heat transfer, electrostatic methods, or photographic systems to produce images on paper.

not-for-profit agency   An agency that the law prohibits from having an excess of income over expenses and receives certain tax benefits as a result.

office manual   A guide containing company policies of importance to all employees.

office professional   A well-trained and capable assistant who provides support to one or more managers.

Official Airline Guide (OAG)   A comprehensive guide containing up-to-date flight information for all airlines to airports throughout the United States.

offset duplication (multilith)   Duplication using a master plate as the basis for producing multiple copies.

optical character reader (OCR)   A device that electronically reads typewritten, computer-printed, or hand-printed characters from documents. Used by the U.S. Postal Service to read addresses and speed up delivery.

optical disk   A disk that uses a laser device to store large amounts of data on 12-inch disks. These disks allow random access to and storage for all images; however, the data cannot be revised.

out folder   A folder that holds materials to be stored when a file is removed.

out guide   A marker that shows where a removed file is to be replaced and records the charge-out information.

passport   A document issued by the U.S. government giving a citizen official approval to travel to another country.

pending file   A file containing a list of major tasks or actual documents in progress to be completed by specific dates.

person-to-person call   A form of long-distance call in which the caller identifies for the operator the person to be reached and is not charged unless a connection is made.

persuasive (sales) message   A message designed to build up to the main point, which is a request for some action on the reader's part.

petty-cash fund   A fund kept for purchases of small items.

phototypesetter   A device that transforms typewritten copy into print with various typefaces and spacing.

plagiarism   Using someone else's words or ideas without indicating the source.

portable terminal   A small, lightweight terminal consisting of a standard-size keyboard and a built-in printing device that combine both input and output capabilities.

positive attitude   An approach to one's work, co-workers, and managers that is consistently upbeat and optimistic.

post-interview letter   A letter sent to a potential employer at the conclusion of an interview to express appreciation for being seen.

presorted mail Mail that has been sorted by ZIP code prior to sending to speed up delivery.

printer A unit used for printing information from a computer.

priority mail First-class mail weighing from ½ ounce to 70 pounds with a size limit of 100 inches.

probationary period A limited time period during which the qualifications and abilities of an individual are tested.

problem-solving skill The ability of an office professional to identify the cause of a difficulty, determine appropriate and effective solutions, and take action.

proceedings A report of what was done at a meeting.

professionalism A quality demonstrated by an office professional by exhibiting competence, attention to details, job knowledge, and other abilities valued by managers.

Professional Secretaries International (PSI) An international organization that provides educational programs and services to office professionals.

proofreading Checking typewritten copy for errors or omissions.

pseudonym A name used by a writer instead of his or her real name.

public stenographer An individual available to prepare written information on a job-by-job basis.

quotation Words written by someone else repeated exactly as in the original, with recognition of the author.

random access searching A software feature that enables the user to locate certain data stored in a computer's memory.

recirculating document feeder A device that feeds originals into the copier and back out.

recommendation A statement that suggests a specific action to solve an identified problem.

reconcile To determine whether there are any discrepancies between the ending balance on a bank statement and the checkbook balance and make any necessary corrections.

reference (1) A note that gives credit to the original source of material used in another publication; (2) A person who agrees to provide information on a job applicant's experiences and qualifications for a position.

registered mail A service for first-class or priority mail that provides additional protection for items of clear value such as checks, bonds, or stock certificates.

remote user network A communications network that serves workstations located beyond a single or adjacent group of buildings.

release mark An indication placed on a document that the item is ready to be filed.

reprographics The process of duplicating materials.

research   The process of gathering facts to support opinions or recommendations.

responsibility   Accountability for an action, individual, or project.

résumé   A job applicant's statement of education, past experience, and qualifications for a particular position.

retention and disposal procedures   Methods for determining which materials are kept and which are thrown out.

return receipt   A receipt showing evidence that a mailed item was delivered to the addressee.

return-to-position   A feature that returns the copier to its original state after a job is completed.

Robert's Rules of Order, Newly Revised   The accepted guidelines for conducting formal meetings.

routine message   A message used repeatedly in the daily course of conducting business.

routing slip   An office form attached to a document indicating who is to read or otherwise use it.

second-class mail   A class of mail that includes newspapers and periodicals, sent at a lower bulk mail rate.

secretary   One of a number of titles used for those who provide support to one or more managers.

self-motivation   The willingness to create goals or incentives directed toward specific accomplishments.

shared-logic word processor   A word processor that shares the memory and logic of a single central processing unit.

shortcut trap   The tendency of experienced individuals to explain assignments too quickly, sometimes eliminating necessary steps because they have learned shortcuts.

sight draft   A type of draft that is payable upon presentation.

software   Computer programs that control the operation of a data processing system.

sort   To arrange items in alphabetical, numerical, or geographic order, or by subject.

sorting   A software feature that enables data to be arranged for easy use.

span of control   A supervisory principle emphasizing that only a limited number of individuals and tasks can be handled well at a given time.

special delivery   A daily service for all classes of mail in which a messenger delivers to the addressee after post office hours, on Sundays, or on holidays.

special-events file   A collection of details and other information on periodic and nonroutine activities.

special handling   A service for third- and fourth-class mail used to speed up its delivery.

specialist   A person who develops expertise in a narrowly defined area of activity.

spiral binding   A plastic comb or wire thread that fits through machine-punched holes in the pages of a document to hold them together.

spirit duplicator A duplicator that uses a master and a moistening solution.

spreadsheet package A software package that performs arithmetic operations with columns of data.

station-to-station call A call made to another number with the intent of talking to whoever answers the phone.

statistical package A software package that contains stored formulas with which to make calculations rapidly.

stencil duplicator A duplicator that uses a plastic-coated sheet (stencil).

store To place documents in a file.

stress Great pressure or force, usually producing discomfort.

subhead A title inserted into a document to introduce a new subtopic.

substitution card A card placed in a file to show that a document has been taken out.

technical assistant An office professional who assists scientists and other researchers in completing their work, especially the preparation of complex reports and similar documents.

temporary service secretary An office professional who chooses to work part-time and is assigned to various employers through a temporary help agency.

text editing The ability to add, delete, or change characters, words, and lines in a document.

thermal binding A type of binding that uses glue along the inside edges of all pages to hold a document together.

third-class mail A class of mail that includes printed matter (e.g., books, catalogs, drawings) weighing under 16 ounces.

tickler file A long-range planning system that enables you to keep track of tasks to be completed and deadlines to be met over a year's time.

tie lines Special telephone connectors to offices in the same area or in distant locations.

time draft A type of draft that gives the purchaser more time to make payment.

toll charges Costs involved in placing calls.

tone A manner of writing that demonstrates a positive attitude of the writer toward the reader.

touch sensing A method of inputting data in which the user points to words, drawings, diagrams, or symbols displayed on the screen and the screen responds to the touch as it would if the information were being keyboarded.

transcribe Writing, typing, or entering information such as notes, letters, memos, reports, and testimony.

transfax *See* facsimile transmission (fax).

transparency A reproduction of a document, made with a copier using special film, that can be projected on a screen with an overhead projector.

travel advance   A sum of money given to a traveler before a trip begins to cover a portion of the expenses.

typographical error   A mistake made in the spelling of a word, the inclusion of an inappropriate word, or the exclusion of a needed word.

unity of command   A supervisory principle stating that a person cannot report to two individuals.

utility   A program that manages files, disks, and subdocuments.

validate   To support with facts.

velo-binding   A form of binding that uses two plastic strips—one with teeth threaded through the document and another with holes that hold the teeth tightly and keep the pages together.

verbatim   Word for word.

visa   An official endorsement for a passport from the embassy or office of a country allowing the passport holder to travel to that country.

visualize   To form a mental picture of something invisible or absent.

voice mail   A computerized system for answering, recording, and directing calls that can't be taken immediately.

voice messaging   The ability to enter data and issue commands to a computer with spoken words.

voucher   A receipt or other written evidence of a payment.

Wide Area Telephone Service (WATS)   A system of unlimited long-distance telephone service for a flat monthly fee; used by businesses and industries.

Winchester disk   A type of hard disk often used in microcomputers.

word processing specialist   An office professional who supports several managers by working in and/or supervising a unit that inputs and prepares information.

workstation   An area in which an individual employee works in semiprivacy with necessary equipment and material easily accessible.

"you" approach   An approach to writing correspondence in which the writer thinks of the reader first to create a comfortable tone.

ZIP code (Zone Improvement Program)   A five-digit number used by the U.S. Postal Service to identify each postal delivery area in the United States.

ZIP plus 4   An expanded ZIP code designation for moving mail to its destination more rapidly.

INDEX

Note: Page numbers in italic indicate illustrations.